鳥　山　明

I like movies. When I was younger, I used to go to the movies about four times a week. When I was in elementary school, I even used to ride my bike to the movie theater in Nagoya, boxed lunch in hand, and spend all day inside the theater. All of these movies that I watched when I was younger are reflected in my manga. When coming up with a story or sequence for a manga, I often think of it as a movie sequence, which helps my pencil to flow with ideas. Ahhh, the good 'ol days...

—*Akira Toriyama, 1991*

Artist/writer Akira Toriyama burst onto the manga scene in 1980 with the wildly popular **Dr. Slump**, a science fiction comedy about the adventures of a mad scientist and his android "daughter." In 1984 he created his hit series **Dragon Ball**, which ran until 1995 in Shueisha's bestselling magazine **Weekly Shonen Jump**, and was translated into foreign languages around the world. Since **Dragon Ball**, he has worked on a variety of short series, including **Cowa!**, **Kajika**, **Sand Land**, and **Neko Majin**, as well as a children's book, **Toccio the Angel**. He is also known for his design work on video games, particularly the **Dragon Warrior** RPG series. He lives with his family in Japan.

DRAGON BALL Z VOL. 9
The SHONEN JUMP Graphic Novel Edition

This graphic novel is number 25 in a series of 42.

STORY AND ART BY
AKIRA TORIYAMA

ENGLISH ADAPTATION BY
GERARD JONES

Translation/Lillian Olsen
Touch-Up Art & Lettering/Wayne Truman
Cover Design/Sean Lee & Dan Ziegler
Graphics & Design/Sean Lee
Senior Editor/Jason Thompson

Managing Editor/Annette Roman
Editor in Chief/Hyoe Narita
Director, Licensing and Acquisitions/Rika Inouye
V.P. of Sales and Marketing/Liza Coppola
V.P. of Strategic Development/Yumi Hoashi
Publisher/Seiji Horibuchi

In the original Japanese edition, DRAGON BALL and DRAGON BALL Z
are known collectively as the 42-volume series DRAGON BALL. The
English DRAGON BALL Z was originally volumes 17-42 of the Japanese
DRAGON BALL.

Published by VIZ, LLC
P.O. Box 77010 • San Francisco, CA 94107

The SHONEN JUMP Graphic Novel Edition
10 9 8 7 6 5 4 3 2 1
First printing, May 2003

www.viz.com

THE WORLD'S
MOST POPULAR MANGA

SHONEN JUMP
GRAPHIC NOVEL
www.shonenjump.com

SHONEN JUMP GRAPHIC NOVEL

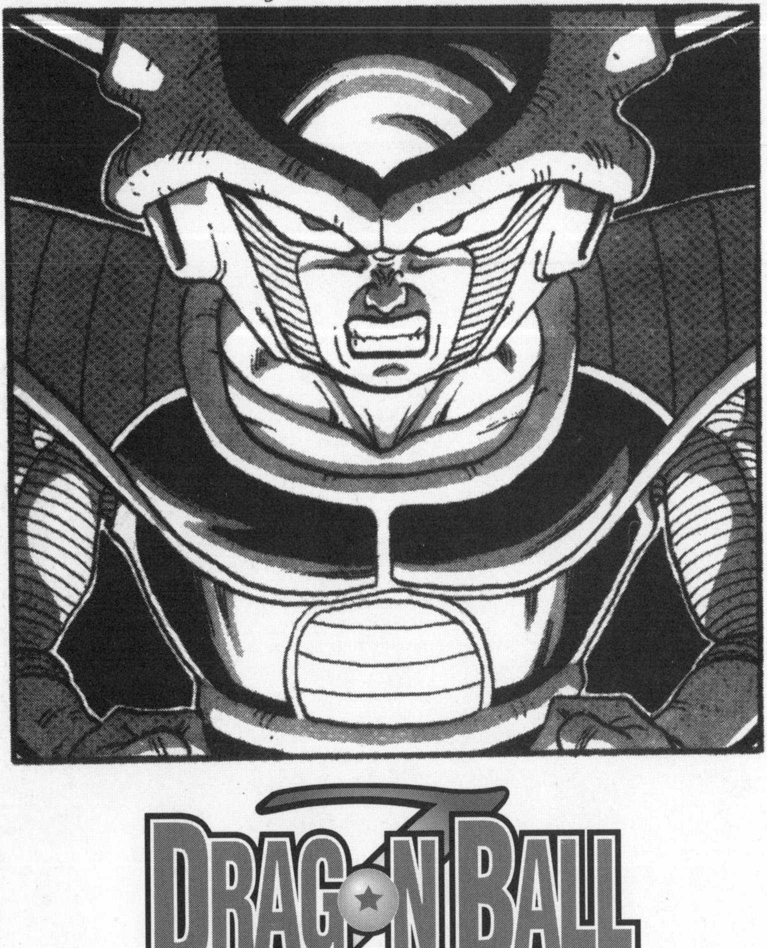

DRAGON BALL Z

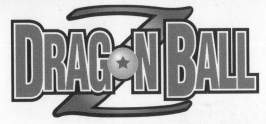

Vol. 9

DB: 25 of 42

STORY AND ART BY

AKIRA TORIYAMA

THE MAIN CHARACTERS

Bulma

Goku's oldest friend, Bulma is a scientific genius. She met Goku while on a quest for the seven magical Dragon Balls which, when gathered together, can grant any wish.

Son Goku

The greatest martial artist on Earth, he owes his strength to the training of Kame-Sen'nin and Kaiô-sama, and the fact that he's an alien Saiyan. To get even stronger, he has trained under 100 times Earth's gravity.

The Great Elder

The oldest living Namekian, its children include Dende and Nail. It created Namek's Dragon Balls in the same way that Kami-sama (Piccolo's twin) created Earth's Dragon Balls, and they are bound to its life force.

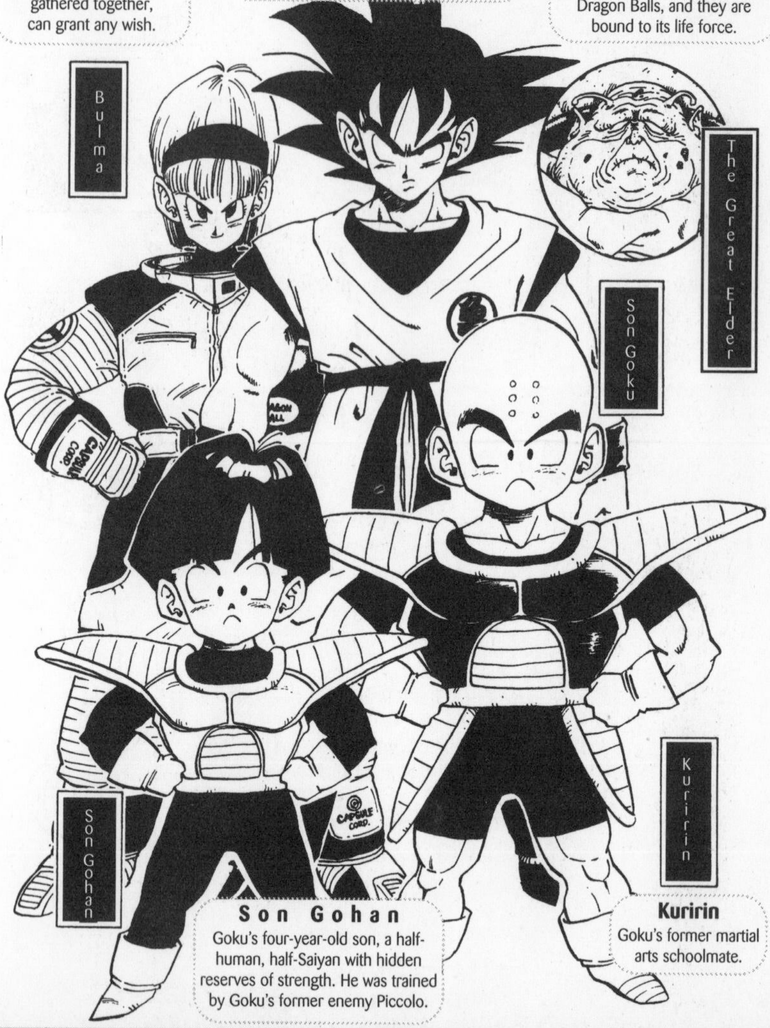

Bulma
The Great Elder
Son Goku
Kuririn
Son Gohan

Son Gohan

Goku's four-year-old son, a half-human, half-Saiyan with hidden reserves of strength. He was trained by Goku's former enemy Piccolo.

Kuririn

Goku's former martial arts schoolmate.

The Ginyu Force

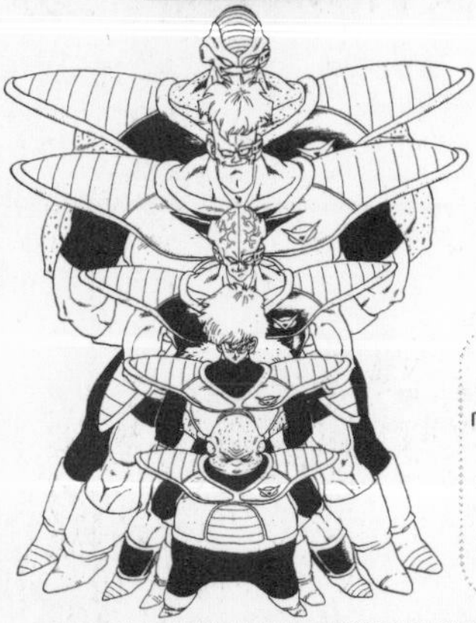

Freeza

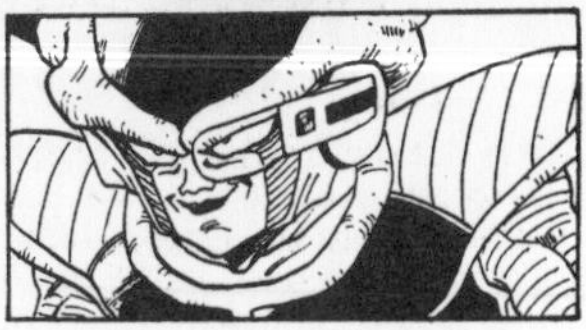

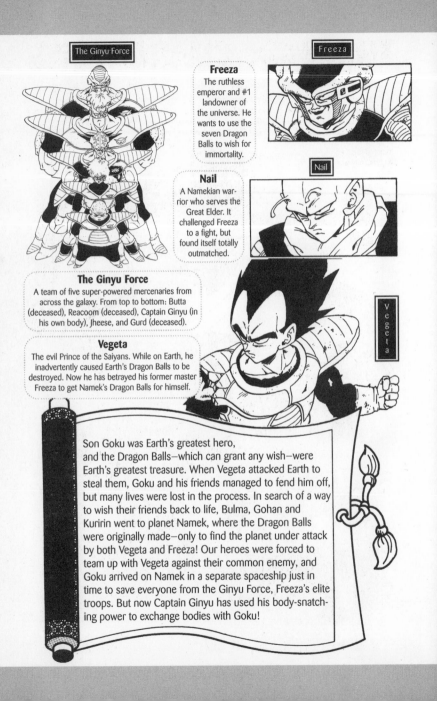

Freeza

The ruthless emperor and #1 landowner of the universe. He wants to use the seven Dragon Balls to wish for immortality.

Nail

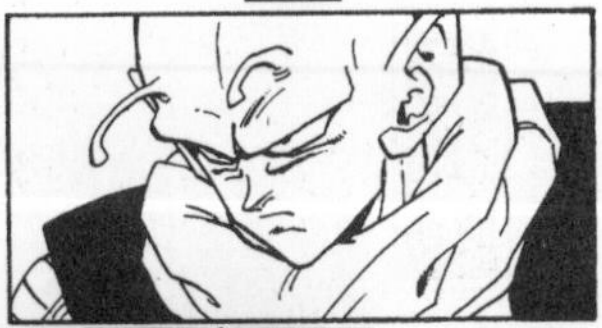

Nail

A Namekian warrior who serves the Great Elder. It challenged Freeza to a fight, but found itself totally outmatched.

The Ginyu Force

A team of five super-powered mercenaries from across the galaxy. From top to bottom: Butta (deceased), Reacoom (deceased), Captain Ginyu (in his own body), Jheese, and Gurd (deceased).

Vegeta

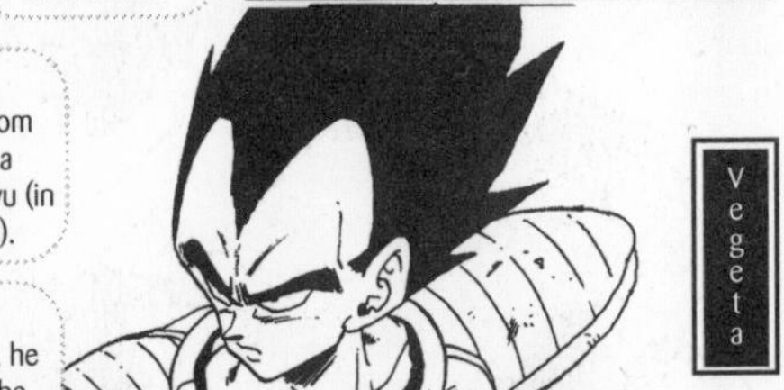

Vegeta

The evil Prince of the Saiyans. While on Earth, he inadvertently caused Earth's Dragon Balls to be destroyed. Now he has betrayed his former master Freeza to get Namek's Dragon Balls for himself.

Son Goku was Earth's greatest hero, and the Dragon Balls—which can grant any wish—were Earth's greatest treasure. When Vegeta attacked Earth to steal them, Goku and his friends managed to fend him off, but many lives were lost in the process. In search of a way to wish their friends back to life, Bulma, Gohan and Kuririn went to planet Namek, where the Dragon Balls were originally made—only to find the planet under attack by both Vegeta and Freeza! Our heroes were forced to team up with Vegeta against their common enemy, and Goku arrived on Namek in a separate spaceship just in time to save everyone from the Ginyu Force, Freeza's elite troops. But now Captain Ginyu has used his body-snatching power to exchange bodies with Goku!

DRAGON BALL Z 9

CONTENTS

DRAGON BALL

DBZ:95 • Ginyu's Mistake!

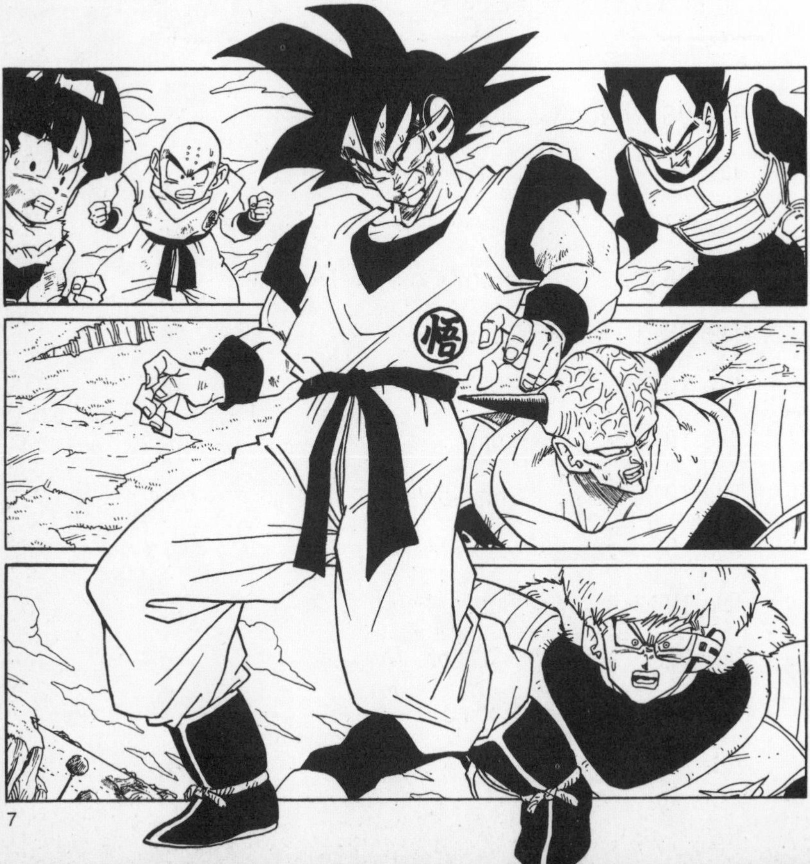
悟

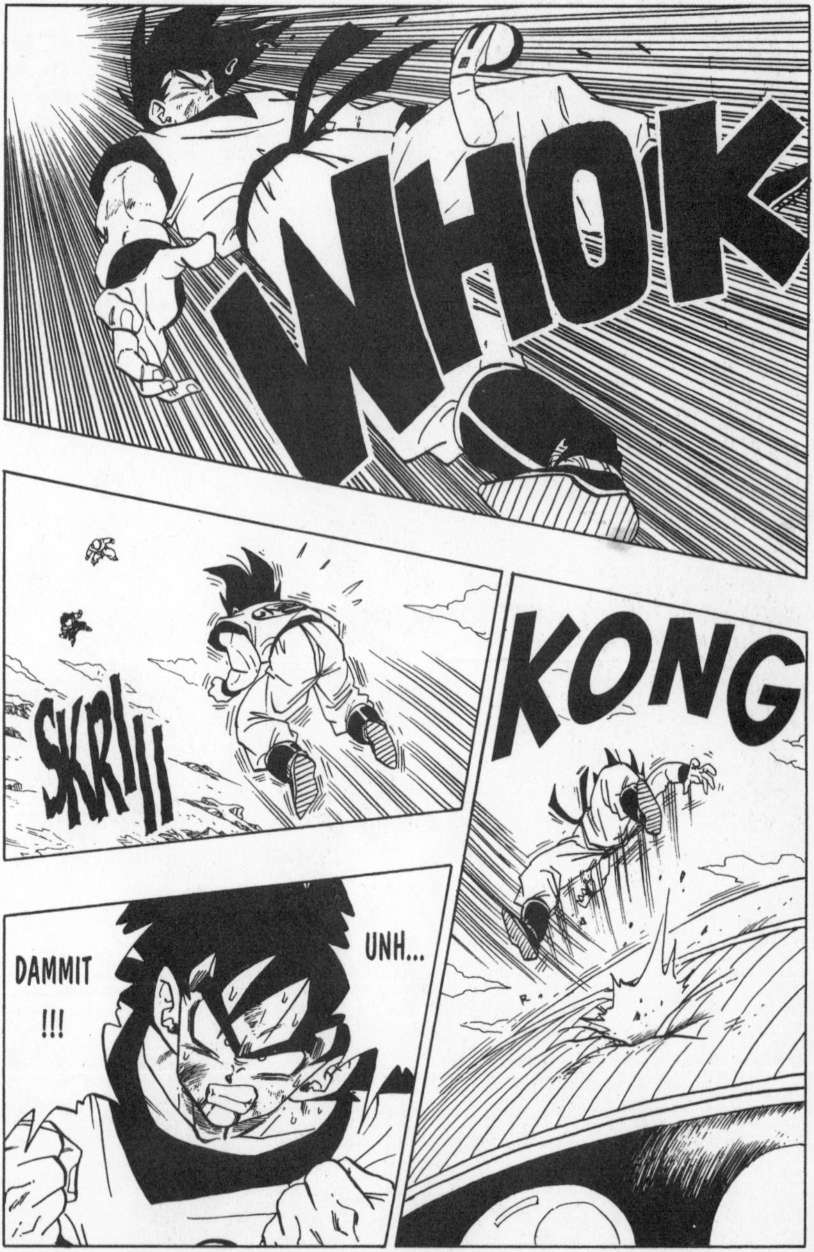
WHOK
KONG
SKRIII
UNH...
DAMMIT !!!

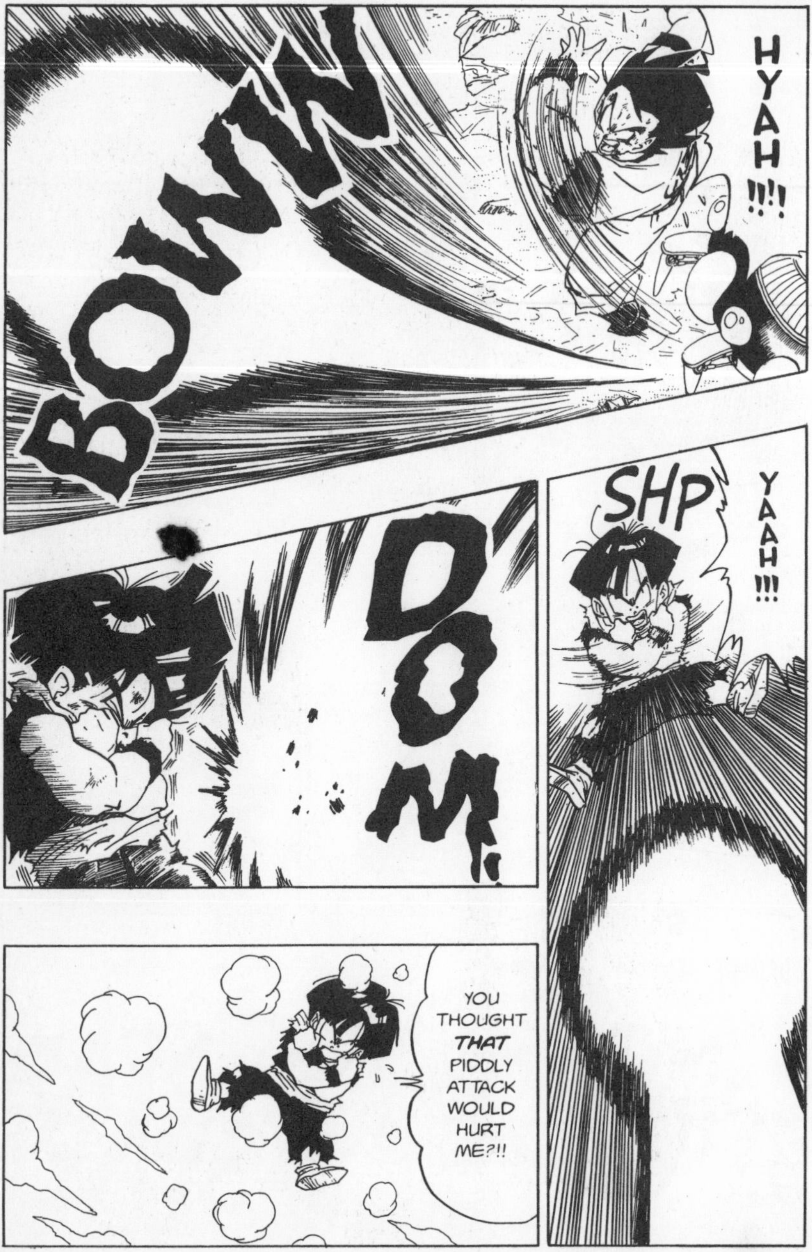
HYAH!!!!
BOWN
SHP
YAAH!!!
DOOM!
YOU THOUGHT *THAT* PIDDLY ATTACK WOULD HURT ME?!!

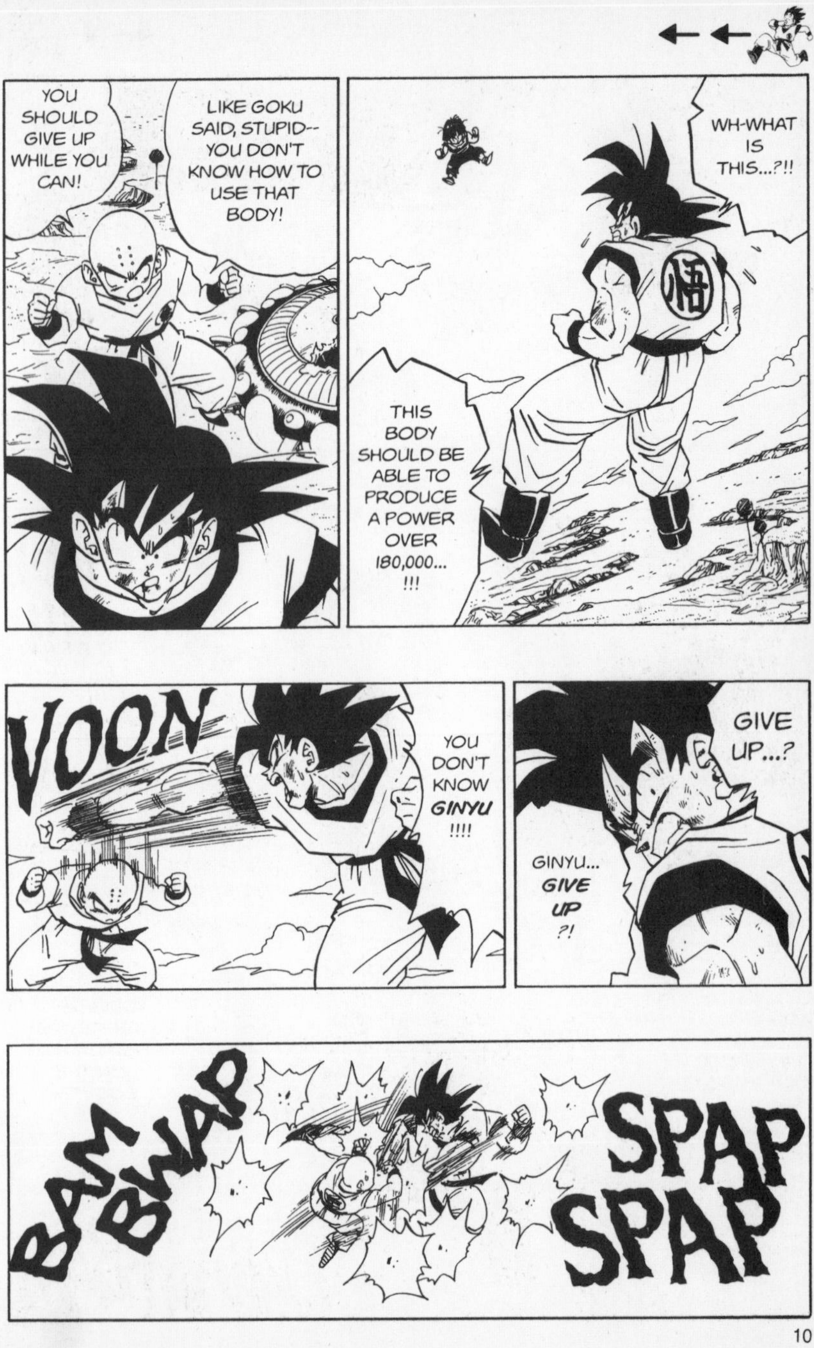
WH-WHAT IS THIS...?!!
THIS BODY SHOULD BE ABLE TO PRODUCE A POWER OVER 180,000... !!!
LIKE GOKU SAID, STUPID-- YOU DON'T KNOW HOW TO USE THAT BODY!
YOU SHOULD GIVE UP WHILE YOU CAN!
GIVE UP...?
GINYU... **GIVE UP** ?!
YOU DON'T KNOW **GINYU** !!!!
VOON
SPAP
SPAP
BWAP
BAM

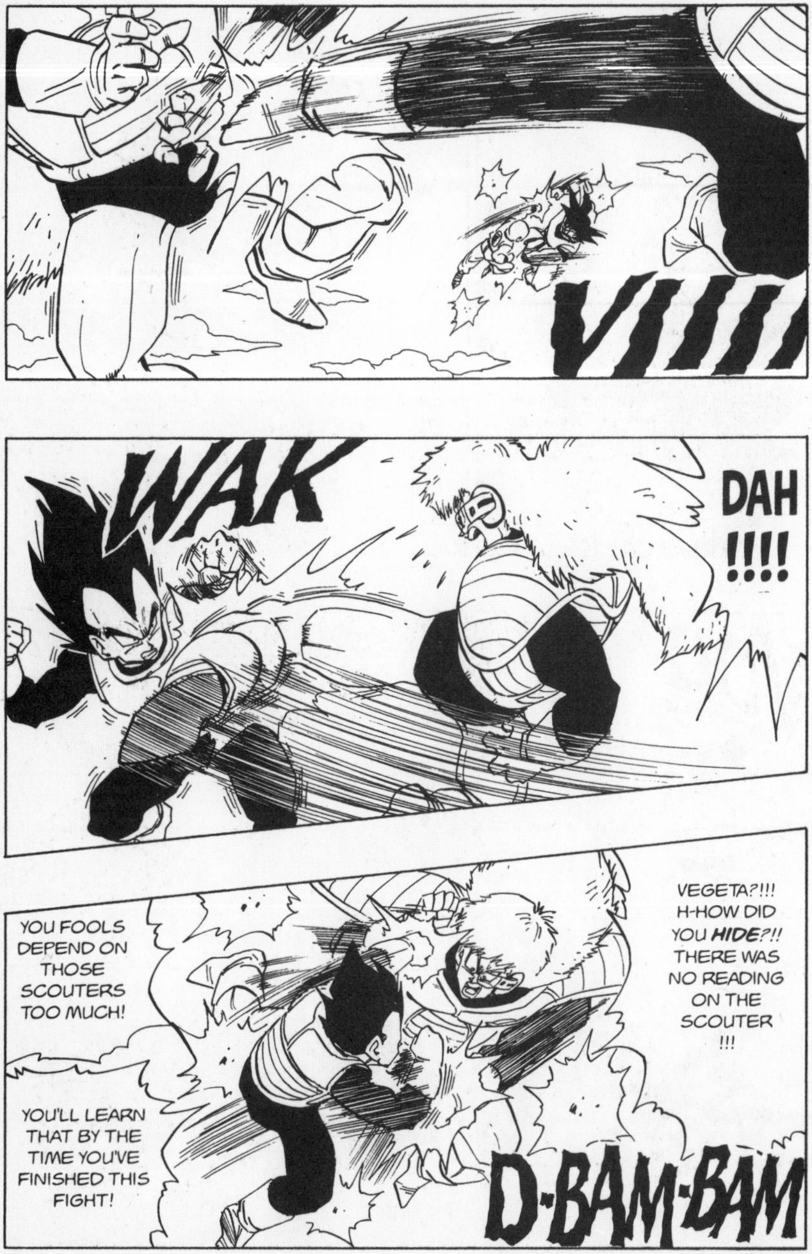
VIIII
DAH !!!!
WAK
VEGETA?!!! H-HOW DID YOU *HIDE?!!* THERE WAS NO READING ON THE SCOUTER !!!
YOU FOOLS DEPEND ON THOSE SCOUTERS TOO MUCH!
YOU'LL LEARN THAT BY THE TIME YOU'VE FINISHED THIS FIGHT!
D-BAM-BAM

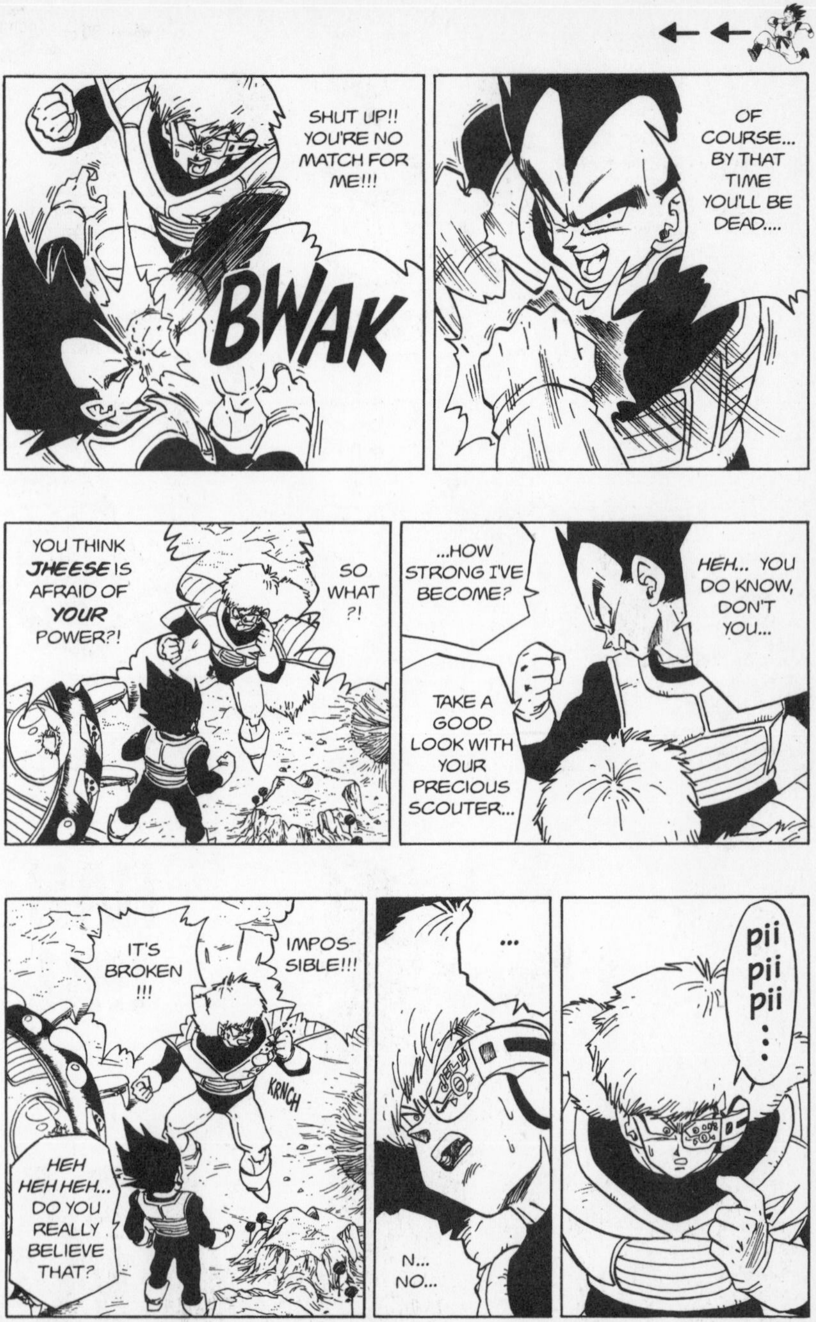
OF COURSE... BY THAT TIME YOU'LL BE DEAD....
SHUT UP!! YOU'RE NO MATCH FOR ME!!!
BWAK
HEH... YOU DO KNOW, DON'T YOU...
...HOW STRONG I'VE BECOME?
TAKE A GOOD LOOK WITH YOUR PRECIOUS SCOUTER...
SO WHAT ?!
YOU THINK JHEESE IS AFRAID OF YOUR POWER?!
pii pii pii ...
...
N... NO...
IMPOSSIBLE!!!
IT'S BROKEN !!!
KRNCH
HEH HEH HEH... DO YOU REALLY BELIEVE THAT?

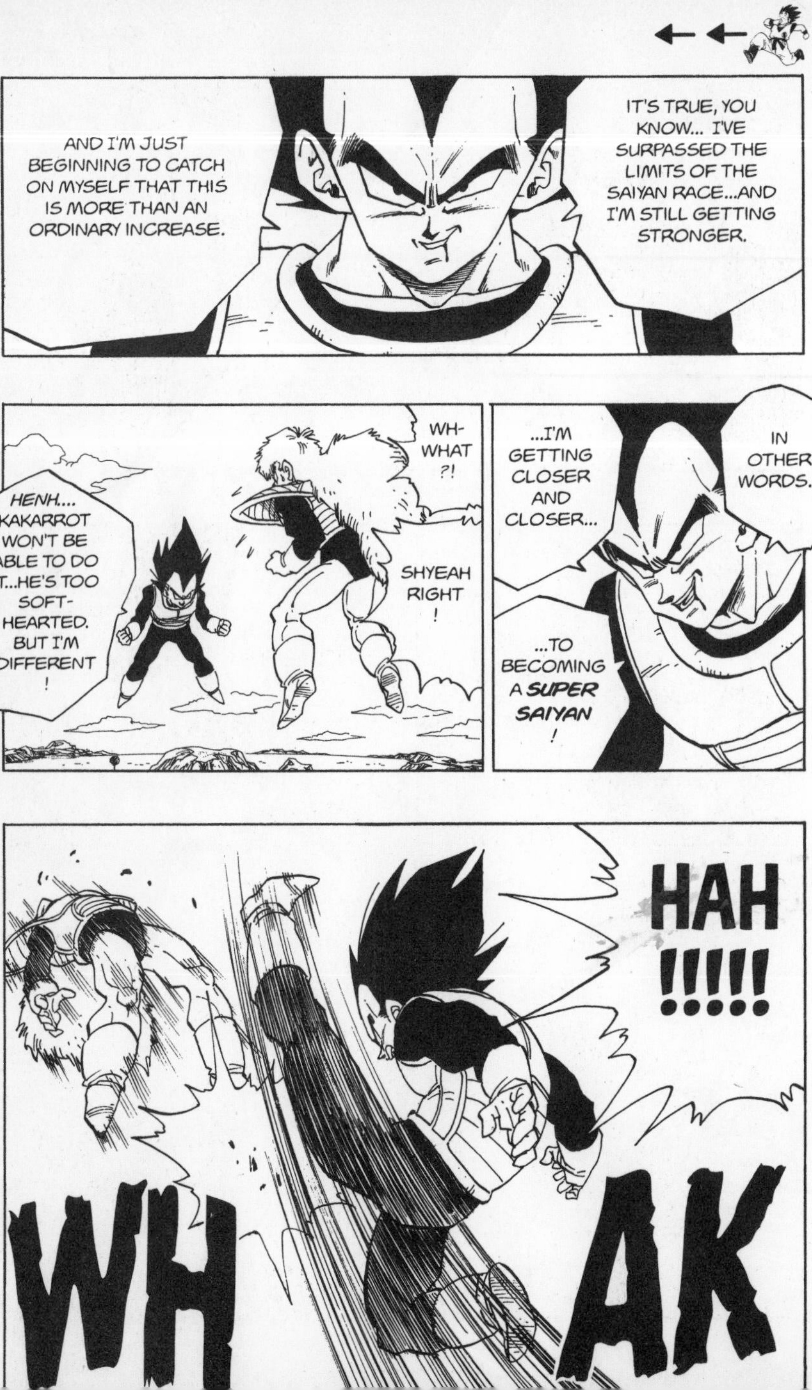
IT'S TRUE, YOU KNOW... I'VE SURPASSED THE LIMITS OF THE SAIYAN RACE...AND I'M STILL GETTING STRONGER.
AND I'M JUST BEGINNING TO CATCH ON MYSELF THAT THIS IS MORE THAN AN ORDINARY INCREASE.
IN OTHER WORDS...
...I'M GETTING CLOSER AND CLOSER...
...TO BECOMING A *SUPER SAIYAN*!
WH-WHAT?!
SHYEAH RIGHT!
HENH.... KAKARROT WON'T BE ABLE TO DO IT...HE'S TOO SOFT-HEARTED. BUT I'M DIFFERENT!
HAH!!!!!
WHAK

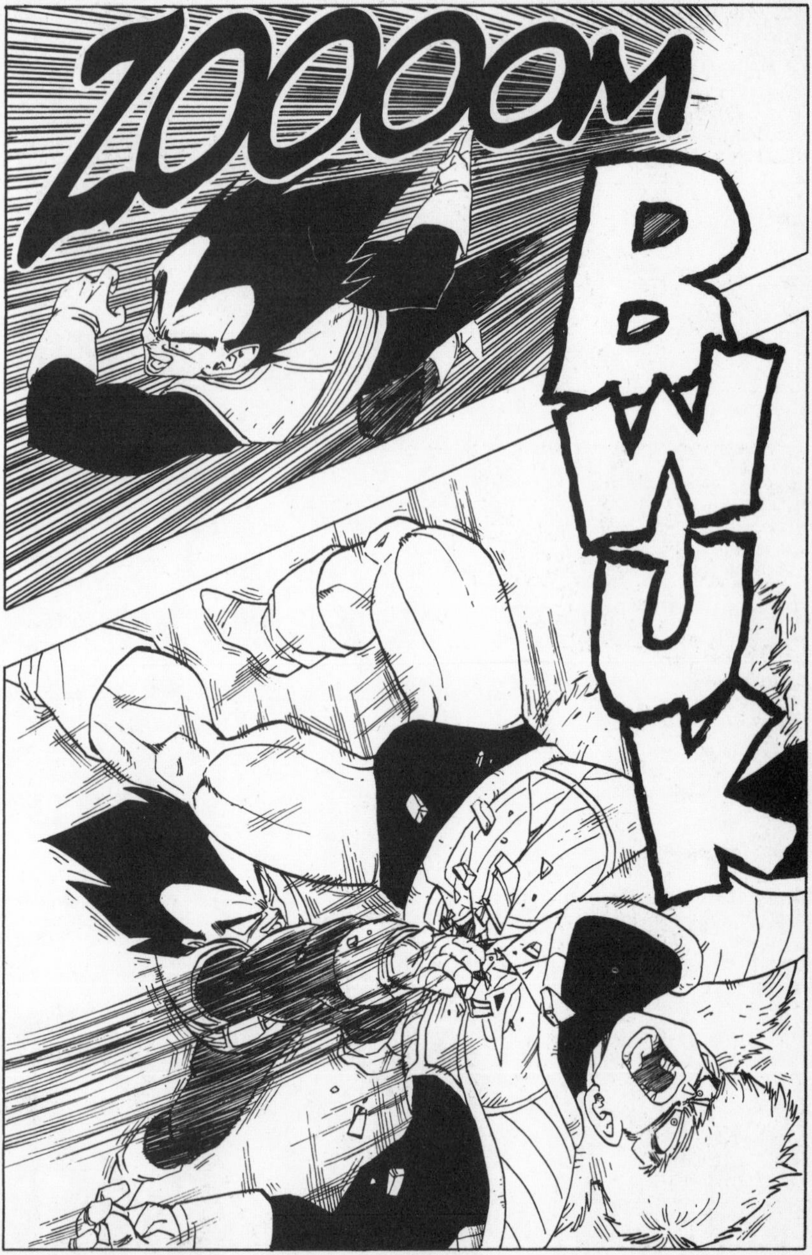
ZOOOOM
BWUK

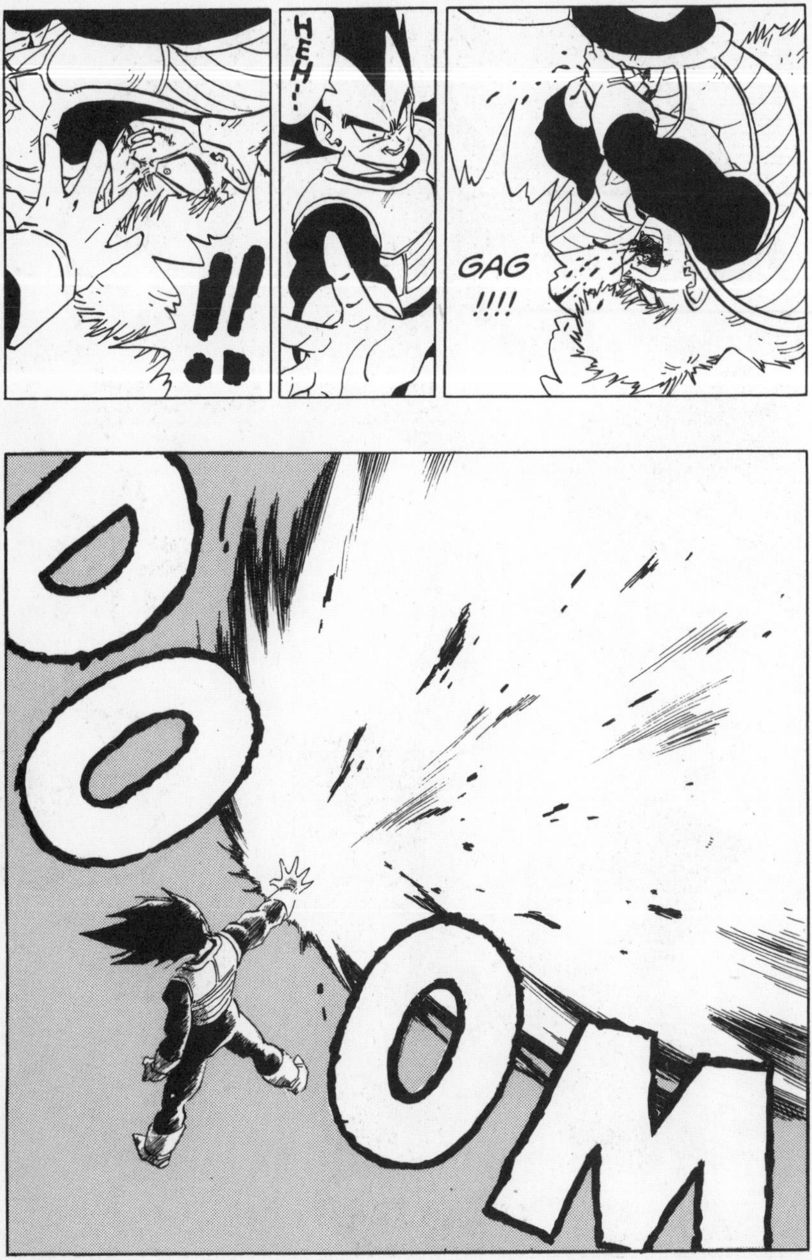
GAG !!!!
HEH!!
!!
DOOM

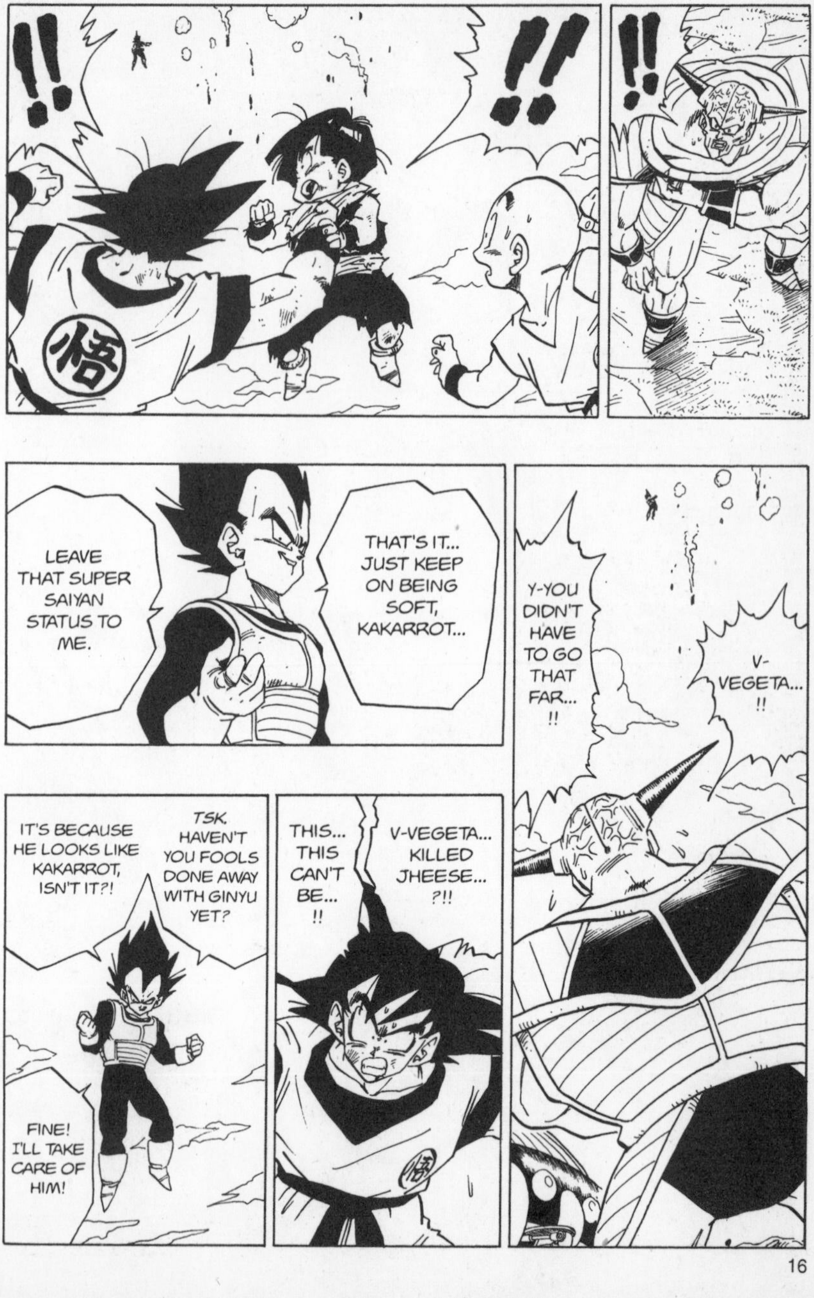
!!
!!
!!
V-
VEGETA...
!!
Y-YOU DIDN'T HAVE TO GO THAT FAR... !!
THAT'S IT... JUST KEEP ON BEING SOFT, KAKARROT...
LEAVE THAT SUPER SAIYAN STATUS TO ME.
V-VEGETA... KILLED JHEESE... ?!!
THIS... THIS CAN'T BE... !!
TSK. HAVEN'T YOU FOOLS DONE AWAY WITH GINYU YET?
IT'S BECAUSE HE LOOKS LIKE KAKARROT, ISN'T IT?!
FINE! I'LL TAKE CARE OF HIM!

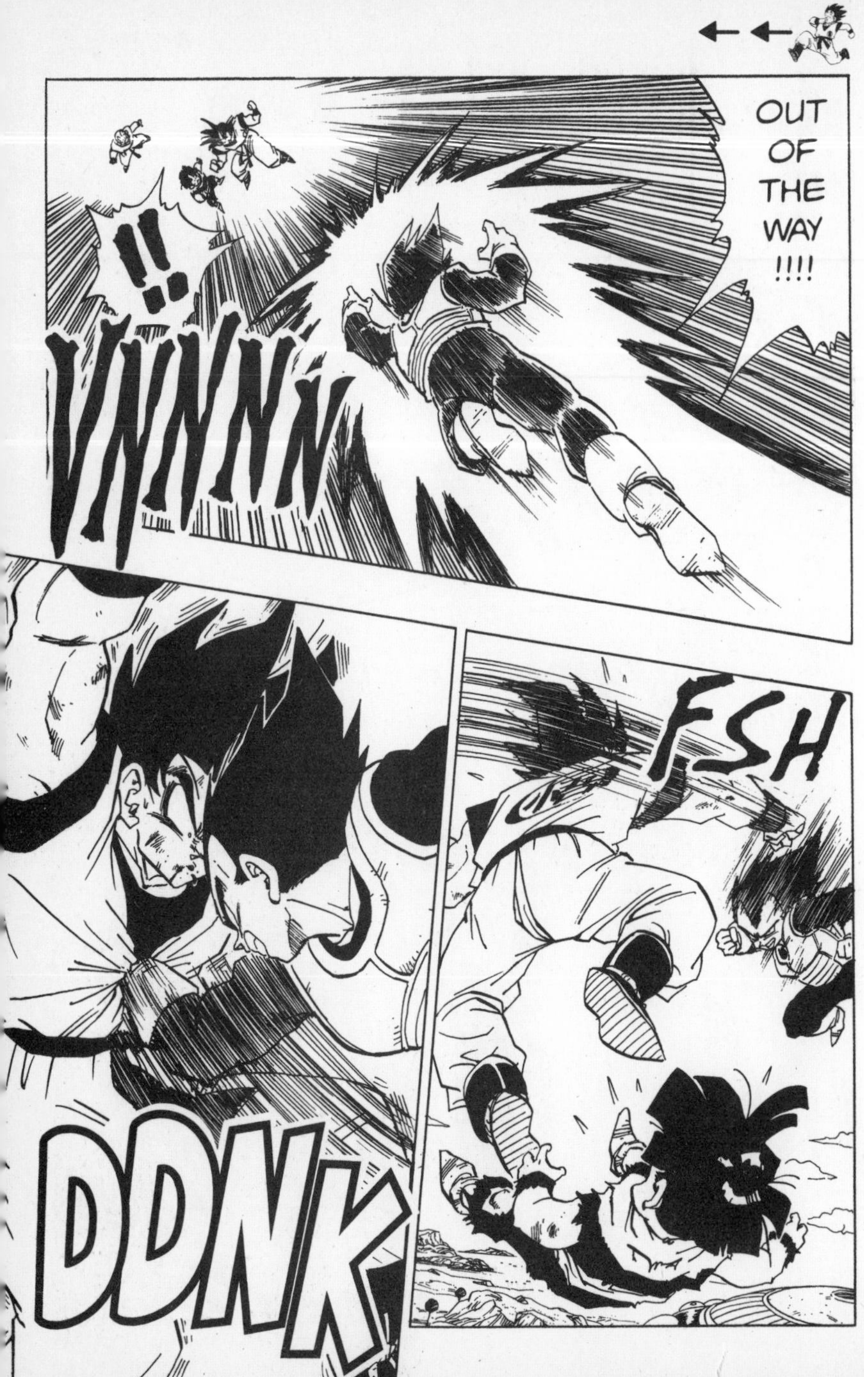
OUT OF THE WAY !!!!
!!
VNNNN
FSH
DDNK

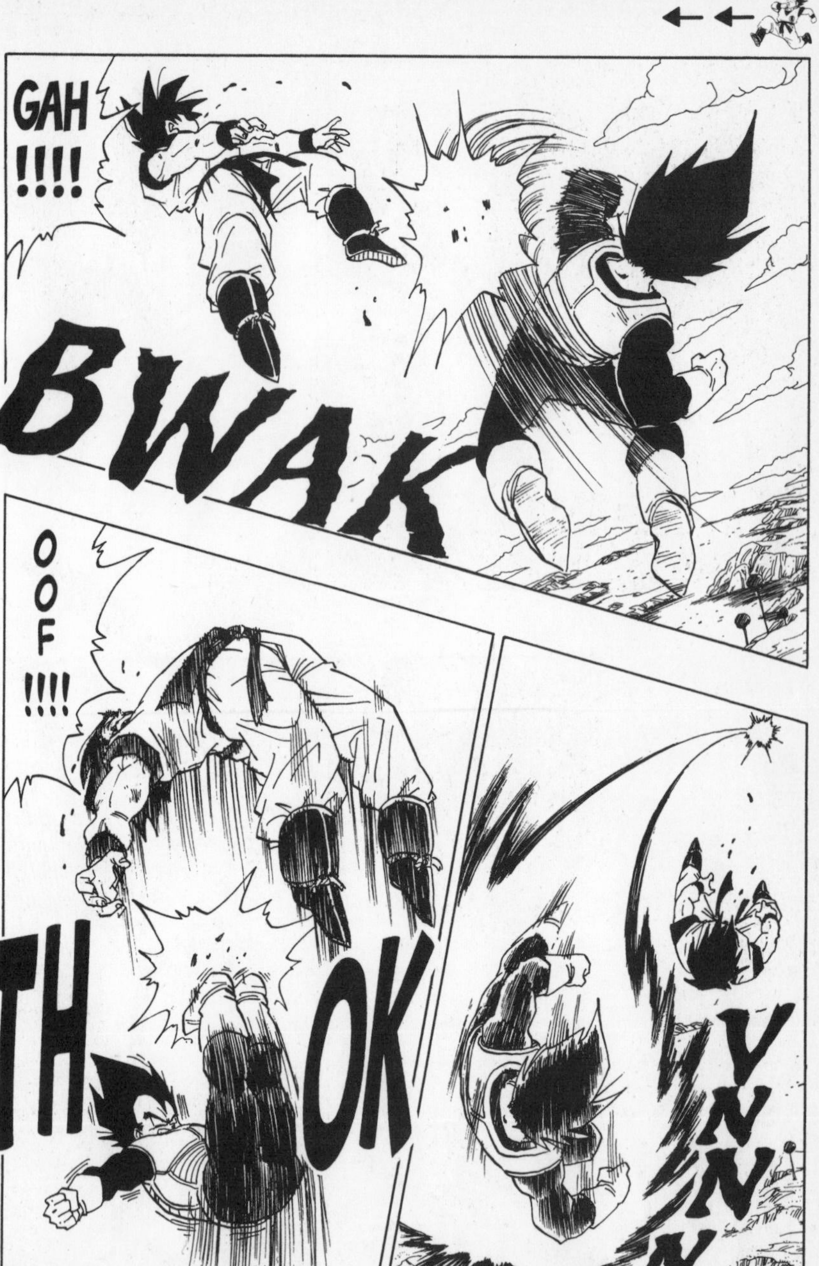
GAH !!!!
BWAK
VNNNN
OOF !!!!
TH OK

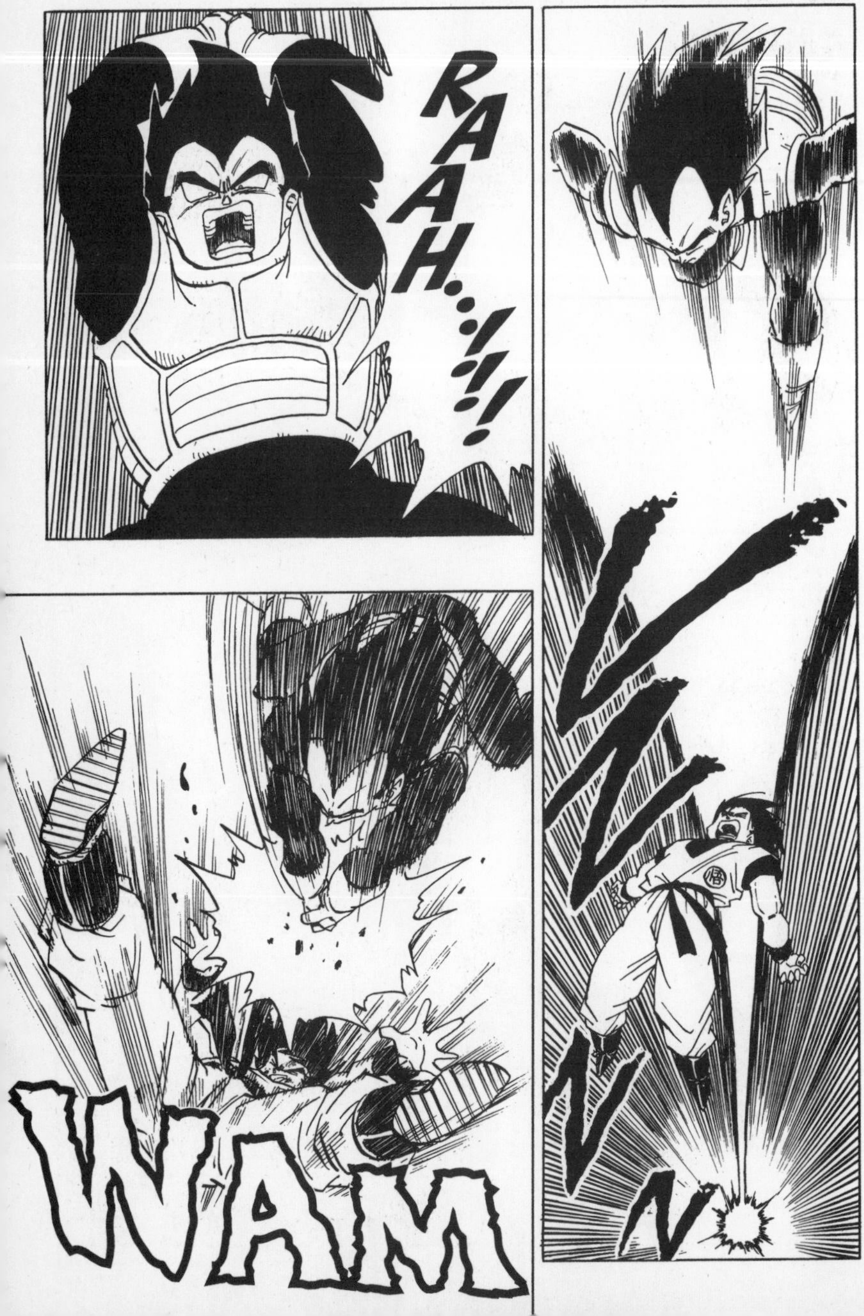
RAAH...!!!
WAM

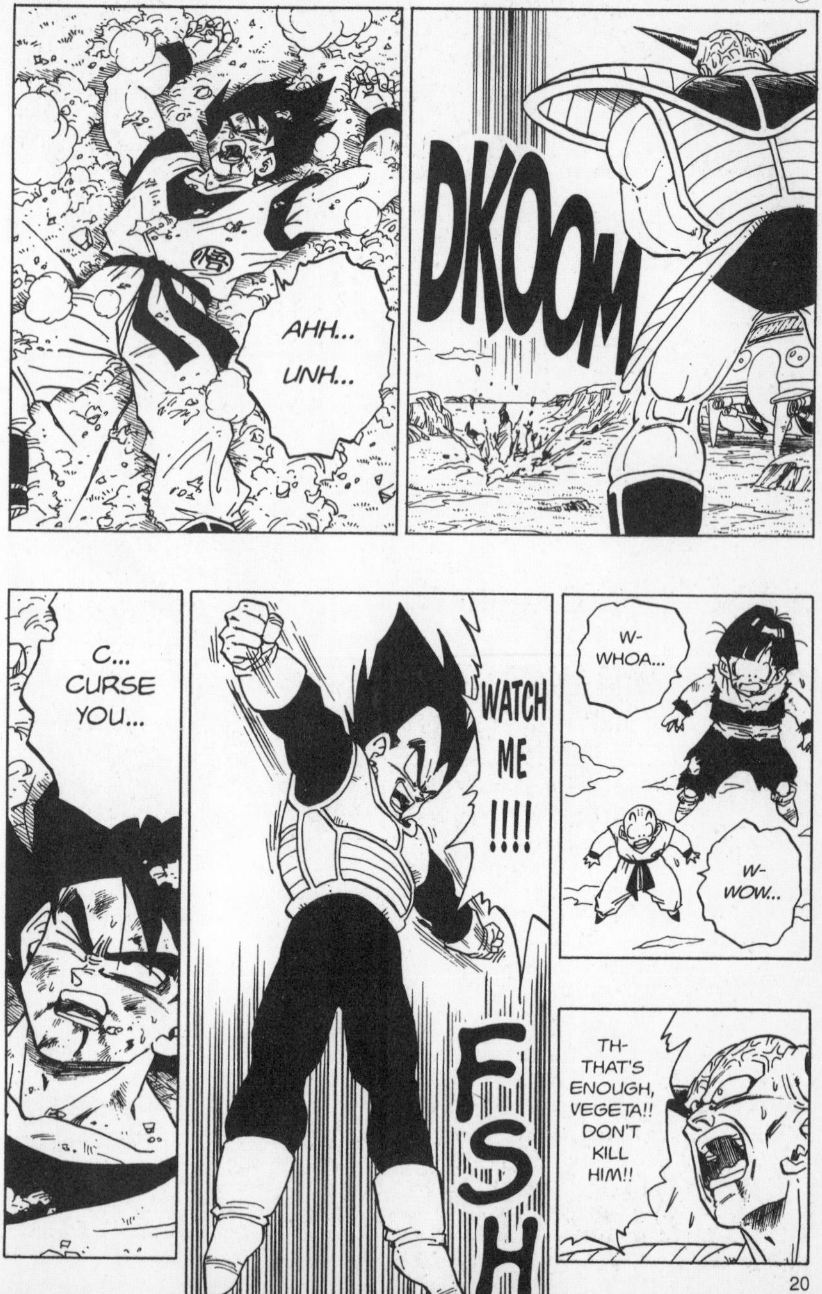
DKOOM
AHH... UNH...
W-WHOA...
W-WOW...
TH-THAT'S ENOUGH, VEGETA!! DON'T KILL HIM!!
WATCH ME !!!!
FSH
C... CURSE YOU...

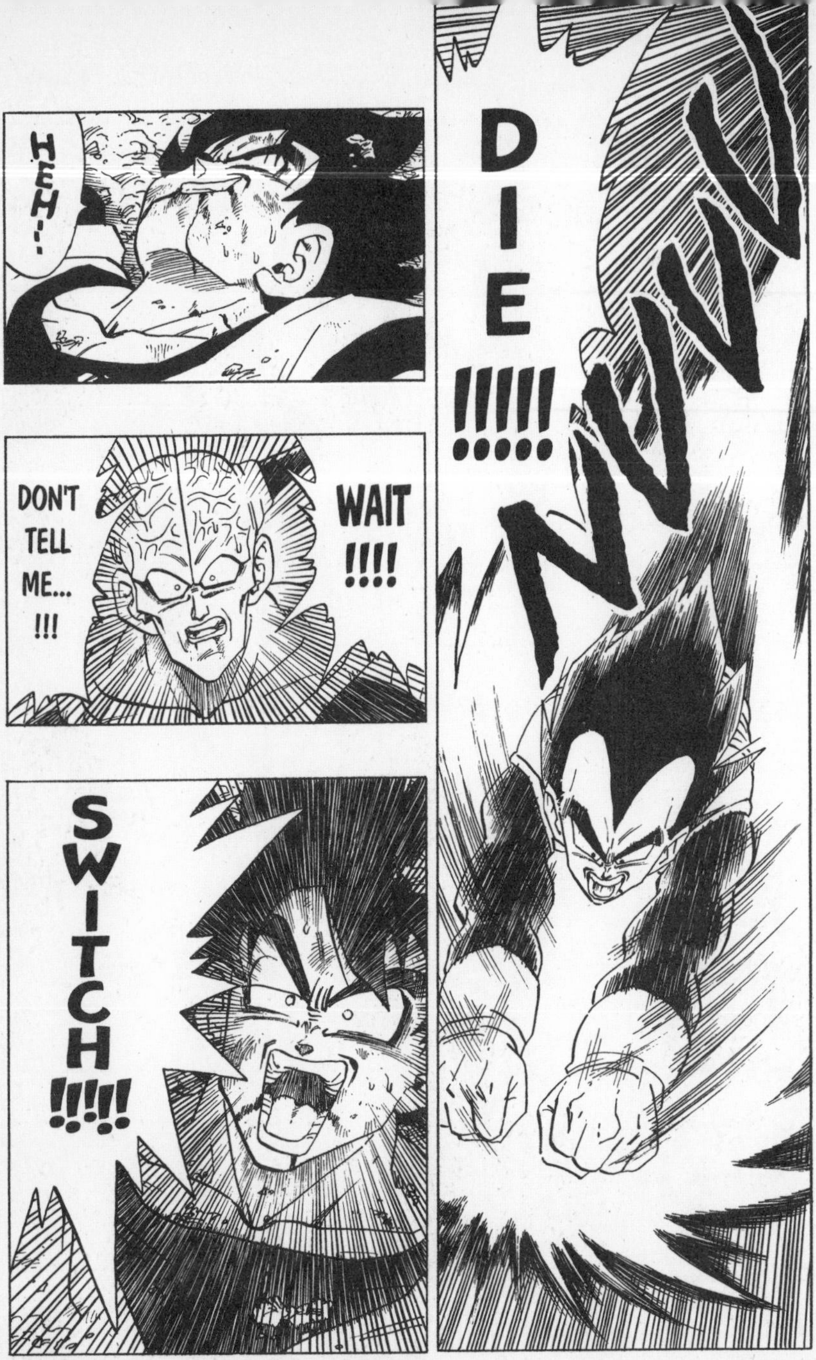
DIE!!!!!
HEH!..
WAIT!!!!
DON'T TELL ME...!!!
SWITCH!!!!!

NEXT: Is This the End?!

DBZ:96 • The Final Switch

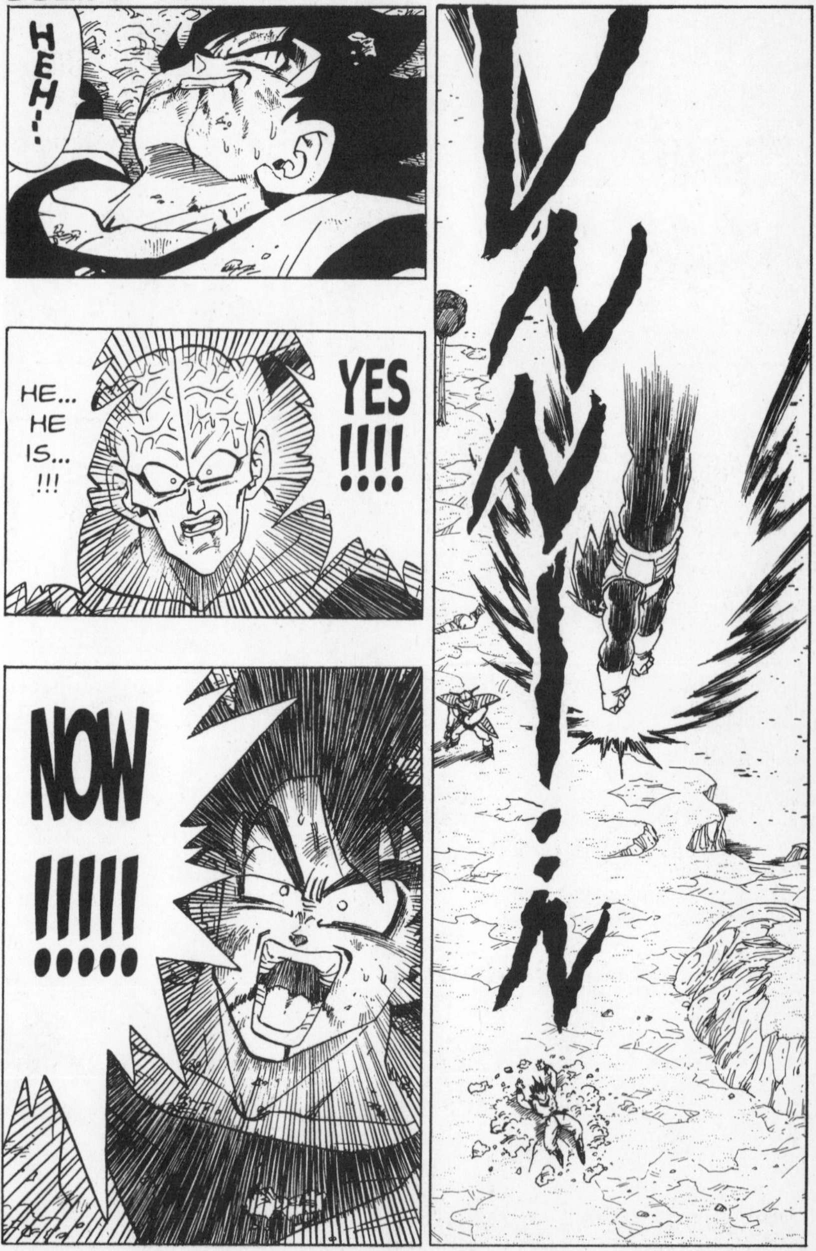
HEH...
HE... HE IS... !!!
YES !!!!
NOW !!!!!

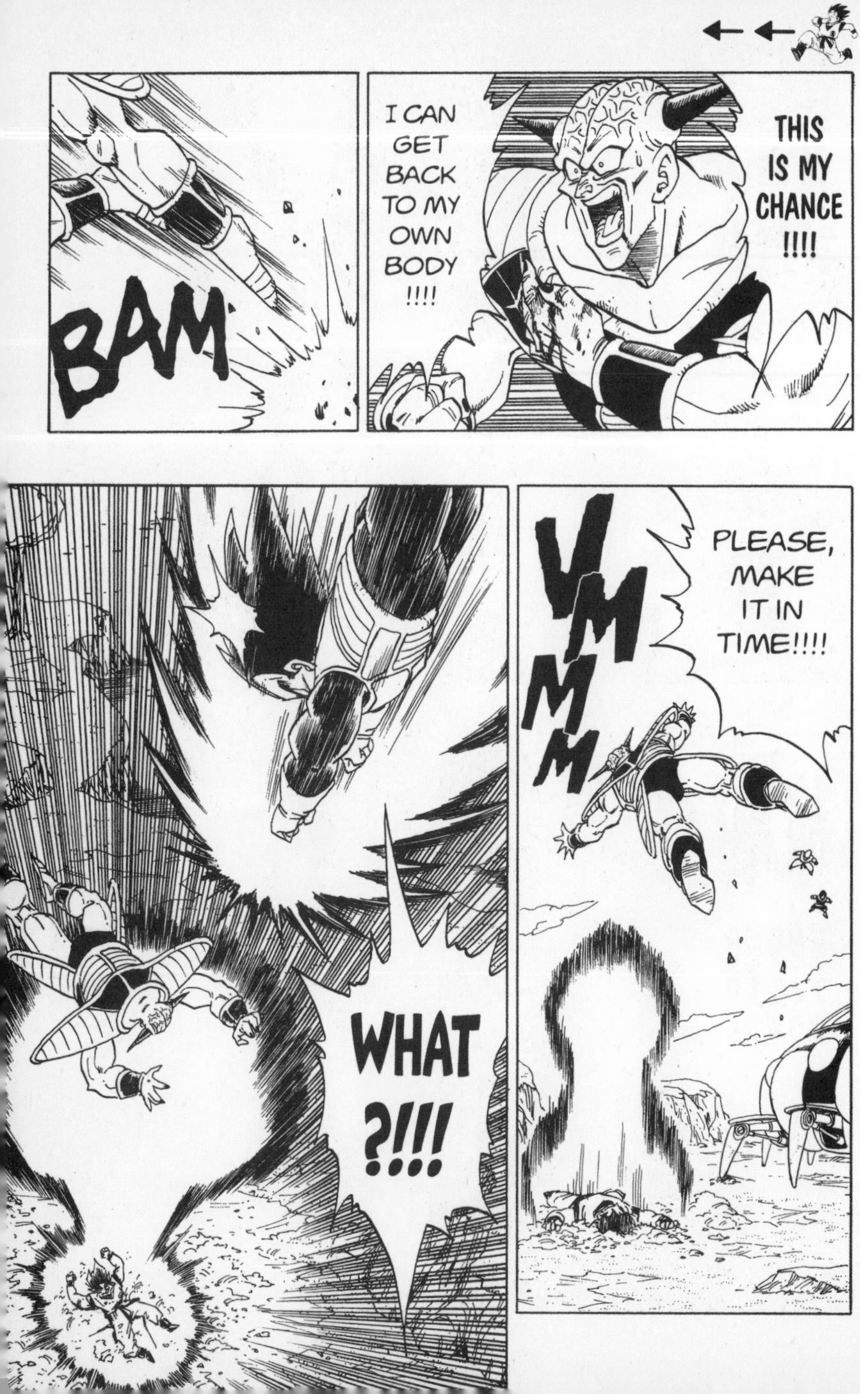

THIS IS MY CHANCE!!!!
I CAN GET BACK TO MY OWN BODY!!!!
BAM
PLEASE, MAKE IT IN TIME!!!!
VMMM
WHAT?!!!

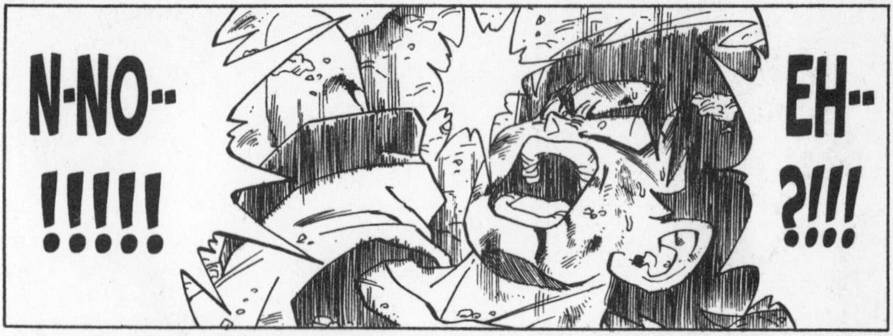
EH--?!!!
N-NO--!!!!!!
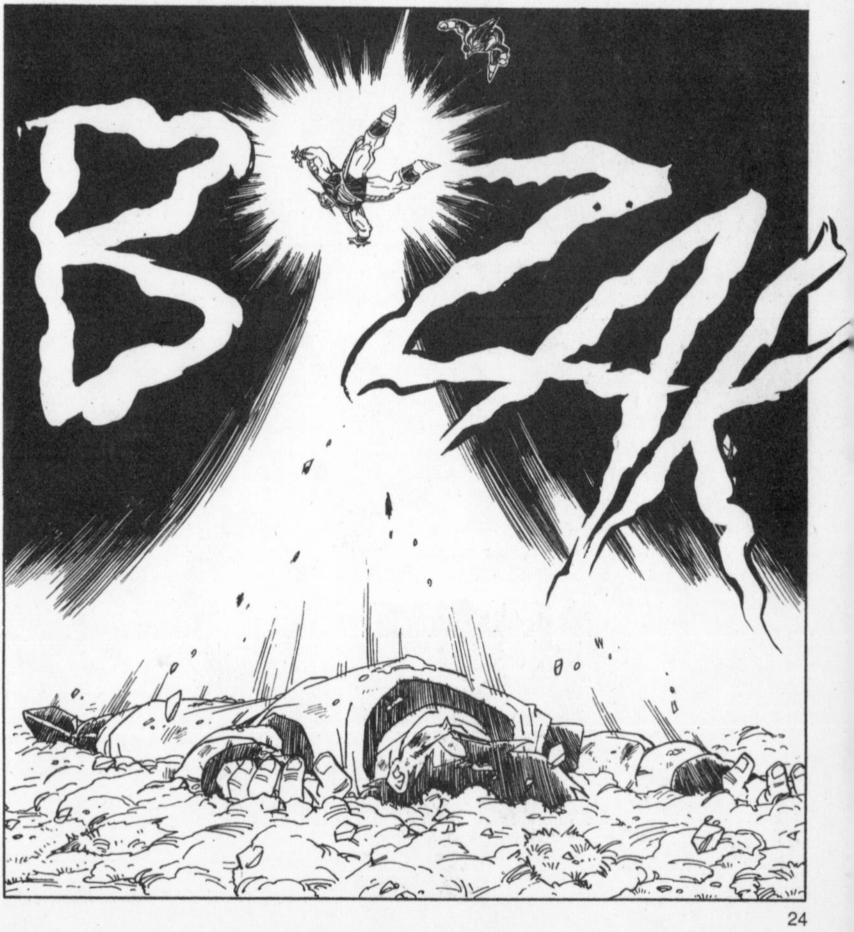

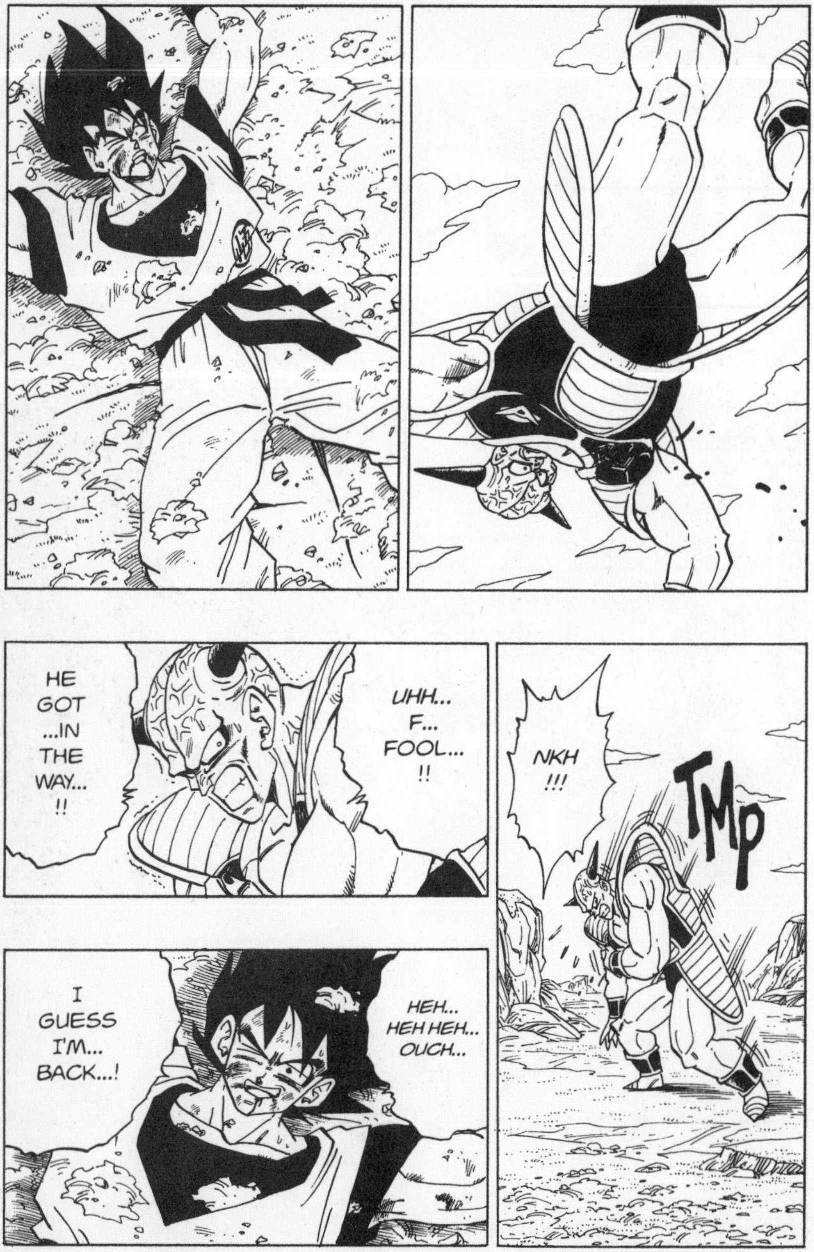
NKH!!!
TMP
UHH... F... FOOL... !!
HE GOT ...IN THE WAY... !!
HEH... HEH HEH... OUCH...
I GUESS I'M... BACK...!

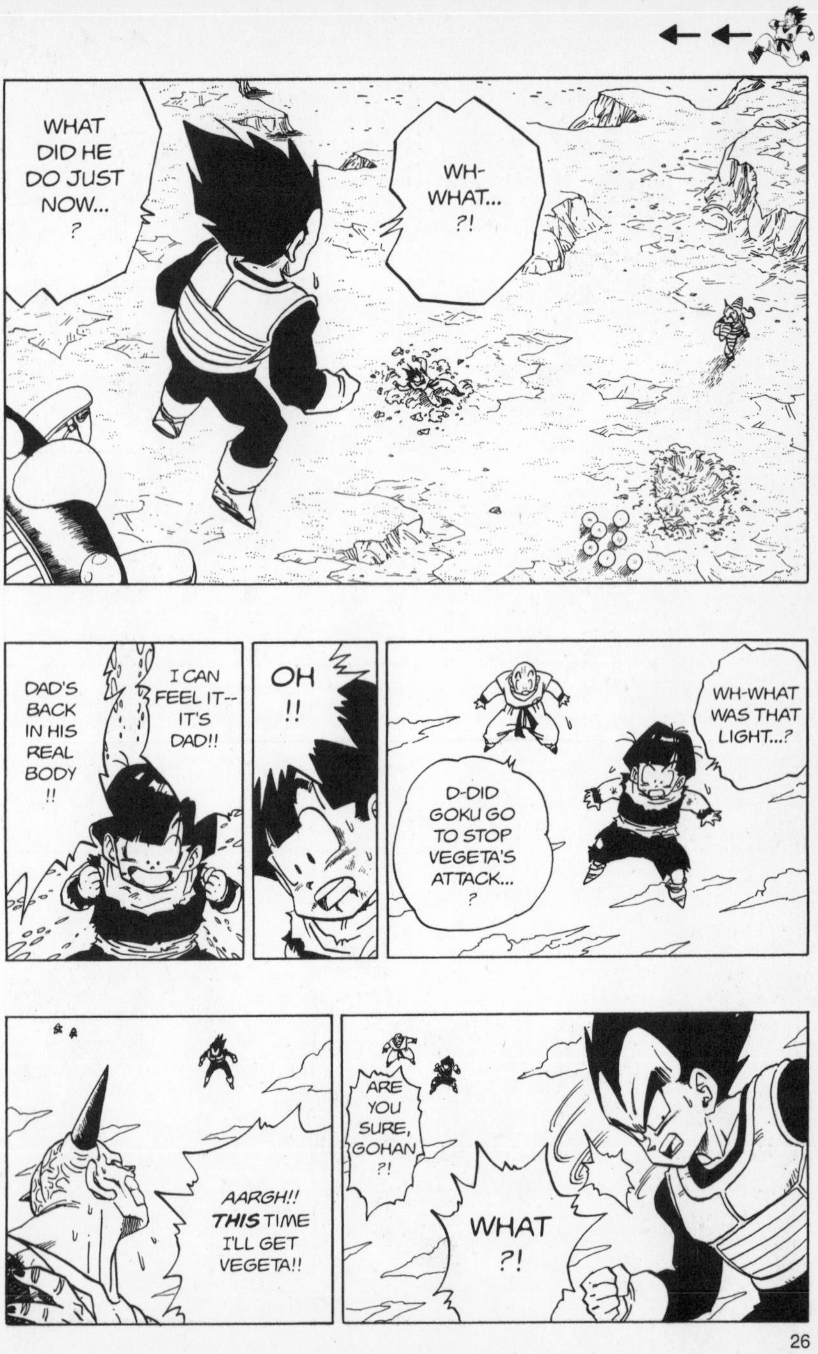
WH-WHAT...?!
WHAT DID HE DO JUST NOW...?
WH-WHAT WAS THAT LIGHT...?
D-DID GOKU GO TO STOP VEGETA'S ATTACK...?
OH!!
I CAN FEEL IT-- IT'S DAD!!
DAD'S BACK IN HIS REAL BODY!!
ARE YOU SURE, GOHAN?!
WHAT?!
AARGH!! THIS TIME I'LL GET VEGETA!!

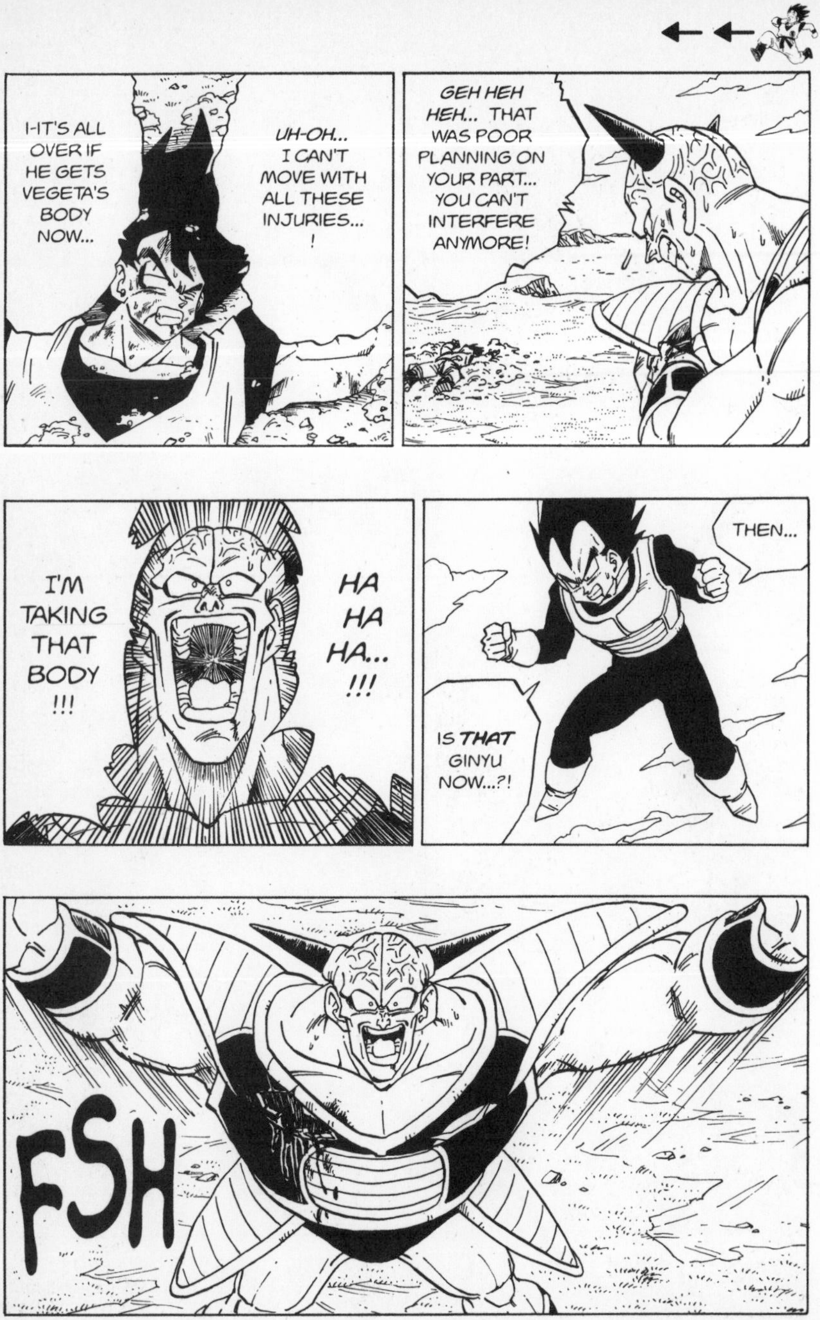
GEH HEH HEH... THAT WAS POOR PLANNING ON YOUR PART... YOU CAN'T INTERFERE ANYMORE!
UH-OH... I CAN'T MOVE WITH ALL THESE INJURIES...!
I-IT'S ALL OVER IF HE GETS VEGETA'S BODY NOW...
THEN...
IS THAT GINYU NOW...?!
HA HA HA...!!!
I'M TAKING THAT BODY!!!
FSH

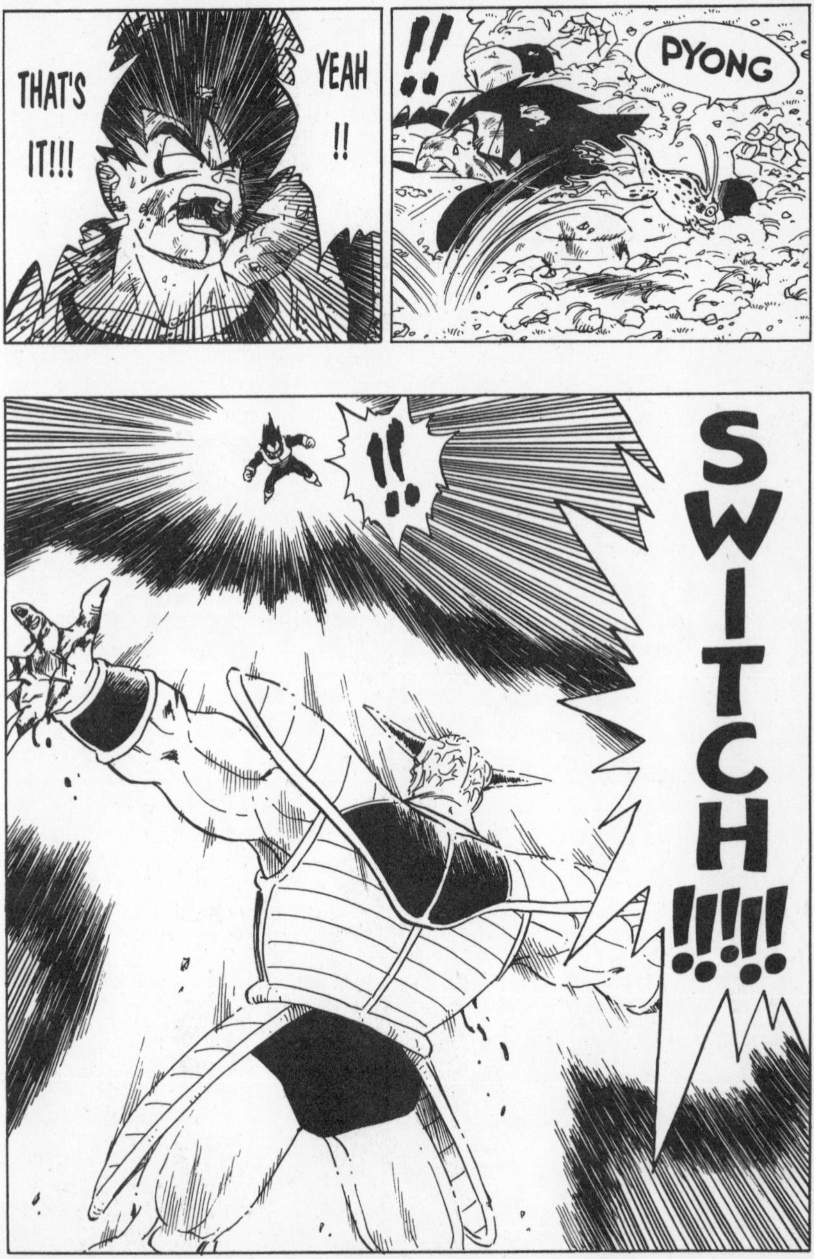
!!
PYONG
YEAH!!
THAT'S IT!!!!
!!
SWITCH!!!!!

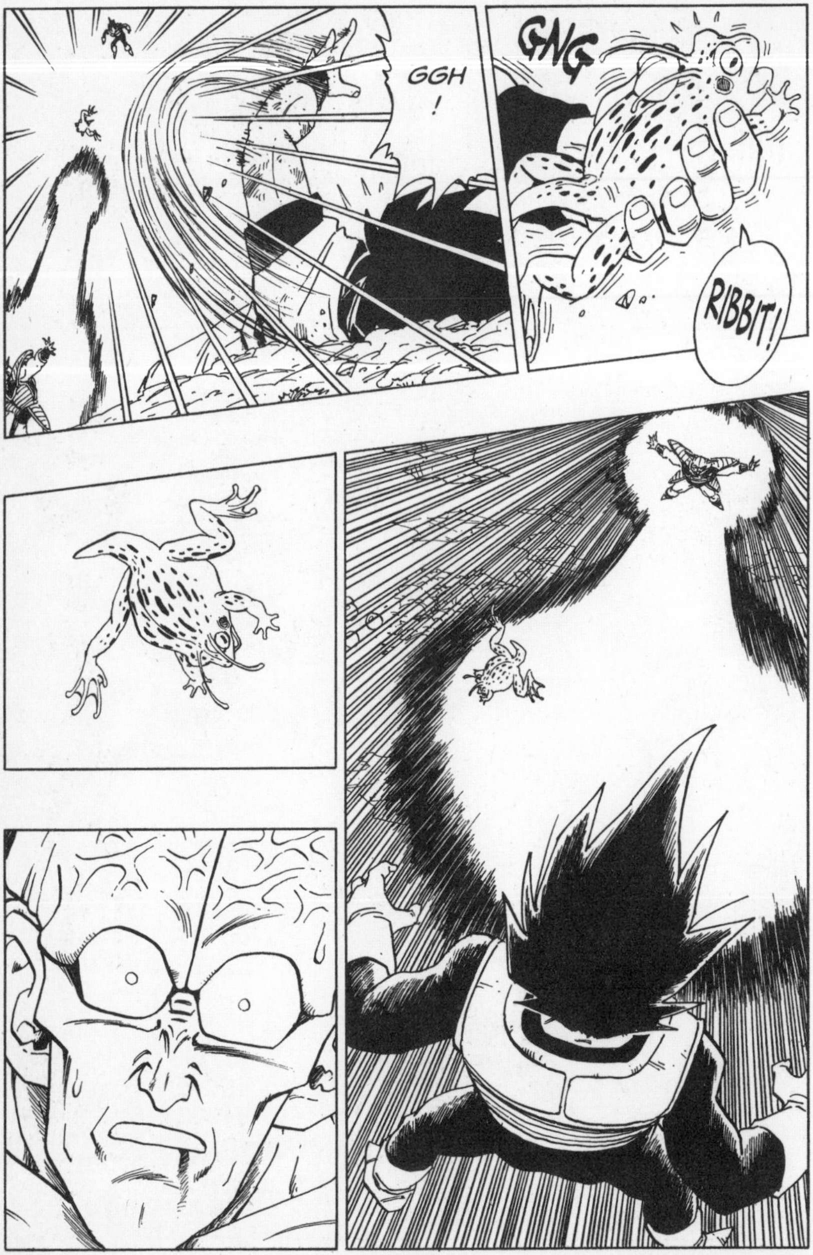
GNG
RIBBIT!
GGH
!

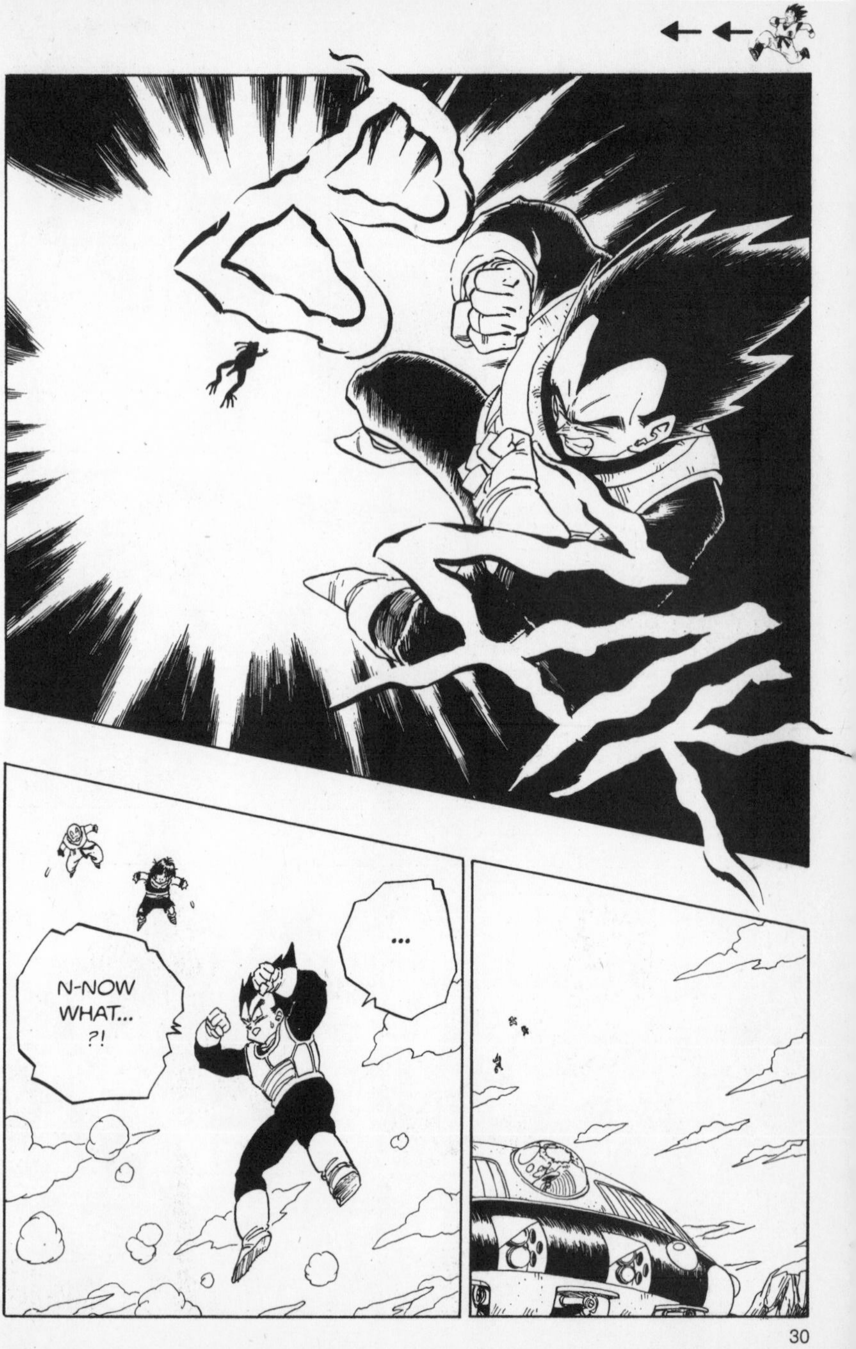
...
N-NOW WHAT... ?!

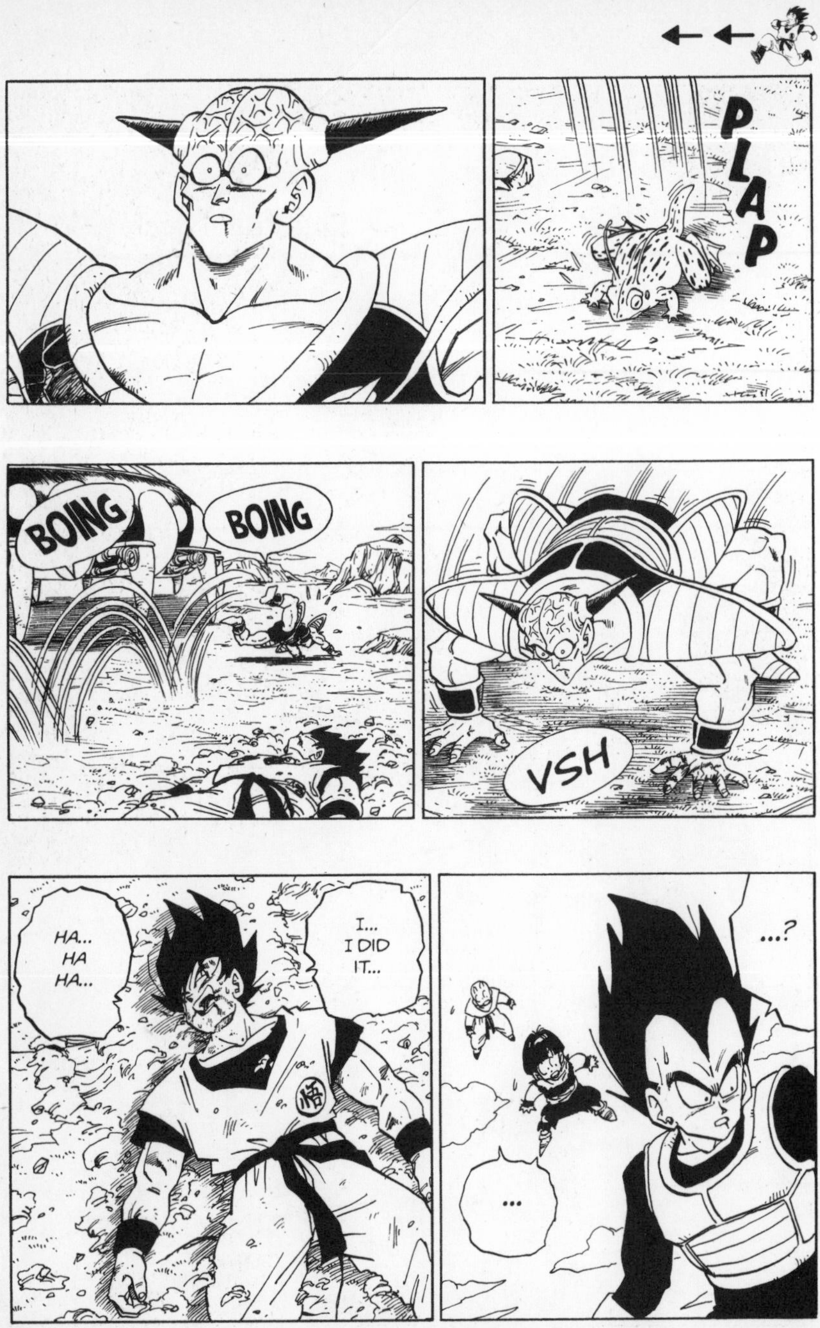
PLAP
VSH
BOING
BOING
...?
...
I... I DID IT...
HA... HA HA...

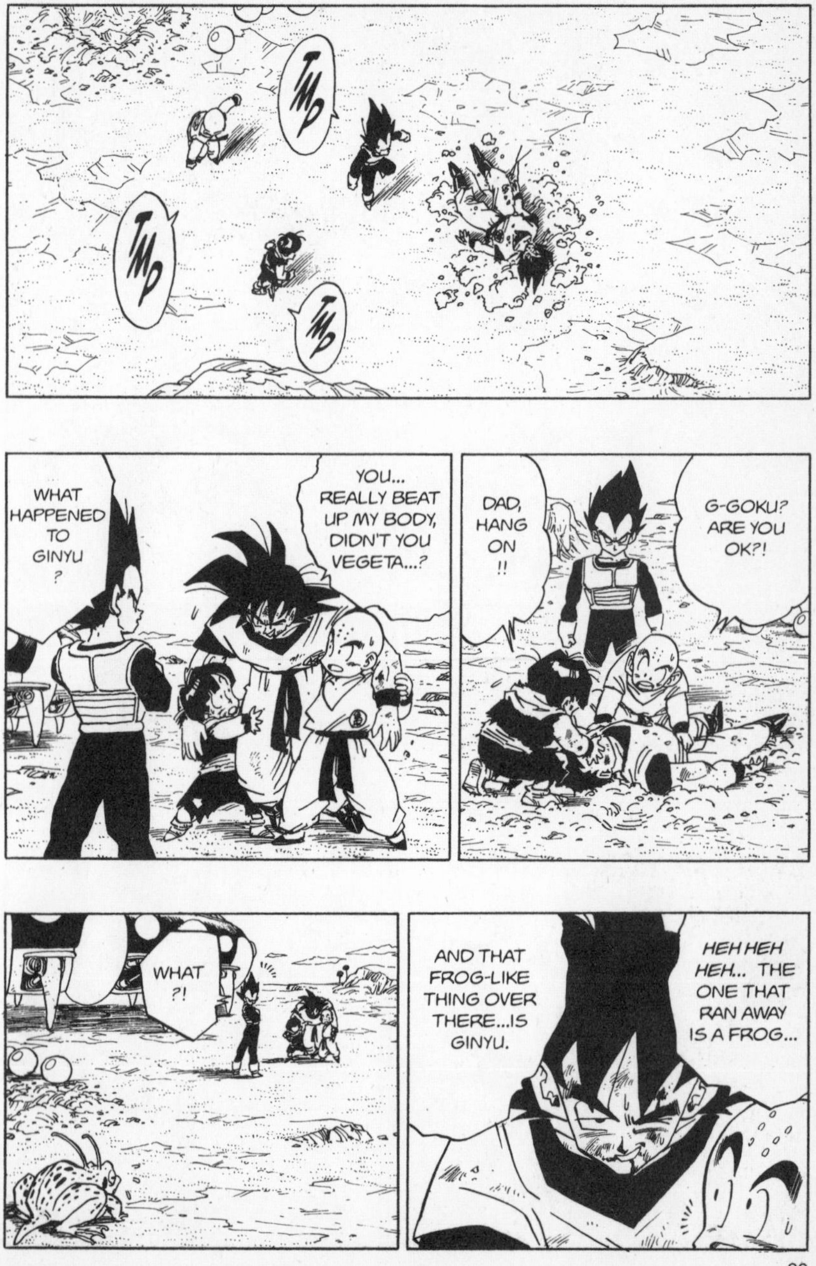
TMP
TMP
TMP
G-GOKU? ARE YOU OK?!
DAD, HANG ON !!
YOU... REALLY BEAT UP MY BODY, DIDN'T YOU VEGETA...?
WHAT HAPPENED TO GINYU ?
HEH HEH HEH... THE ONE THAT RAN AWAY IS A FROG...
AND THAT FROG-LIKE THING OVER THERE...IS GINYU.
WHAT ?!

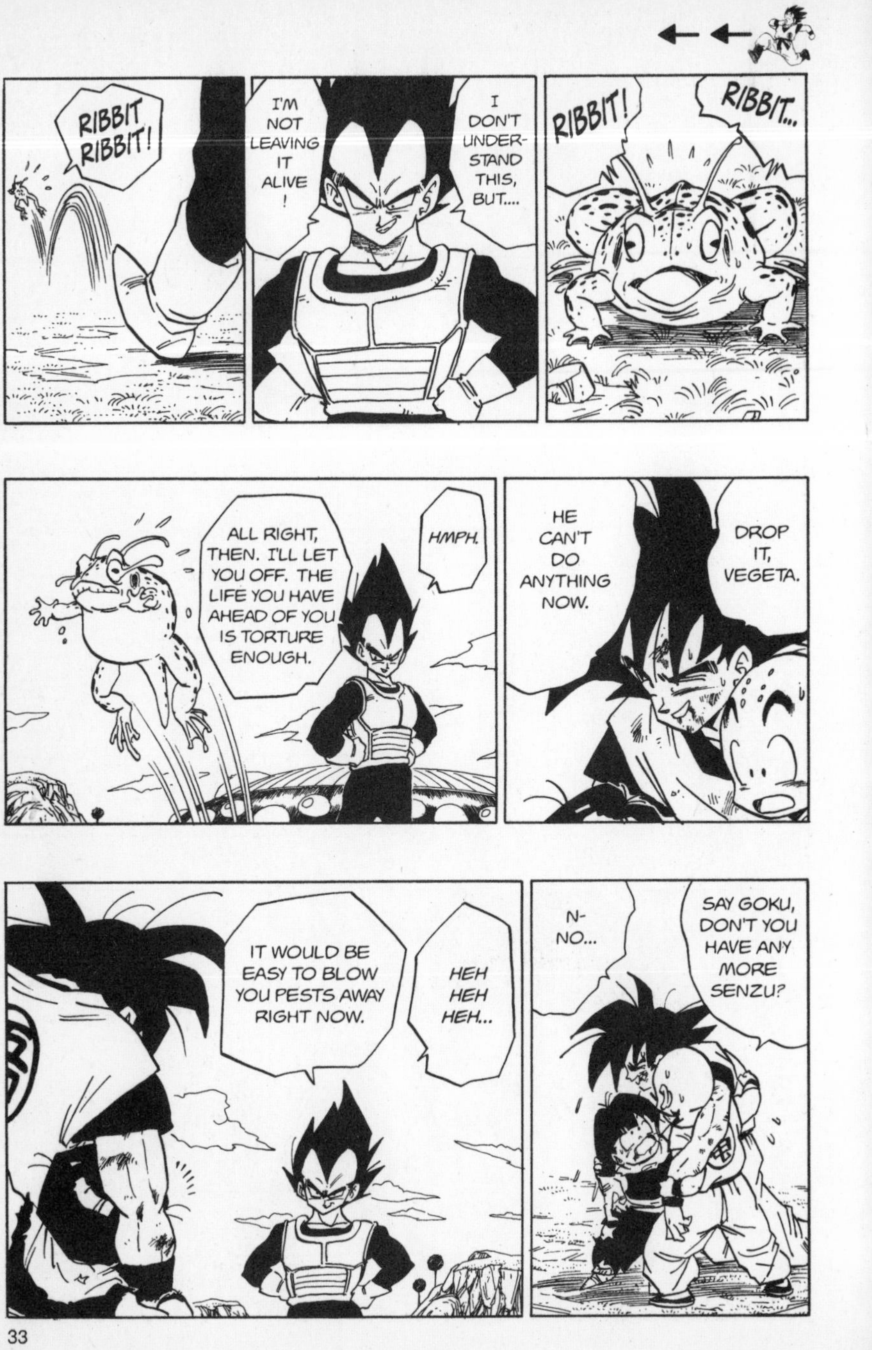
RIBBIT...
RIBBIT!
I DON'T UNDERSTAND THIS, BUT....
I'M NOT LEAVING IT ALIVE!
RIBBIT RIBBIT!
DROP IT, VEGETA.
HE CAN'T DO ANYTHING NOW.
HMPH.
ALL RIGHT, THEN. I'LL LET YOU OFF. THE LIFE YOU HAVE AHEAD OF YOU IS TORTURE ENOUGH.
SAY GOKU, DON'T YOU HAVE ANY MORE SENZU?
N-NO...
HEH HEH HEH...
IT WOULD BE EASY TO BLOW YOU PESTS AWAY RIGHT NOW.

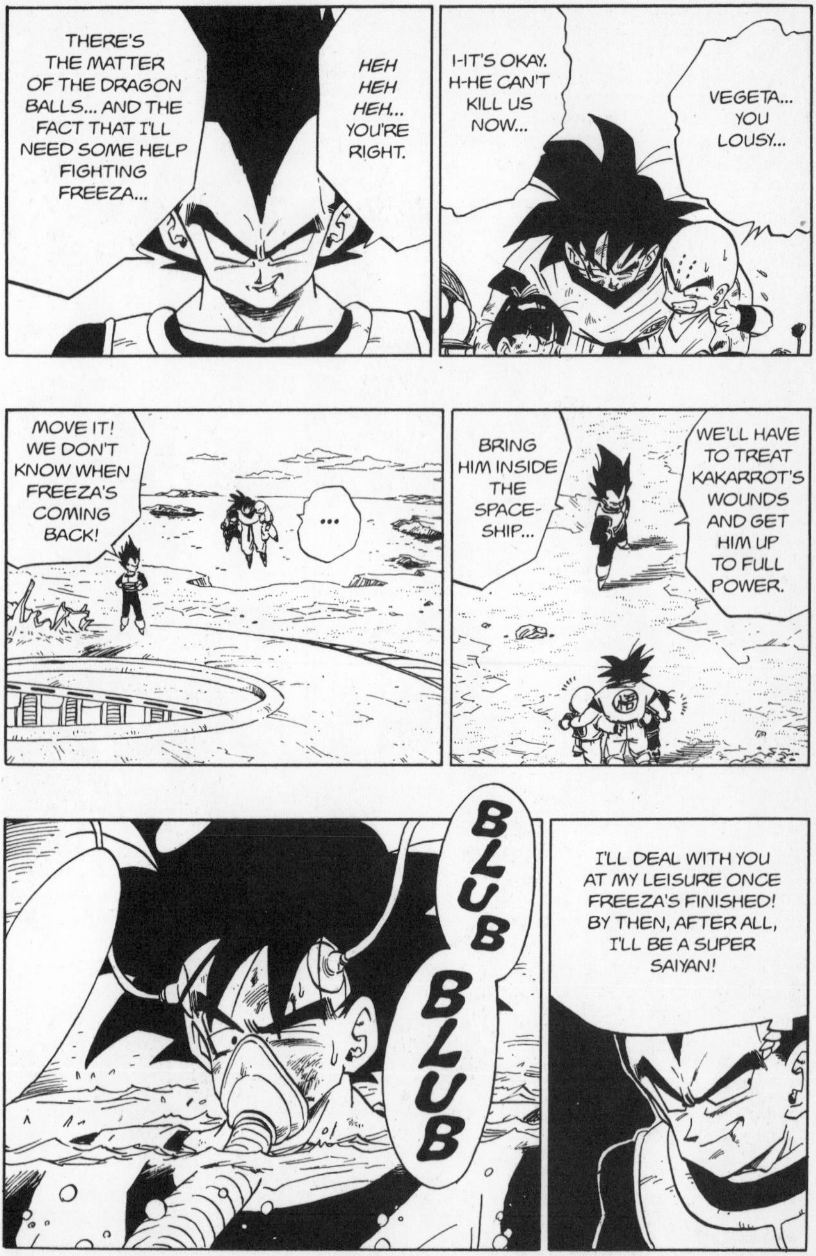
VEGETA... YOU LOUSY...
I-IT'S OKAY. H-HE CAN'T KILL US NOW...
HEH HEH HEH... YOU'RE RIGHT.
THERE'S THE MATTER OF THE DRAGON BALLS... AND THE FACT THAT I'LL NEED SOME HELP FIGHTING FREEZA...
WE'LL HAVE TO TREAT KAKARROT'S WOUNDS AND GET HIM UP TO FULL POWER.
BRING HIM INSIDE THE SPACE-SHIP...
MOVE IT! WE DON'T KNOW WHEN FREEZA'S COMING BACK!
...
I'LL DEAL WITH YOU AT MY LEISURE ONCE FREEZA'S FINISHED! BY THEN, AFTER ALL, I'LL BE A SUPER SAIYAN!
BLUB
BLUB

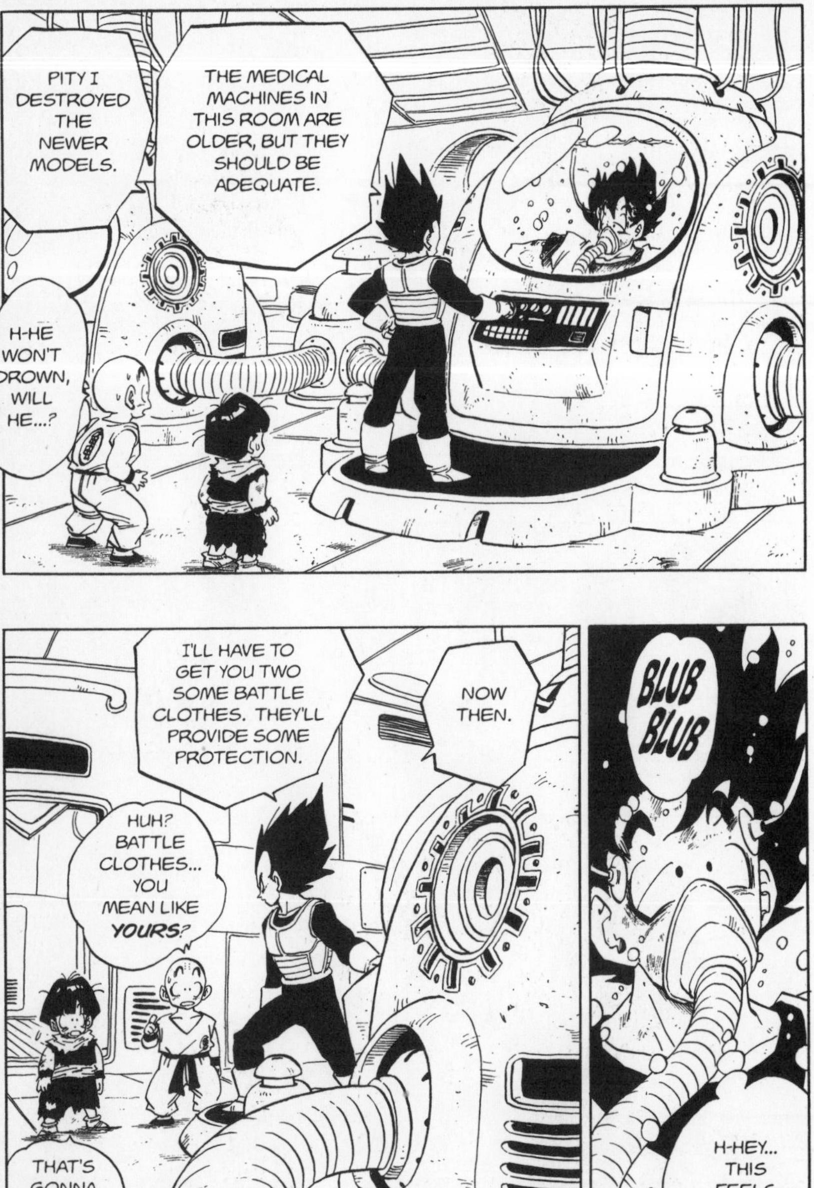
THE MEDICAL MACHINES IN THIS ROOM ARE OLDER, BUT THEY SHOULD BE ADEQUATE.
PITY I DESTROYED THE NEWER MODELS.
H-HE WON'T DROWN, WILL HE...?
BLUB BLUB
H-HEY... THIS FEELS GOOD...
NOW THEN.
I'LL HAVE TO GET YOU TWO SOME BATTLE CLOTHES. THEY'LL PROVIDE SOME PROTECTION.
HUH? BATTLE CLOTHES... YOU MEAN LIKE *YOURS*?
THAT'S GONNA FEEL *WEIRD*....

NEXT: Freeza vs. Nail, Part 2

DBZ:97 • Nail's Sacrifice

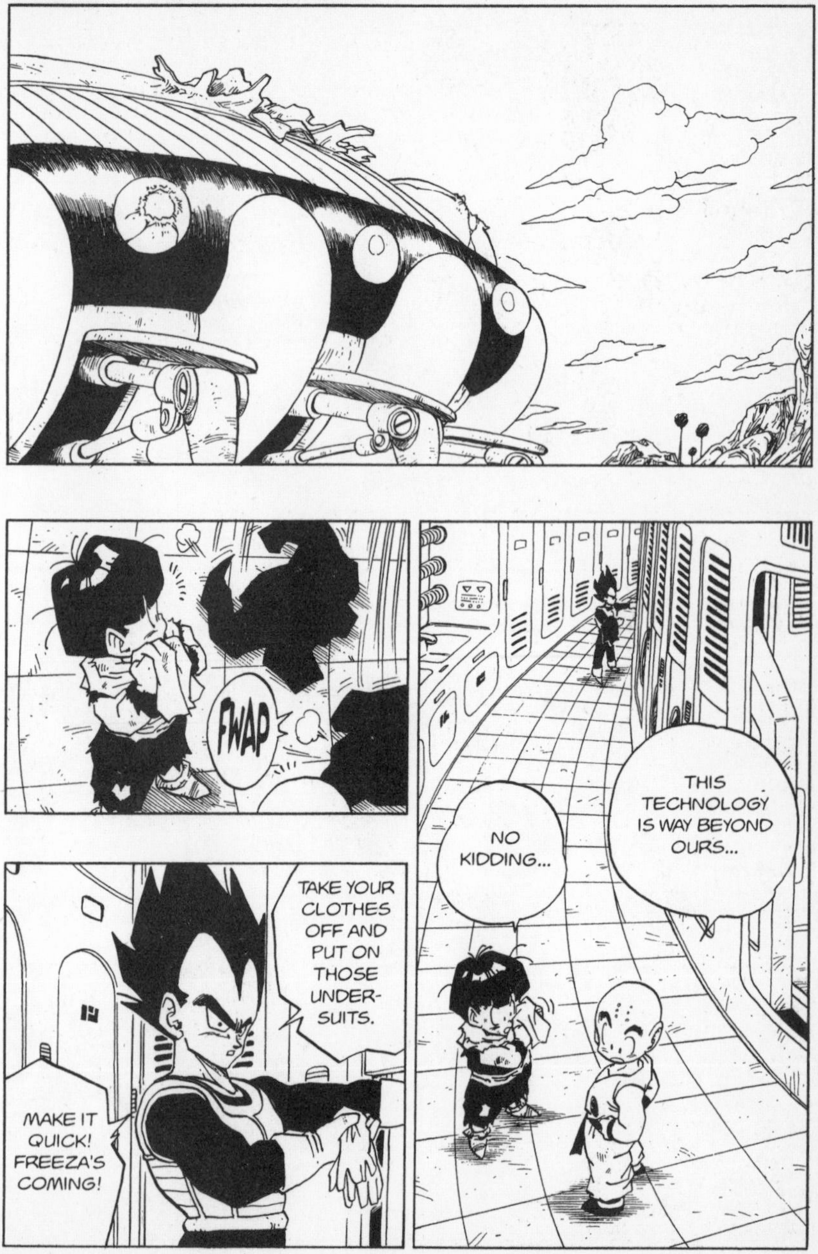
THIS TECHNOLOGY IS WAY BEYOND OURS...
NO KIDDING...
FWAP
TAKE YOUR CLOTHES OFF AND PUT ON THOSE UNDER-SUITS.
MAKE IT QUICK! FREEZA'S COMING!

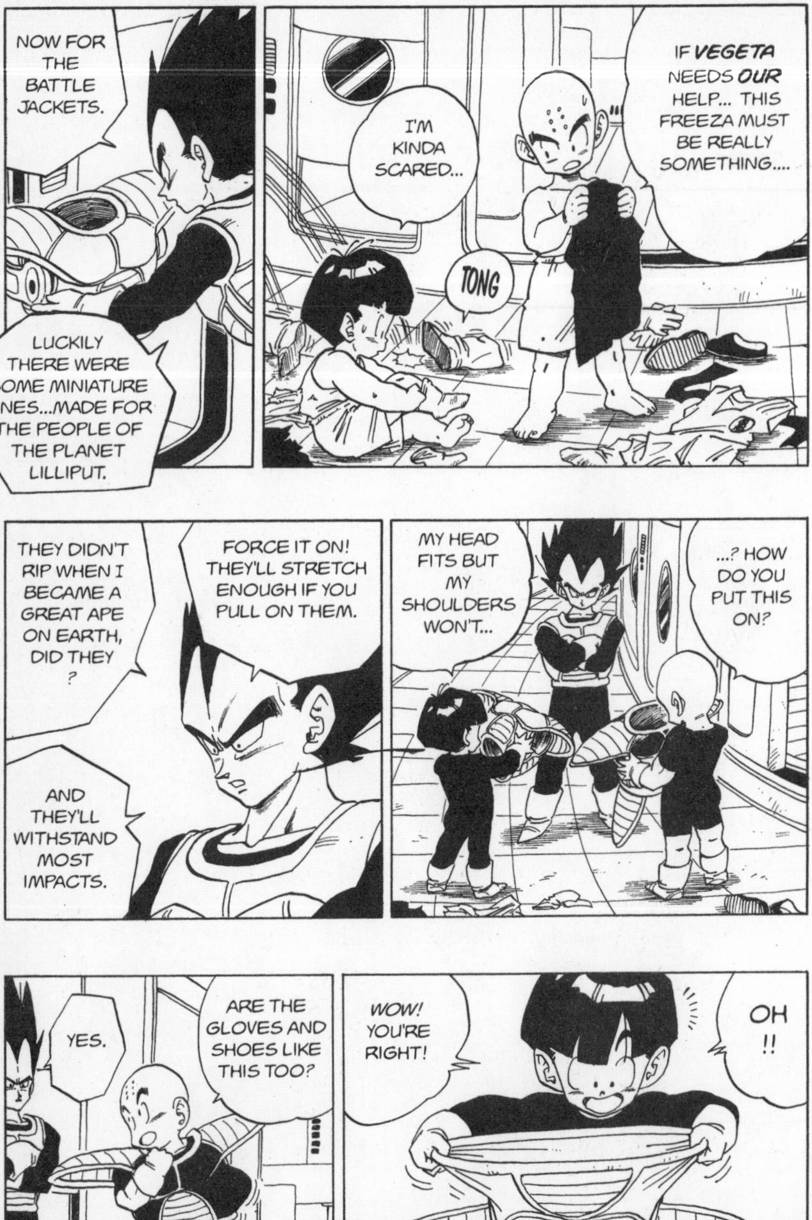
IF **VEGETA** NEEDS **OUR** HELP... THIS FREEZA MUST BE REALLY SOMETHING....
I'M KINDA SCARED...
TONG
NOW FOR THE BATTLE JACKETS.
LUCKILY THERE WERE SOME MINIATURE ONES...MADE FOR THE PEOPLE OF THE PLANET LILLIPUT.
...? HOW DO YOU PUT THIS ON?
MY HEAD FITS BUT MY SHOULDERS WON'T...
FORCE IT ON! THEY'LL STRETCH ENOUGH IF YOU PULL ON THEM.
THEY DIDN'T RIP WHEN I BECAME A GREAT APE ON EARTH, DID THEY ?
AND THEY'LL WITHSTAND MOST IMPACTS.
OH !!
WOW! YOU'RE RIGHT!
ARE THE GLOVES AND SHOES LIKE THIS TOO?
YES.

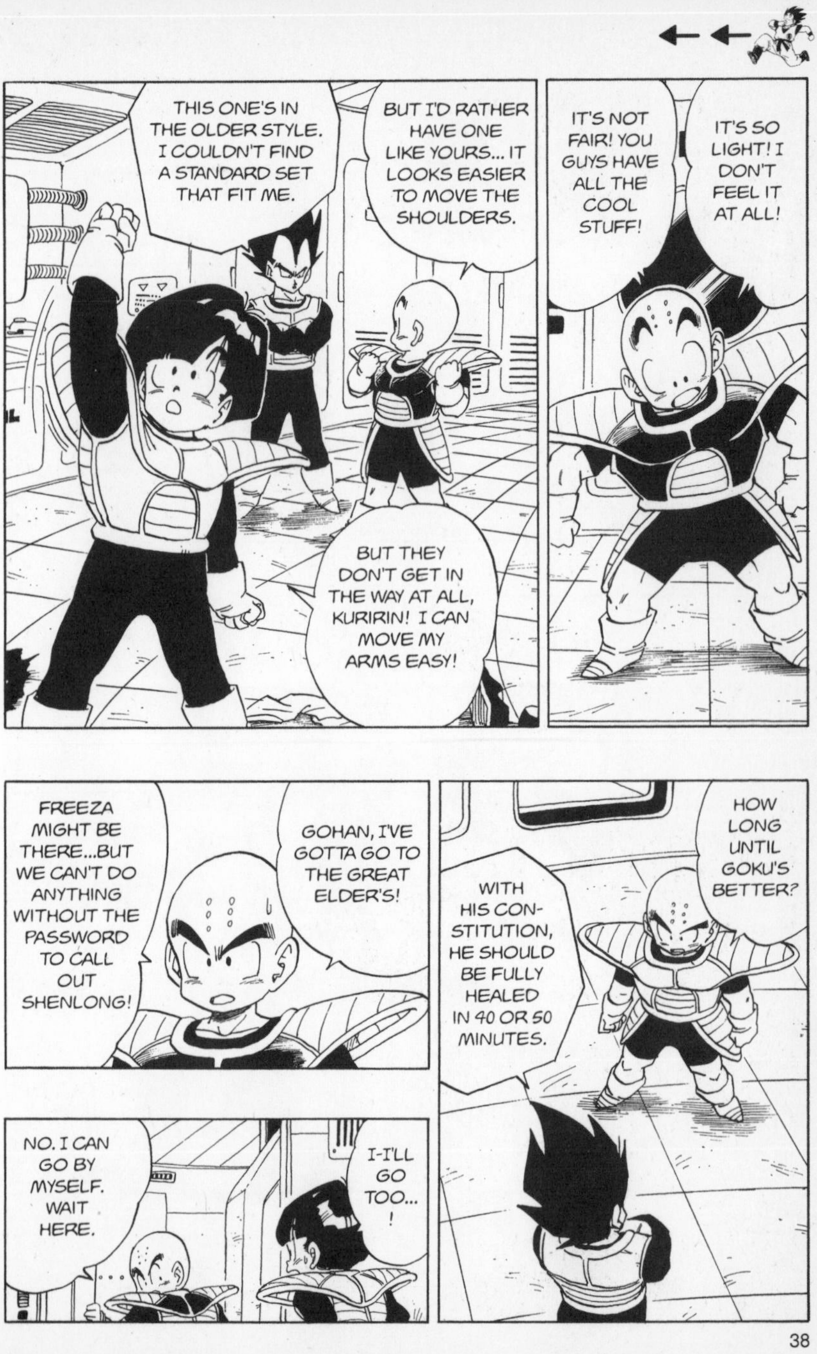
IT'S SO LIGHT! I DON'T FEEL IT AT ALL!
IT'S NOT FAIR! YOU GUYS HAVE ALL THE COOL STUFF!
BUT I'D RATHER HAVE ONE LIKE YOURS... IT LOOKS EASIER TO MOVE THE SHOULDERS.
THIS ONE'S IN THE OLDER STYLE. I COULDN'T FIND A STANDARD SET THAT FIT ME.
BUT THEY DON'T GET IN THE WAY AT ALL, KURIRIN! I CAN MOVE MY ARMS EASY!
HOW LONG UNTIL GOKU'S BETTER?
WITH HIS CON-STITUTION, HE SHOULD BE FULLY HEALED IN 40 OR 50 MINUTES.
GOHAN, I'VE GOTTA GO TO THE GREAT ELDER'S!
FREEZA MIGHT BE THERE...BUT WE CAN'T DO ANYTHING WITHOUT THE PASSWORD TO CALL OUT SHENLONG!
I-I'LL GO TOO... !
NO. I CAN GO BY MYSELF. WAIT HERE.
...

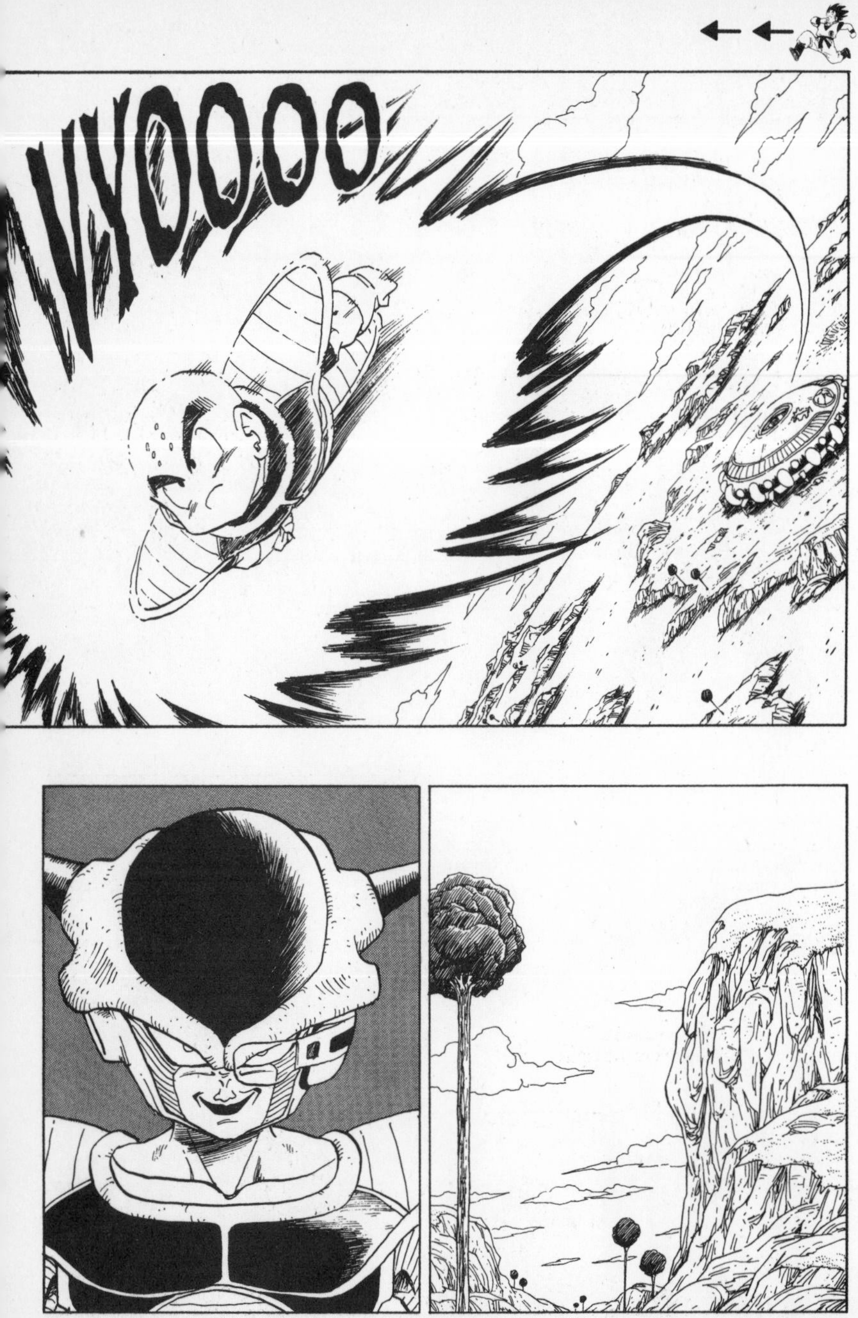
VYOOOO

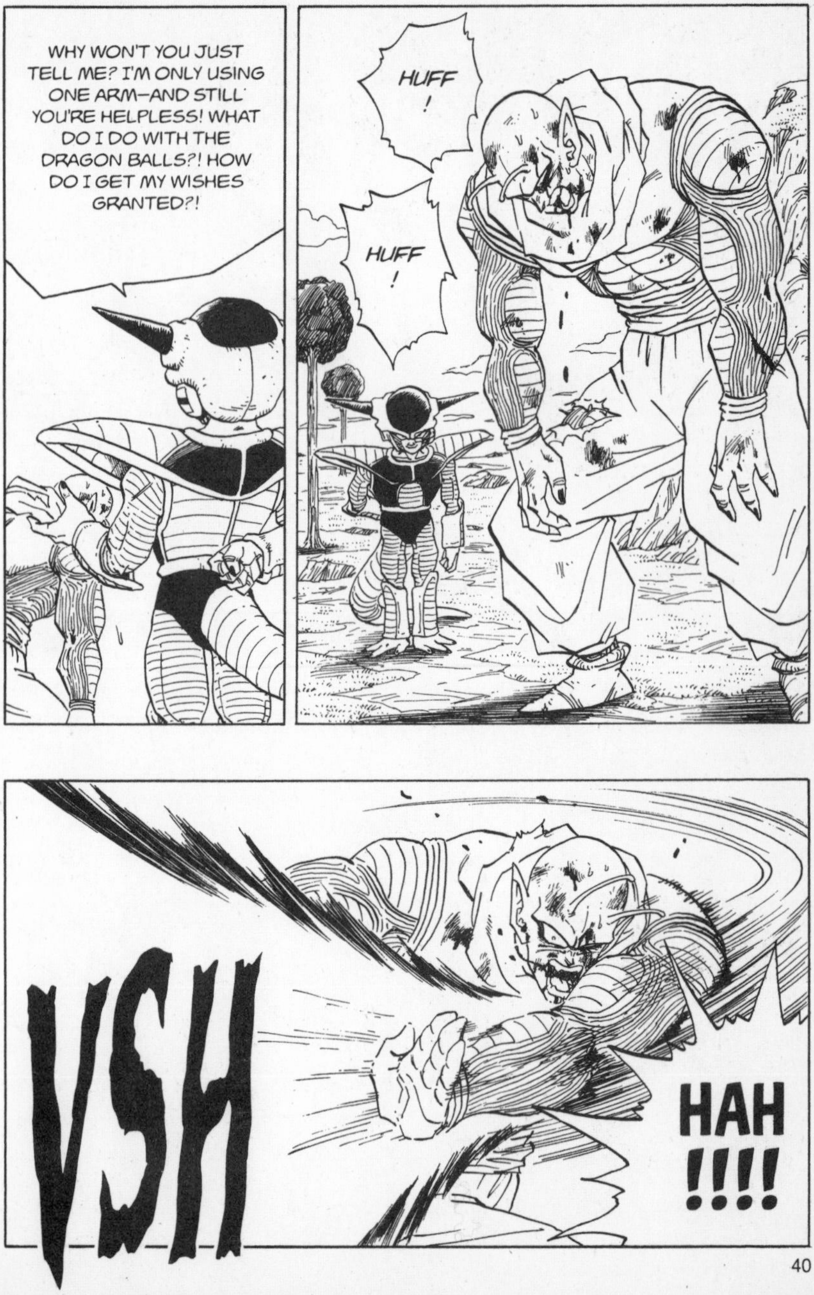
HUFF !
HUFF !
WHY WON'T YOU JUST TELL ME? I'M ONLY USING ONE ARM—AND STILL YOU'RE HELPLESS! WHAT DO I DO WITH THE DRAGON BALLS?! HOW DO I GET MY WISHES GRANTED?!
HAH !!!!
VSH

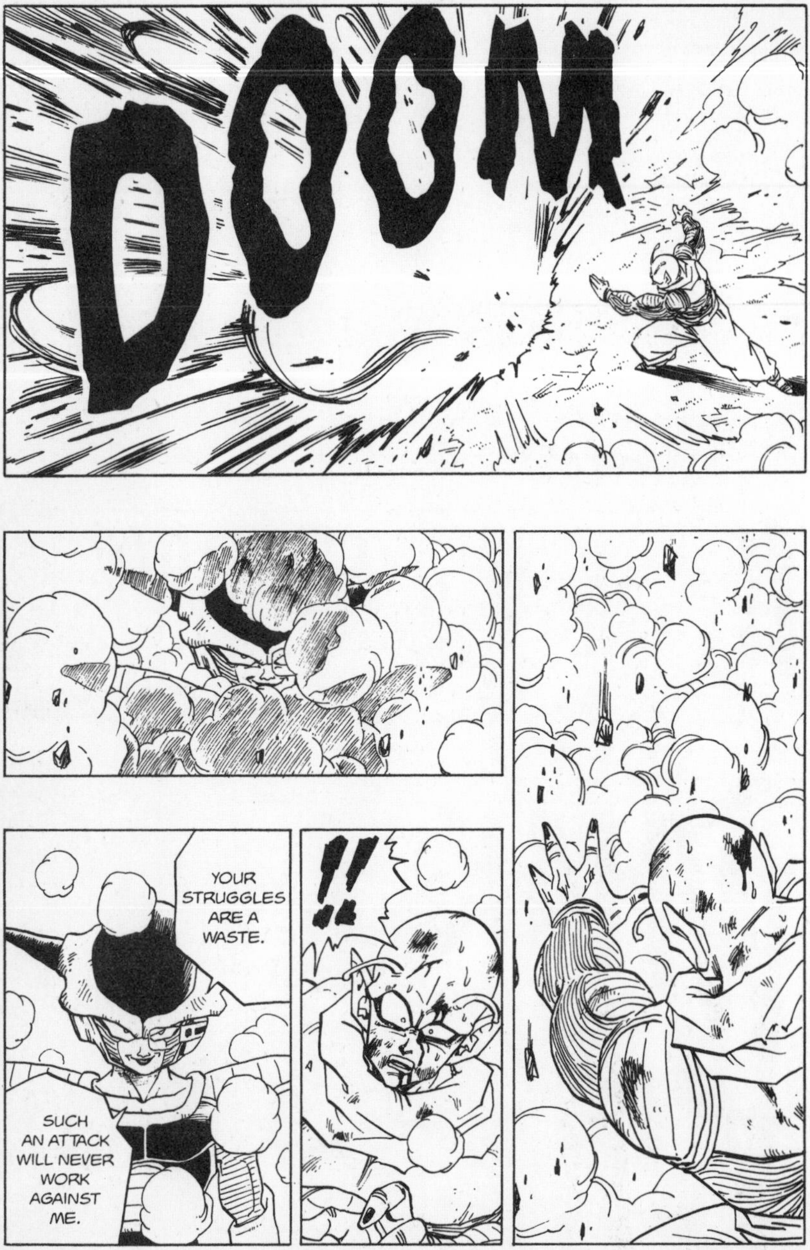
DOOM
!!
YOUR STRUGGLES ARE A WASTE.
SUCH AN ATTACK WILL NEVER WORK AGAINST ME.

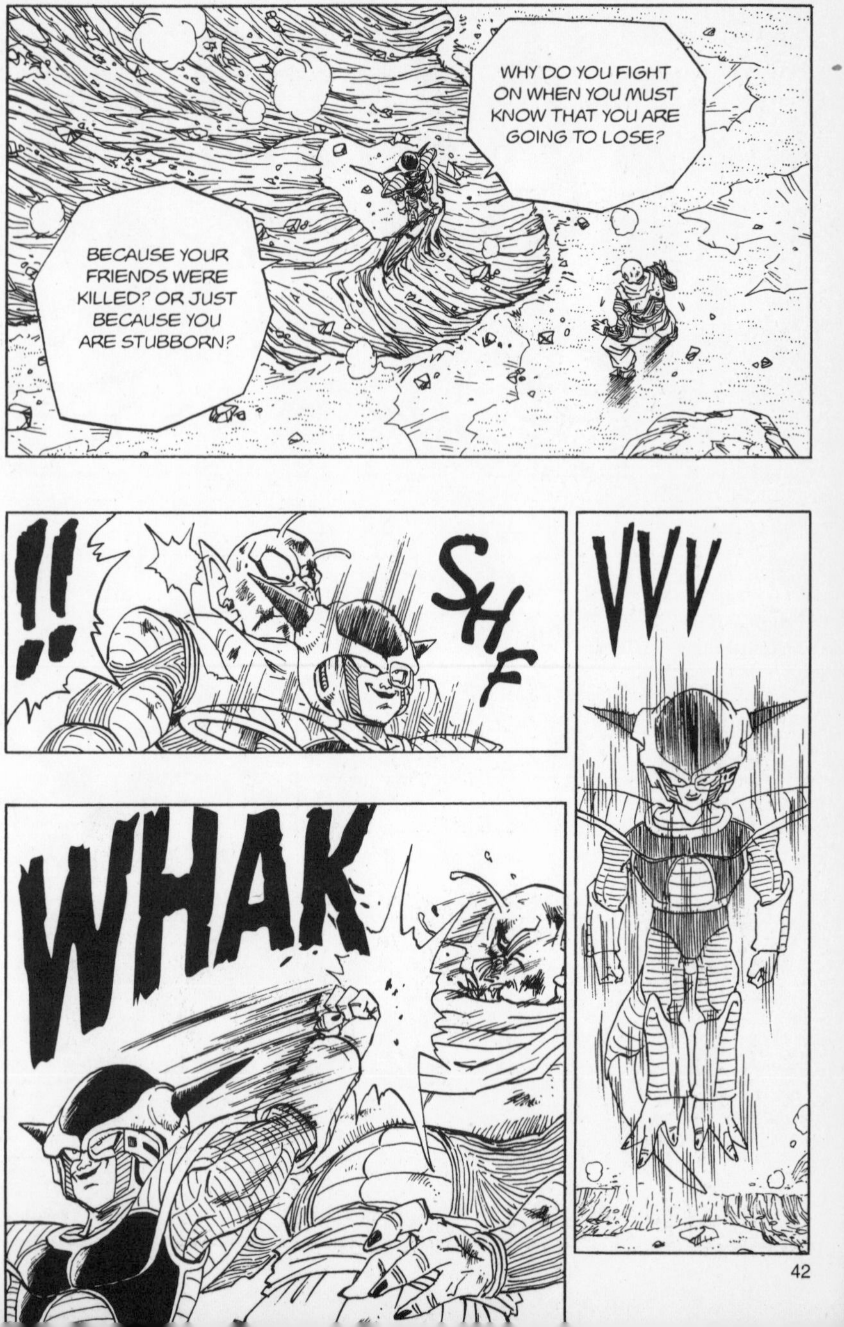
WHY DO YOU FIGHT ON WHEN YOU MUST KNOW THAT YOU ARE GOING TO LOSE?
BECAUSE YOUR FRIENDS WERE KILLED? OR JUST BECAUSE YOU ARE STUBBORN?
VVV
!!
SHF
WHAK

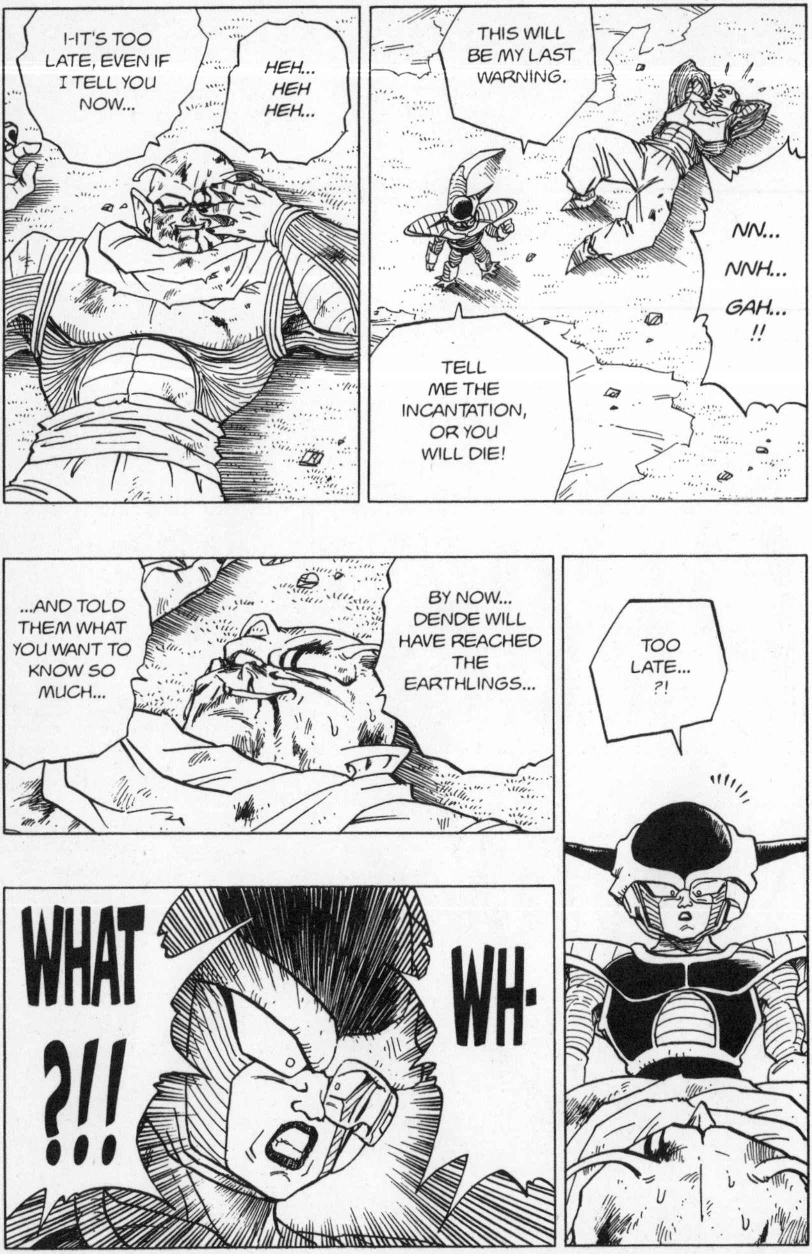
THIS WILL BE MY LAST WARNING.
NN... NNH... GAH... !!
TELL ME THE INCANTATION, OR YOU WILL DIE!
HEH... HEH HEH...
I-IT'S TOO LATE, EVEN IF I TELL YOU NOW...
TOO LATE...?!
BY NOW... DENDE WILL HAVE REACHED THE EARTHLINGS...
...AND TOLD THEM WHAT YOU WANT TO KNOW SO MUCH...
WH-
WHAT ?!!

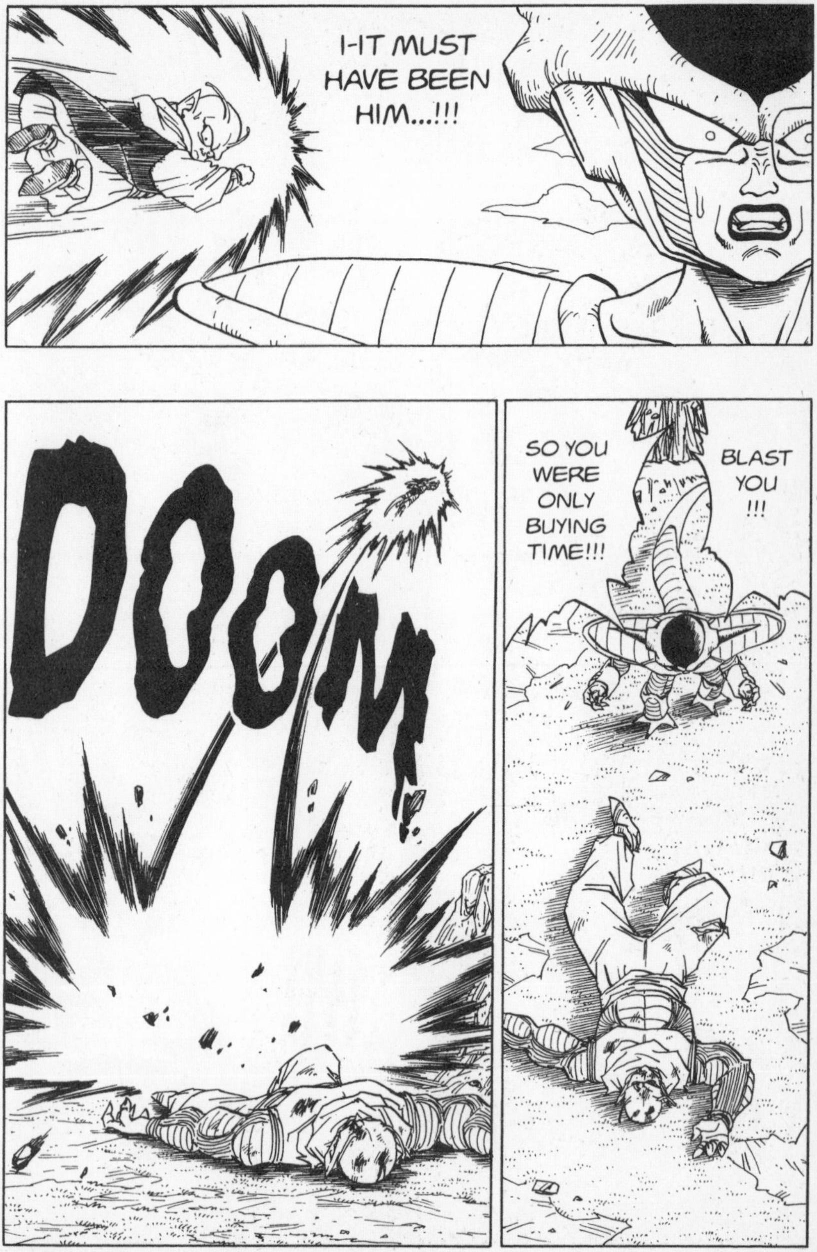
I-IT MUST HAVE BEEN HIM...!!!
BLAST YOU !!!
SO YOU WERE ONLY BUYING TIME!!!
DOOM

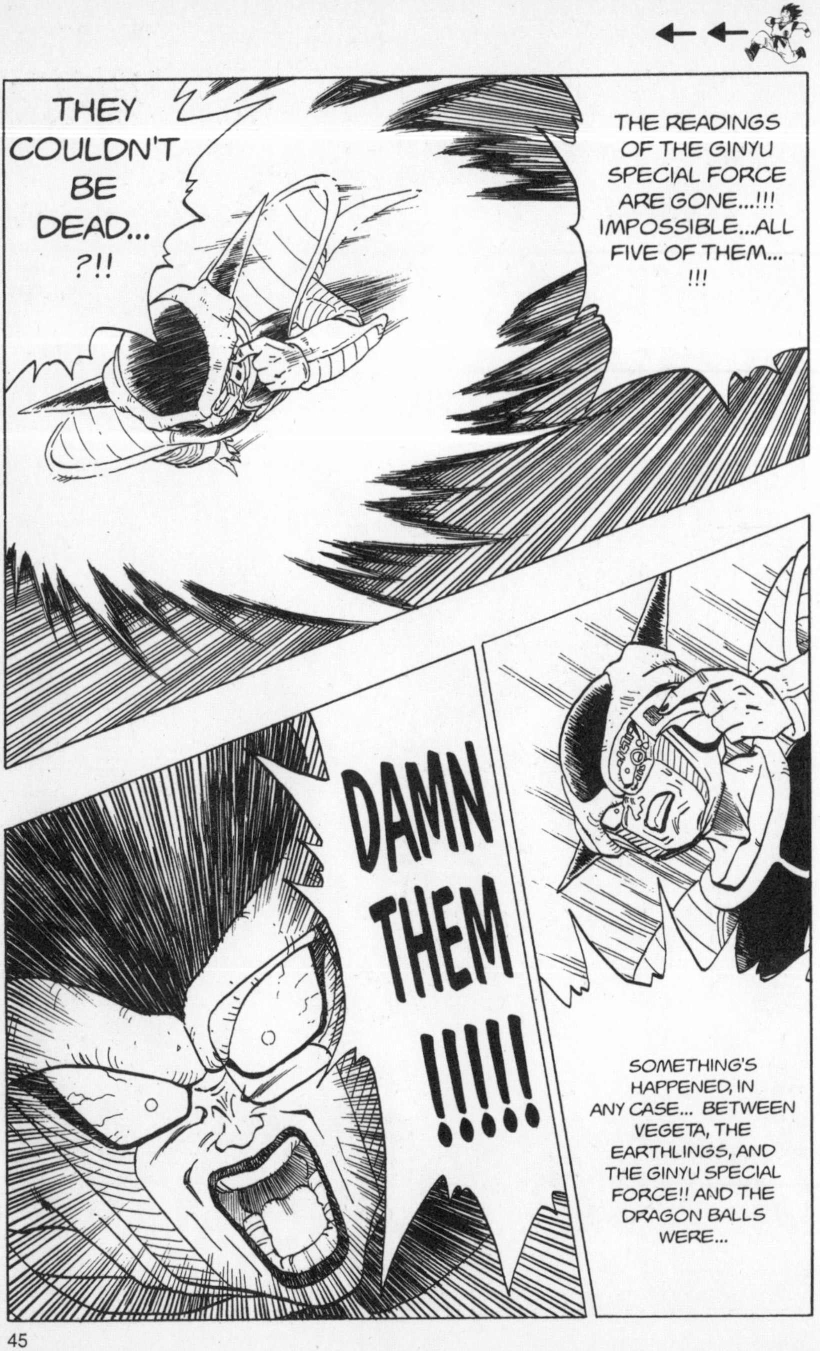
THE READINGS OF THE GINYU SPECIAL FORCE ARE GONE...!!! IMPOSSIBLE...ALL FIVE OF THEM...!!!
THEY COULDN'T BE DEAD...?!!
SOMETHING'S HAPPENED, IN ANY CASE... BETWEEN VEGETA, THE EARTHLINGS, AND THE GINYU SPECIAL FORCE!! AND THE DRAGON BALLS WERE...
DAMN THEM!!!!!

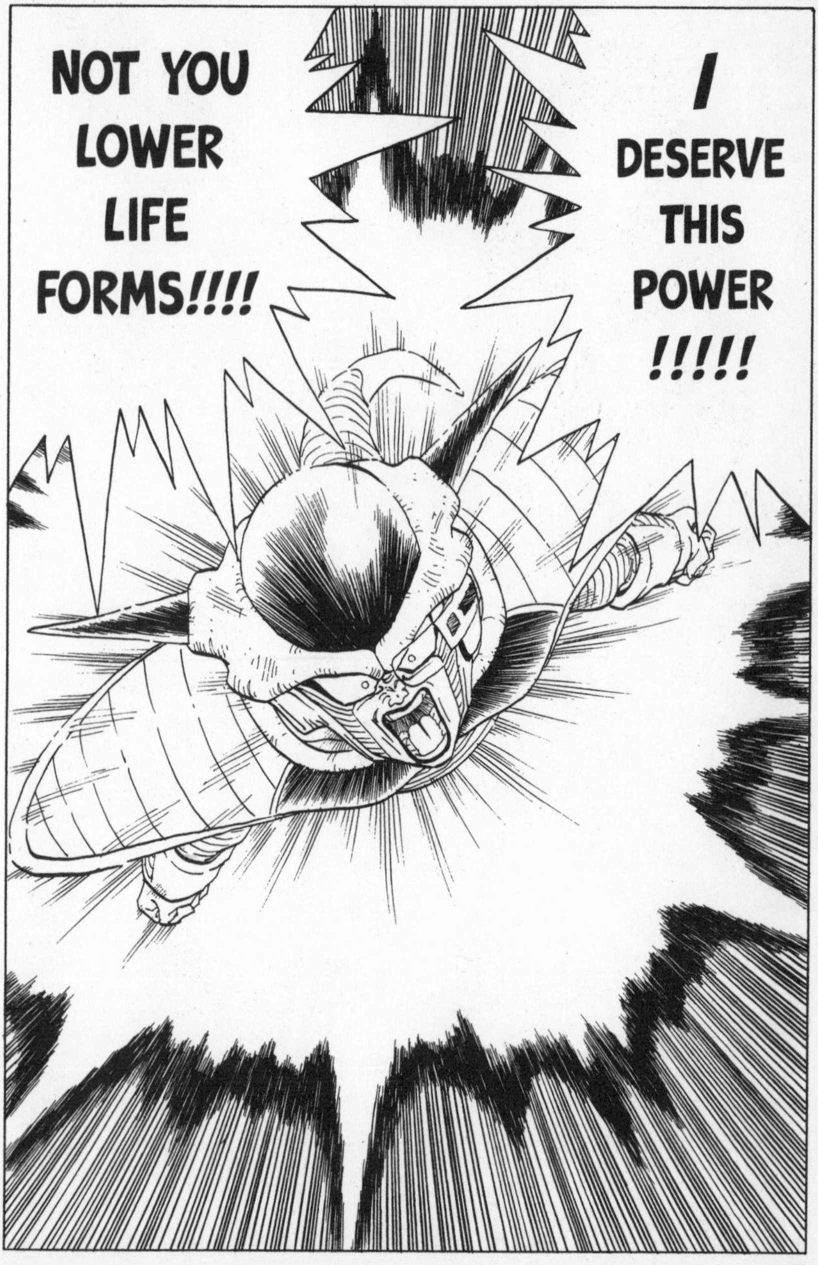
I DESERVE THIS POWER!!!!!
NOT YOU LOWER LIFE FORMS!!!!

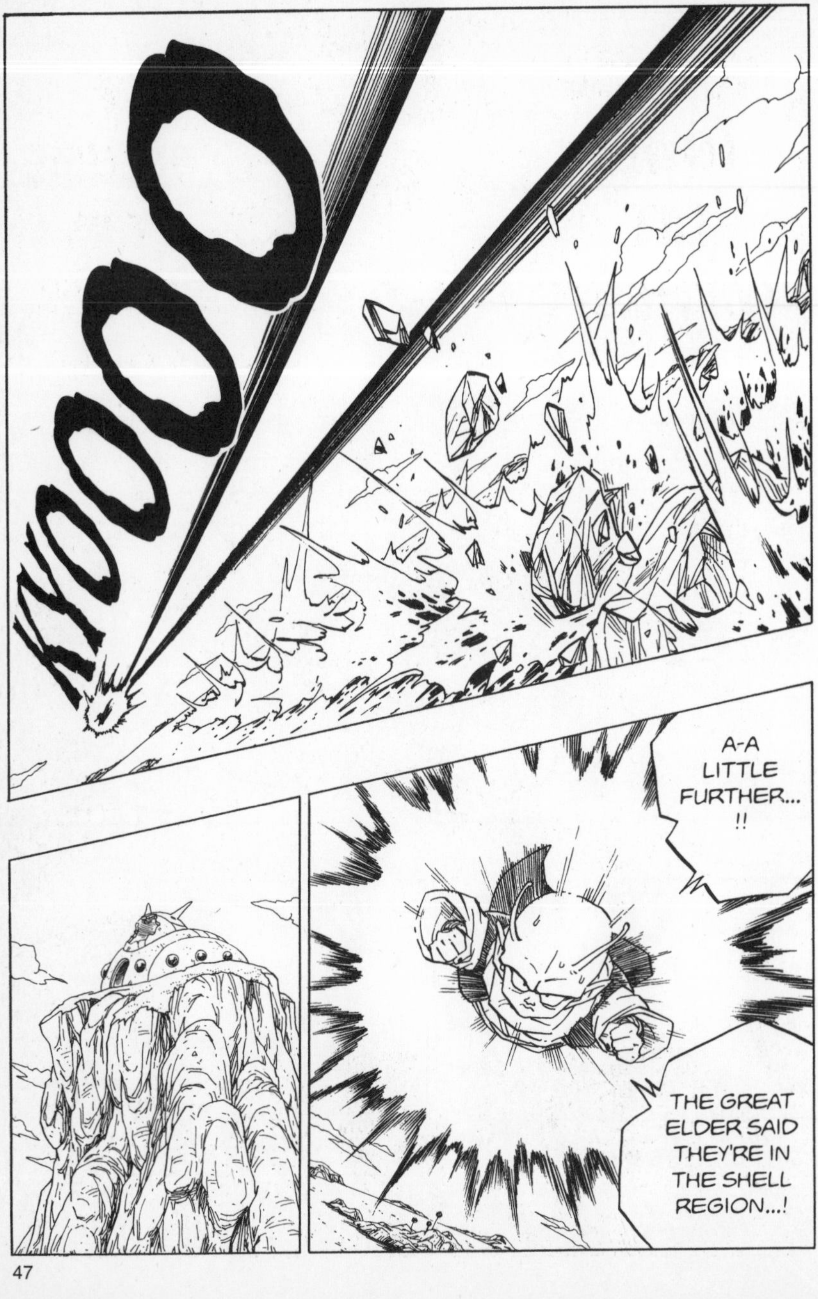
KOOOO
A-A LITTLE FURTHER... !!
THE GREAT ELDER SAID THEY'RE IN THE SHELL REGION...!

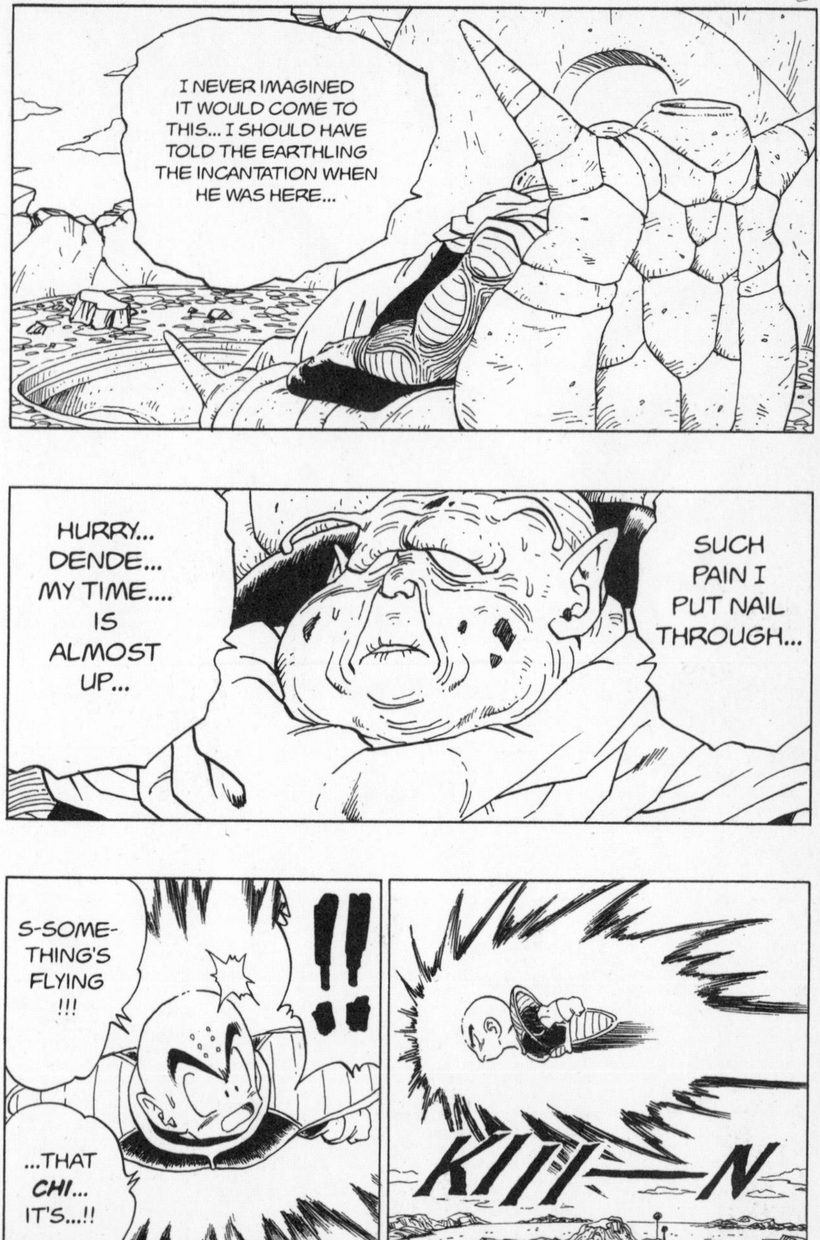
I NEVER IMAGINED IT WOULD COME TO THIS... I SHOULD HAVE TOLD THE EARTHLING THE INCANTATION WHEN HE WAS HERE...
SUCH PAIN I PUT NAIL THROUGH...
HURRY... DENDE... MY TIME.... IS ALMOST UP...
KIT—N
!!
S-SOME-THING'S FLYING !!!
...THAT CHI... IT'S...!!

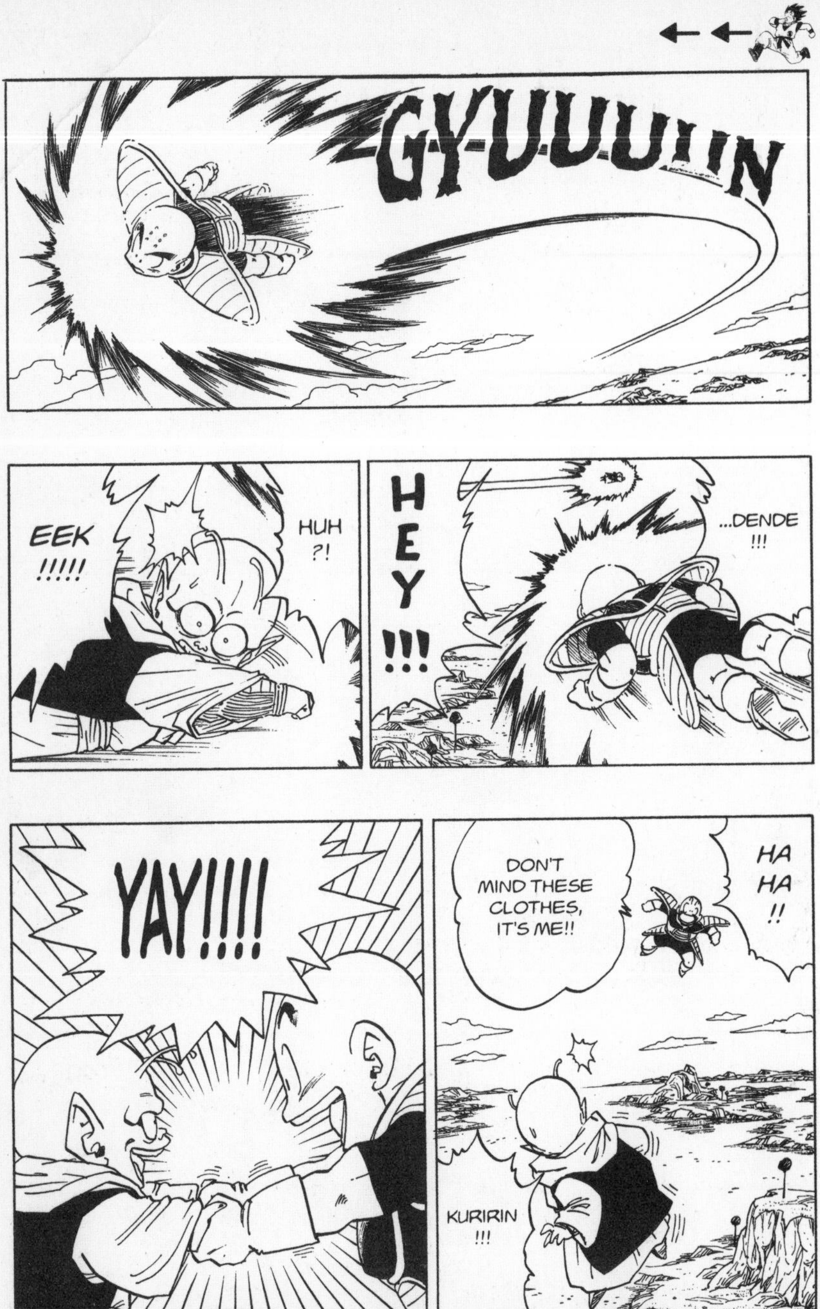

G-Y-U-U-U-I-IN
...DENDE !!!
HEY !!!
HUH ?!
EEK !!!!!
HA HA !!
DON'T MIND THESE CLOTHES, IT'S ME!!
KURIRIN !!!
YAY!!!!

NEXT: The True Shenlong!!

DBZ:98 • The True God Dragon

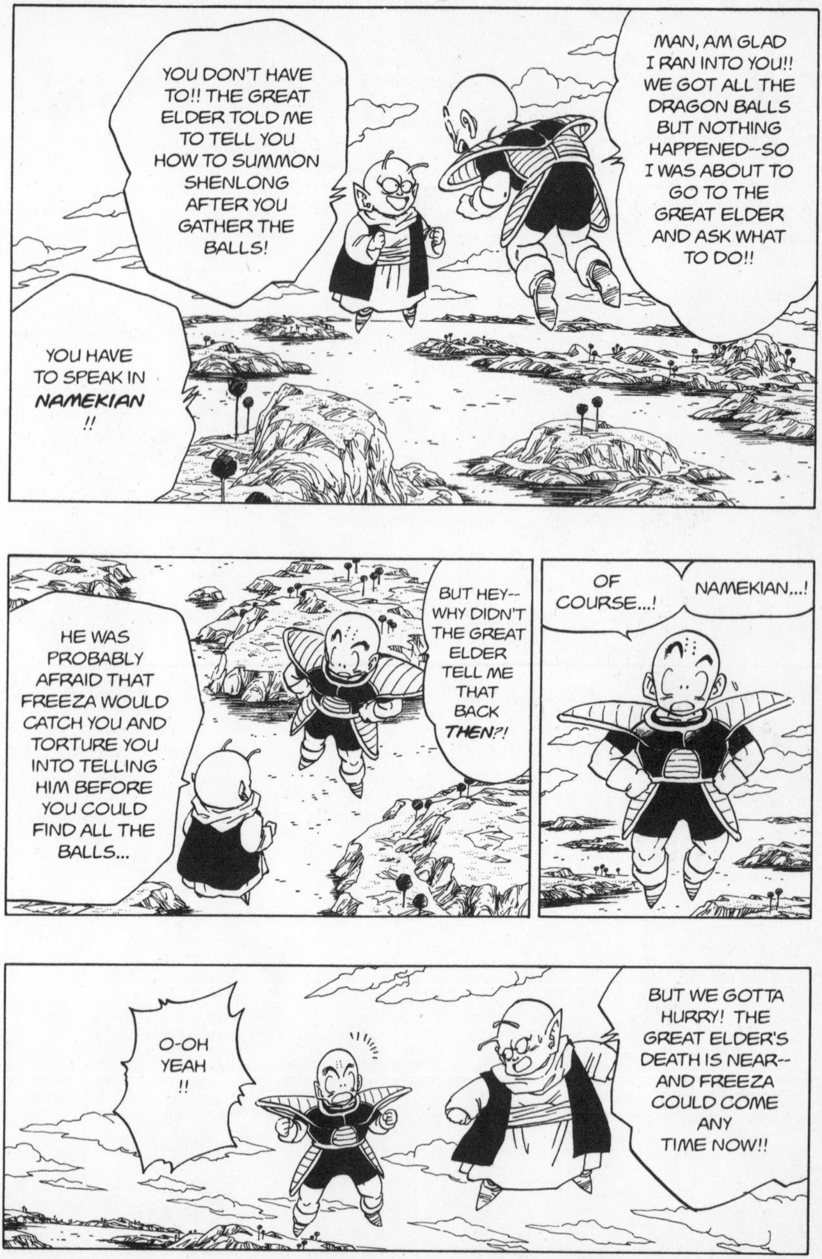
MAN, AM GLAD I RAN INTO YOU!! WE GOT ALL THE DRAGON BALLS BUT NOTHING HAPPENED--SO I WAS ABOUT TO GO TO THE GREAT ELDER AND ASK WHAT TO DO!!
YOU DON'T HAVE TO!! THE GREAT ELDER TOLD ME TO TELL YOU HOW TO SUMMON SHENLONG AFTER YOU GATHER THE BALLS!
YOU HAVE TO SPEAK IN *NAMEKIAN*!!
OF COURSE...!
NAMEKIAN...!
BUT HEY--WHY DIDN'T THE GREAT ELDER TELL ME THAT BACK *THEN*?!
HE WAS PROBABLY AFRAID THAT FREEZA WOULD CATCH YOU AND TORTURE YOU INTO TELLING HIM BEFORE YOU COULD FIND ALL THE BALLS...
BUT WE GOTTA HURRY! THE GREAT ELDER'S DEATH IS NEAR--AND FREEZA COULD COME ANY TIME NOW!!
O-OH YEAH!!

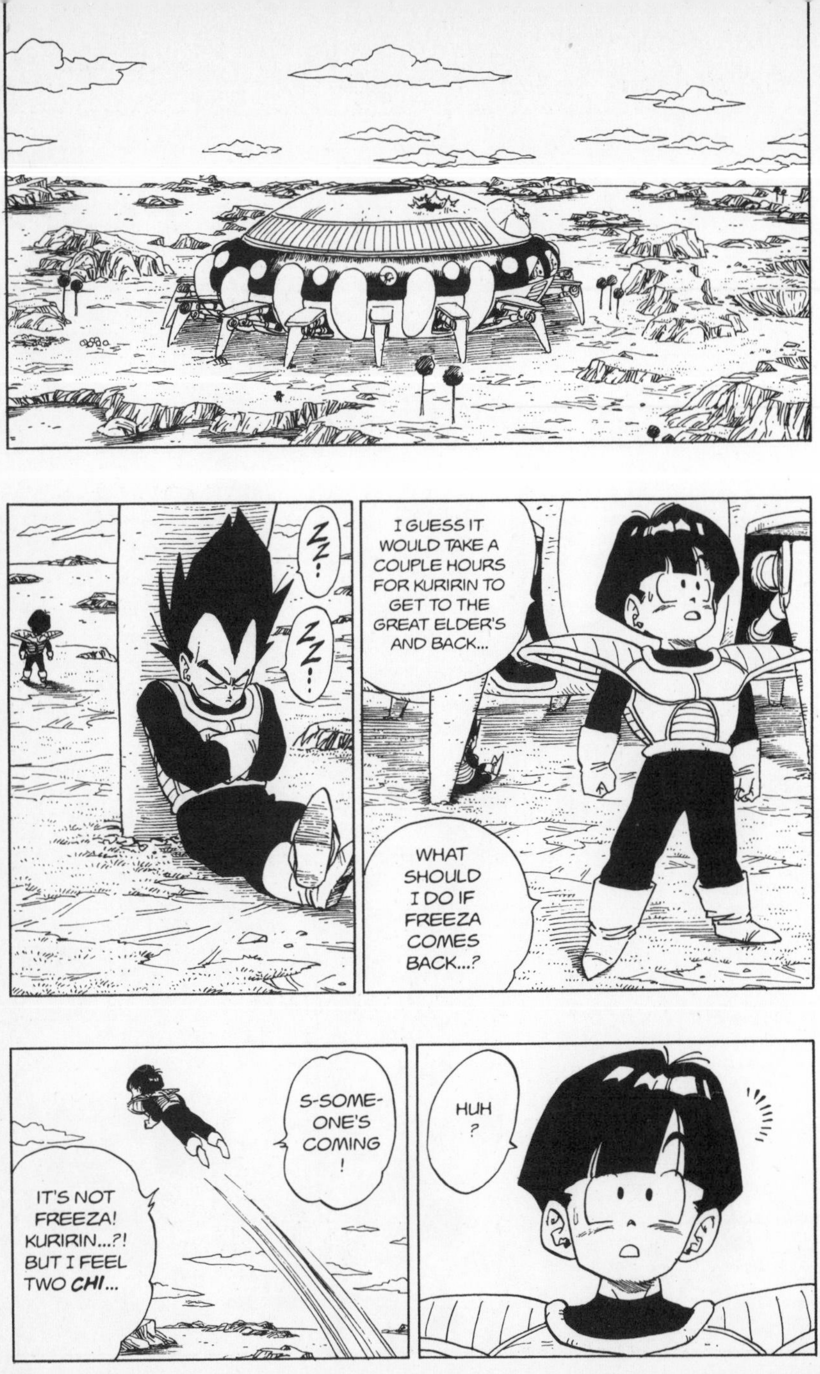
I GUESS IT WOULD TAKE A COUPLE HOURS FOR KURIRIN TO GET TO THE GREAT ELDER'S AND BACK...
WHAT SHOULD I DO IF FREEZA COMES BACK...?
ZZ...
ZZ...
HUH ?
S-SOME-ONE'S COMING !
IT'S NOT FREEZA! KURIRIN...?! BUT I FEEL TWO **CHI**...

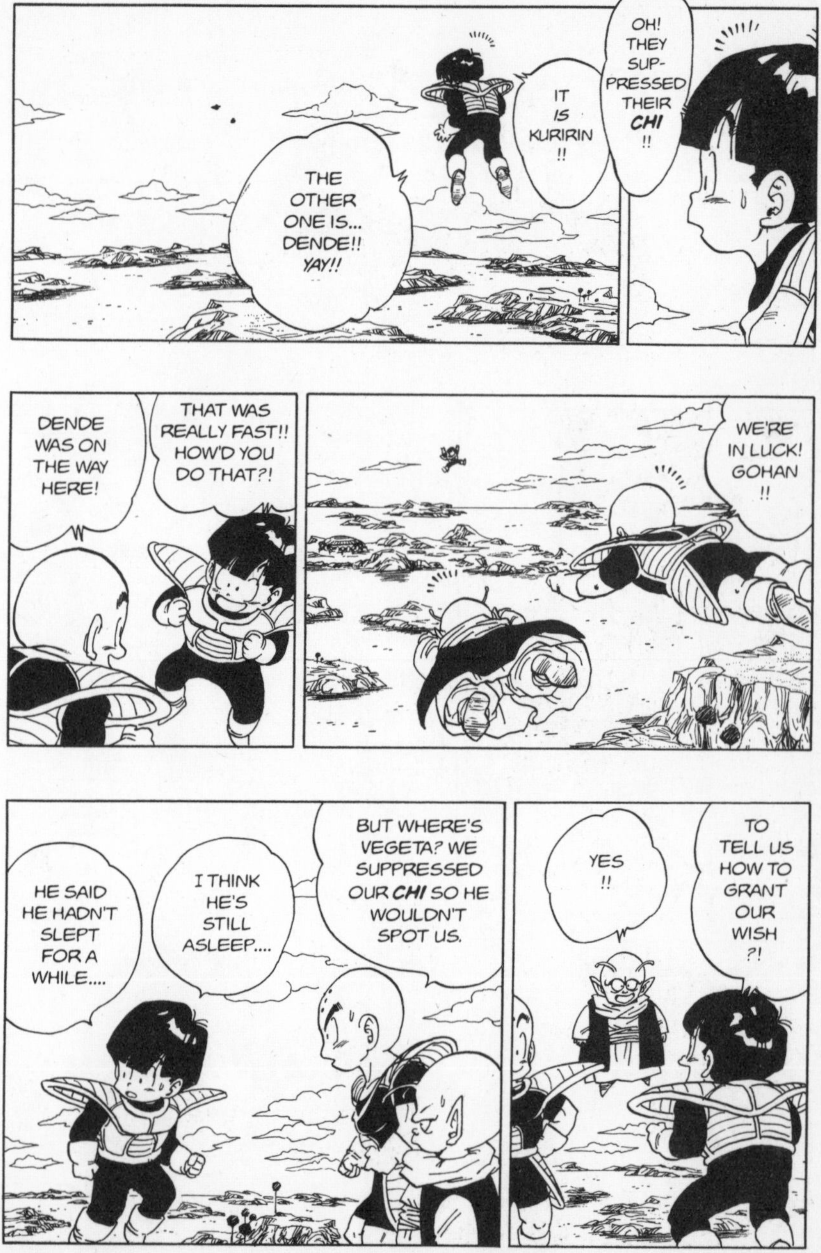
OH! THEY SUPPRESSED THEIR CHI !!
IT IS KURIRIN !!
THE OTHER ONE IS... DENDE!! YAY!!
WE'RE IN LUCK! GOHAN !!
THAT WAS REALLY FAST!! HOW'D YOU DO THAT?!
DENDE WAS ON THE WAY HERE!
TO TELL US HOW TO GRANT OUR WISH ?!
YES !!
BUT WHERE'S VEGETA? WE SUPPRESSED OUR CHI SO HE WOULDN'T SPOT US.
I THINK HE'S STILL ASLEEP....
HE SAID HE HADN'T SLEPT FOR A WHILE....

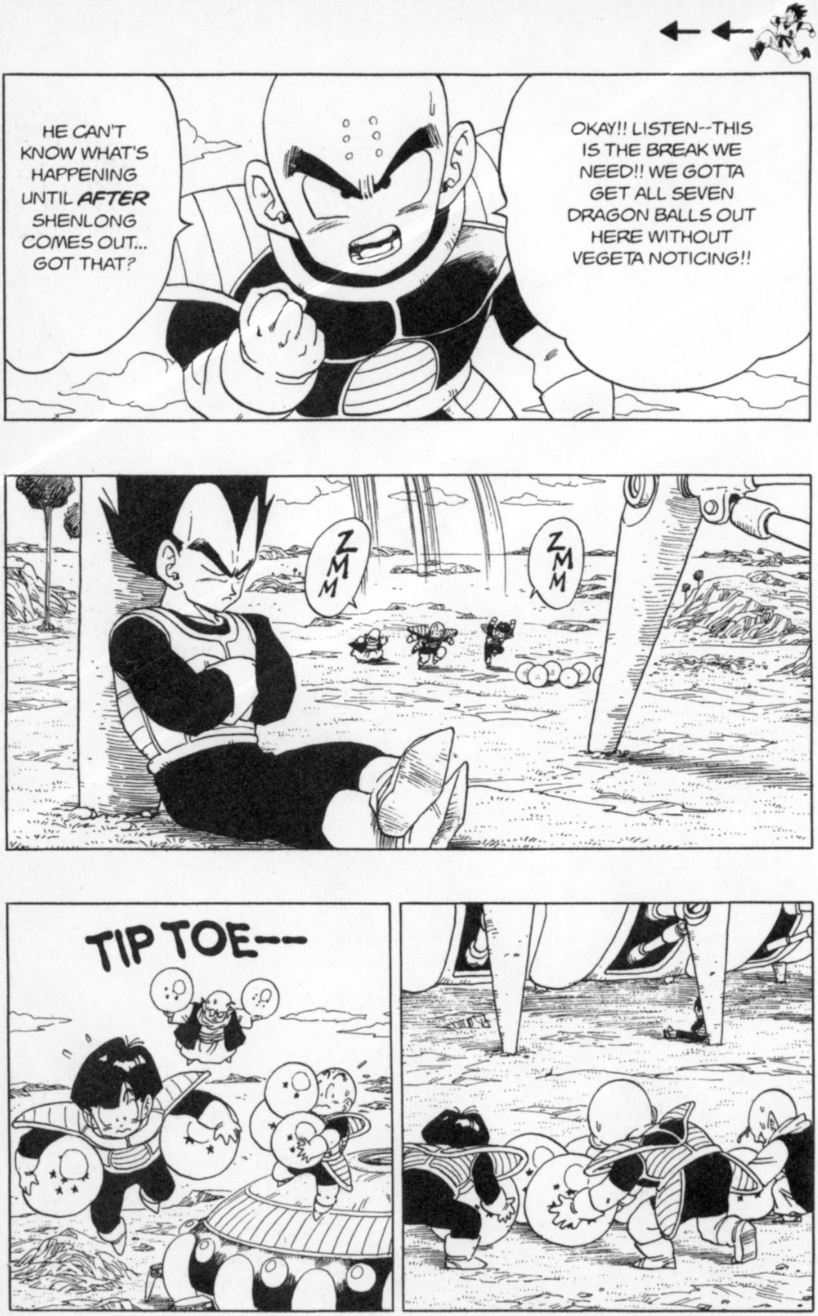
OKAY!! LISTEN--THIS IS THE BREAK WE NEED!! WE GOTTA GET ALL SEVEN DRAGON BALLS OUT HERE WITHOUT VEGETA NOTICING!!
HE CAN'T KNOW WHAT'S HAPPENING UNTIL AFTER SHENLONG COMES OUT... GOT THAT?
ZMM
ZMM
TIP TOE---

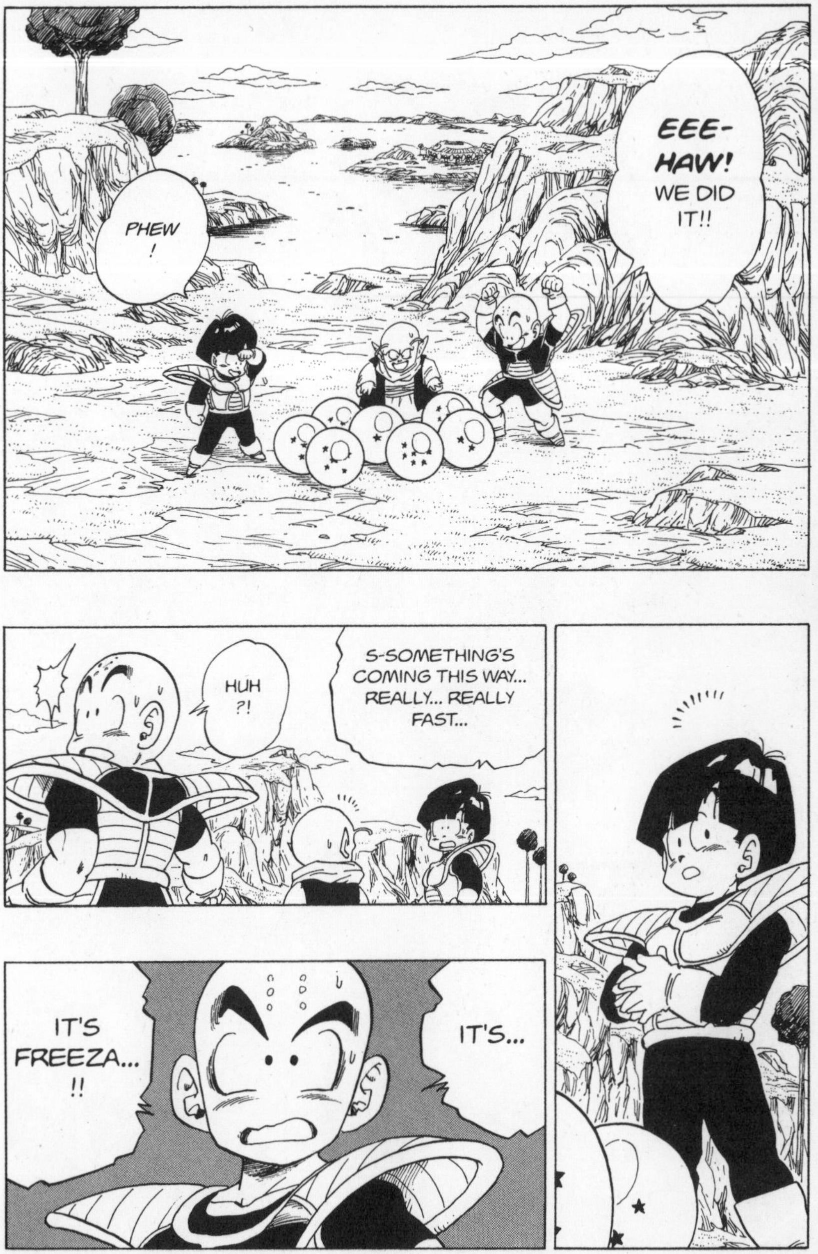
EEE-HAW! WE DID IT!!
PHEW!
S-SOMETHING'S COMING THIS WAY... REALLY... REALLY FAST...
HUH?!
IT'S...
IT'S FREEZA...!!

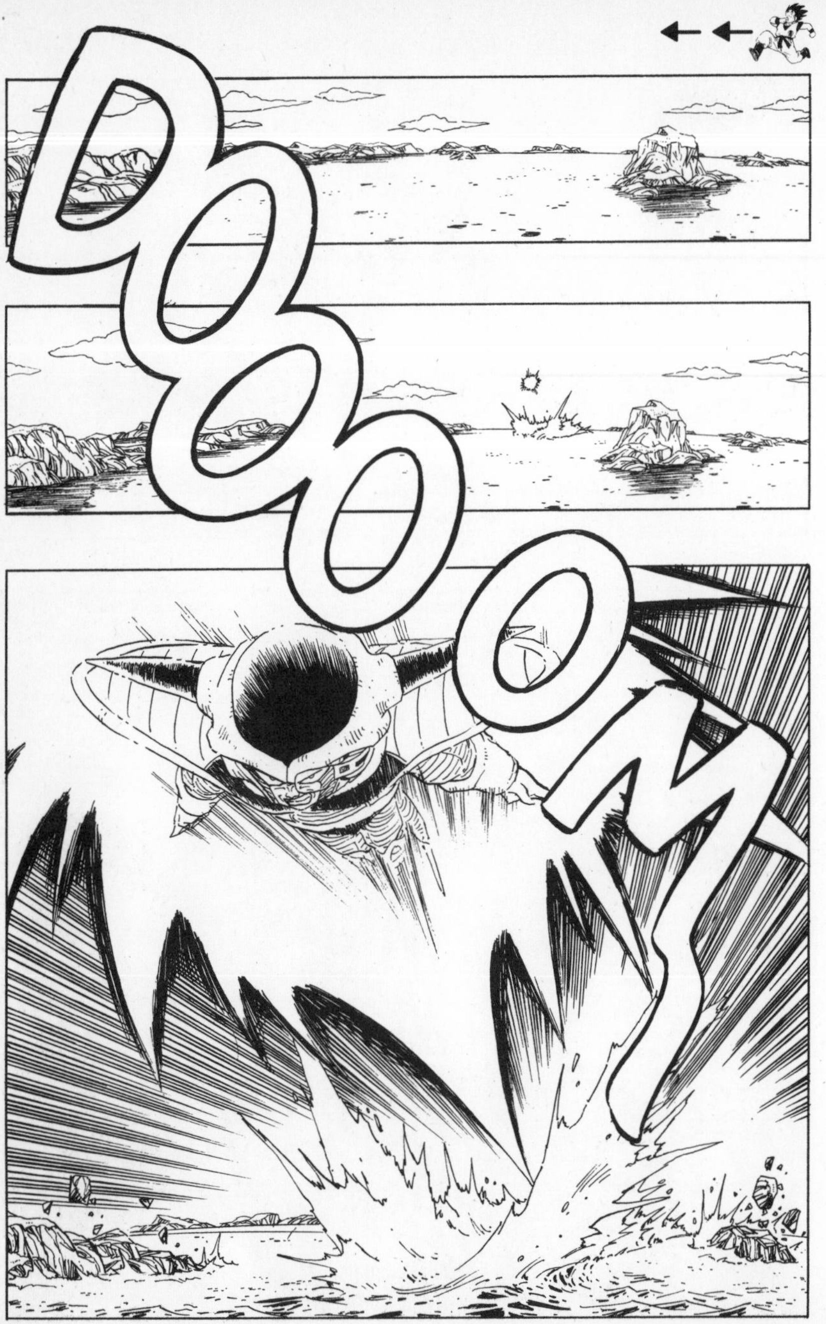
DOOOOM

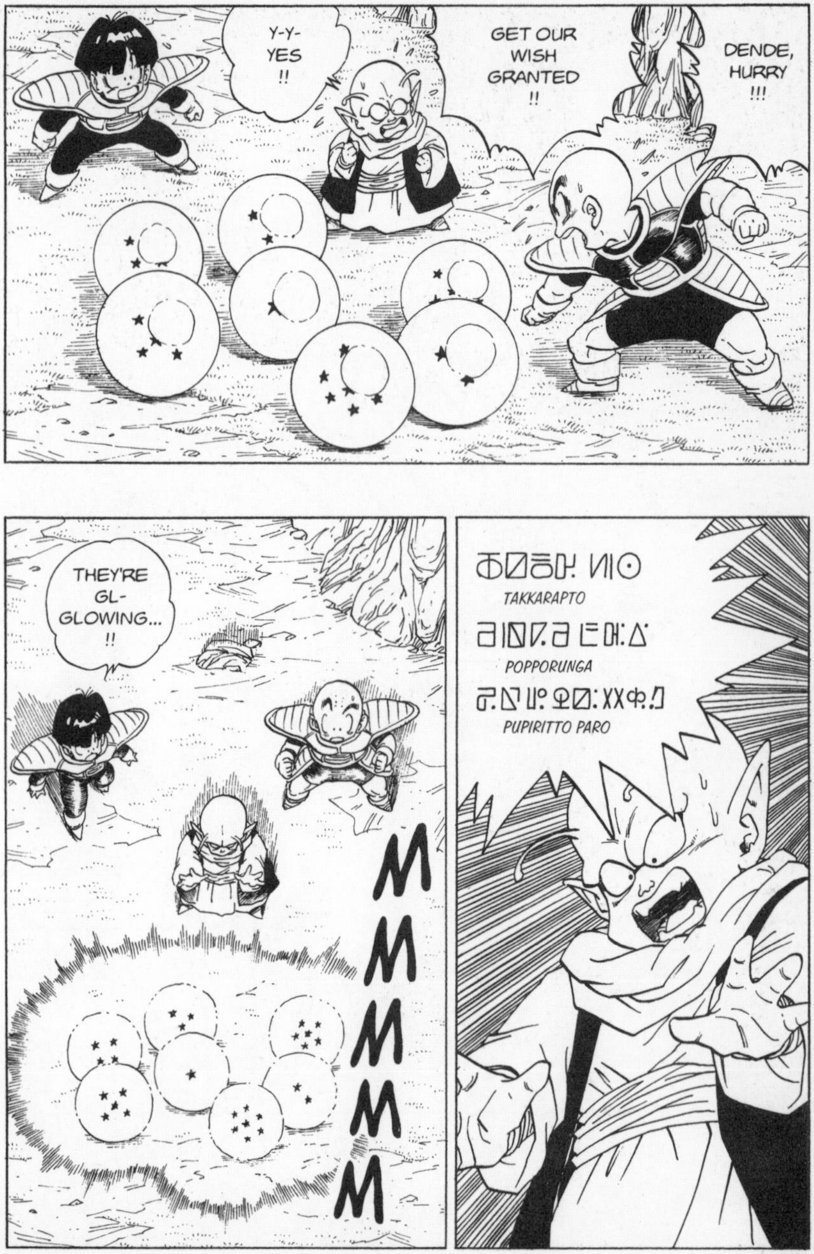
DENDE, HURRY!!!
GET OUR WISH GRANTED!!
Y-Y-YES!!
TAKKARAPTO
POPPORUNGA
PUPIRITTO PARO
THEY'RE GL-GLOWING...!!
MMMMMM

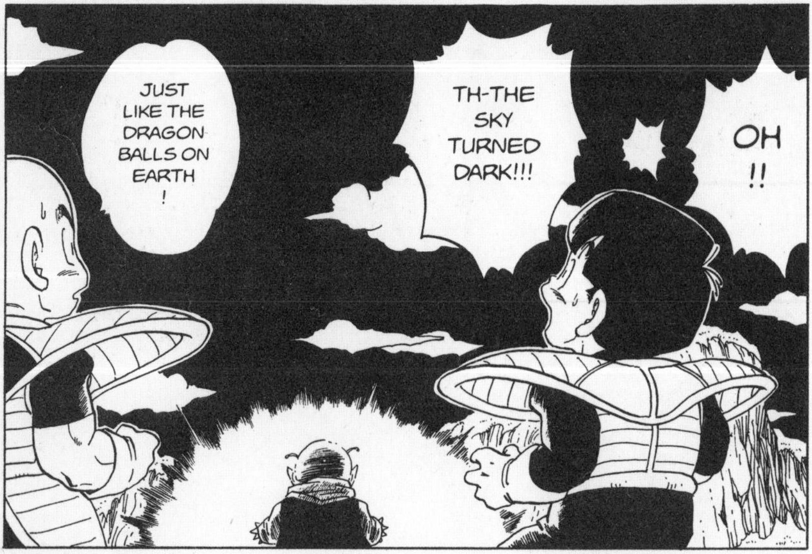
OH !!
TH-THE SKY TURNED DARK!!!
JUST LIKE THE DRAGON BALLS ON EARTH !

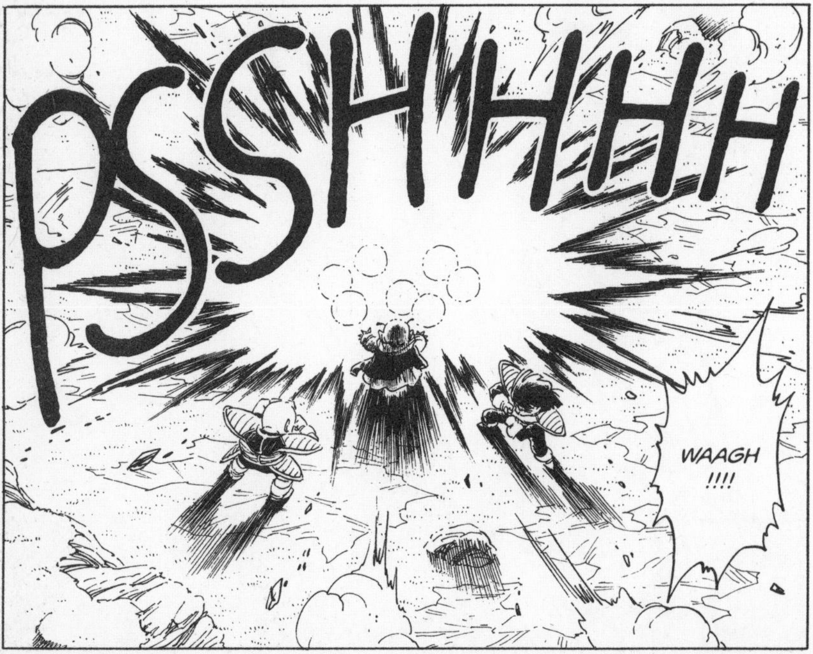
PSSHHHHH
WAAGH !!!!

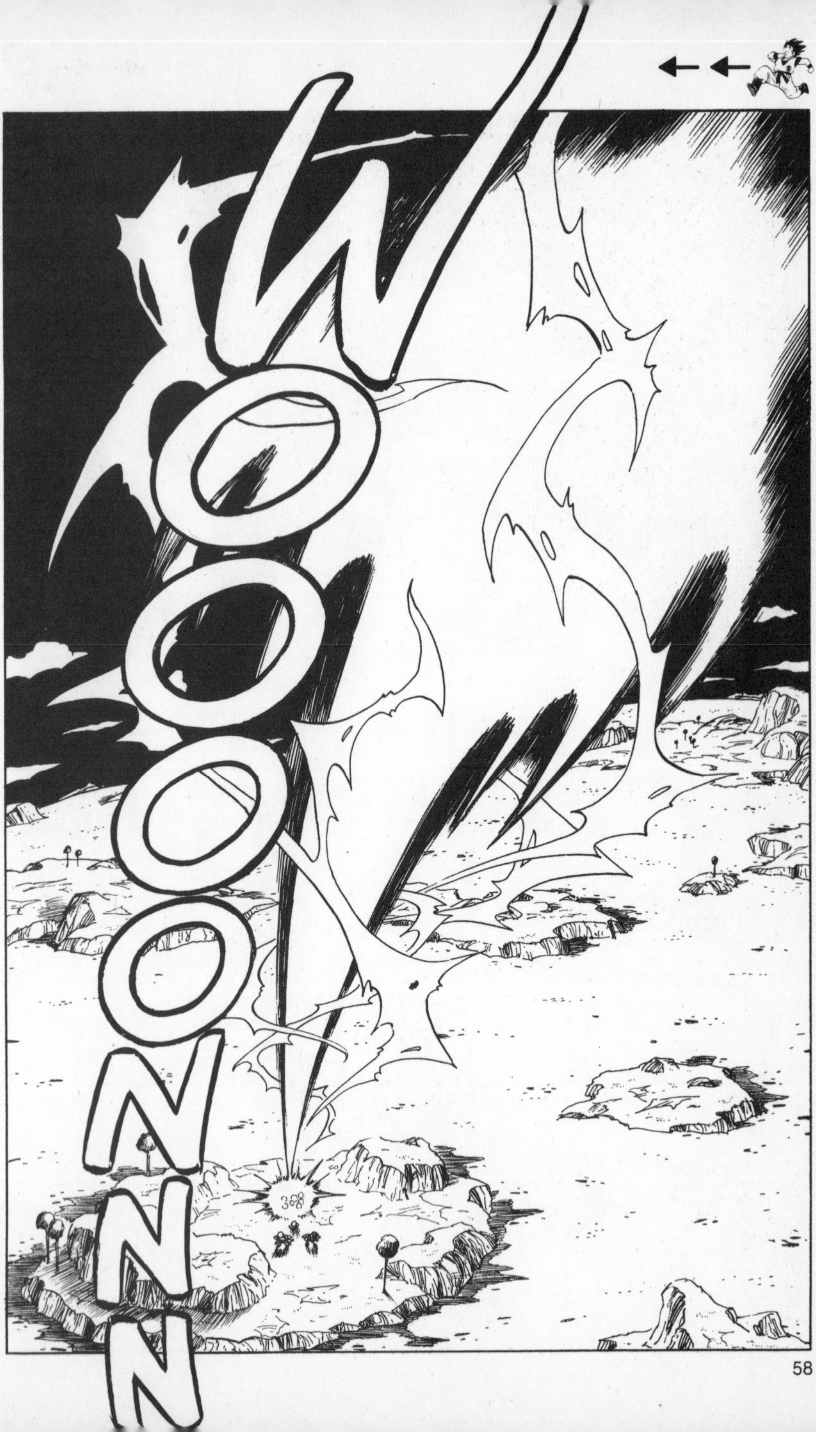
WOOOONNN

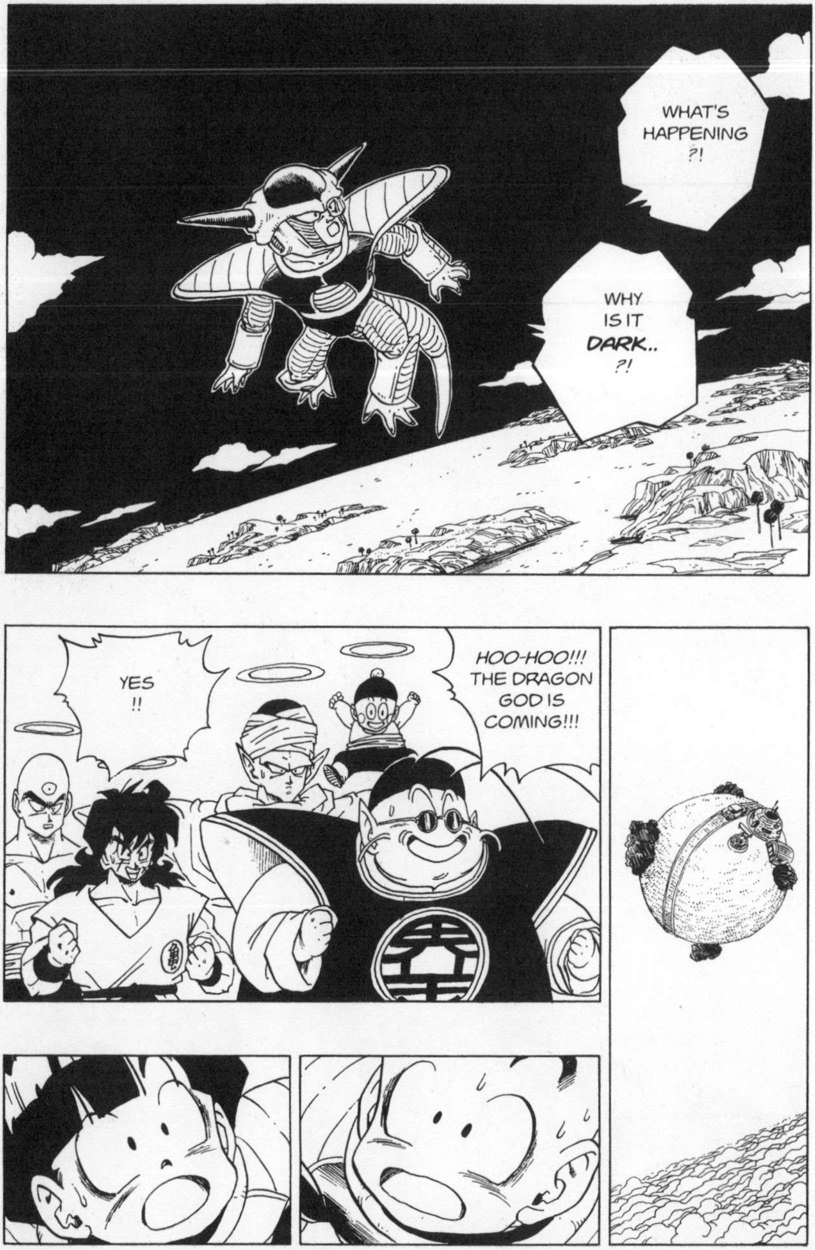
WHAT'S HAPPENING ?!
WHY IS IT DARK.. ?!
HOO-HOO!!! THE DRAGON GOD IS COMING!!!
YES !!

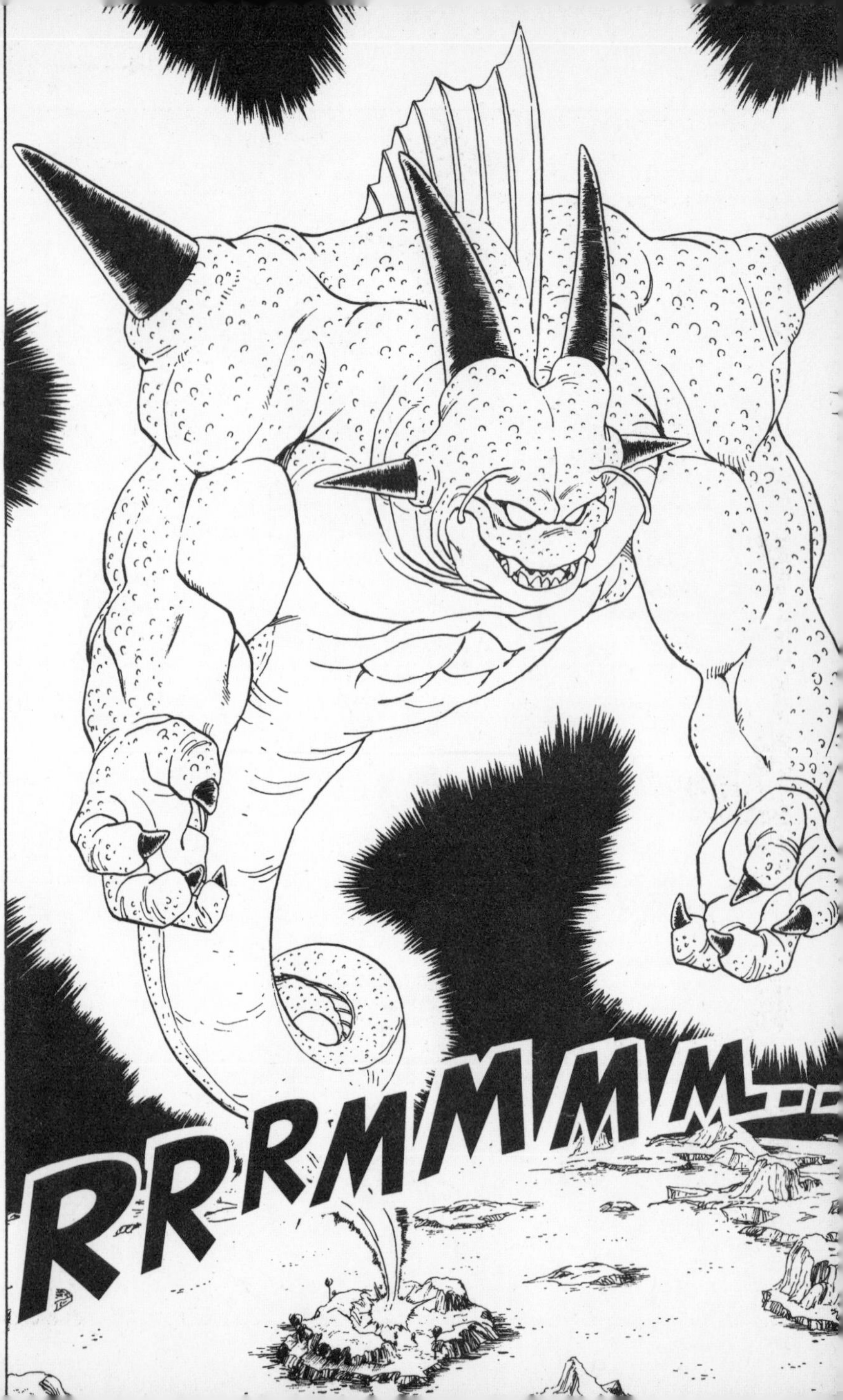
RRRMMMMMM...

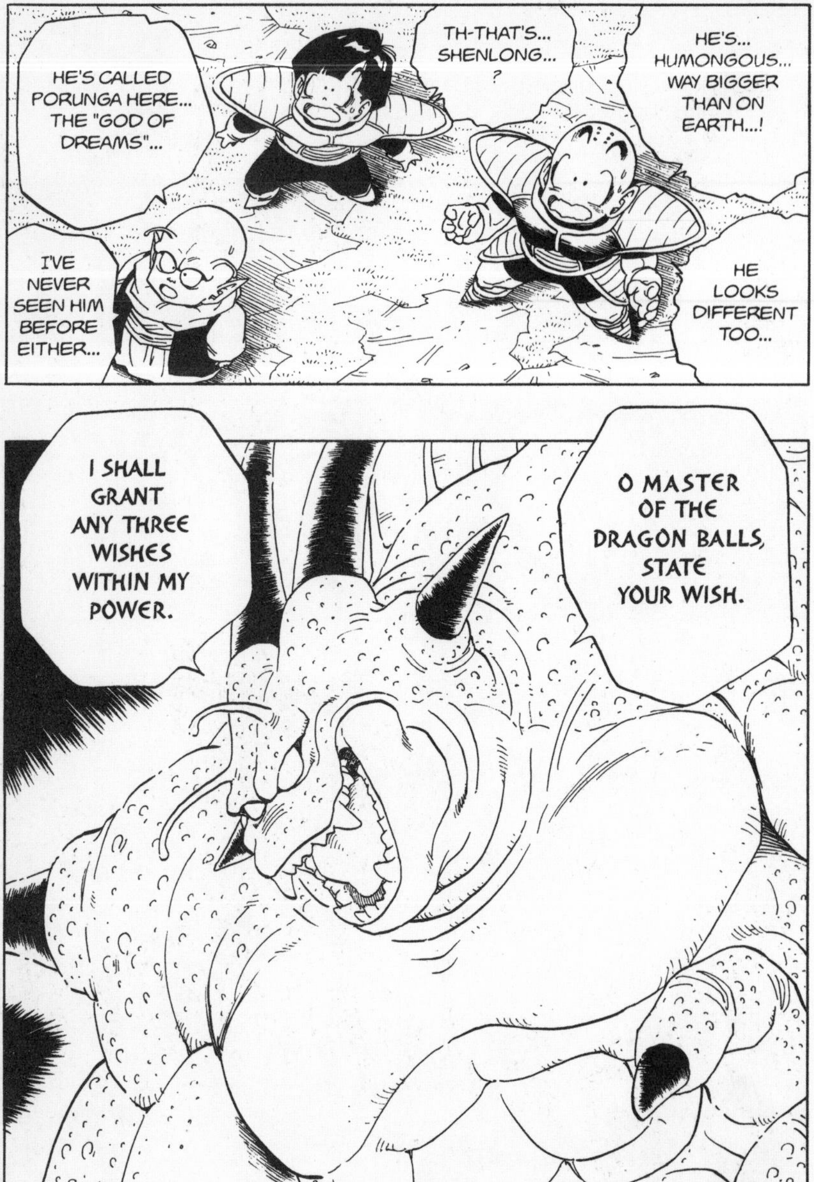
HE'S... HUMONGOUS... WAY BIGGER THAN ON EARTH...!
TH-THAT'S... SHENLONG... ?
HE'S CALLED PORUNGA HERE... THE "GOD OF DREAMS"...
HE LOOKS DIFFERENT TOO...
I'VE NEVER SEEN HIM BEFORE EITHER...
O MASTER OF THE DRAGON BALLS, STATE YOUR WISH.
I SHALL GRANT ANY THREE WISHES WITHIN MY POWER.

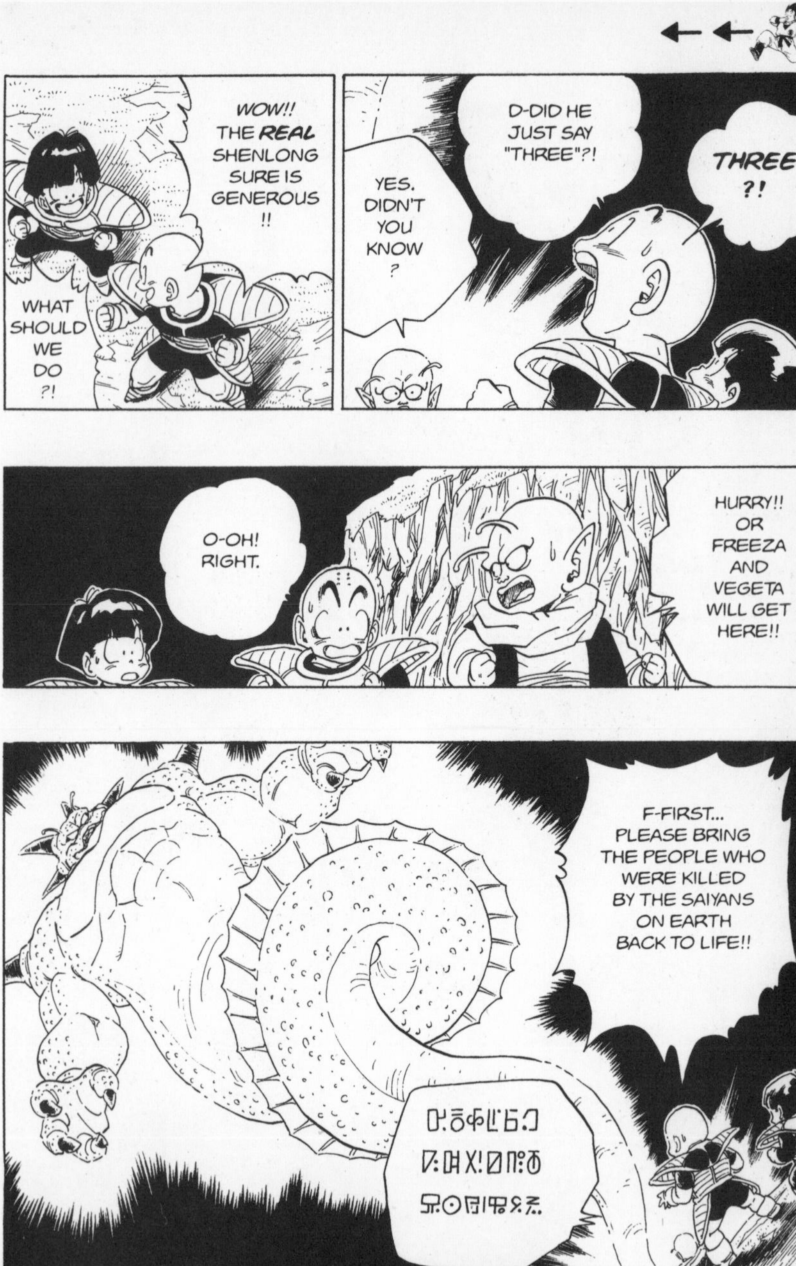
THREE ?!
D-DID HE JUST SAY "THREE"?!
YES. DIDN'T YOU KNOW ?
WOW!! THE REAL SHENLONG SURE IS GENEROUS !!
WHAT SHOULD WE DO ?!
HURRY!! OR FREEZA AND VEGETA WILL GET HERE!!
O-OH! RIGHT.
F-FIRST... PLEASE BRING THE PEOPLE WHO WERE KILLED BY THE SAIYANS ON EARTH BACK TO LIFE!!

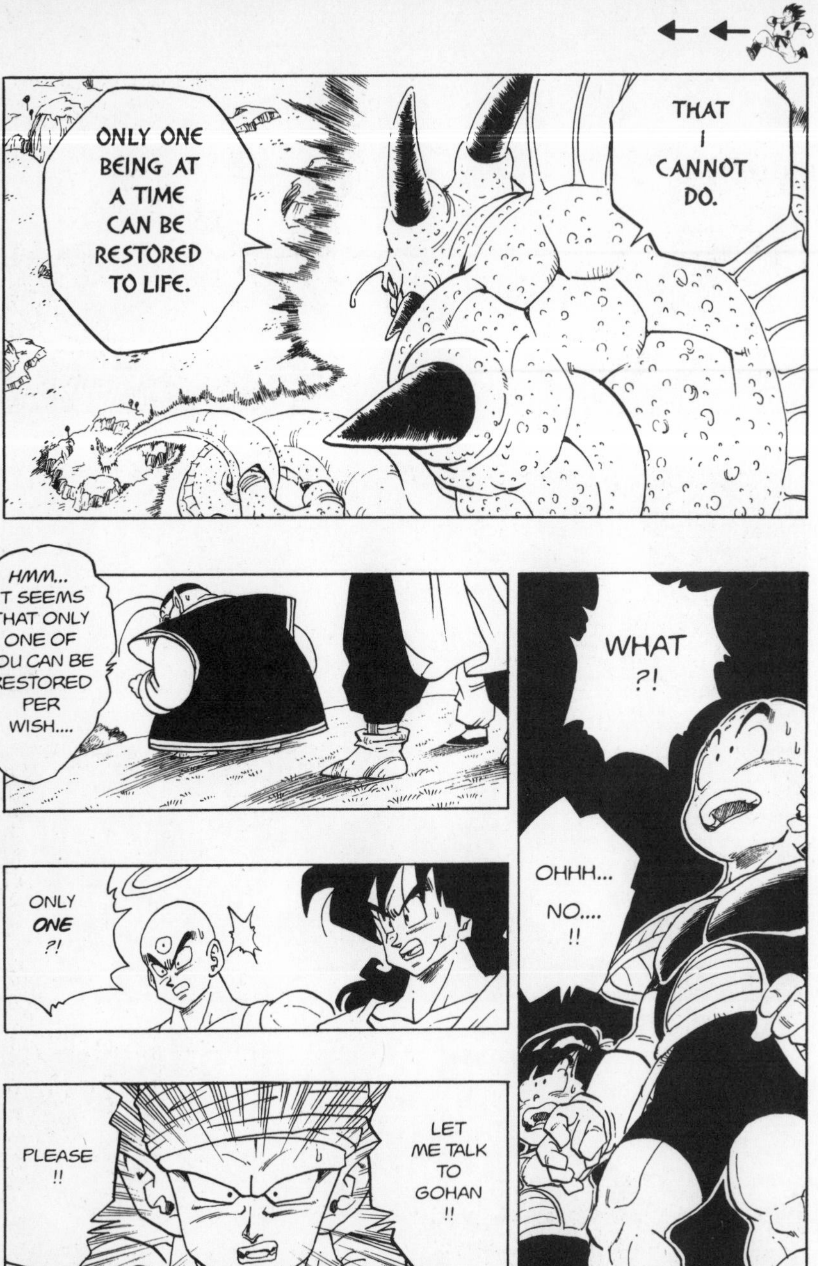
THAT I CANNOT DO.
ONLY ONE BEING AT A TIME CAN BE RESTORED TO LIFE.
WHAT ?!
OHHH... NO.... !!
HMM... IT SEEMS THAT ONLY ONE OF YOU CAN BE RESTORED PER WISH....
ONLY *ONE* ?!
LET ME TALK TO GOHAN !!
PLEASE !!

NEXT: Piccolo's Idea

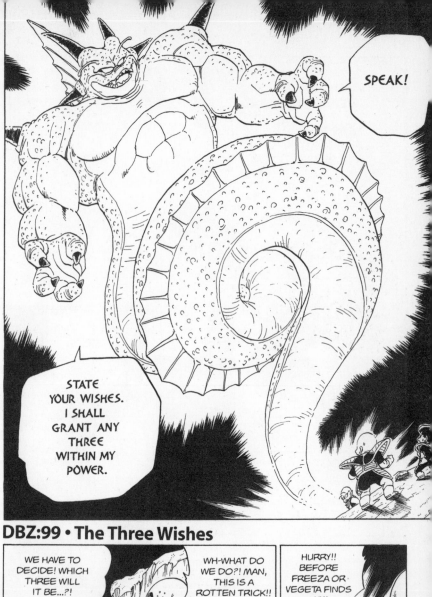

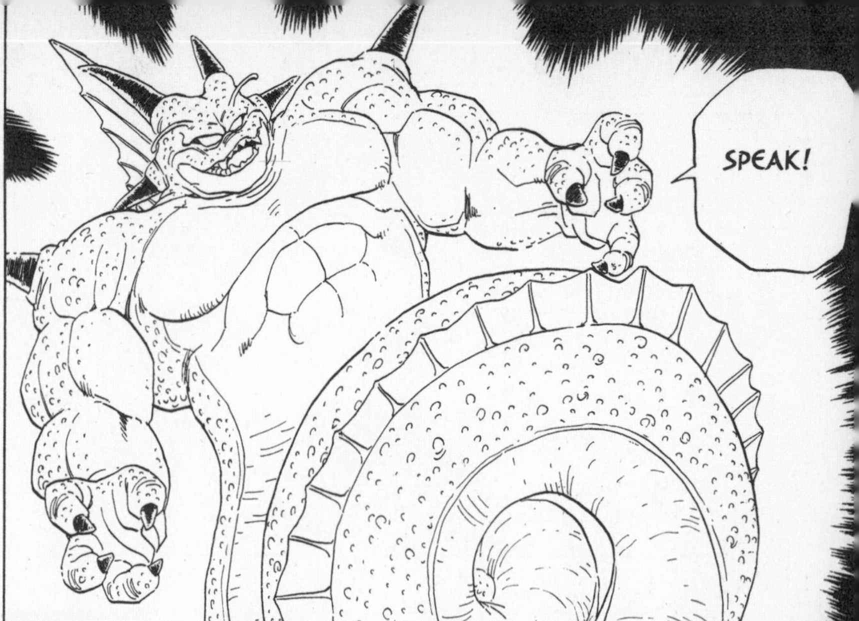
SPEAK!
STATE YOUR WISHES. I SHALL GRANT ANY THREE WITHIN MY POWER.

DBZ:99 • The Three Wishes

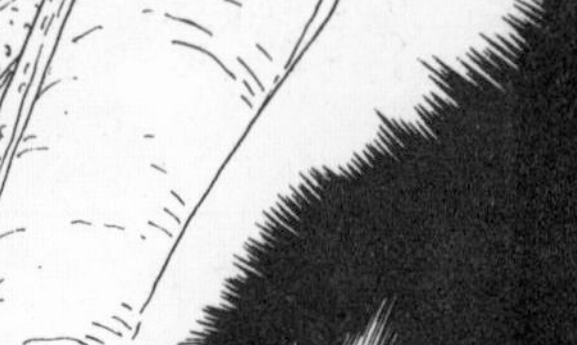
HURRY!! BEFORE FREEZA OR VEGETA FINDS US!!

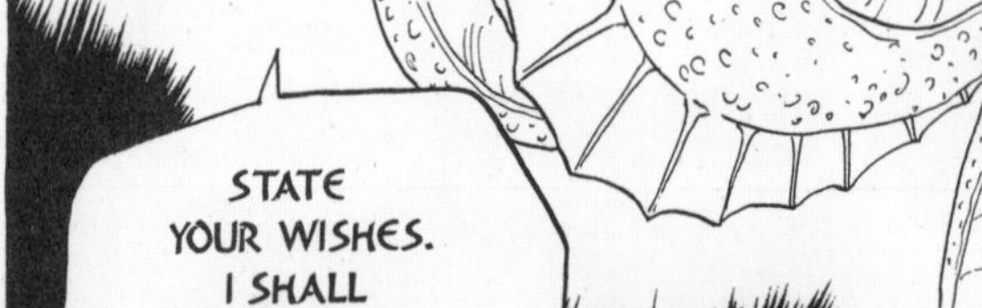
WH-WHAT DO WE DO?! MAN, THIS IS A ROTTEN TRICK!! YOU'D THINK THE REAL SHENLONG COULD--
WE HAVE TO DECIDE! WHICH THREE WILL IT BE...?!

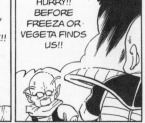

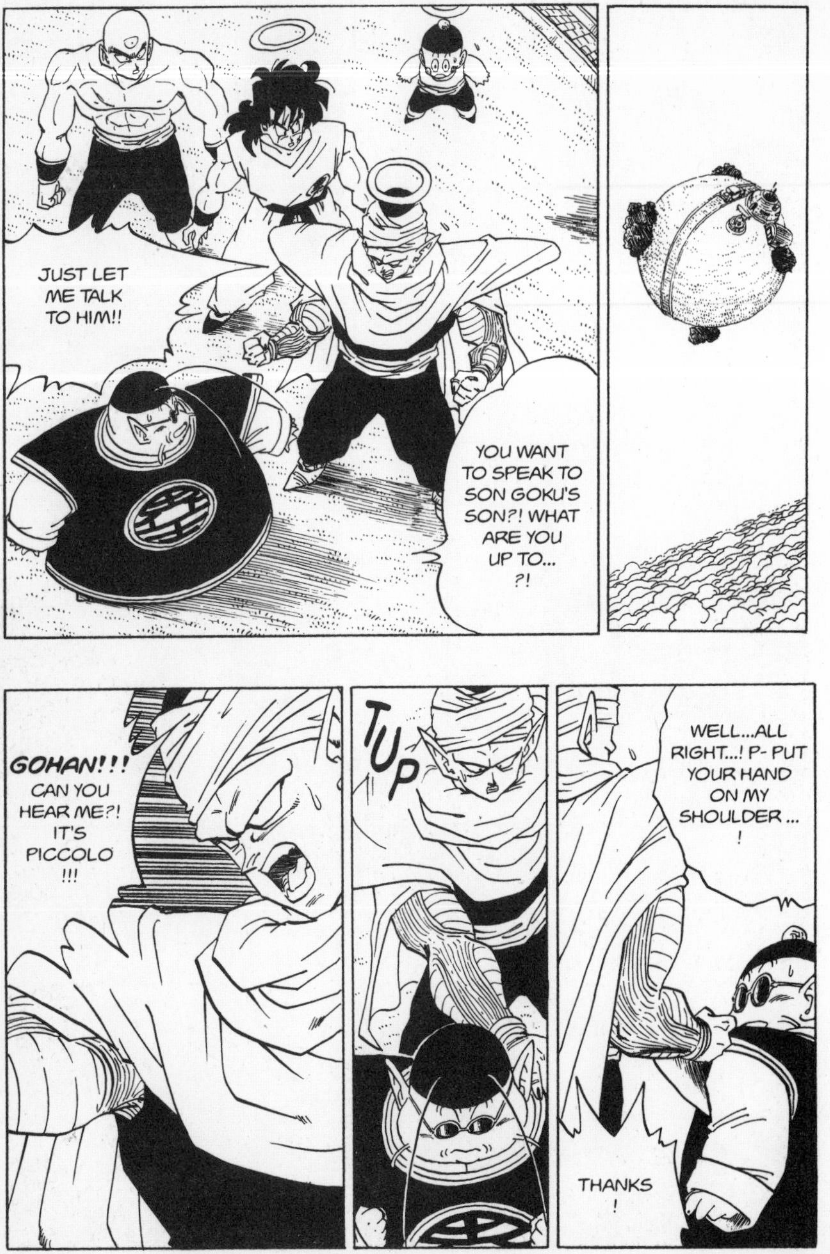
YOU WANT TO SPEAK TO SON GOKU'S SON?! WHAT ARE YOU UP TO... ?!
JUST LET ME TALK TO HIM!!
WELL...ALL RIGHT...! P- PUT YOUR HAND ON MY SHOULDER ... !
THANKS !
TUP
GOHAN!!! CAN YOU HEAR ME?! IT'S PICCOLO !!!

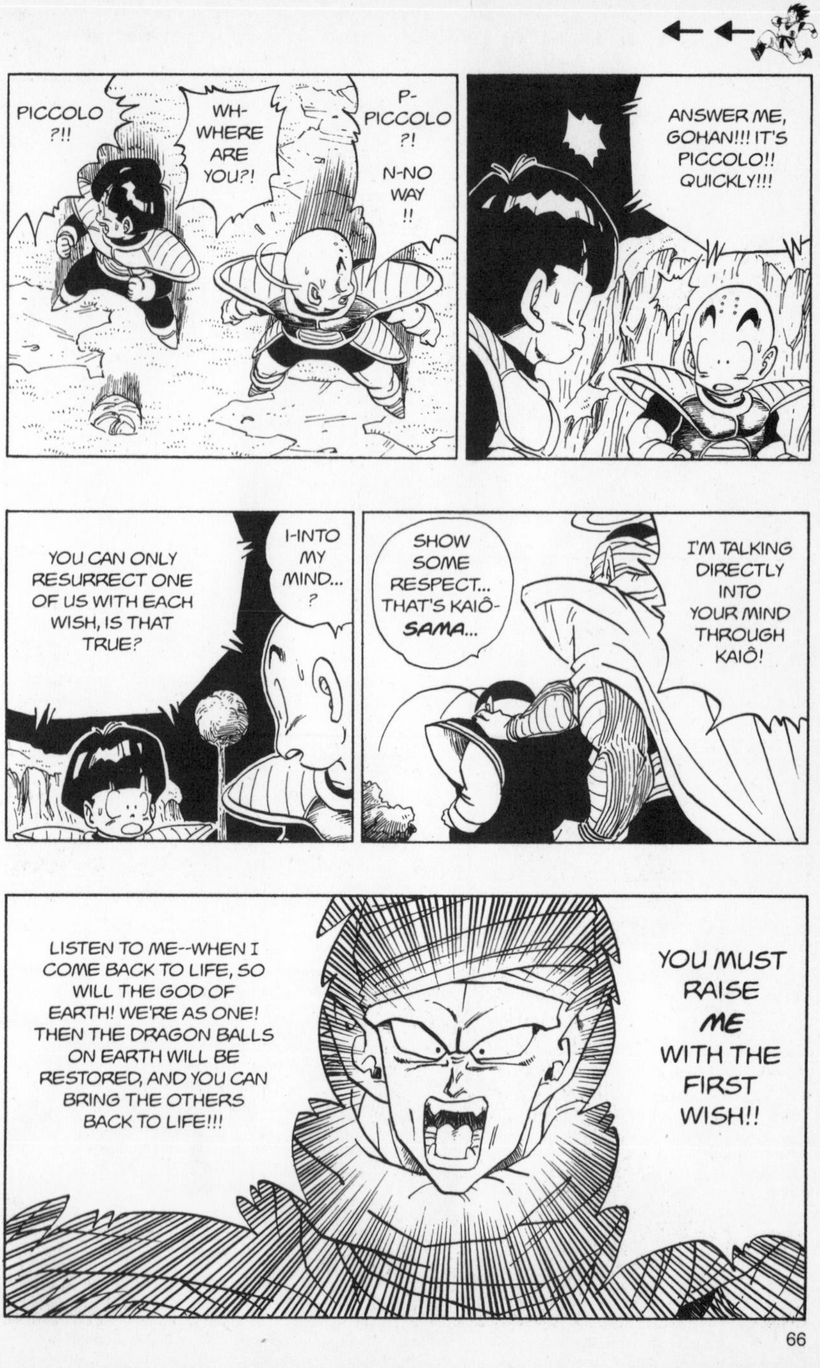
ANSWER ME, GOHAN!!! IT'S PICCOLO!! QUICKLY!!!
P-PICCOLO?!
N-NO WAY!!
WH-WHERE ARE YOU?!
PICCOLO?!!
I'M TALKING DIRECTLY INTO YOUR MIND THROUGH KAIÔ!
SHOW SOME RESPECT... THAT'S KAIÔ-*SAMA*...
I-INTO MY MIND...?
YOU CAN ONLY RESURRECT ONE OF US WITH EACH WISH, IS THAT TRUE?
YOU MUST RAISE *ME* WITH THE FIRST WISH!!
LISTEN TO ME--WHEN I COME BACK TO LIFE, SO WILL THE GOD OF EARTH! WE'RE AS ONE! THEN THE DRAGON BALLS ON EARTH WILL BE RESTORED, AND YOU CAN BRING THE OTHERS BACK TO LIFE!!!

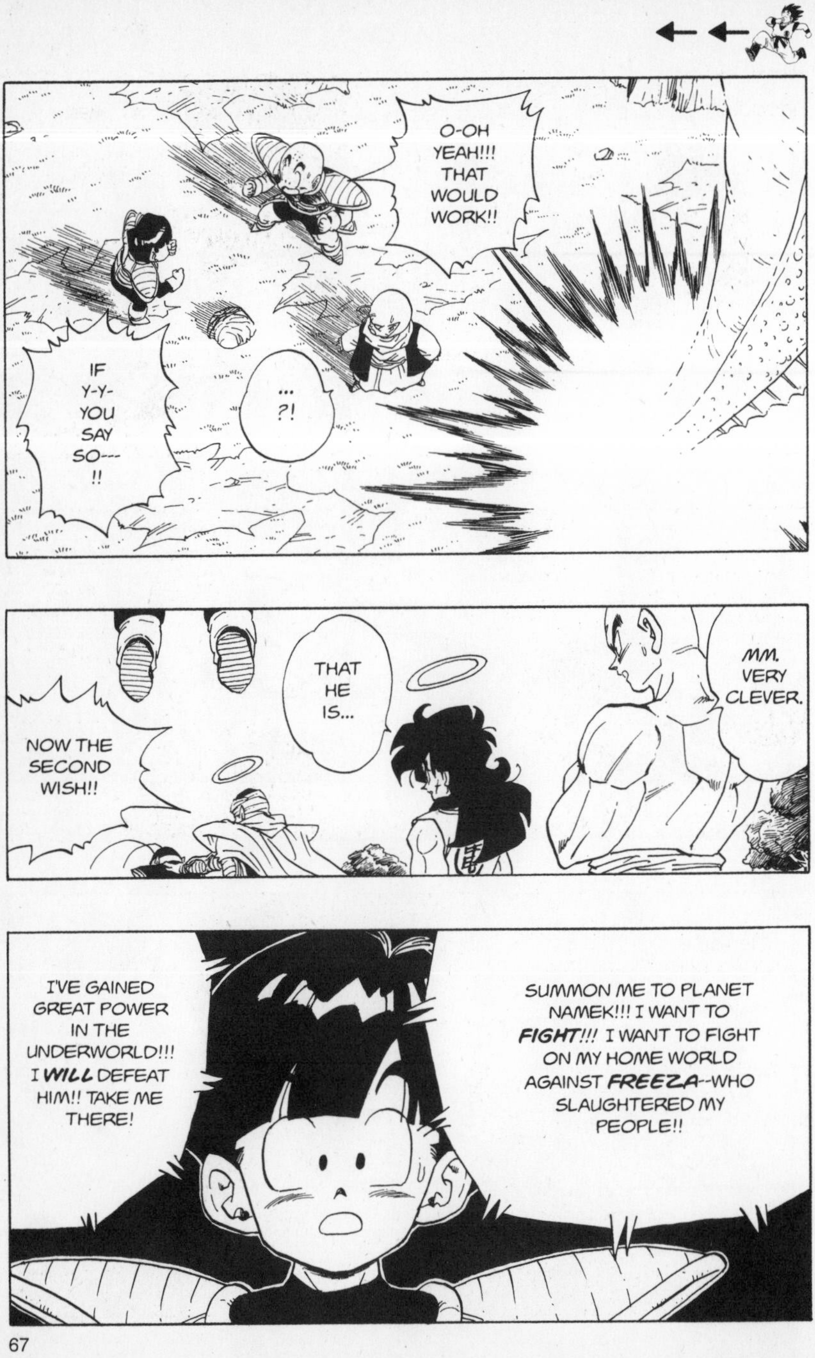
O-OH YEAH!!! THAT WOULD WORK!!
...?!
IF Y-Y-YOU SAY SO---!!
MM. VERY CLEVER.
THAT HE IS...
NOW THE SECOND WISH!!
SUMMON ME TO PLANET NAMEK!!! I WANT TO FIGHT!!! I WANT TO FIGHT ON MY HOME WORLD AGAINST FREEZA--WHO SLAUGHTERED MY PEOPLE!!
I'VE GAINED GREAT POWER IN THE UNDERWORLD!!! I WILL DEFEAT HIM!! TAKE ME THERE!

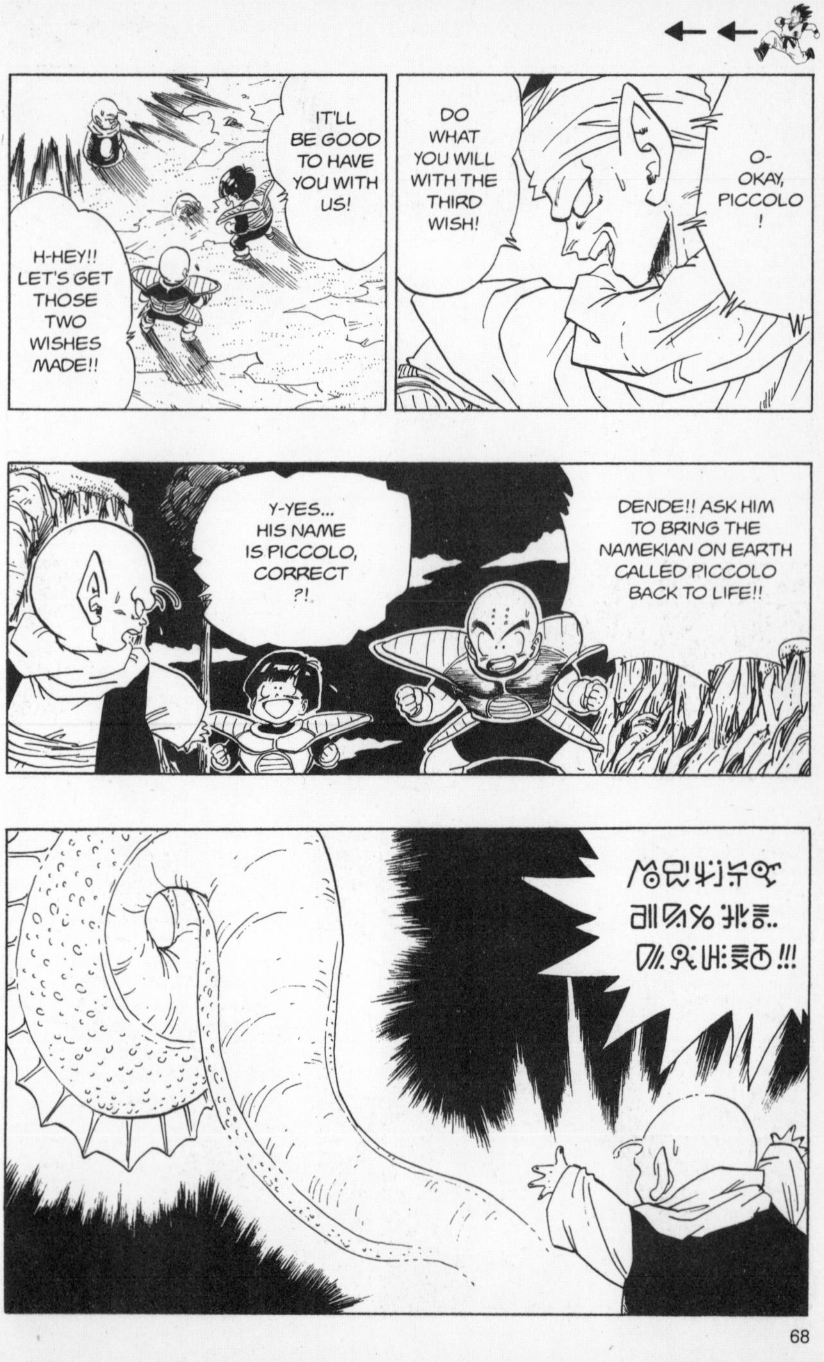
DO WHAT YOU WILL WITH THE THIRD WISH!
O-OKAY, PICCOLO!
IT'LL BE GOOD TO HAVE YOU WITH US!
H-HEY!! LET'S GET THOSE TWO WISHES MADE!!
DENDE!! ASK HIM TO BRING THE NAMEKIAN ON EARTH CALLED PICCOLO BACK TO LIFE!!
Y-YES... HIS NAME IS PICCOLO, CORRECT?!

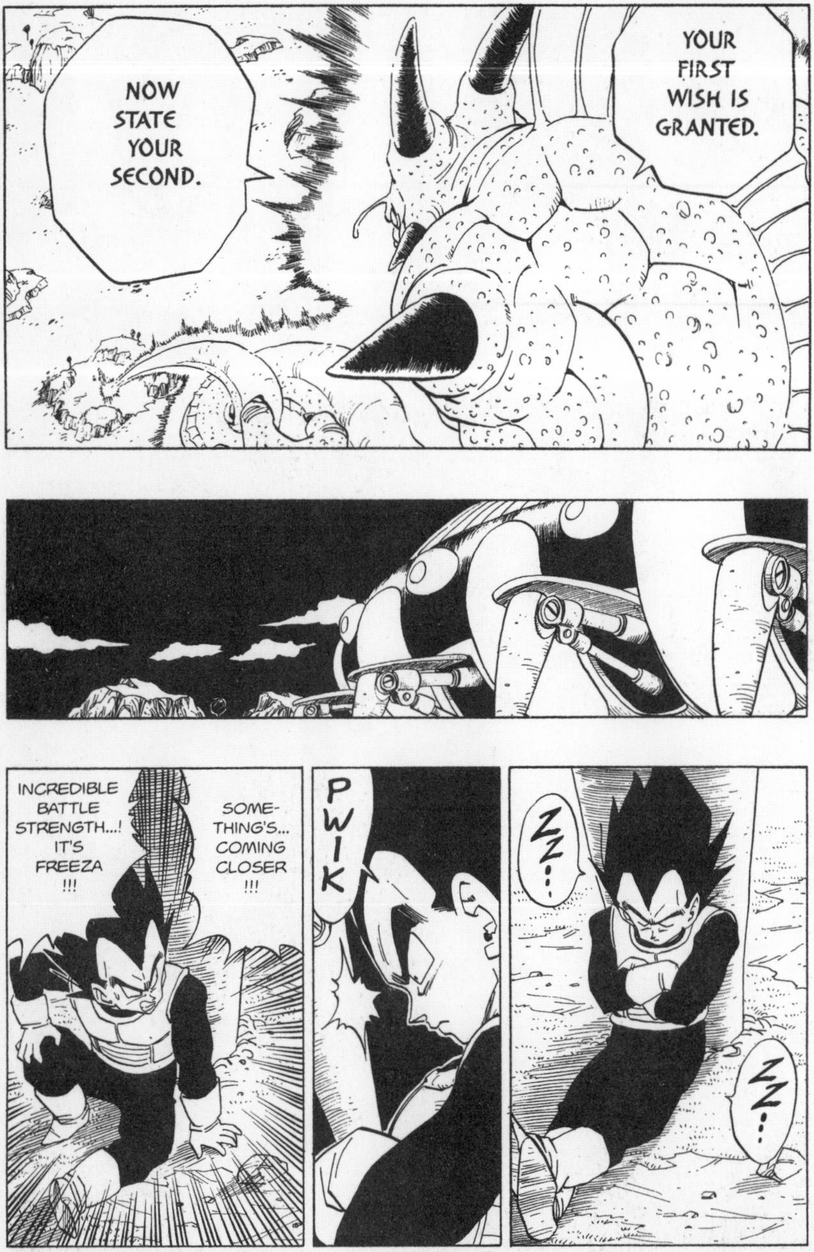
YOUR FIRST WISH IS GRANTED.
NOW STATE YOUR SECOND.
ZZ...
ZZ...
PWIK
SOME-THING'S... COMING CLOSER!!!
INCREDIBLE BATTLE STRENGTH...! IT'S FREEZA!!!

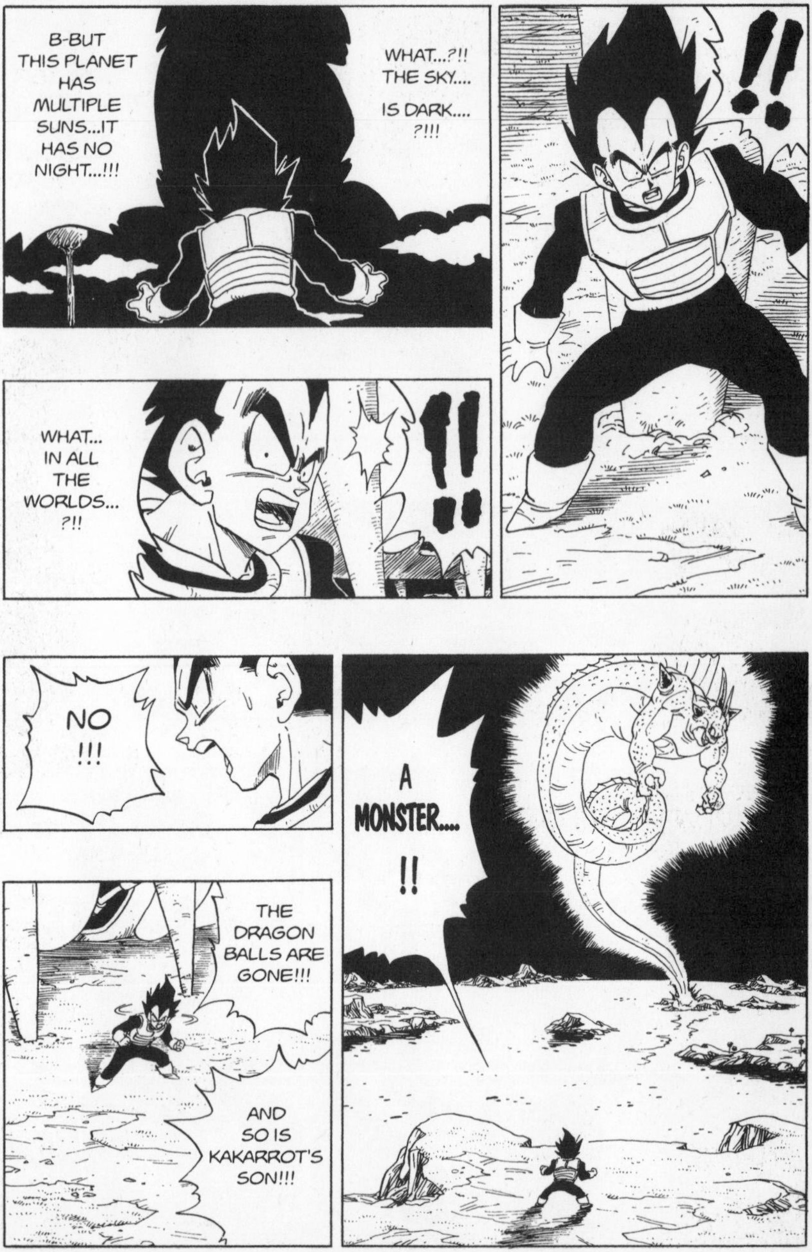
!!
WHAT...?!! THE SKY.... IS DARK....?!!!
B-BUT THIS PLANET HAS MULTIPLE SUNS...IT HAS NO NIGHT...!!!
!!
WHAT... IN ALL THE WORLDS...?!!
A MONSTER.... !!
NO !!!
THE DRAGON BALLS ARE GONE!!!
AND SO IS KAKARROT'S SON!!!

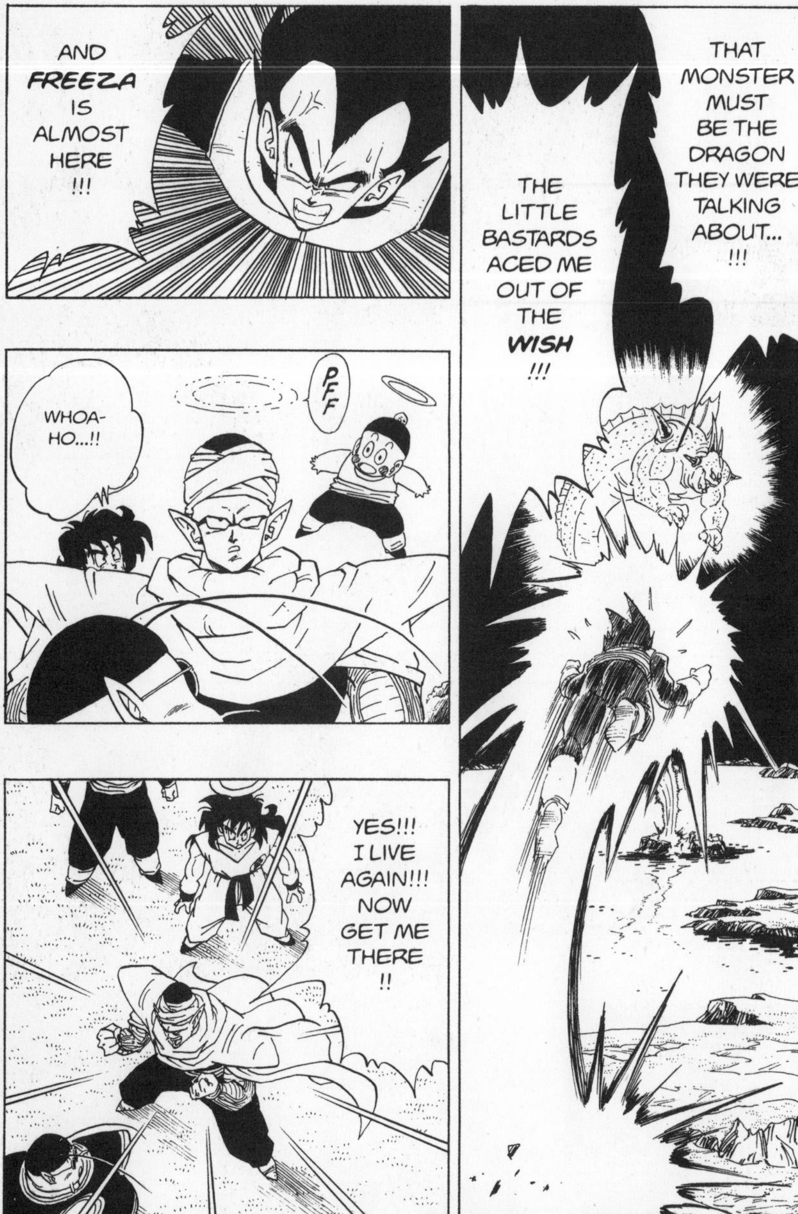
THAT MONSTER MUST BE THE DRAGON THEY WERE TALKING ABOUT... !!!
THE LITTLE BASTARDS ACED ME OUT OF THE WISH !!!
AND FREEZA IS ALMOST HERE !!!
WHOA-HO...!!
PFF
YES!!! I LIVE AGAIN!!! NOW GET ME THERE !!

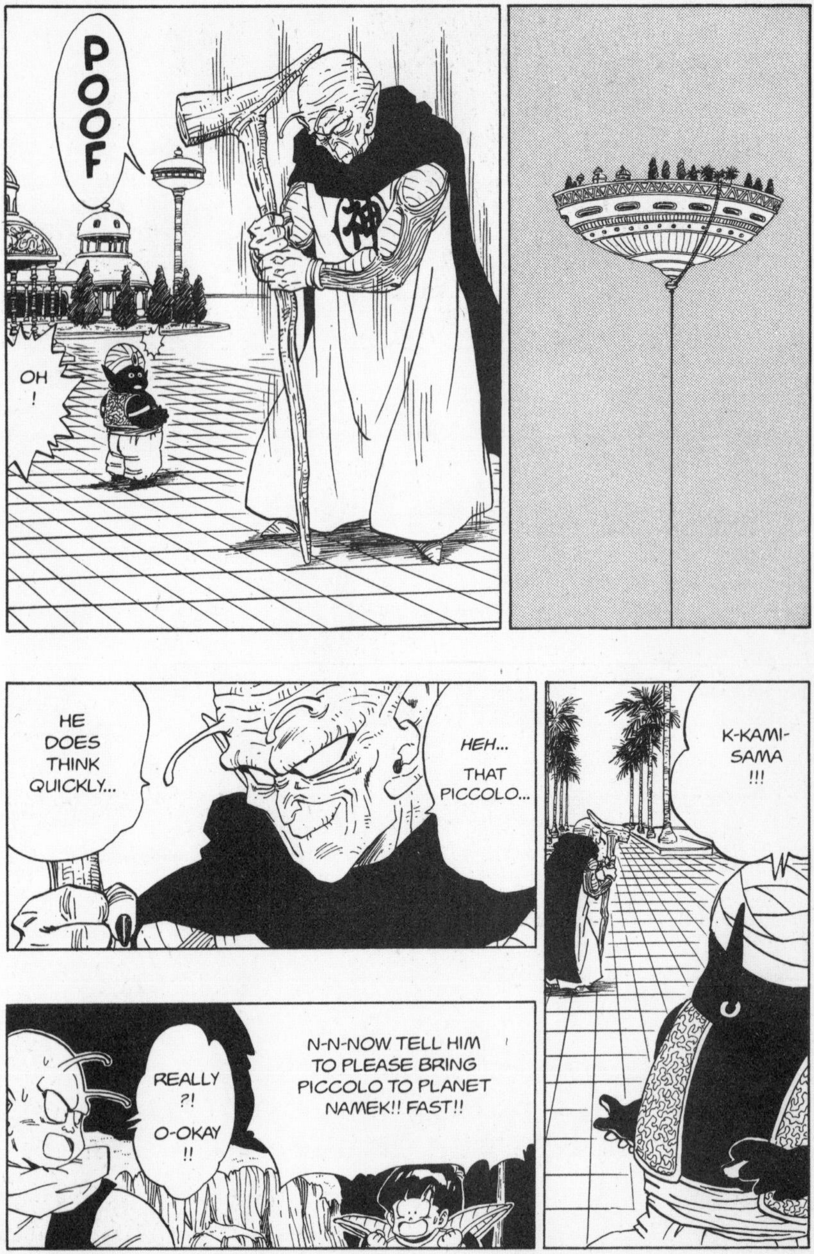
POOF
OH !
K-KAMI-SAMA !!!
HEH... THAT PICCOLO...
HE DOES THINK QUICKLY...
N-N-NOW TELL HIM TO PLEASE BRING PICCOLO TO PLANET NAMEK!! FAST!!
REALLY ?!
O-OKAY !!

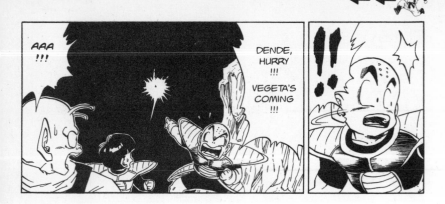

AAA
!!!

DENDE,
HURRY
!!!
VEGETA'S
COMING
!!!

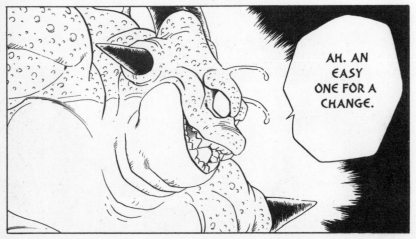

AH. AN
EASY
ONE FOR A
CHANGE.

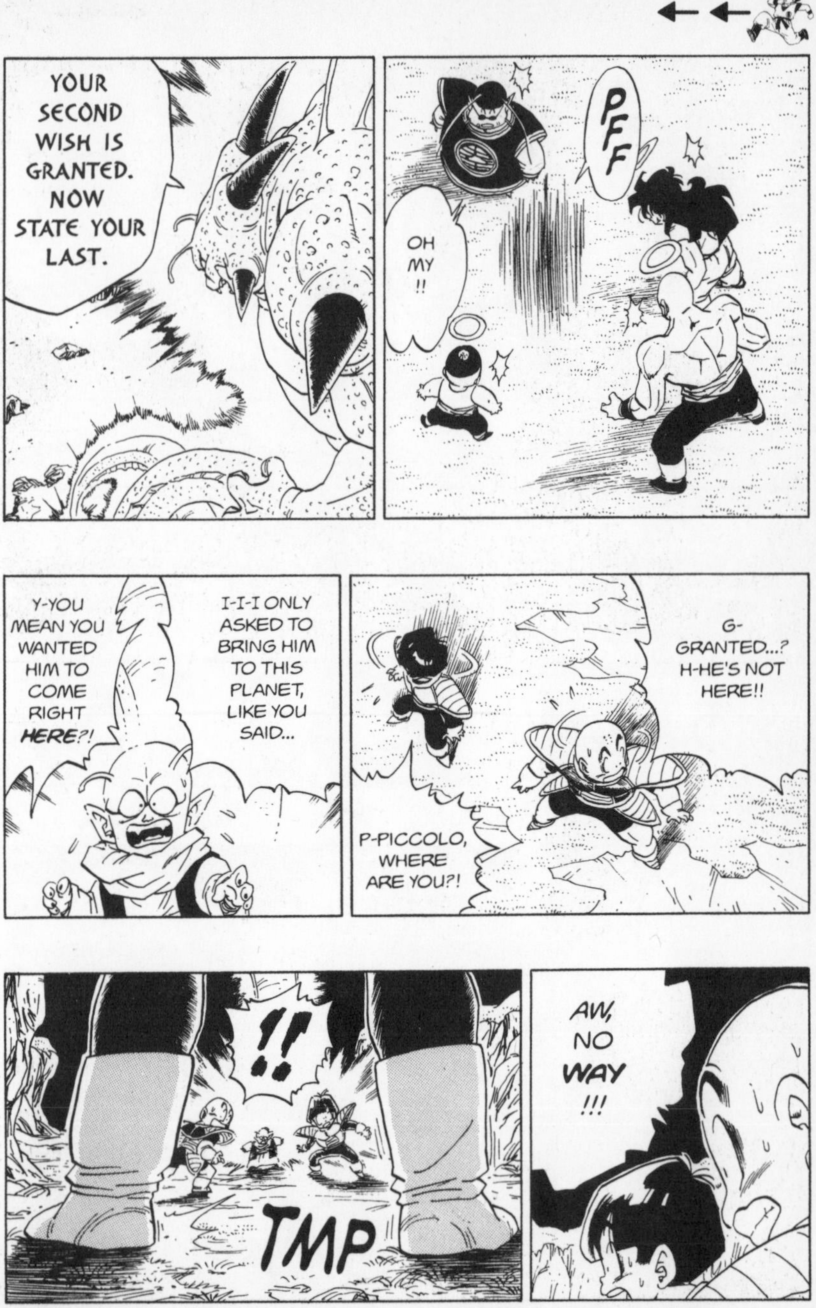

PFF
OH MY !!
YOUR SECOND WISH IS GRANTED. NOW STATE YOUR LAST.
G-GRANTED...? H-HE'S NOT HERE!!
P-PICCOLO, WHERE ARE YOU?!
I-I-I ONLY ASKED TO BRING HIM TO THIS PLANET, LIKE YOU SAID...
Y-YOU MEAN YOU WANTED HIM TO COME RIGHT HERE?!
AW, NO WAY !!!
!!
TMP

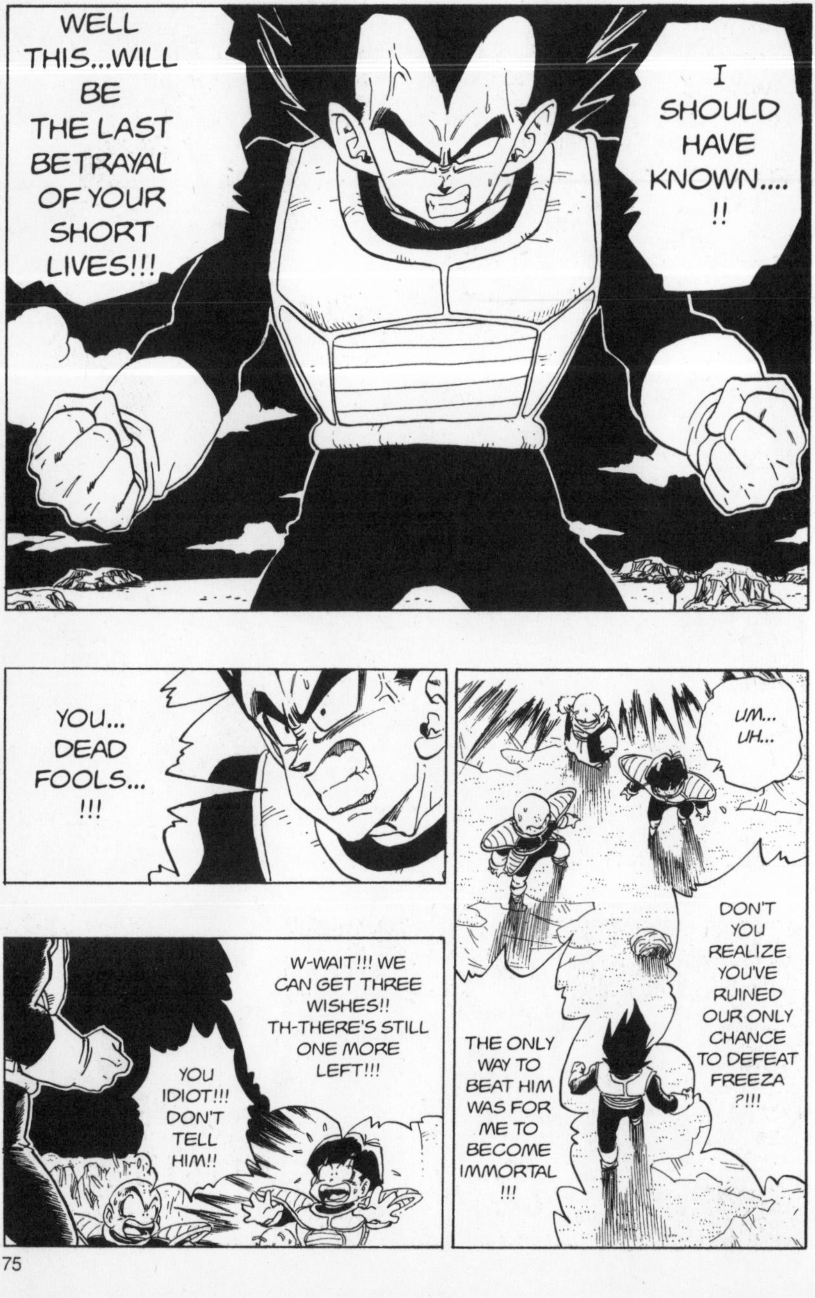
WELL THIS...WILL BE THE LAST BETRAYAL OF YOUR SHORT LIVES!!!
I SHOULD HAVE KNOWN.... !!
YOU... DEAD FOOLS... !!!
UM... UH...
DON'T YOU REALIZE YOU'VE RUINED OUR ONLY CHANCE TO DEFEAT FREEZA ?!!!
THE ONLY WAY TO BEAT HIM WAS FOR ME TO BECOME IMMORTAL !!!
W-WAIT!!! WE CAN GET THREE WISHES!! TH-THERE'S STILL ONE MORE LEFT!!!
YOU IDIOT!!! DON'T TELL HIM!!

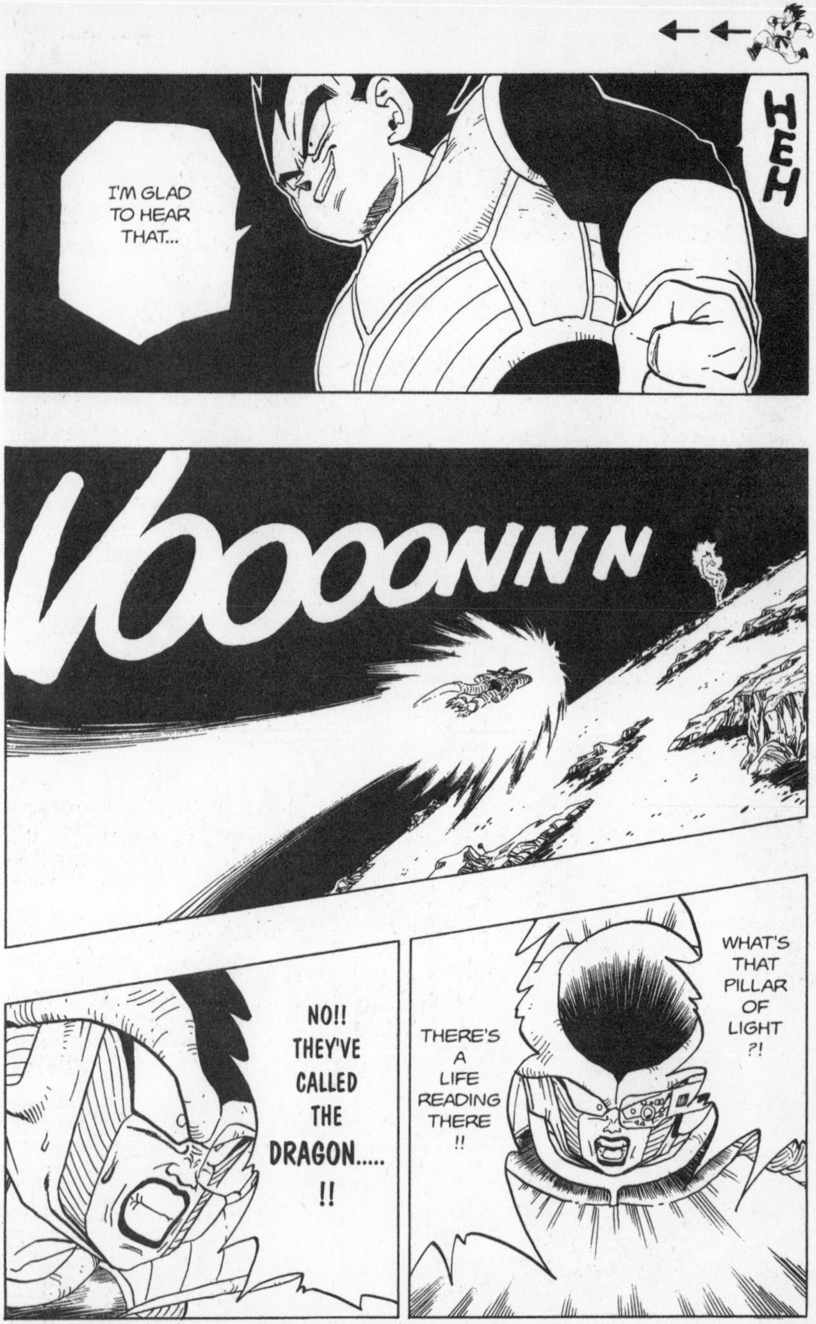
HEH
I'M GLAD TO HEAR THAT...
VOOOONNN
WHAT'S THAT PILLAR OF LIGHT ?!
THERE'S A LIFE READING THERE !!
NO!! THEY'VE CALLED THE DRAGON..... !!

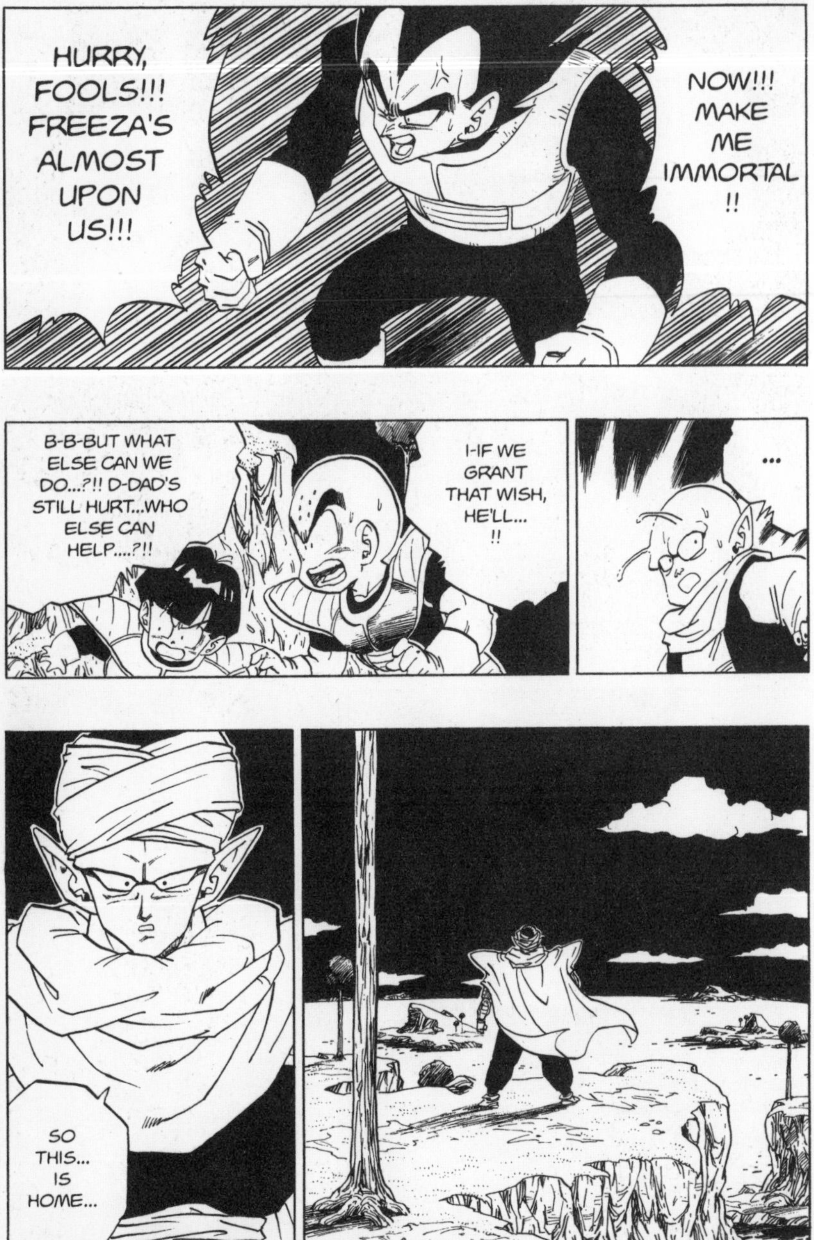
NOW!!! MAKE ME IMMORTAL !!
HURRY, FOOLS!!! FREEZA'S ALMOST UPON US!!!
...
I-IF WE GRANT THAT WISH, HE'LL... !!
B-B-BUT WHAT ELSE CAN WE DO...?!! D-DAD'S STILL HURT...WHO ELSE CAN HELP....?!!
SO THIS... IS HOME...

NEXT: One Wish to Go...

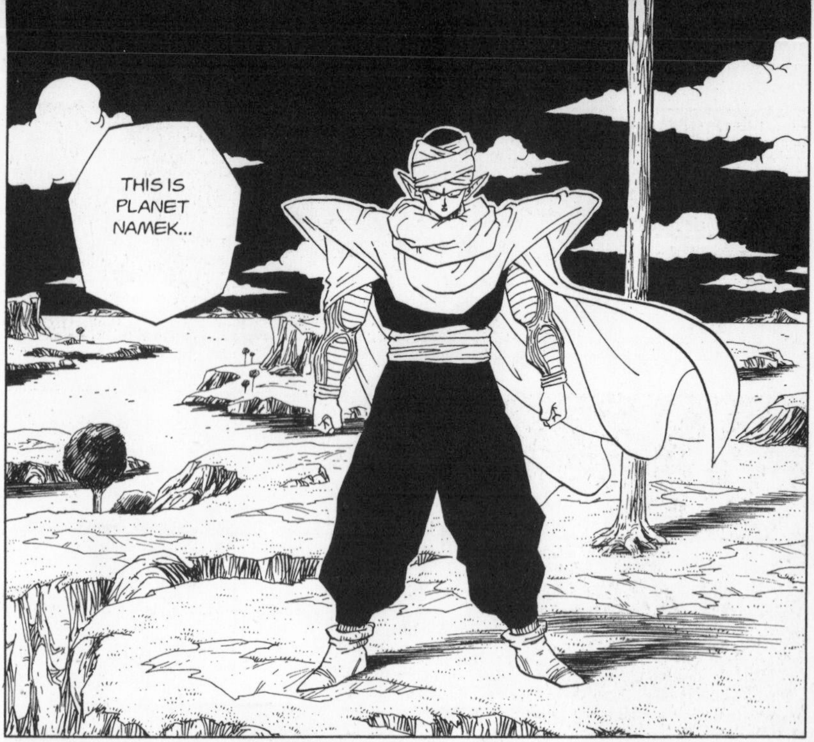
THIS IS PLANET NAMEK...

DBZ:100 • The Last Wish

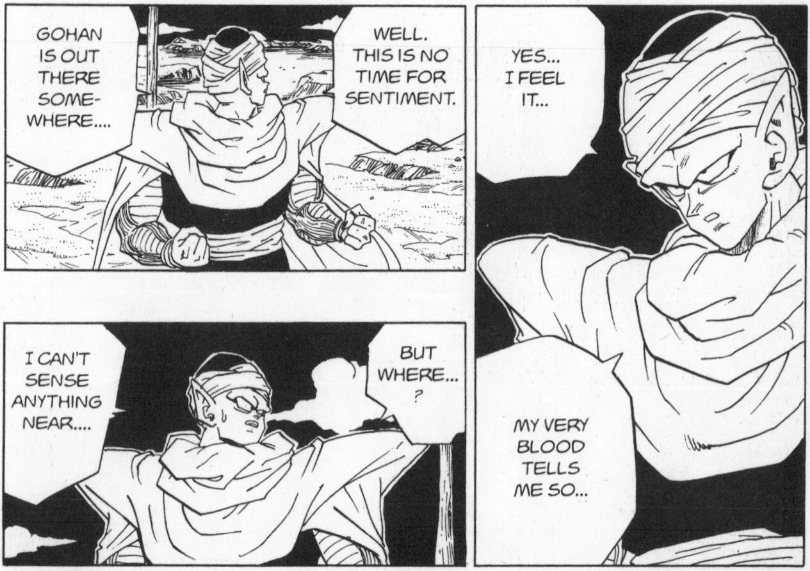
GOHAN IS OUT THERE SOME-WHERE....
WELL. THIS IS NO TIME FOR SENTIMENT.
I CAN'T SENSE ANYTHING NEAR....
BUT WHERE... ?
YES... I FEEL IT...
MY VERY BLOOD TELLS ME SO...

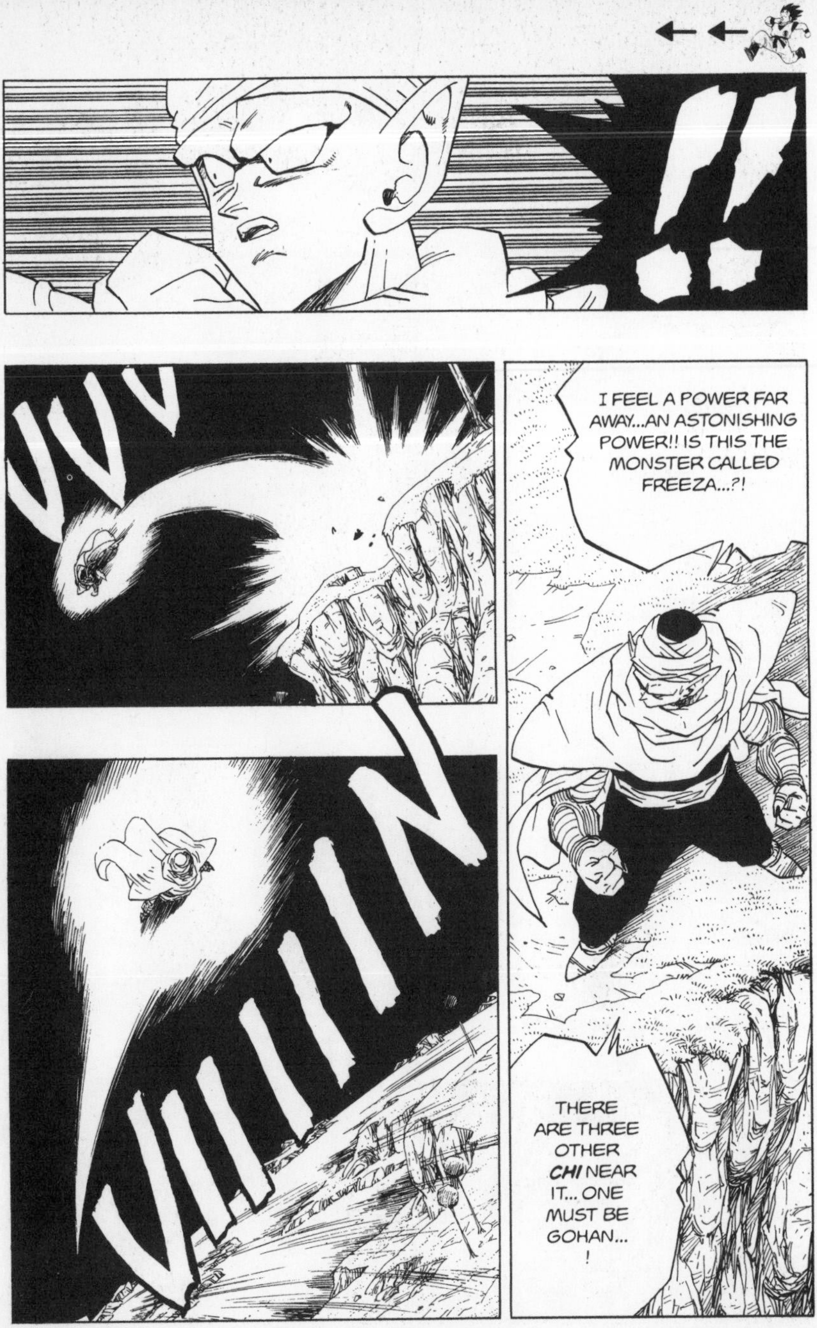
I FEEL A POWER FAR AWAY...AN ASTONISHING POWER!! IS THIS THE MONSTER CALLED FREEZA...?!
THERE ARE THREE OTHER *CHI* NEAR IT... ONE MUST BE GOHAN...!

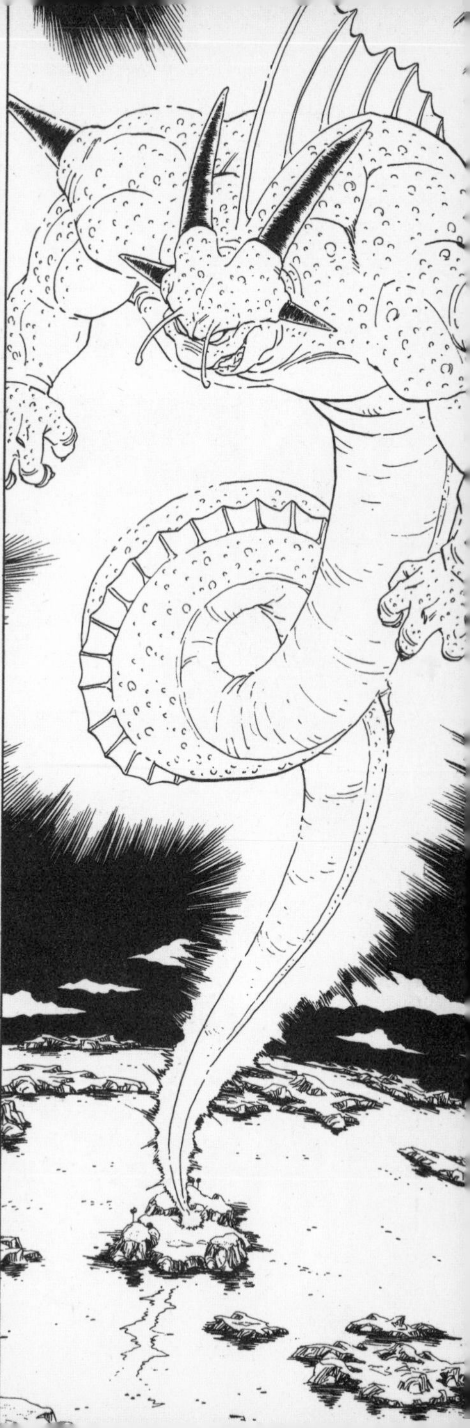

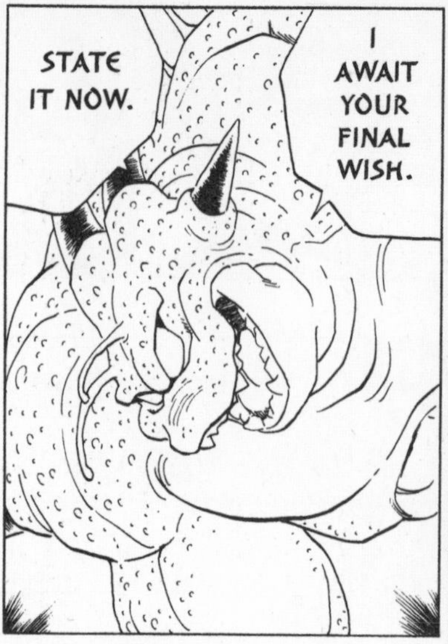
I AWAIT YOUR FINAL WISH.
STATE IT NOW.

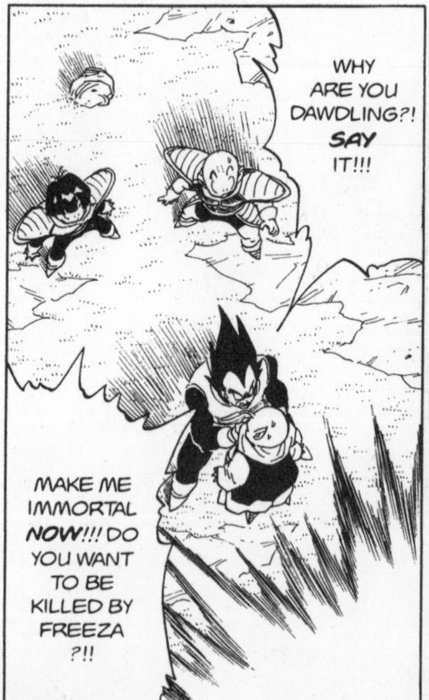
WHY ARE YOU DAWDLING?! **SAY** IT!!!
MAKE ME IMMORTAL ***NOW!!!*** DO YOU WANT TO BE KILLED BY FREEZA ?!!

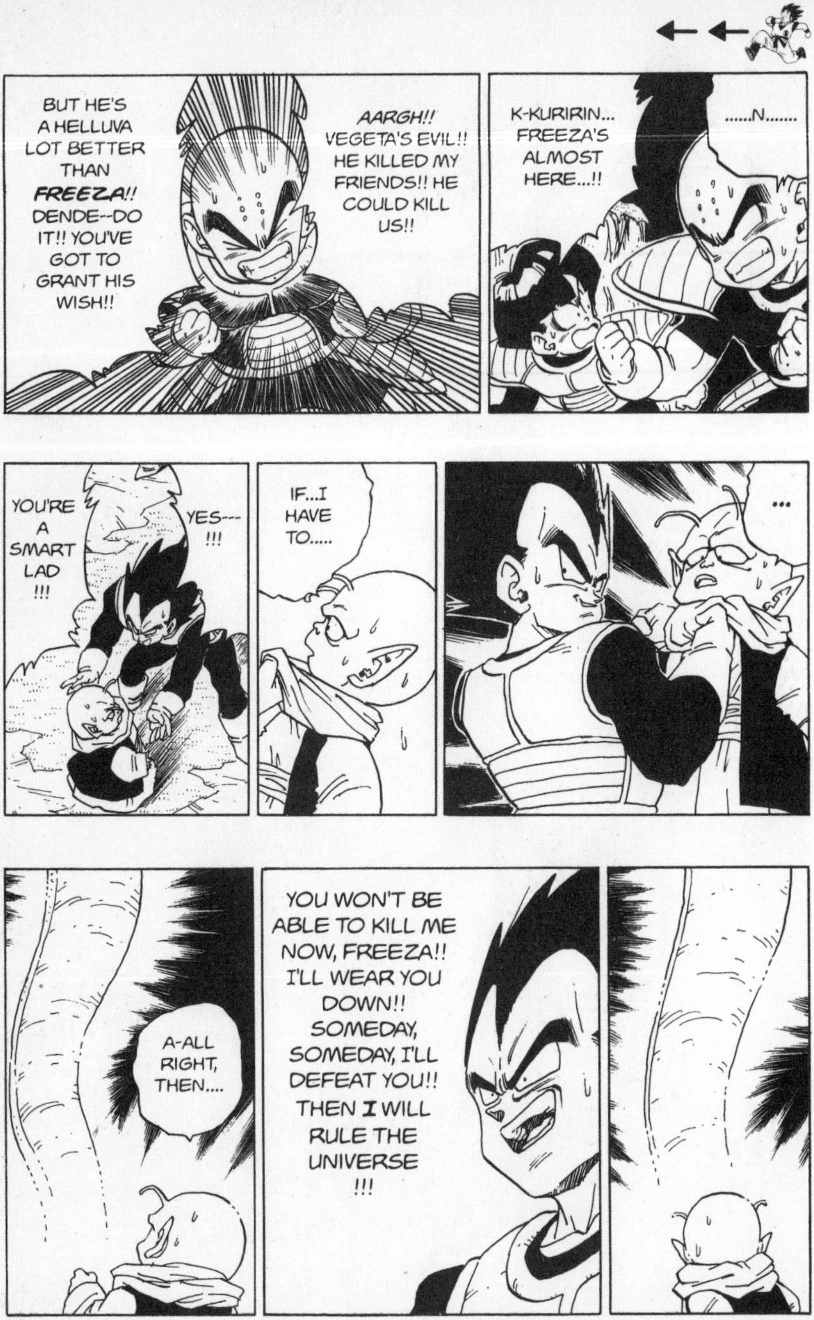
......N.......
K-KURIRIN... FREEZA'S ALMOST HERE...!!
AARGH!! VEGETA'S EVIL!! HE KILLED MY FRIENDS!! HE COULD KILL US!!
BUT HE'S A HELLUVA LOT BETTER THAN FREEZA!! DENDE--DO IT!! YOU'VE GOT TO GRANT HIS WISH!!
...
IF...I HAVE TO.....
YES---!!!
YOU'RE A SMART LAD!!!
YOU WON'T BE ABLE TO KILL ME NOW, FREEZA!! I'LL WEAR YOU DOWN!! SOMEDAY, SOMEDAY, I'LL DEFEAT YOU!! THEN I WILL RULE THE UNIVERSE!!!
A-ALL RIGHT, THEN....

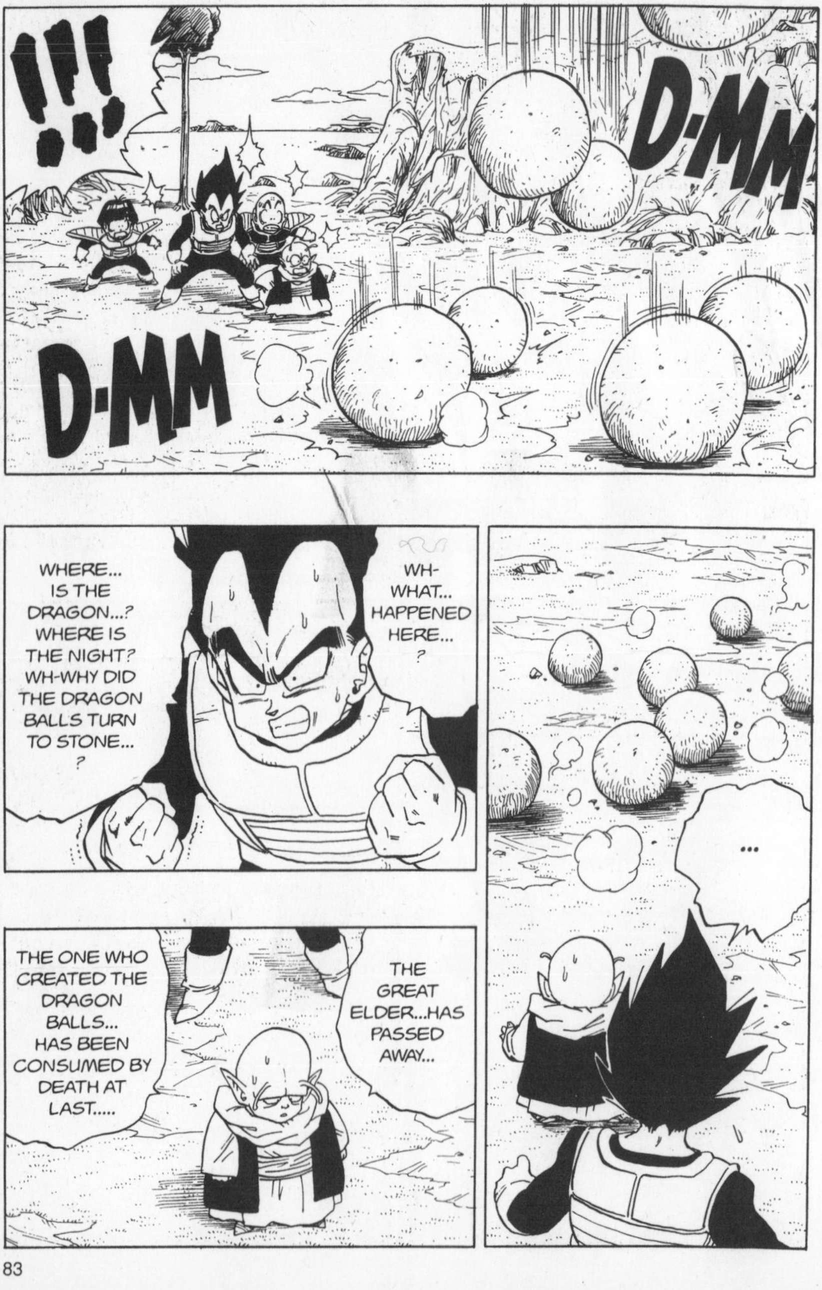

D-MM
!!!
D-MM
...
WH-WHAT... HAPPENED HERE...?
WHERE... IS THE DRAGON...? WHERE IS THE NIGHT? WH-WHY DID THE DRAGON BALLS TURN TO STONE...?
THE GREAT ELDER...HAS PASSED AWAY...
THE ONE WHO CREATED THE DRAGON BALLS... HAS BEEN CONSUMED BY DEATH AT LAST.....

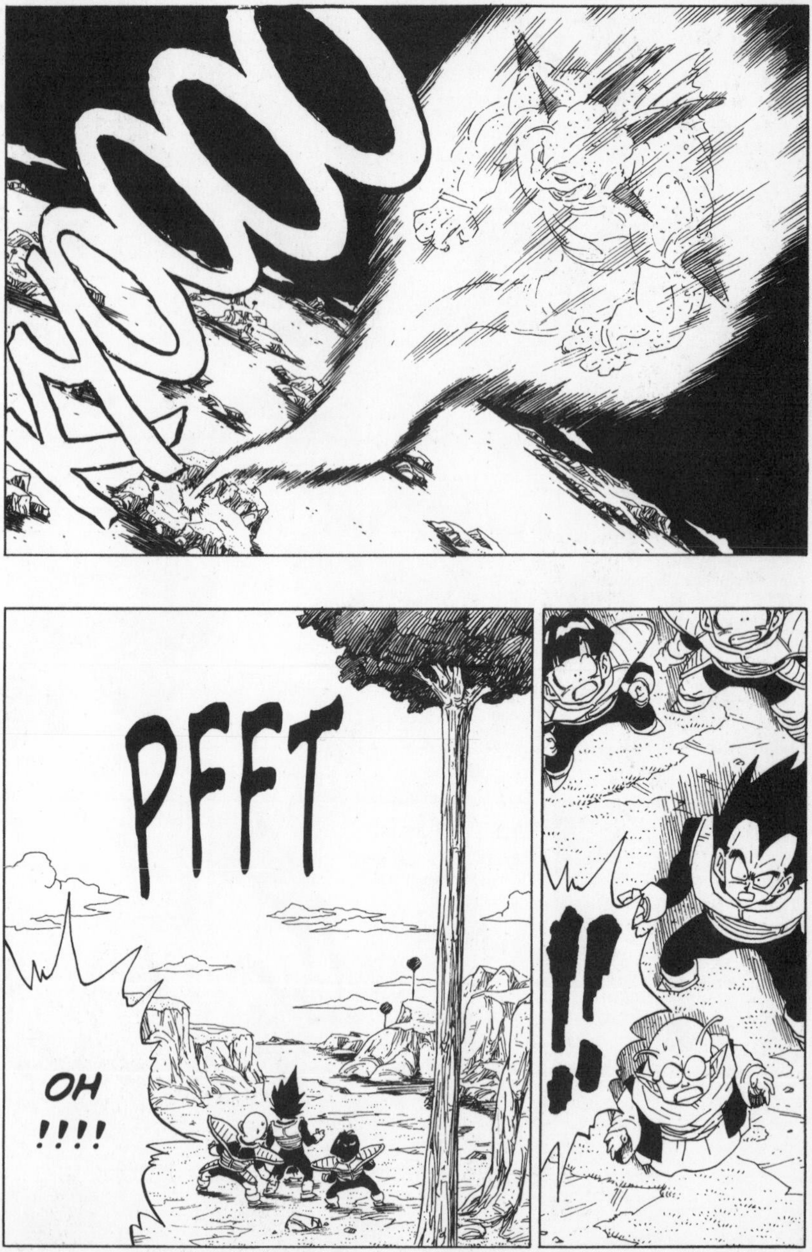
!!
PFFT
OH !!!!

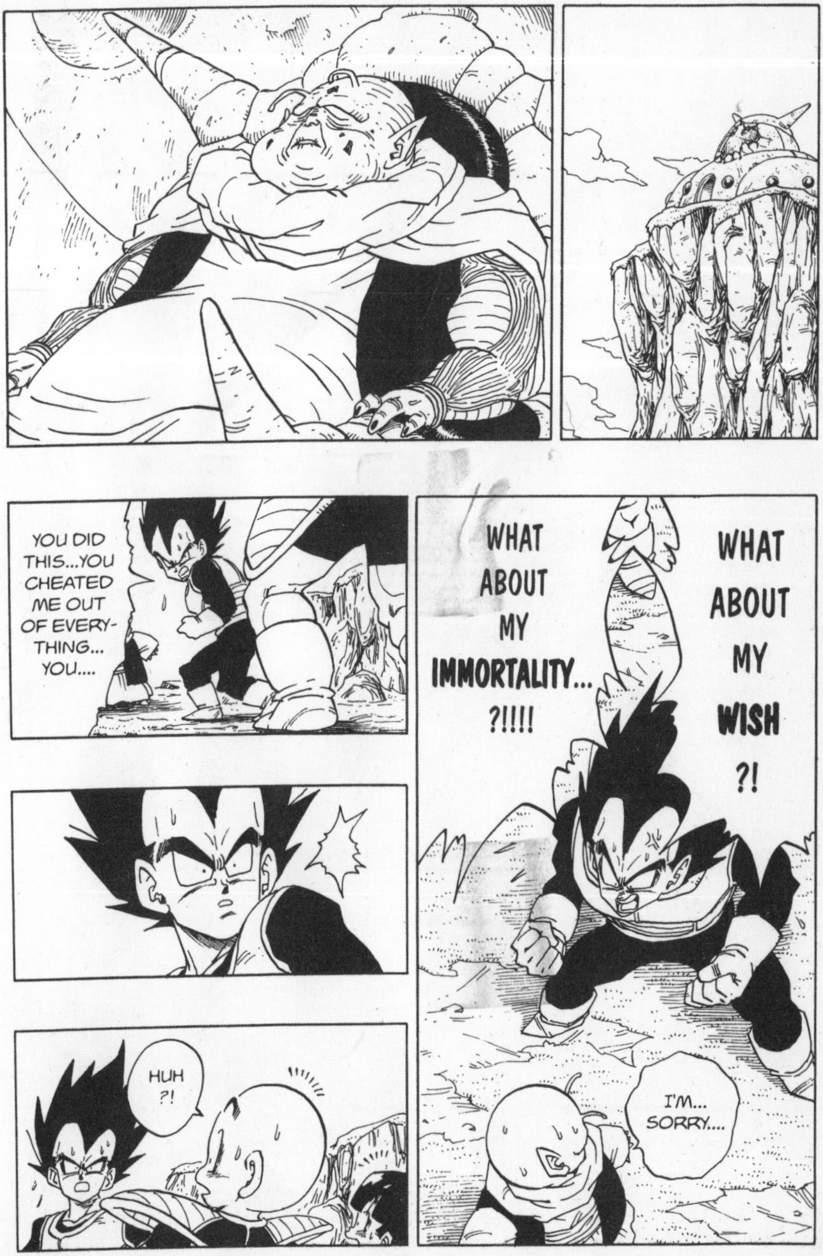
WHAT ABOUT MY WISH ?!
WHAT ABOUT MY IMMORTALITY... ?!!!!
I'M... SORRY....
YOU DID THIS...YOU CHEATED ME OUT OF EVERY-THING... YOU....
HUH ?!

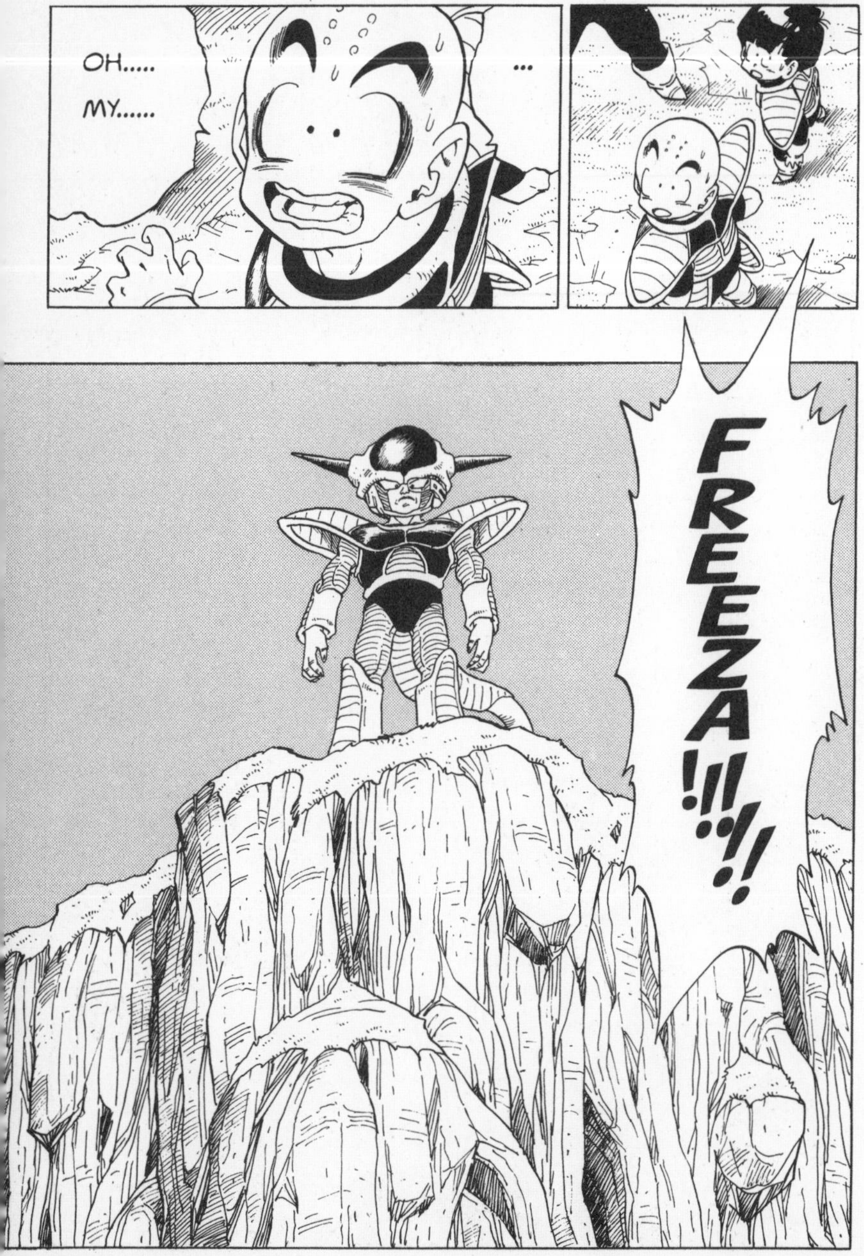
...
OH.....
MY......
FREEZA!!!?!!

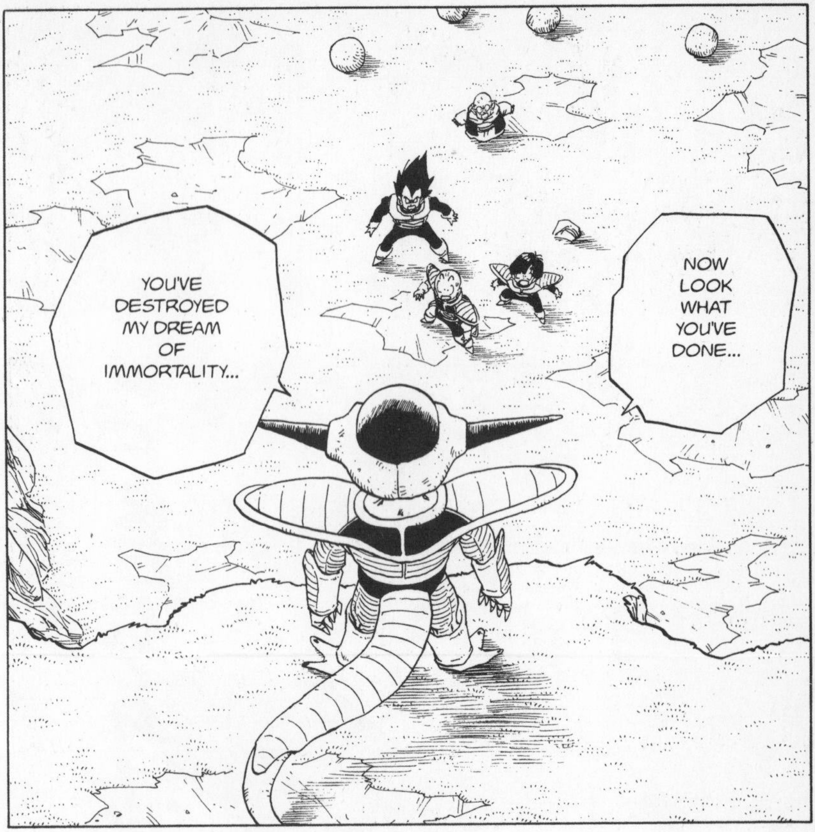
NOW LOOK WHAT YOU'VE DONE...
YOU'VE DESTROYED MY DREAM OF IMMORTALITY...

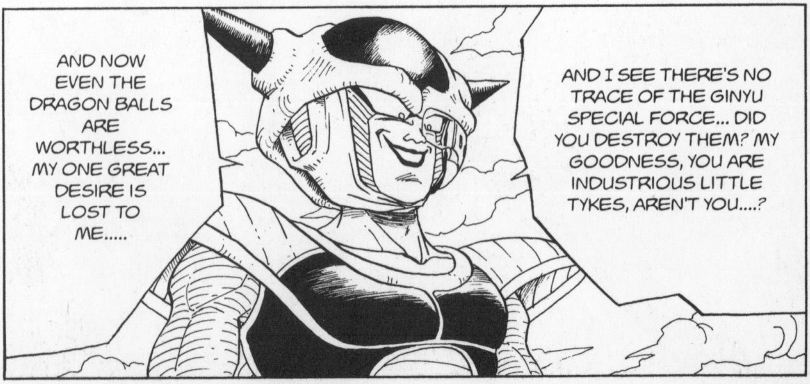
AND I SEE THERE'S NO TRACE OF THE GINYU SPECIAL FORCE... DID YOU DESTROY THEM? MY GOODNESS, YOU ARE INDUSTRIOUS LITTLE TYKES, AREN'T YOU....?
AND NOW EVEN THE DRAGON BALLS ARE WORTHLESS... MY ONE GREAT DESIRE IS LOST TO ME.....

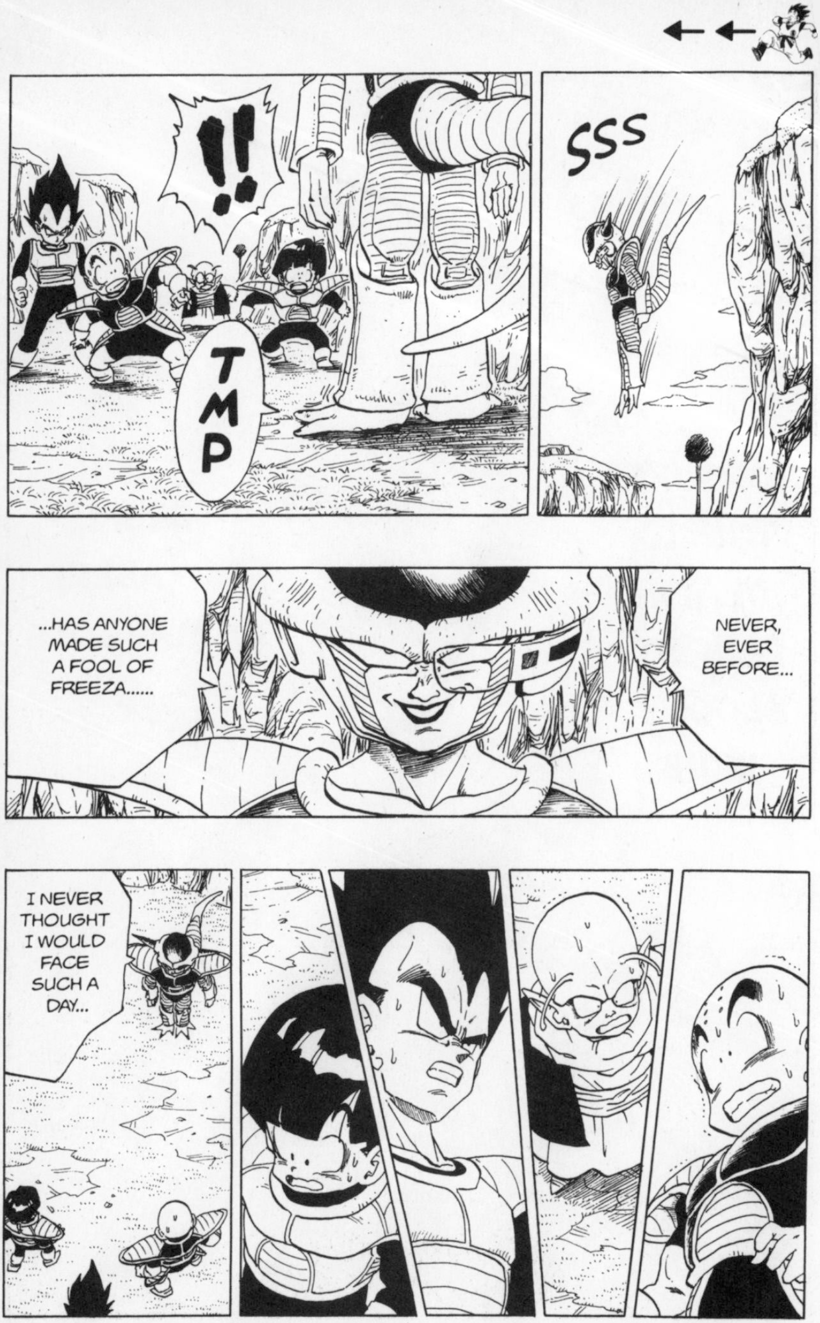
SSS
!!
TMP
NEVER, EVER BEFORE...
...HAS ANYONE MADE SUCH A FOOL OF FREEZA......
I NEVER THOUGHT I WOULD FACE SUCH A DAY...

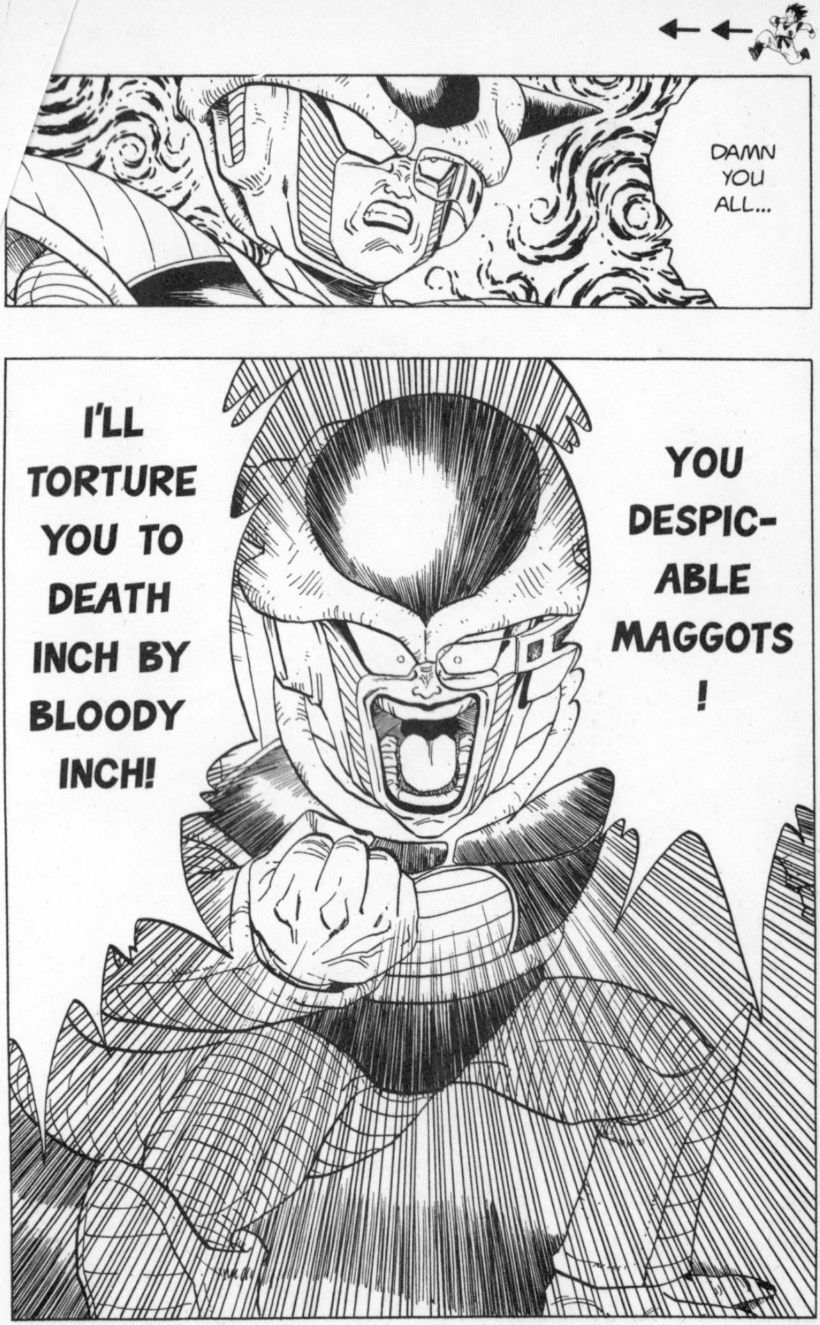

←←
DAMN YOU ALL...
YOU DESPIC-ABLE MAGGOTS!
I'LL TORTURE YOU TO DEATH INCH BY BLOODY INCH!

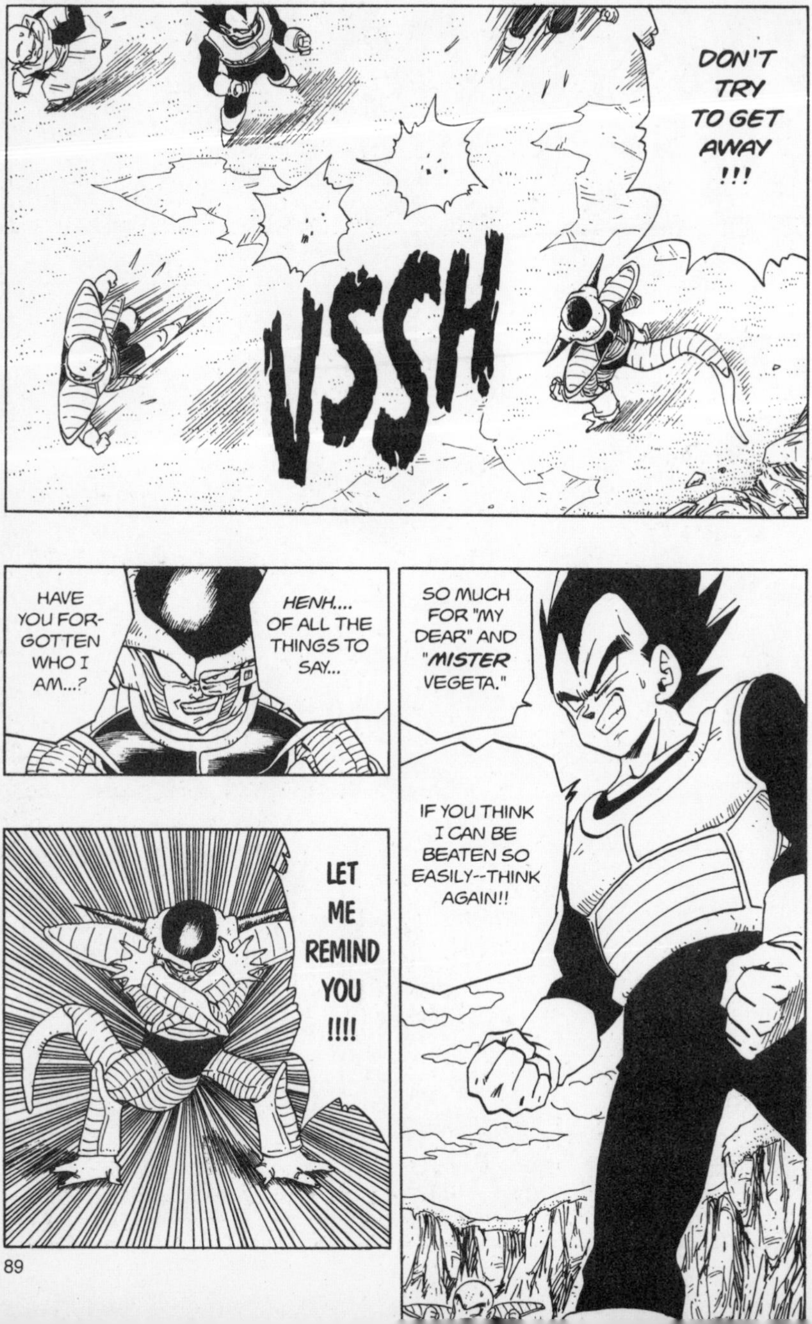
DON'T TRY TO GET AWAY !!!
VSSH
SO MUCH FOR "MY DEAR" AND "*MISTER* VEGETA."
IF YOU THINK I CAN BE BEATEN SO EASILY--THINK AGAIN!!
HENH.... OF ALL THE THINGS TO SAY...
HAVE YOU FOR-GOTTEN WHO I AM...?
LET ME REMIND YOU !!!!

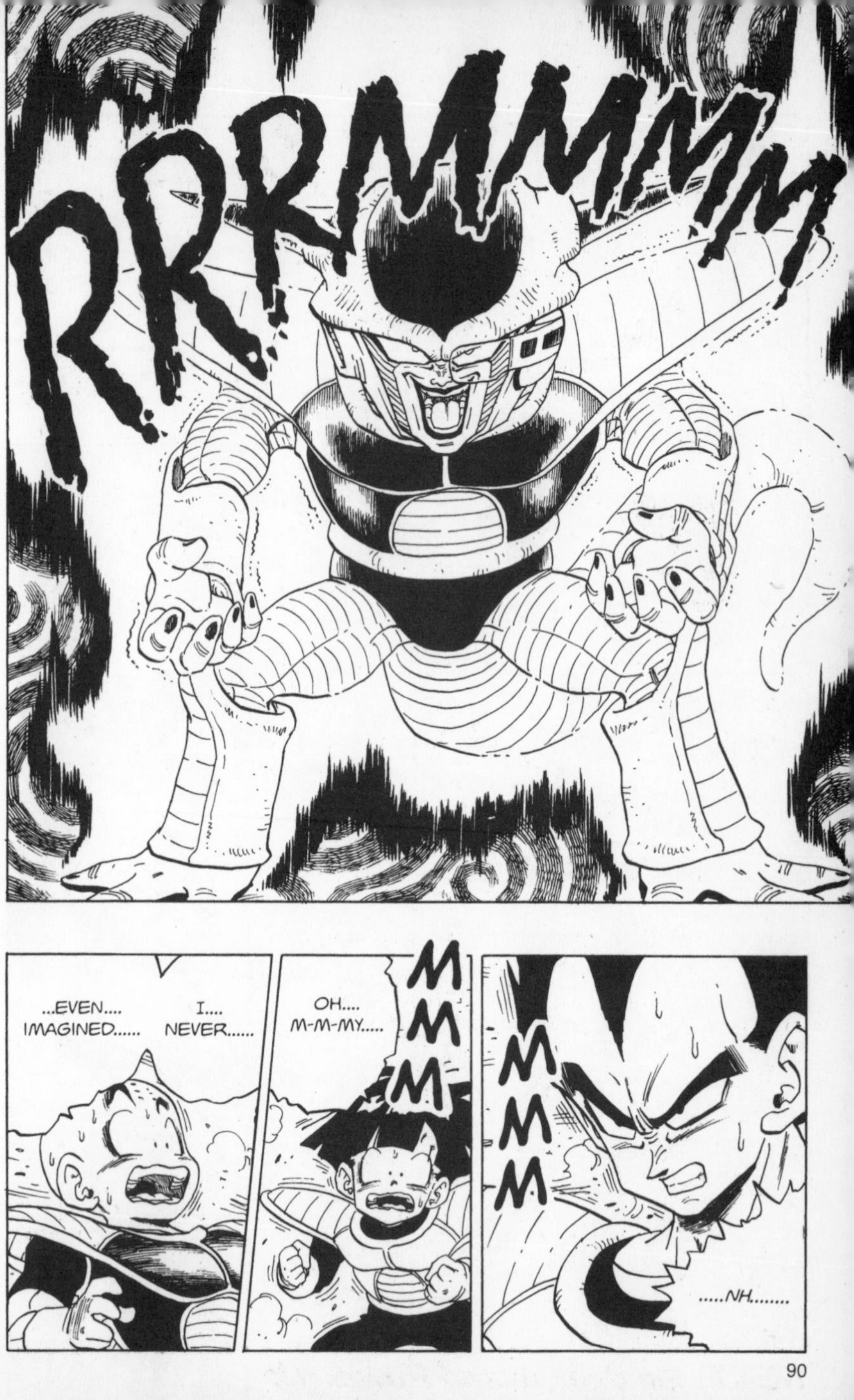
RRRMMMMM
MMMM
.....NH........
OH....
M-M-MY.....
MMMM
I....
NEVER......
...EVEN....
IMAGINED......

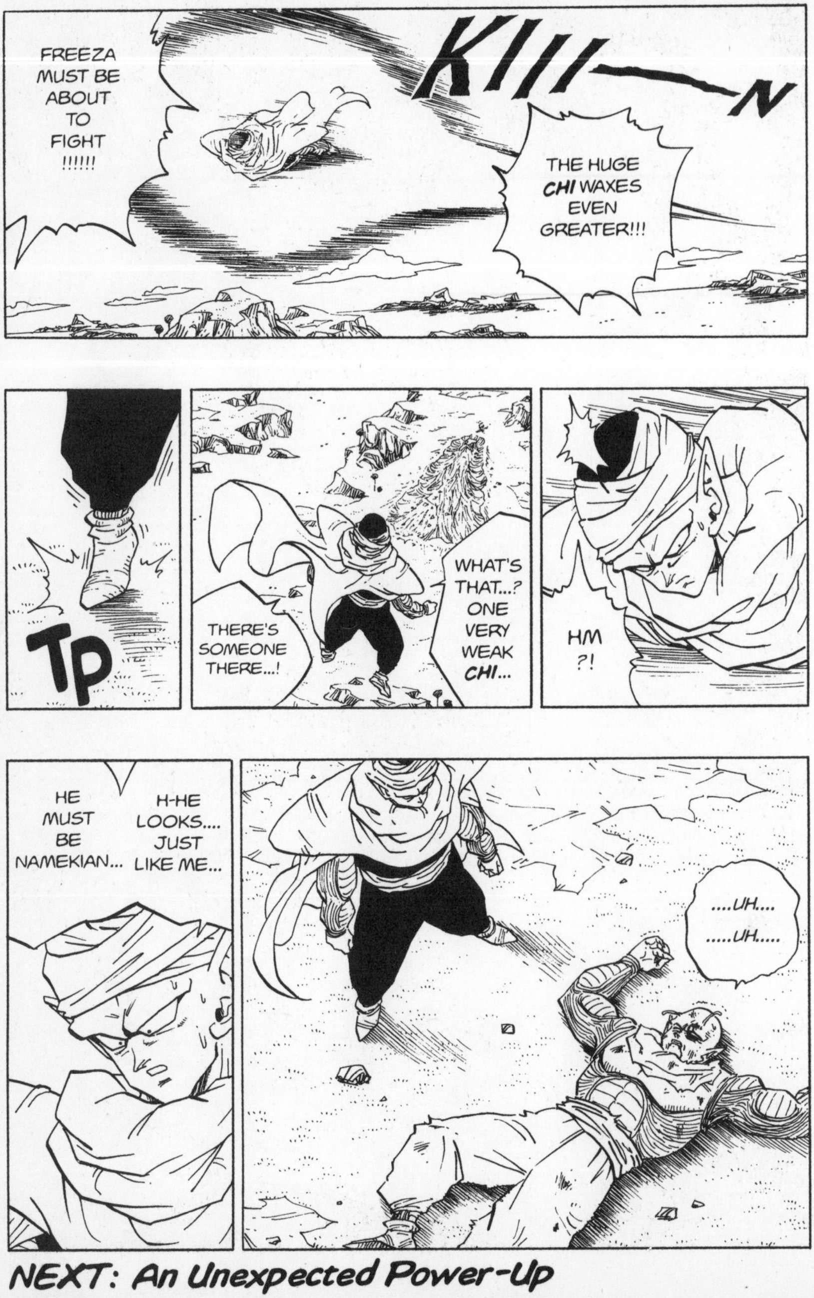
KIII—N
THE HUGE CHI WAXES EVEN GREATER!!!
FREEZA MUST BE ABOUT TO FIGHT !!!!!!
HM ?!
WHAT'S THAT...? ONE VERY WEAK CHI...
THERE'S SOMEONE THERE...!
TP
....UH.... .....UH.....
H-HE LOOKS.... JUST LIKE ME...
HE MUST BE NAMEKIAN...

NEXT: An Unexpected Power-Up

DBZ:101 • The Assimilation

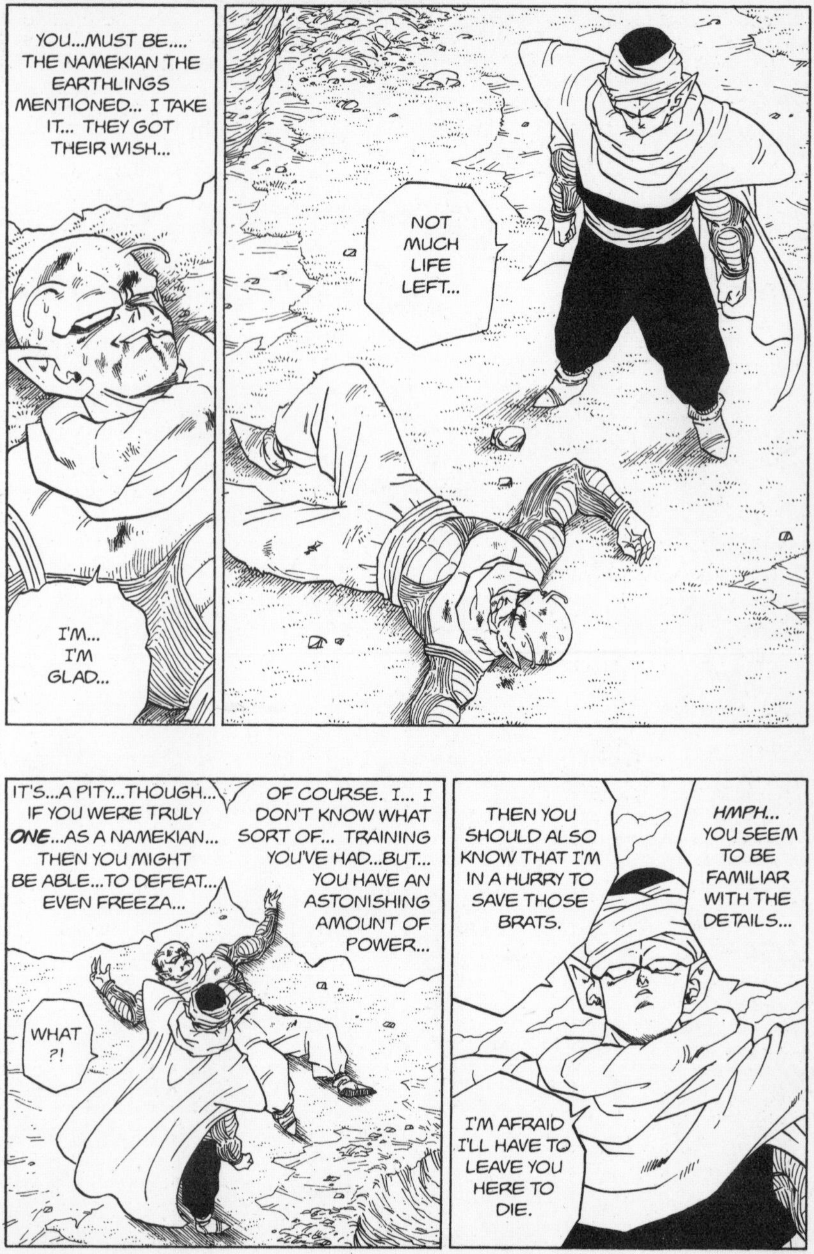
NOT MUCH LIFE LEFT...
YOU...MUST BE.... THE NAMEKIAN THE EARTHLINGS MENTIONED... I TAKE IT... THEY GOT THEIR WISH...
I'M... I'M GLAD...
HMPH... YOU SEEM TO BE FAMILIAR WITH THE DETAILS...
THEN YOU SHOULD ALSO KNOW THAT I'M IN A HURRY TO SAVE THOSE BRATS.
I'M AFRAID I'LL HAVE TO LEAVE YOU HERE TO DIE.
OF COURSE. I... I DON'T KNOW WHAT SORT OF... TRAINING YOU'VE HAD...BUT... YOU HAVE AN ASTONISHING AMOUNT OF POWER...
IT'S...A PITY...THOUGH... IF YOU WERE TRULY *ONE*...AS A NAMEKIAN... THEN YOU MIGHT BE ABLE...TO DEFEAT... EVEN FREEZA...
WHAT?!

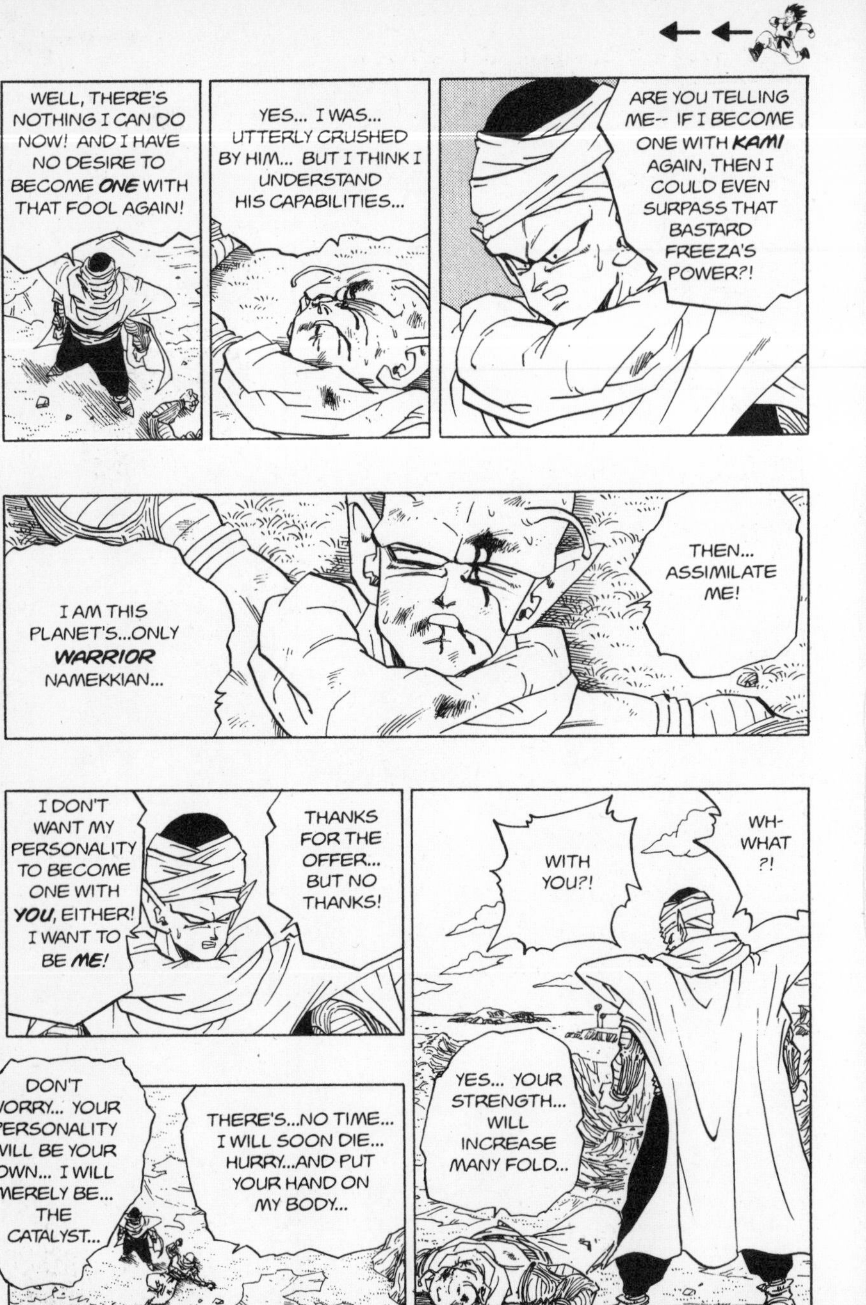
ARE YOU TELLING ME-- IF I BECOME ONE WITH KAMI AGAIN, THEN I COULD EVEN SURPASS THAT BASTARD FREEZA'S POWER?!
YES... I WAS... UTTERLY CRUSHED BY HIM... BUT I THINK I UNDERSTAND HIS CAPABILITIES...
WELL, THERE'S NOTHING I CAN DO NOW! AND I HAVE NO DESIRE TO BECOME ONE WITH THAT FOOL AGAIN!
THEN... ASSIMILATE ME!
I AM THIS PLANET'S...ONLY WARRIOR NAMEKKIAN...
WH- WHAT ?!
WITH YOU?!
YES... YOUR STRENGTH... WILL INCREASE MANY FOLD...
THANKS FOR THE OFFER... BUT NO THANKS!
I DON'T WANT MY PERSONALITY TO BECOME ONE WITH YOU, EITHER! I WANT TO BE ME!
DON'T WORRY... YOUR PERSONALITY WILL BE YOUR OWN... I WILL MERELY BE... THE CATALYST...
THERE'S...NO TIME... I WILL SOON DIE... HURRY...AND PUT YOUR HAND ON MY BODY...

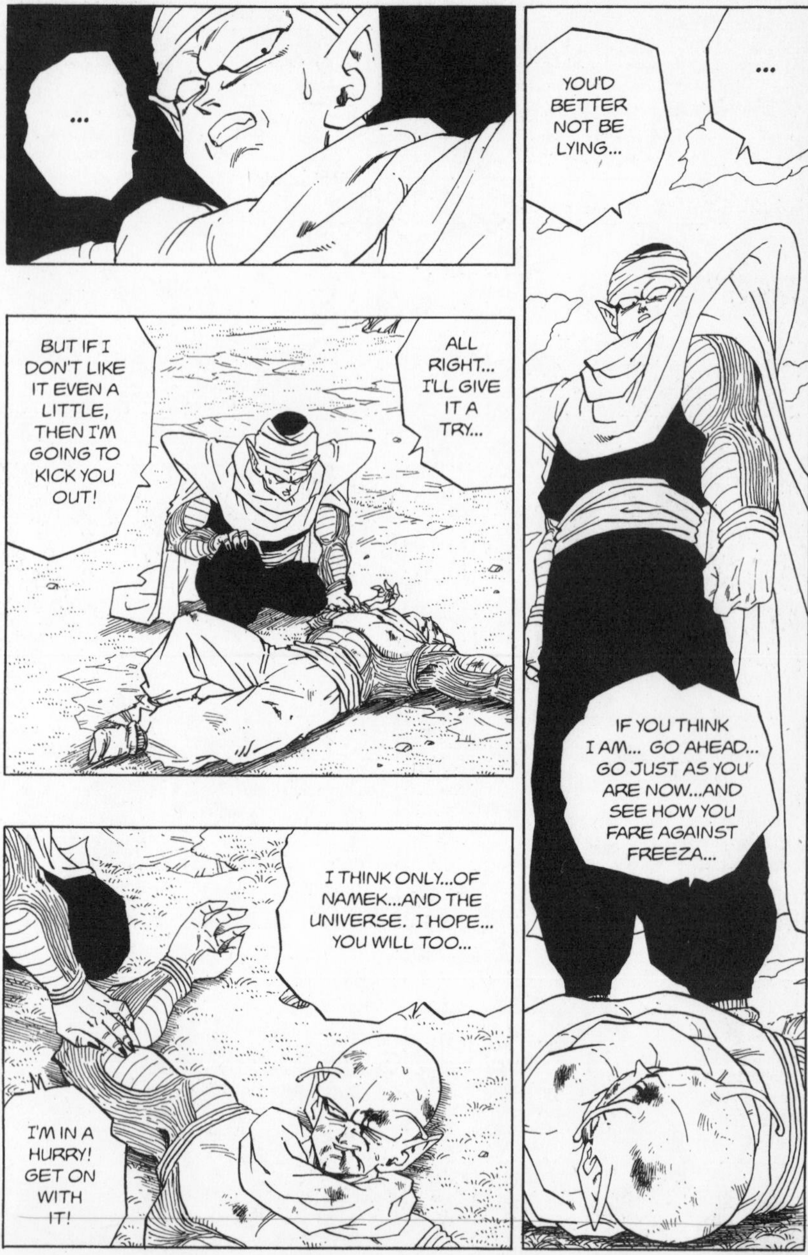
...
YOU'D BETTER NOT BE LYING...
IF YOU THINK I AM... GO AHEAD... GO JUST AS YOU ARE NOW...AND SEE HOW YOU FARE AGAINST FREEZA...
...
ALL RIGHT... I'LL GIVE IT A TRY...
BUT IF I DON'T LIKE IT EVEN A LITTLE, THEN I'M GOING TO KICK YOU OUT!
I THINK ONLY...OF NAMEK...AND THE UNIVERSE. I HOPE... YOU WILL TOO...
I'M IN A HURRY! GET ON WITH IT!

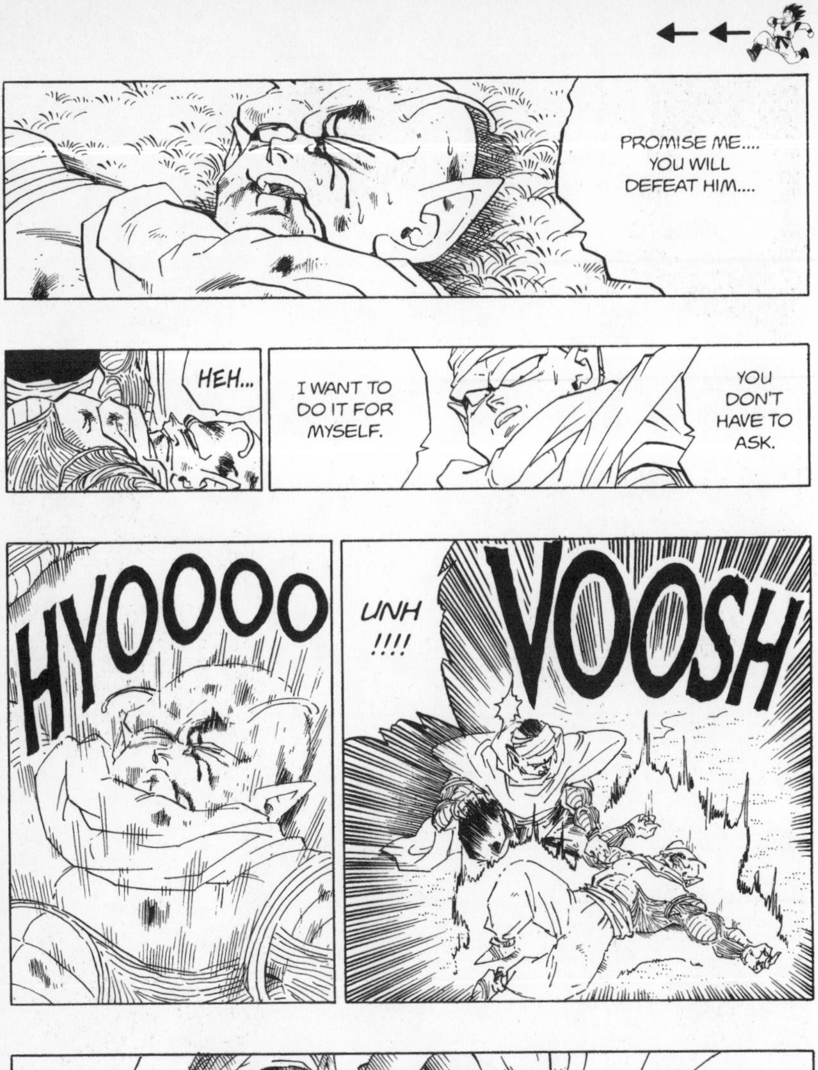
PROMISE ME.... YOU WILL DEFEAT HIM....
YOU DON'T HAVE TO ASK.
I WANT TO DO IT FOR MYSELF.
HEH...
VOOSH
UNH !!!!
HYOOOO
UGH... GH... !!

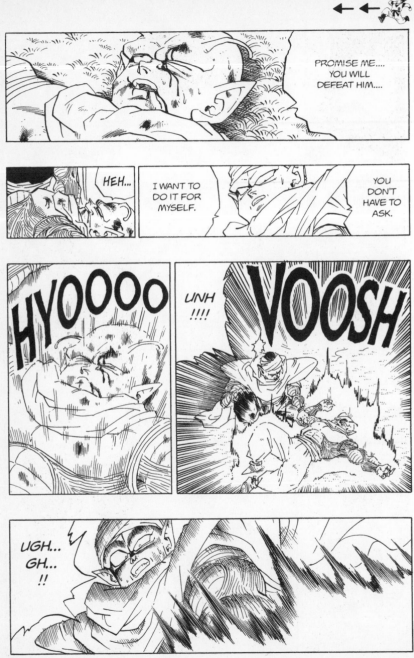

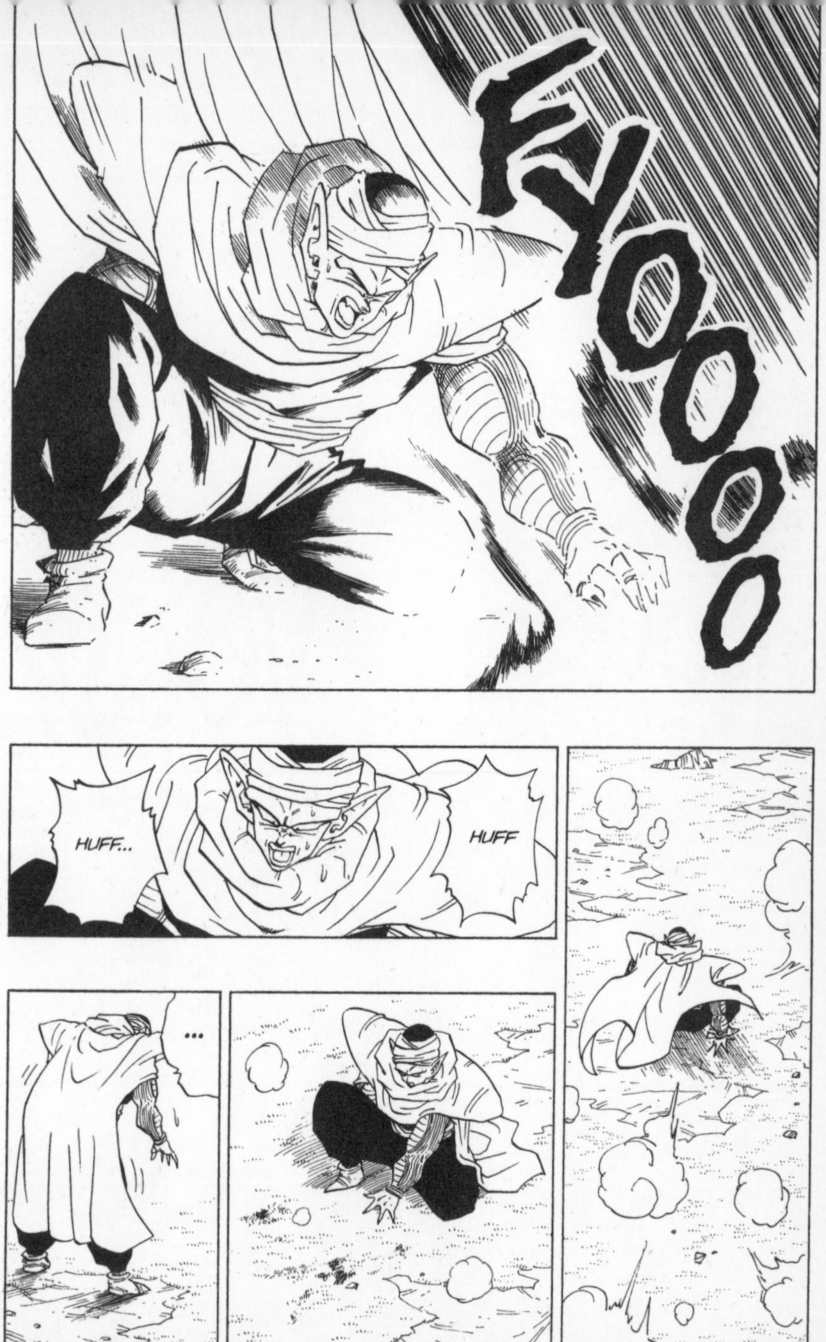
FYOOOOO
HUFF
HUFF...
...

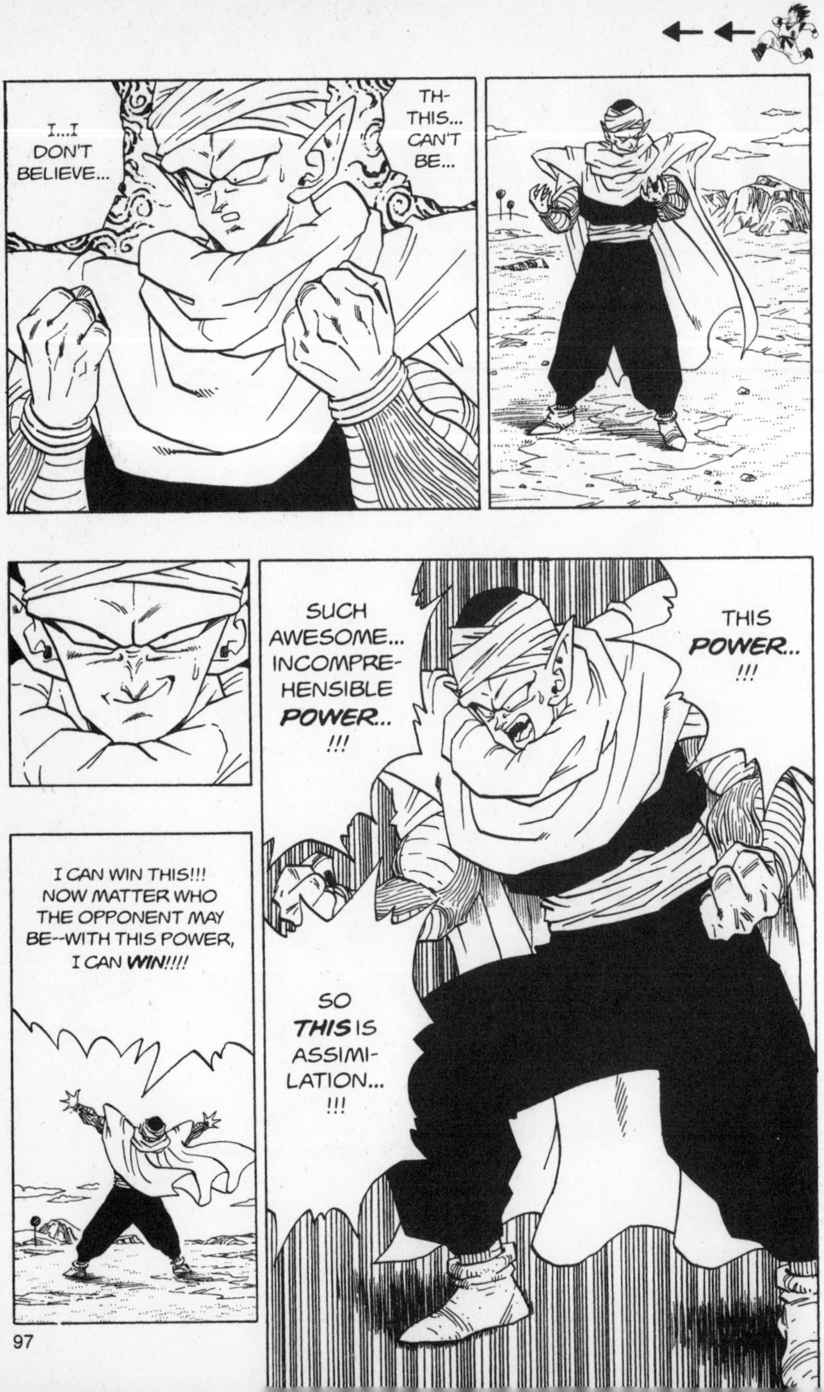
TH- THIS... CAN'T BE...
I...I DON'T BELIEVE...
THIS POWER... !!!
SUCH AWESOME... INCOMPRE-HENSIBLE POWER... !!!
SO THIS IS ASSIMI-LATION... !!!
I CAN WIN THIS!!! NOW MATTER WHO THE OPPONENT MAY BE--WITH THIS POWER, I CAN WIN!!!!

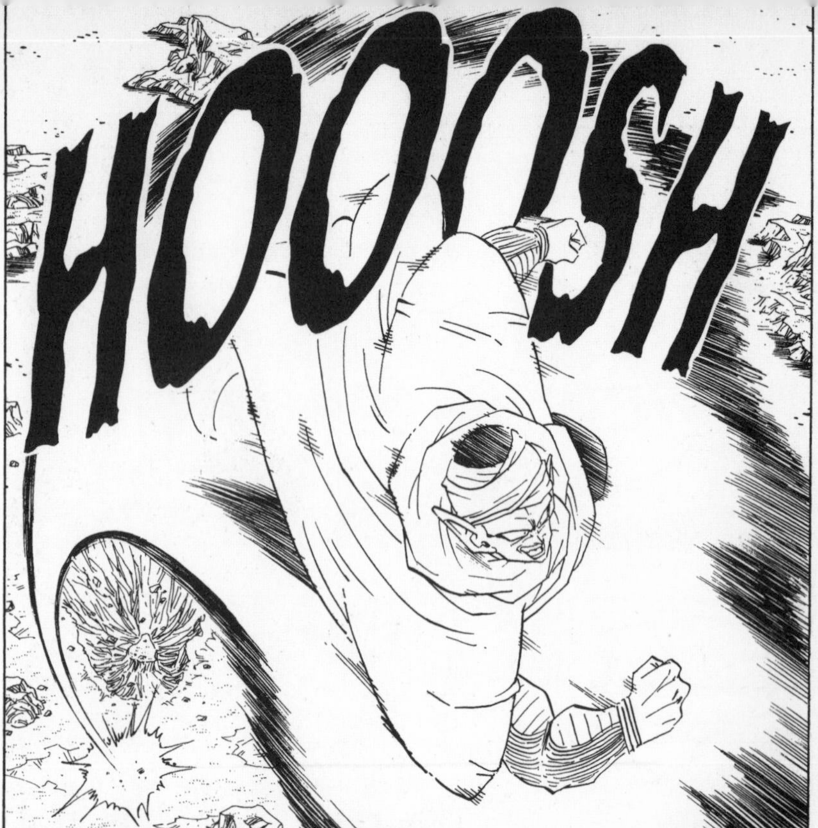
HOOOSH

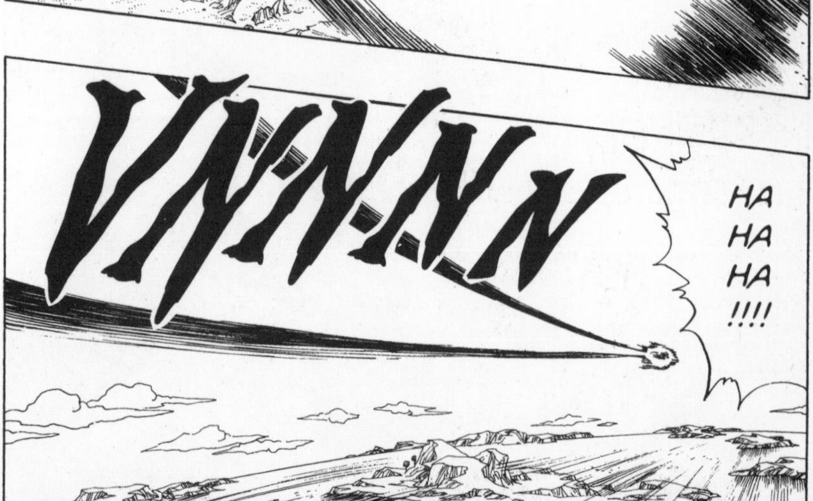
VNNNN
HA HA HA !!!!

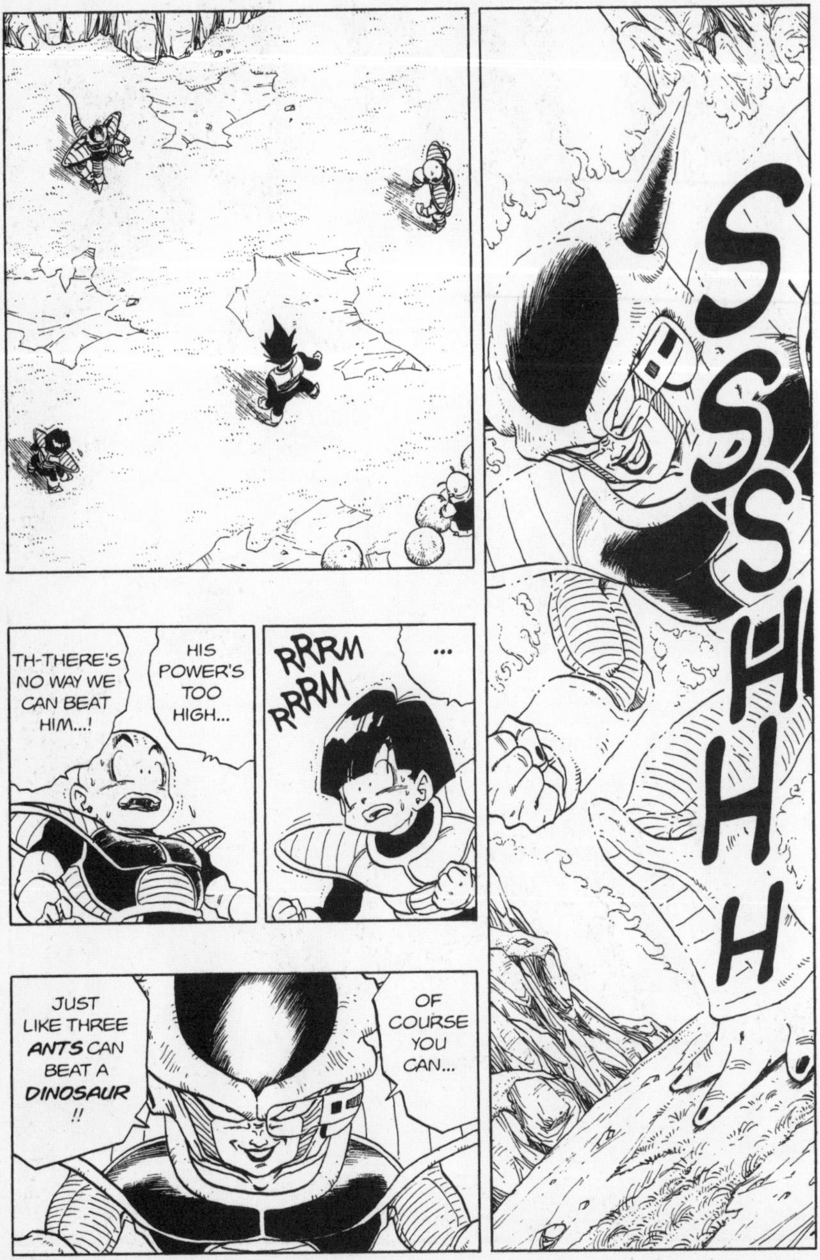
SSSHHHH
...
RRRM RRRM
HIS POWER'S TOO HIGH...
TH-THERE'S NO WAY WE CAN BEAT HIM...!
OF COURSE YOU CAN...
JUST LIKE THREE ANTS CAN BEAT A DINOSAUR !!

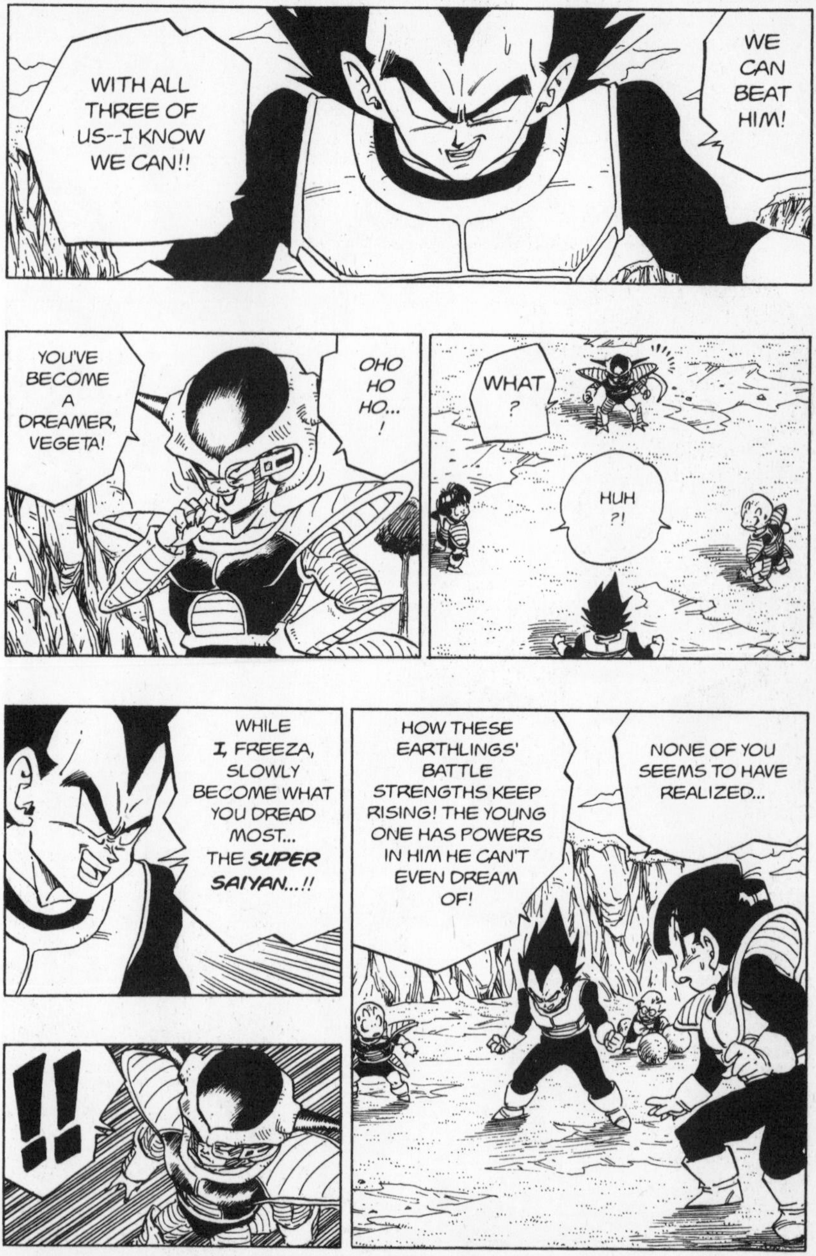
WE CAN BEAT HIM!
WITH ALL THREE OF US--I KNOW WE CAN!!
WHAT ?
HUH ?!
OHO HO HO... !
YOU'VE BECOME A DREAMER, VEGETA!
NONE OF YOU SEEMS TO HAVE REALIZED...
HOW THESE EARTHLINGS' BATTLE STRENGTHS KEEP RISING! THE YOUNG ONE HAS POWERS IN HIM HE CAN'T EVEN DREAM OF!
WHILE I, FREEZA, SLOWLY BECOME WHAT YOU DREAD MOST... THE SUPER SAIYAN...!!
!!

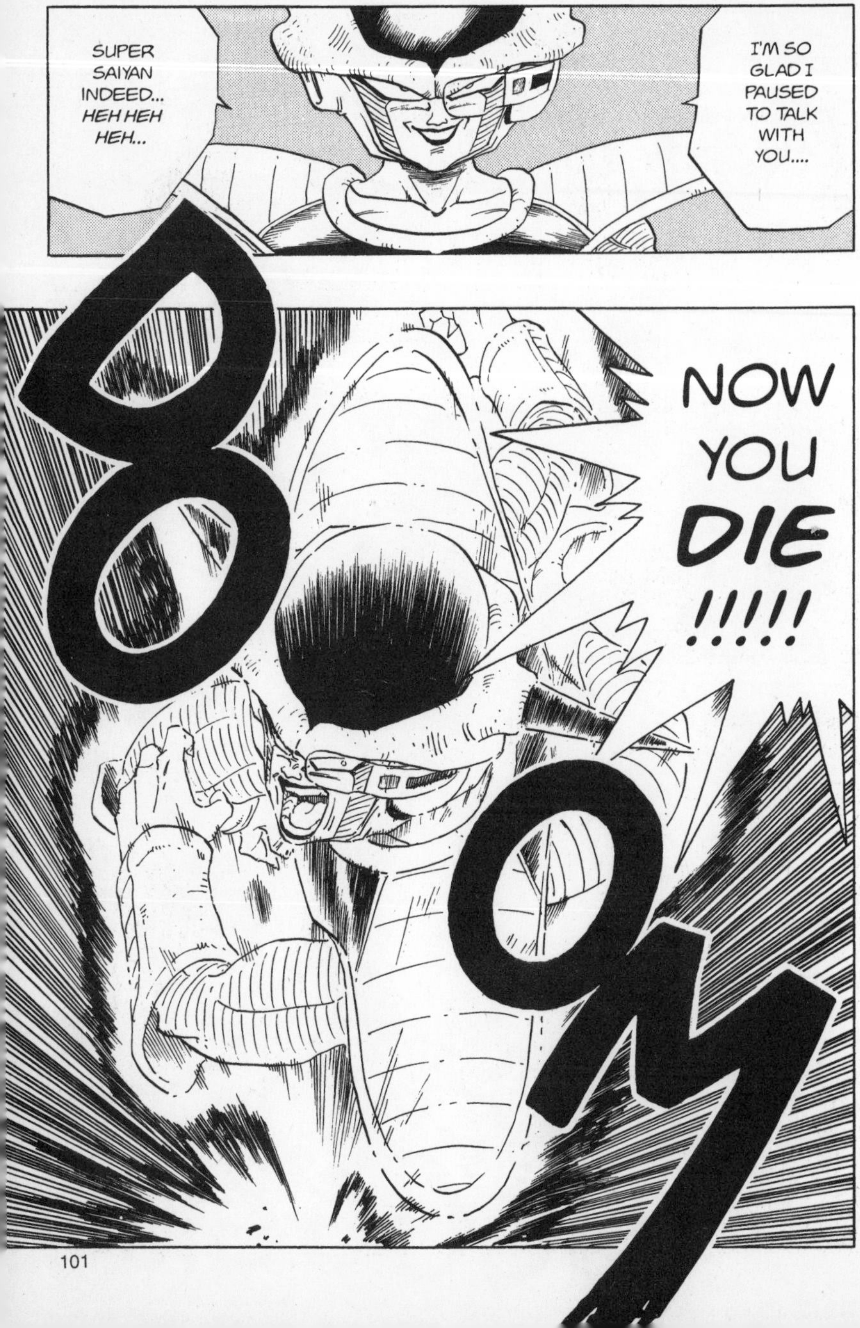
I'M SO GLAD I PAUSED TO TALK WITH YOU....
SUPER SAIYAN INDEED... *HEH HEH HEH...*
NOW YOU **DIE** !!!!!

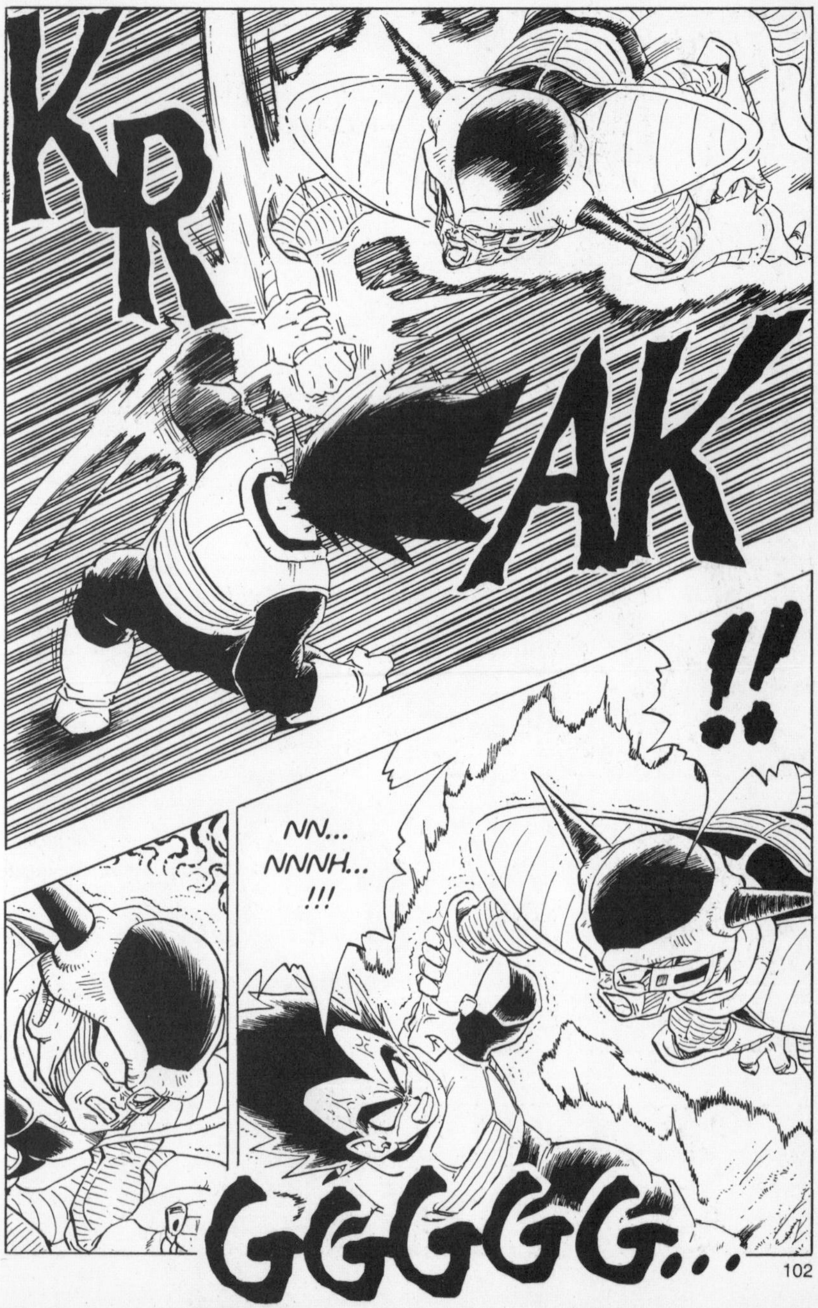
KRAK!!
NN...
NNNH...
!!!
GGGGG...

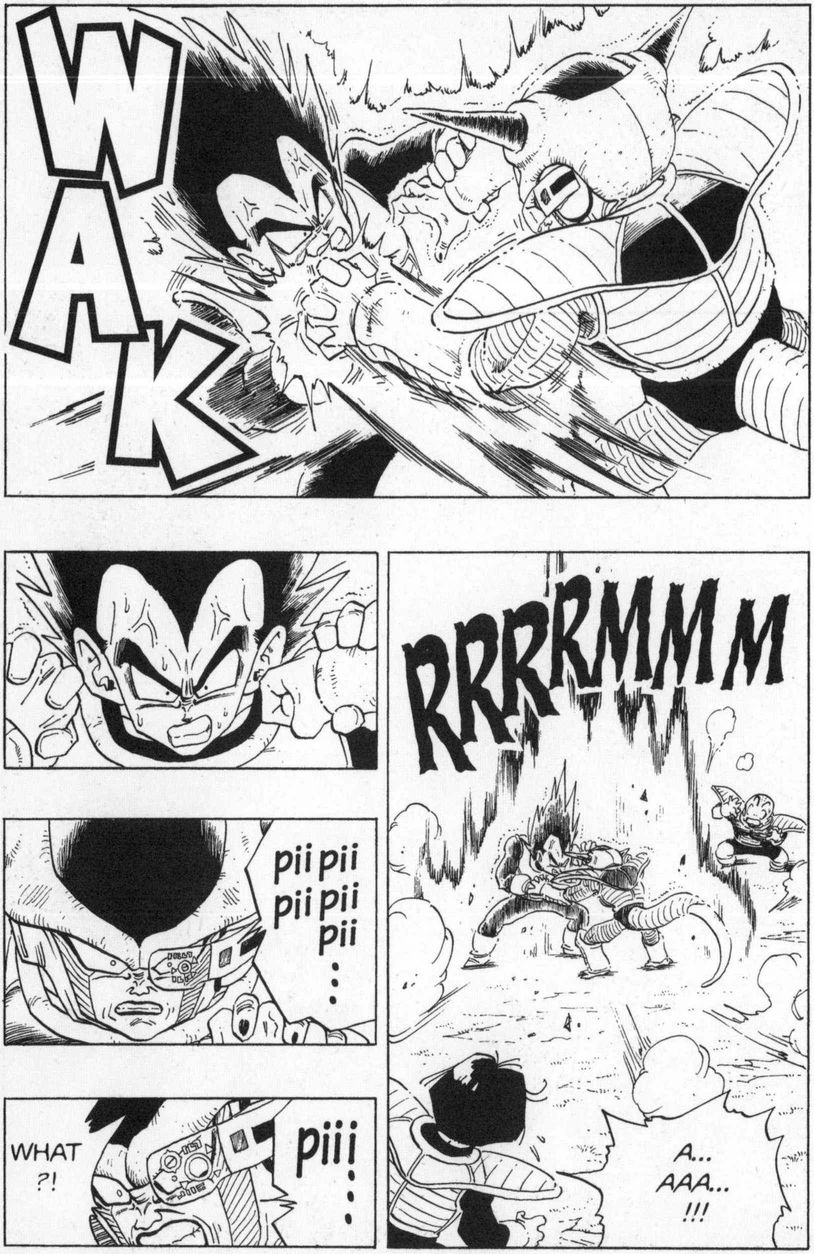
WAK
RRRRMMMM
A... AAA... !!!
pii pii pii pii pii ...
piii...
WHAT ?!

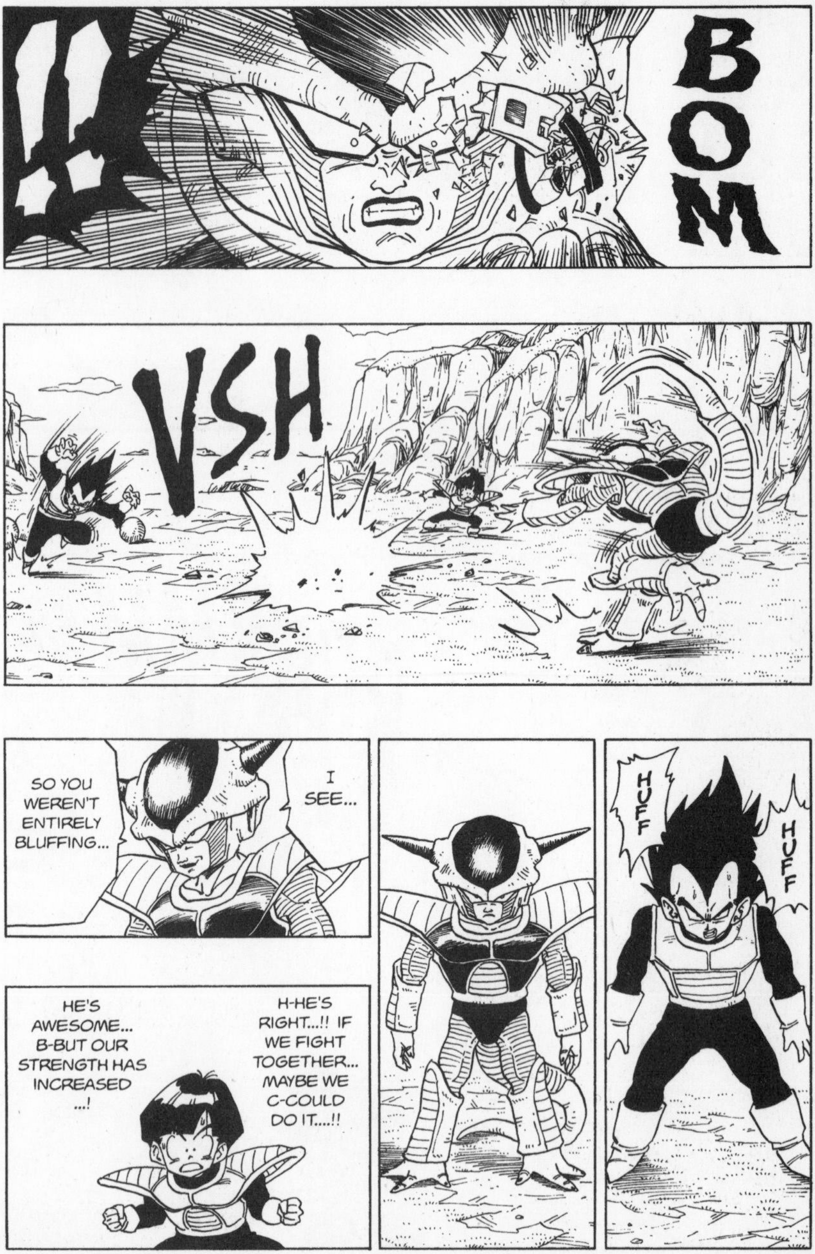
BOM
!!
VSH
HUFF
HUFF
I SEE...
SO YOU WEREN'T ENTIRELY BLUFFING...
H-HE'S RIGHT...!! IF WE FIGHT TOGETHER... MAYBE WE C-COULD DO IT....!!
HE'S AWESOME... B-BUT OUR STRENGTH HAS INCREASED ...!

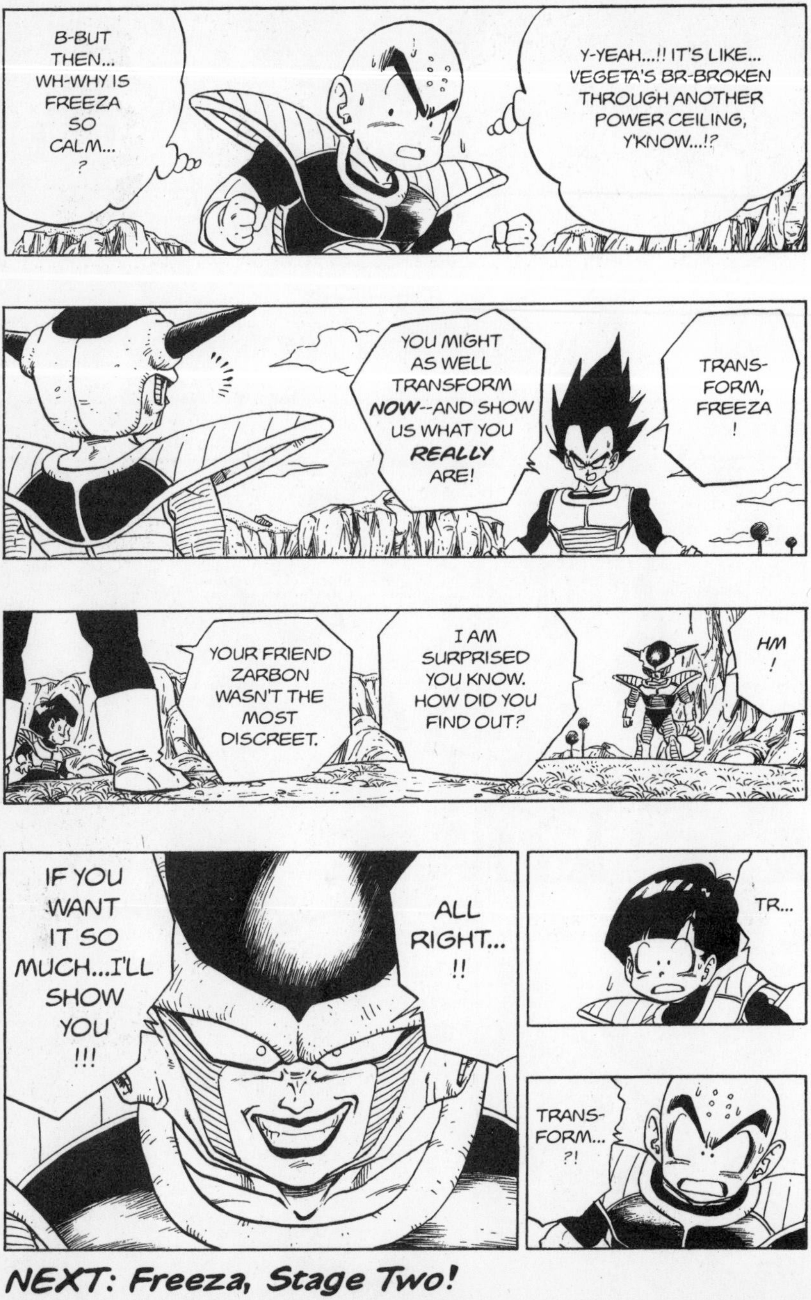
Y-YEAH...!! IT'S LIKE... VEGETA'S BR-BROKEN THROUGH ANOTHER POWER CEILING, Y'KNOW...!?
B-BUT THEN... WH-WHY IS FREEZA SO CALM...?
TRANS-FORM, FREEZA!
YOU MIGHT AS WELL TRANSFORM NOW--AND SHOW US WHAT YOU REALLY ARE!
HM!
I AM SURPRISED YOU KNOW. HOW DID YOU FIND OUT?
YOUR FRIEND ZARBON WASN'T THE MOST DISCREET.
TR...
TRANS-FORM...?!
ALL RIGHT...!!
IF YOU WANT IT SO MUCH...I'LL SHOW YOU!!!

***NEXT*: Freeza, Stage Two!**

DBZ:102 • The Transformation

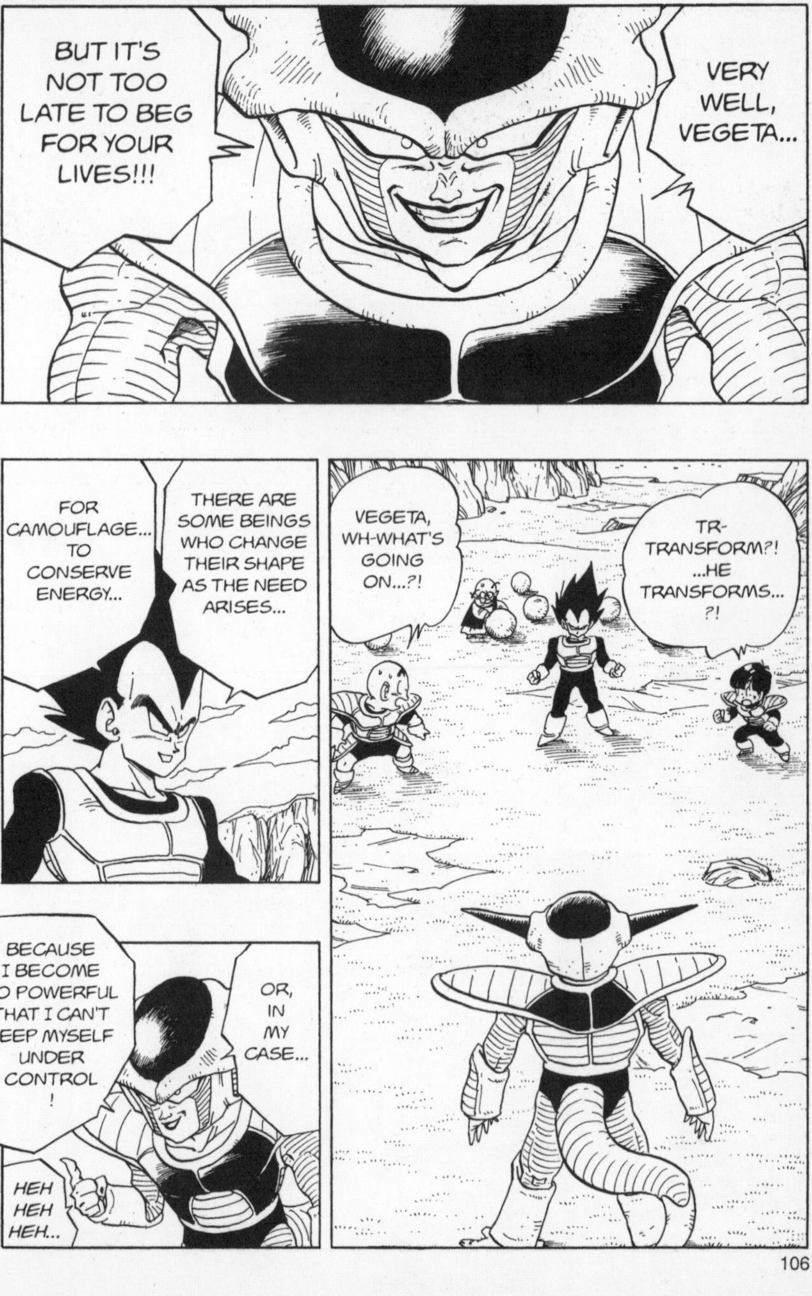
VERY WELL, VEGETA...
BUT IT'S NOT TOO LATE TO BEG FOR YOUR LIVES!!!
TR- TRANSFORM?! ...HE TRANSFORMS...?!
VEGETA, WH-WHAT'S GOING ON...?!
THERE ARE SOME BEINGS WHO CHANGE THEIR SHAPE AS THE NEED ARISES...
FOR CAMOUFLAGE... TO CONSERVE ENERGY...
OR, IN MY CASE...
BECAUSE I BECOME SO POWERFUL THAT I CAN'T KEEP MYSELF UNDER CONTROL!
HEH HEH HEH...

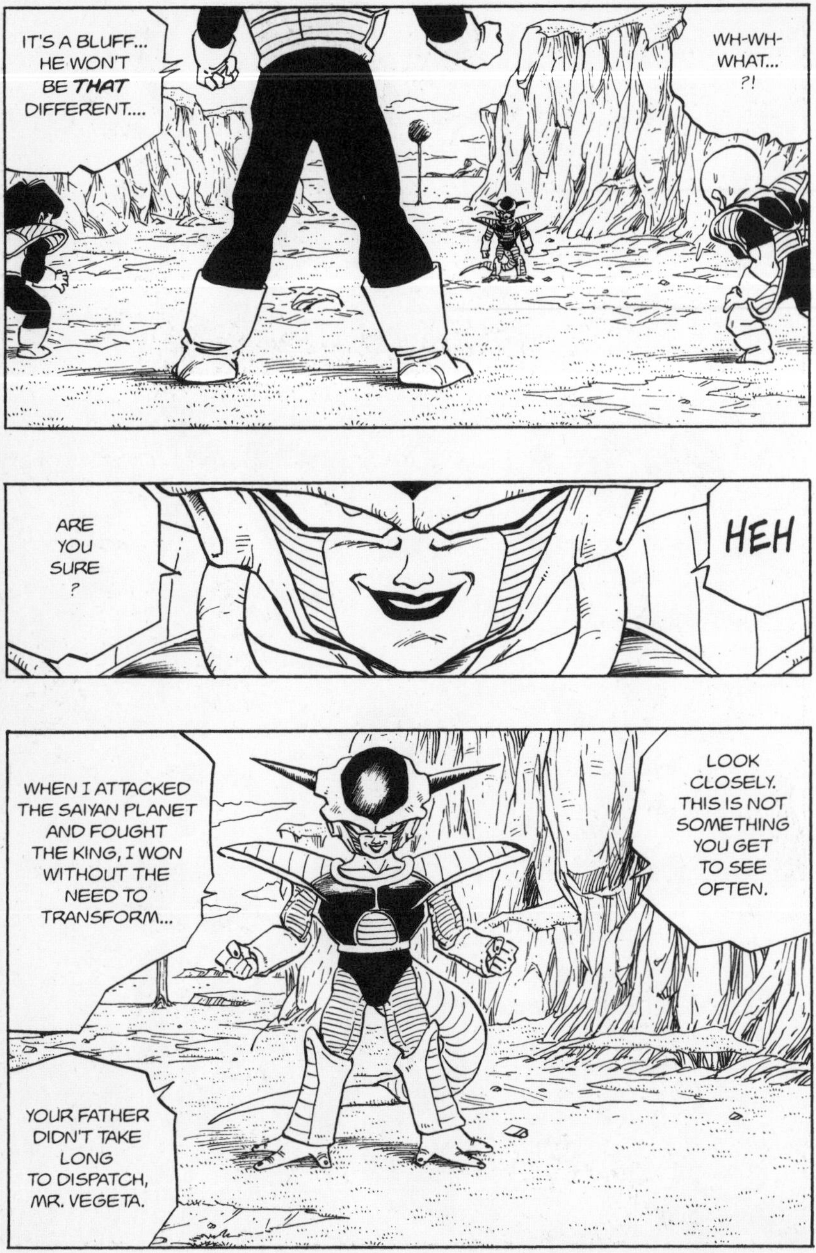
WH-WH-WHAT...?!
IT'S A BLUFF... HE WON'T BE *THAT* DIFFERENT....
HEH
ARE YOU SURE?
LOOK CLOSELY. THIS IS NOT SOMETHING YOU GET TO SEE OFTEN.
WHEN I ATTACKED THE SAIYAN PLANET AND FOUGHT THE KING, I WON WITHOUT THE NEED TO TRANSFORM...
YOUR FATHER DIDN'T TAKE LONG TO DISPATCH, MR. VEGETA.

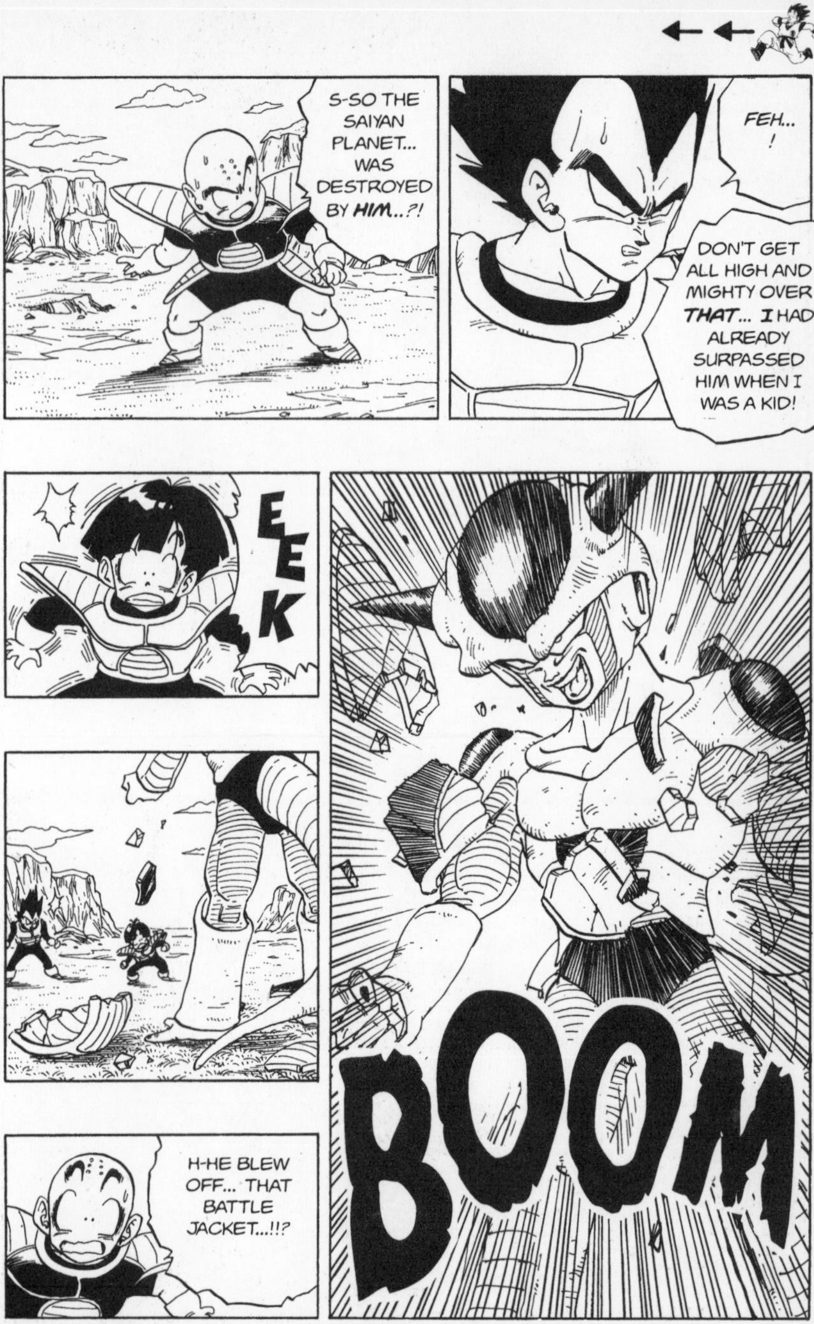
FEH... !
DON'T GET ALL HIGH AND MIGHTY OVER **THAT**... I HAD ALREADY SURPASSED HIM WHEN I WAS A KID!
S-SO THE SAIYAN PLANET... WAS DESTROYED BY **HIM**...?!
BOOM
EEK
H-HE BLEW OFF... THAT BATTLE JACKET...!!?

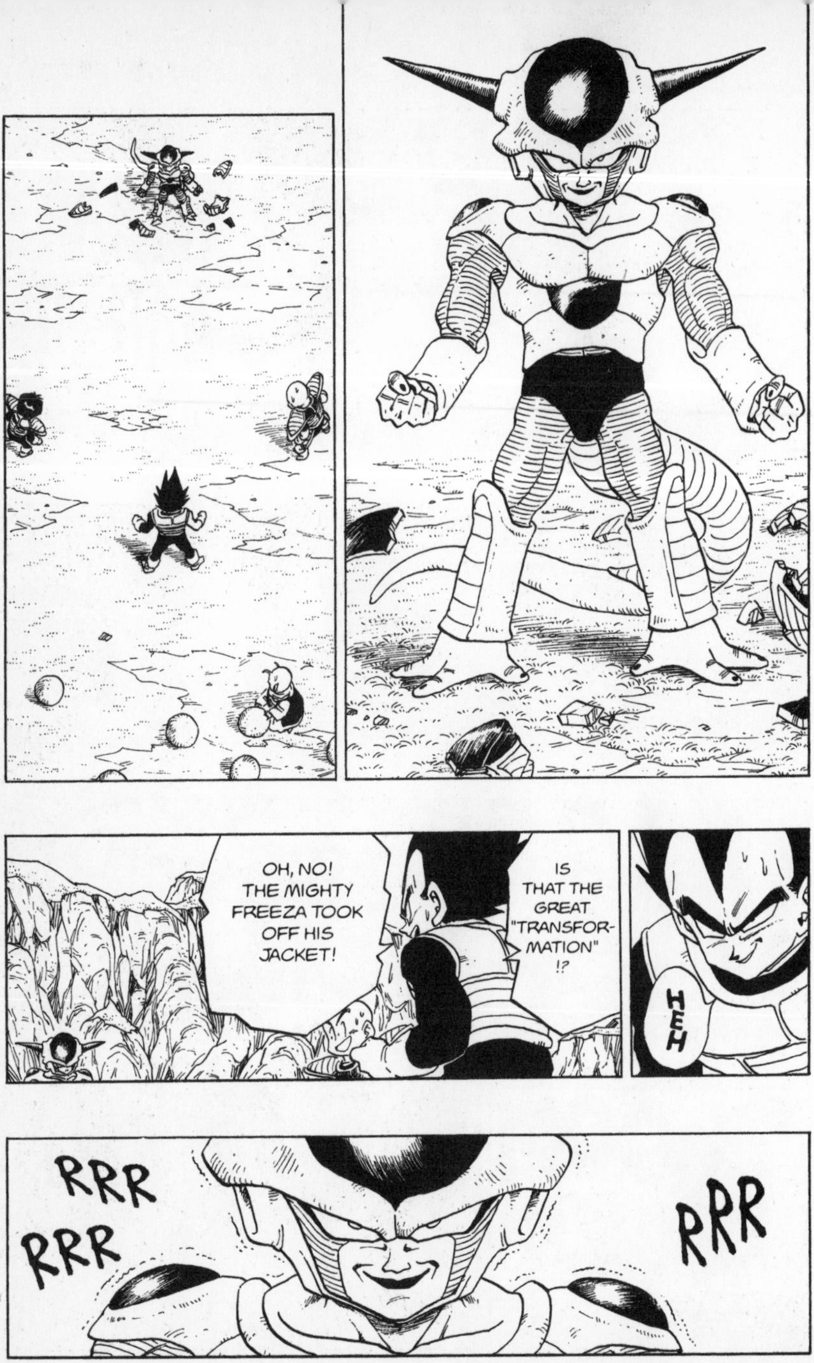
HEH
IS THAT THE GREAT "TRANSFORMATION" !?
OH, NO! THE MIGHTY FREEZA TOOK OFF HIS JACKET!
RRR
RRR
RRR

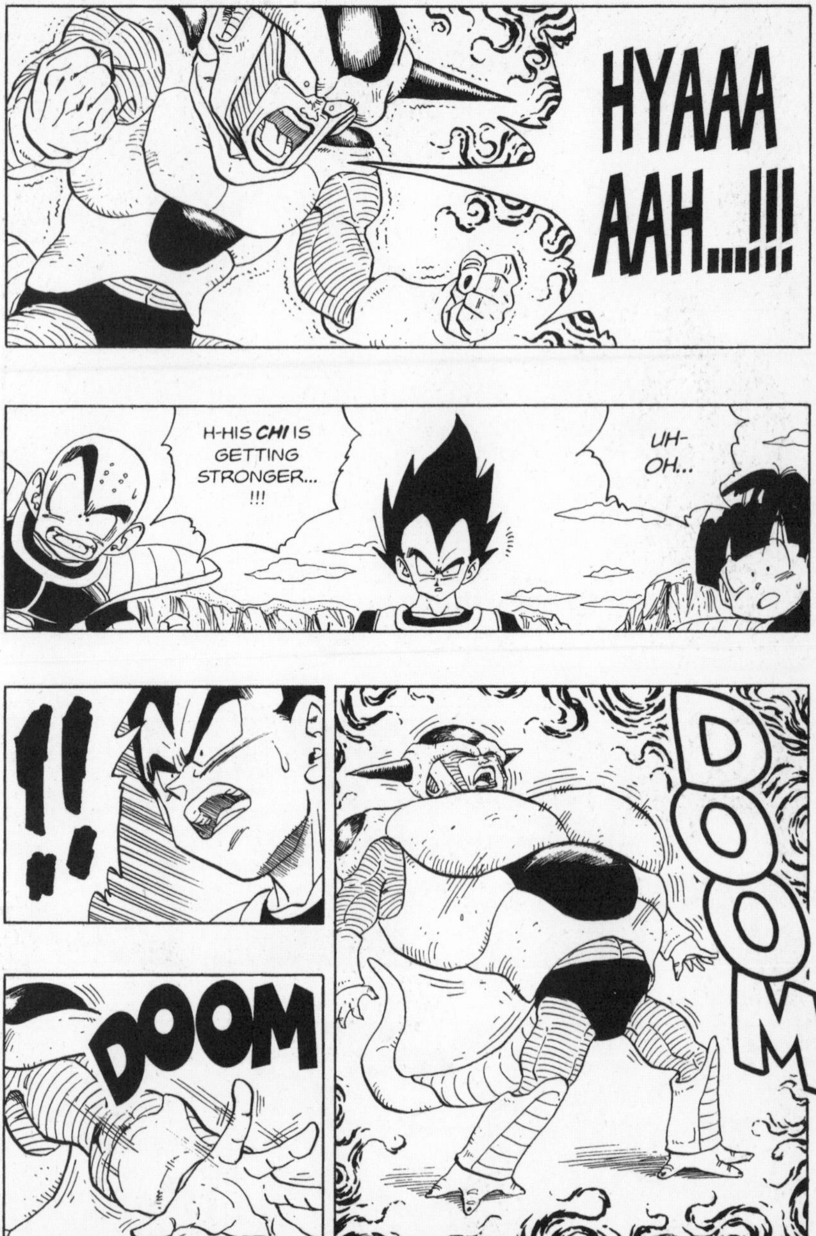
HYAAA AAH...!!!
UH-OH...
H-HIS CHI IS GETTING STRONGER...!!!
DOOOM
!!
DOOM

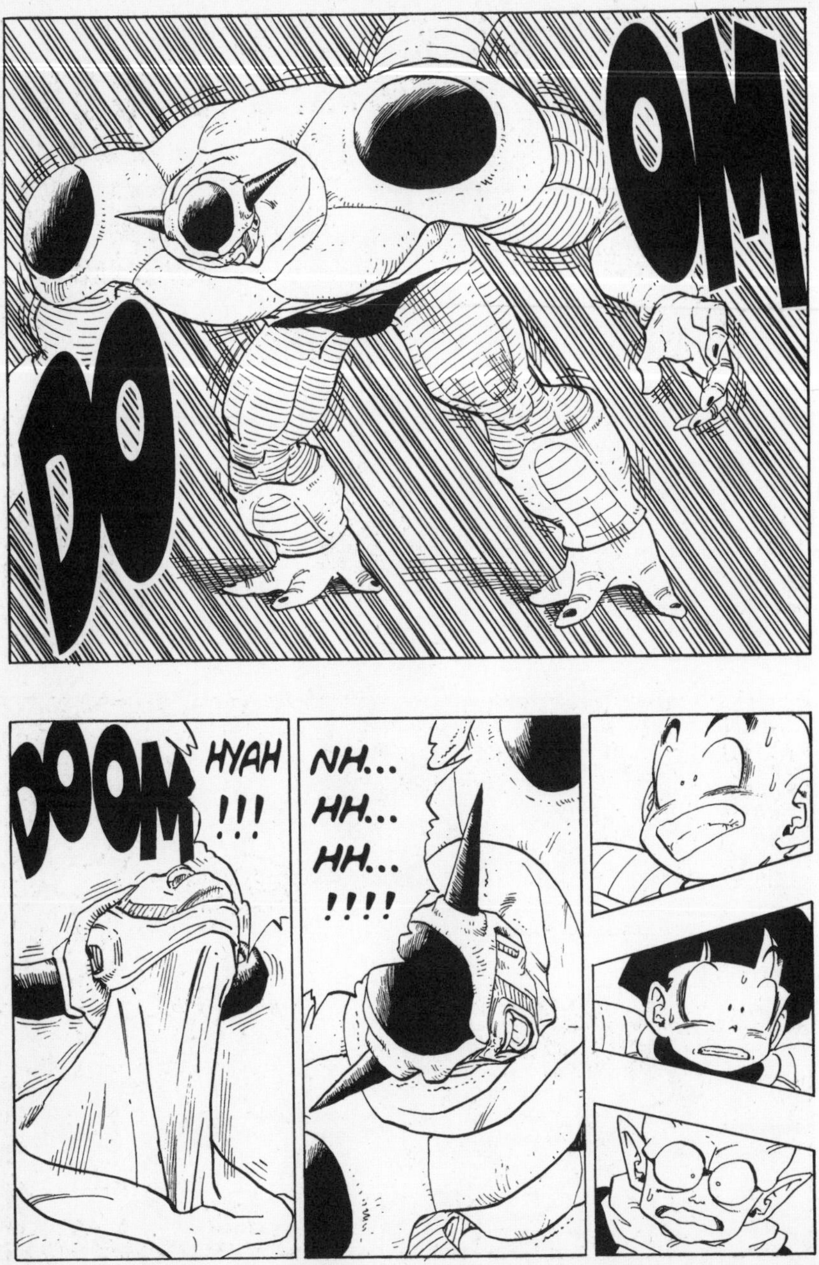
DOOM
NH...
HH...
HH...
!!!!
DOOM
HYAH
!!!

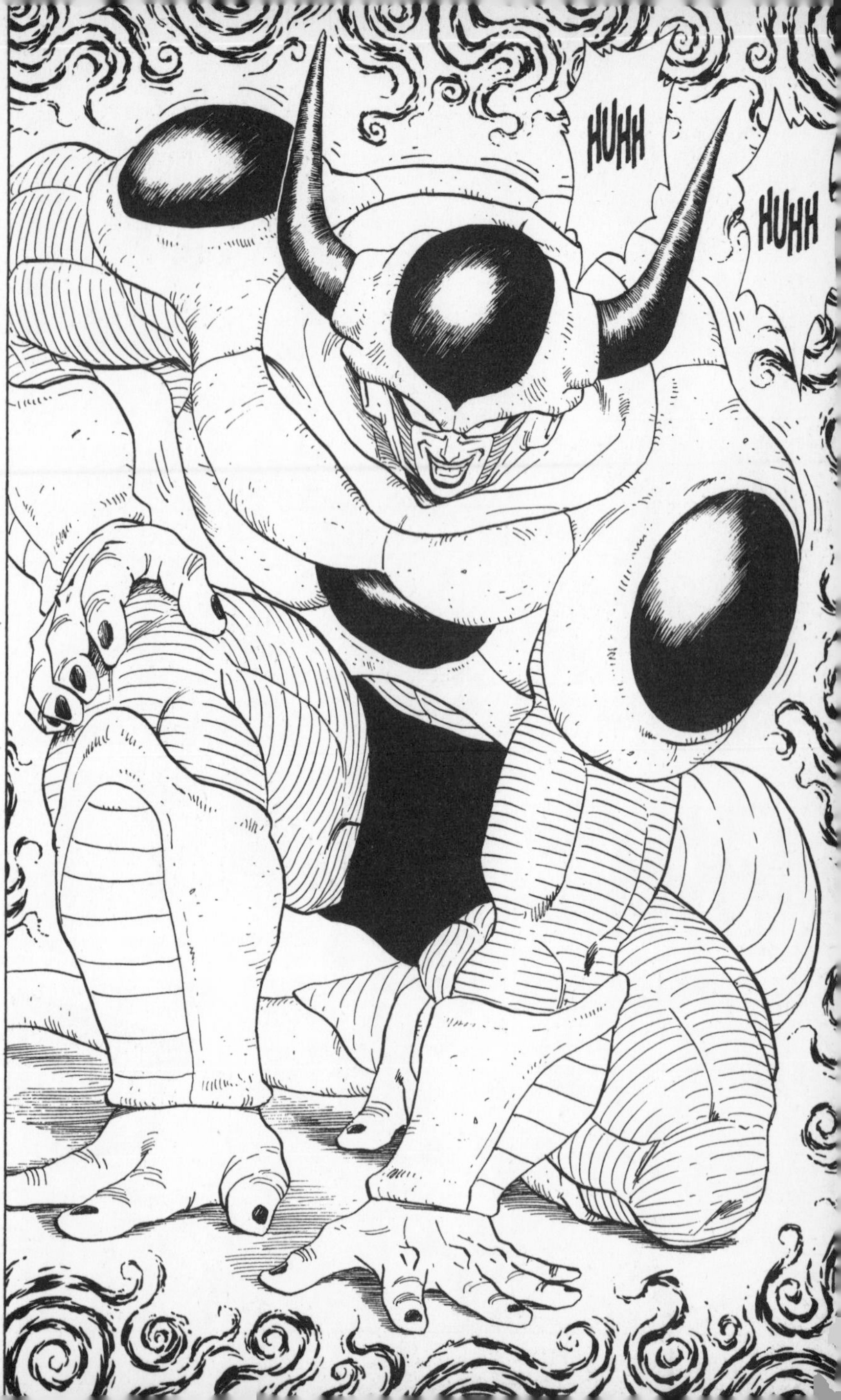
HUHH
HUHH

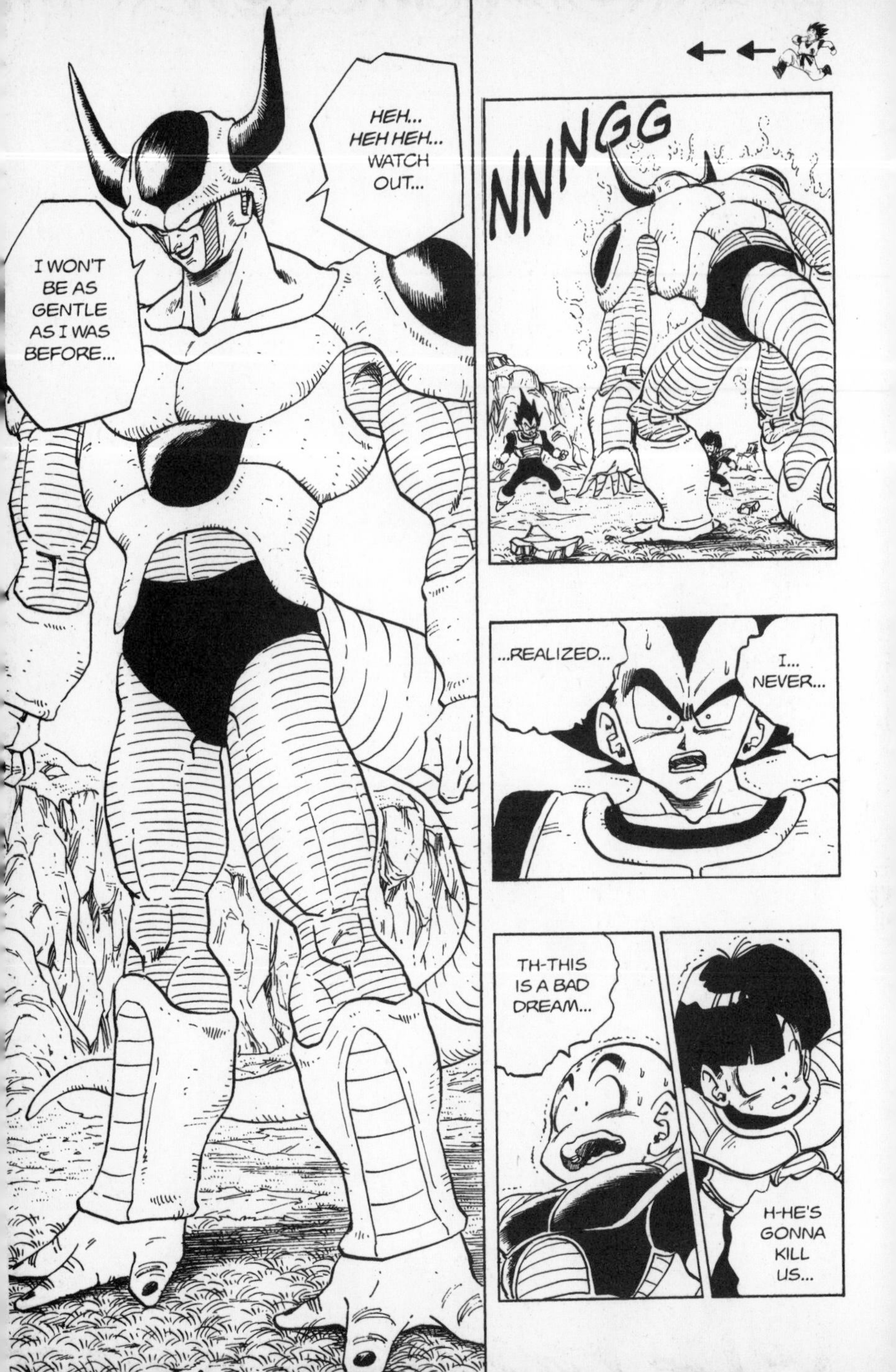
NNNGG
I... NEVER...
...REALIZED...
H-HE'S GONNA KILL US...
TH-THIS IS A BAD DREAM...
HEH... HEH HEH... WATCH OUT...
I WON'T BE AS GENTLE AS I WAS BEFORE...

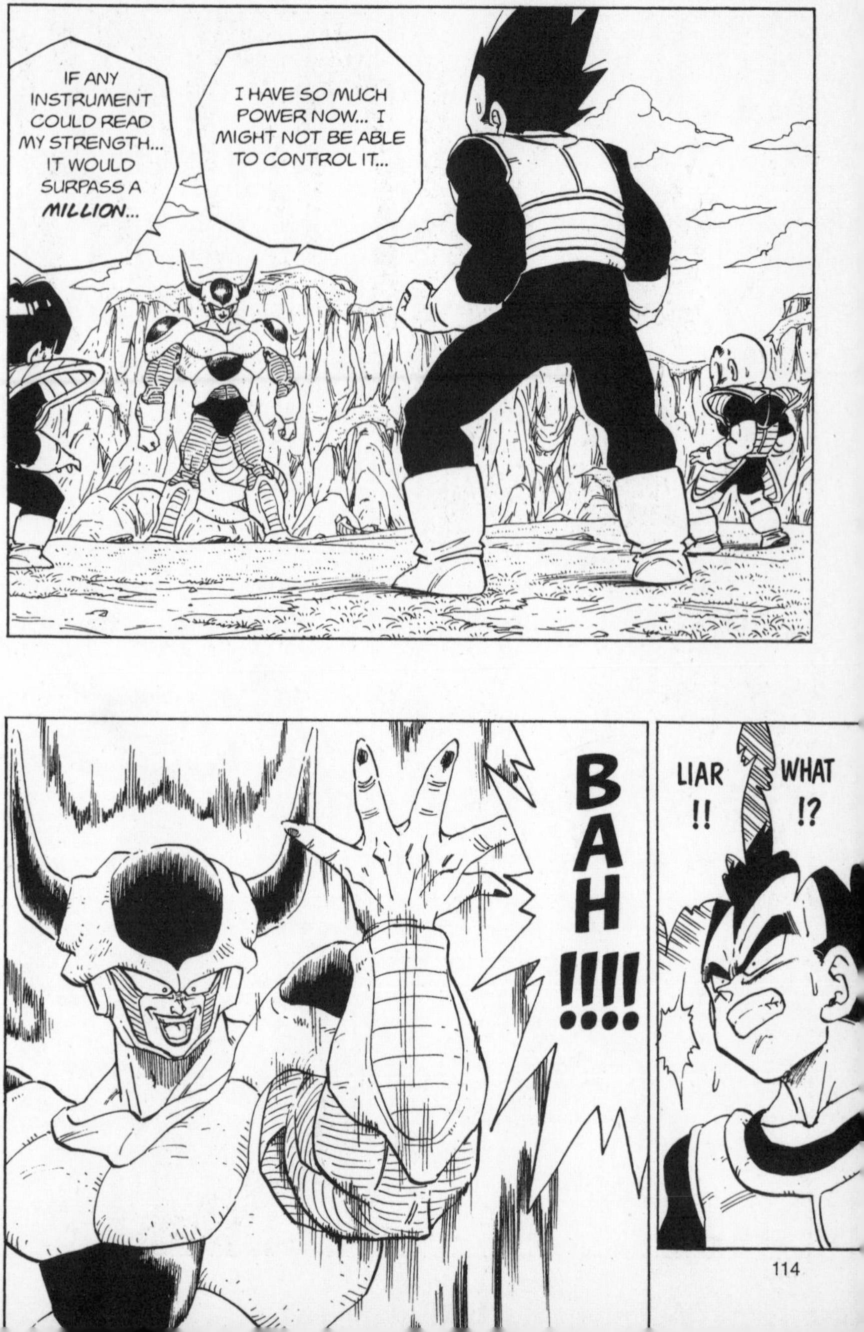
I HAVE SO MUCH POWER NOW... I MIGHT NOT BE ABLE TO CONTROL IT...
IF ANY INSTRUMENT COULD READ MY STRENGTH... IT WOULD SURPASS A MILLION...
WHAT !?
LIAR !!
BAH !!!!

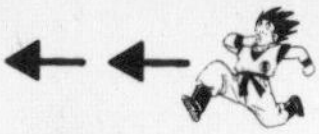

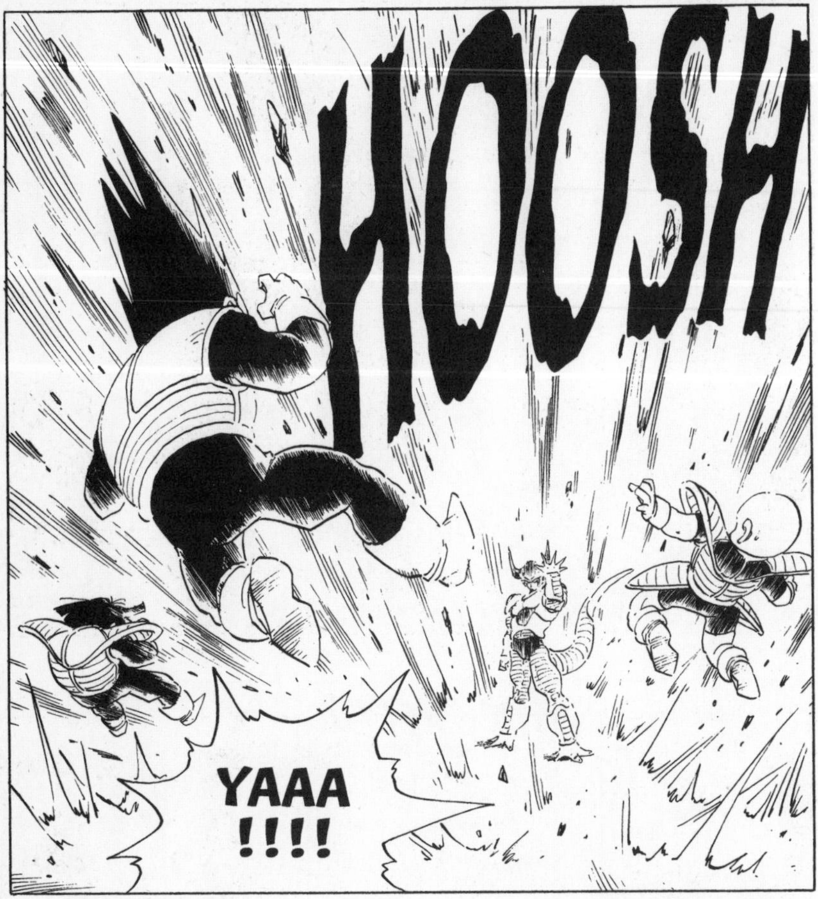
WHOOSH
YAAA !!!!

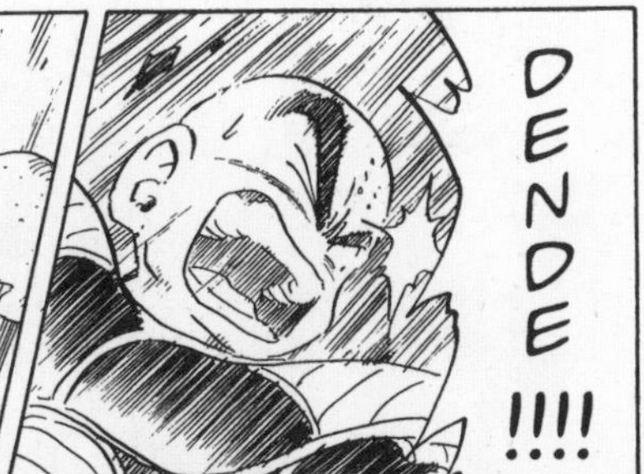
DENDE !!!!

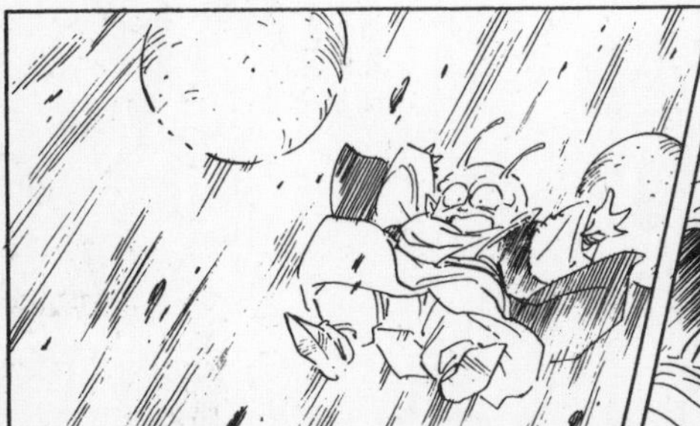

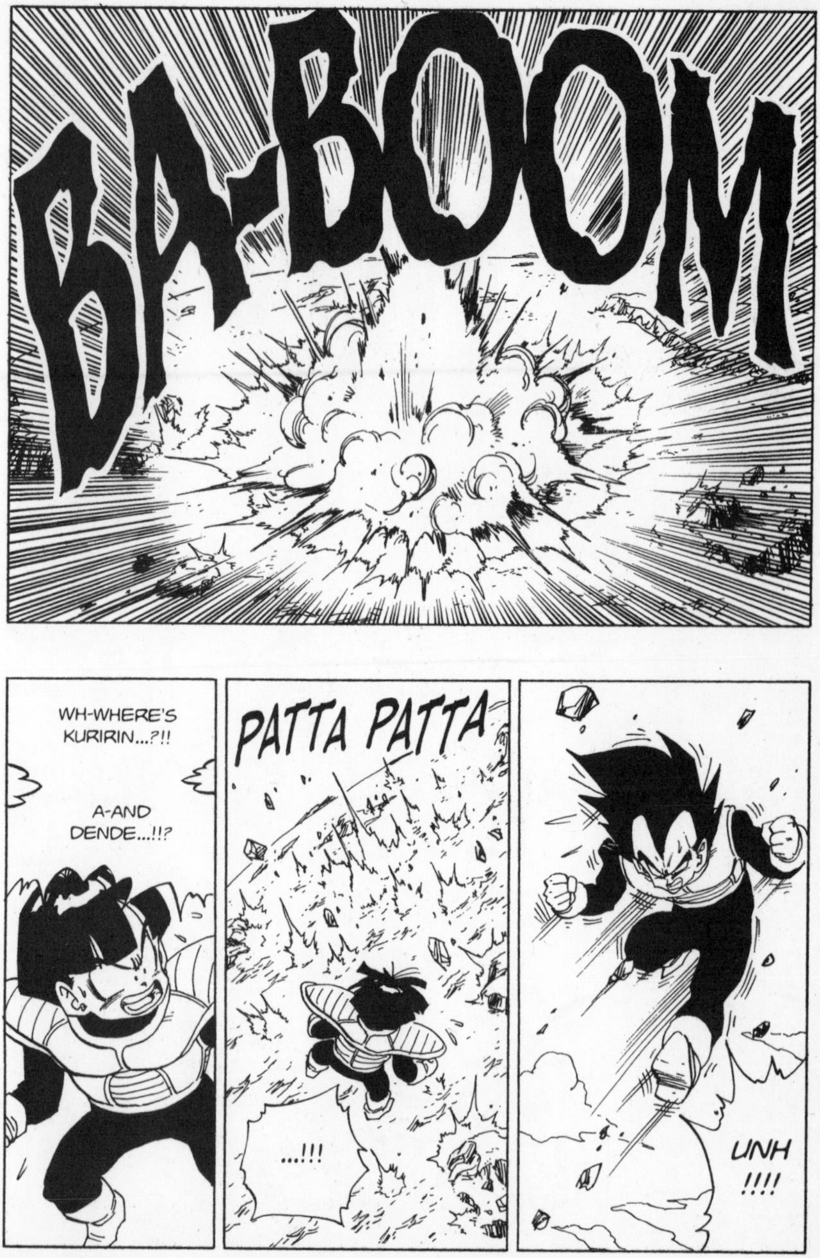
BA-BOOM
UNH !!!!
PATTA PATTA
...!!!
WH-WHERE'S KURIRIN...?!!
A-AND DENDE...!!?

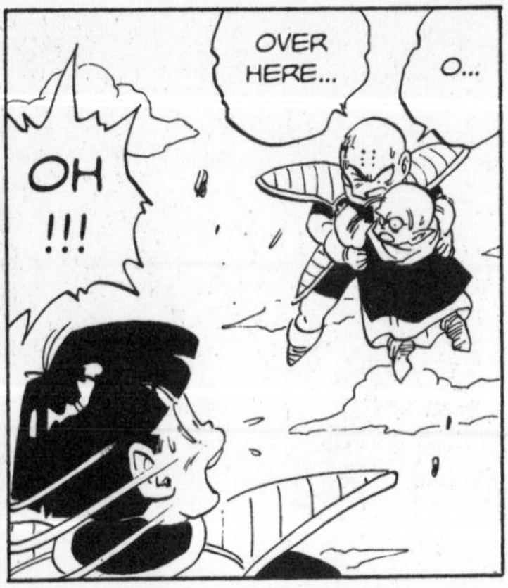
O...
OVER HERE...
OH !!!
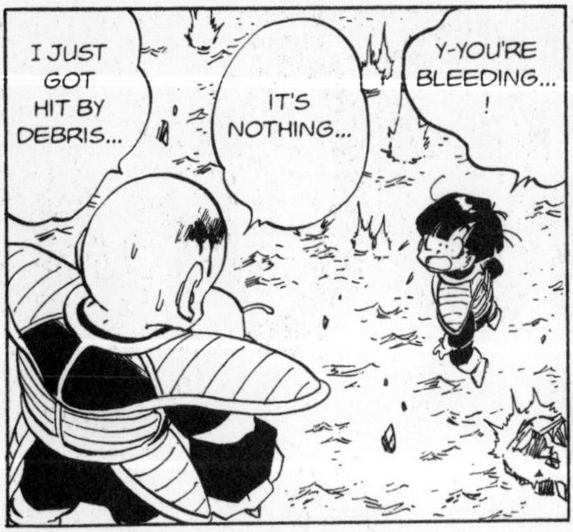
Y-YOU'RE BLEEDING... !
IT'S NOTHING...
I JUST GOT HIT BY DEBRIS...
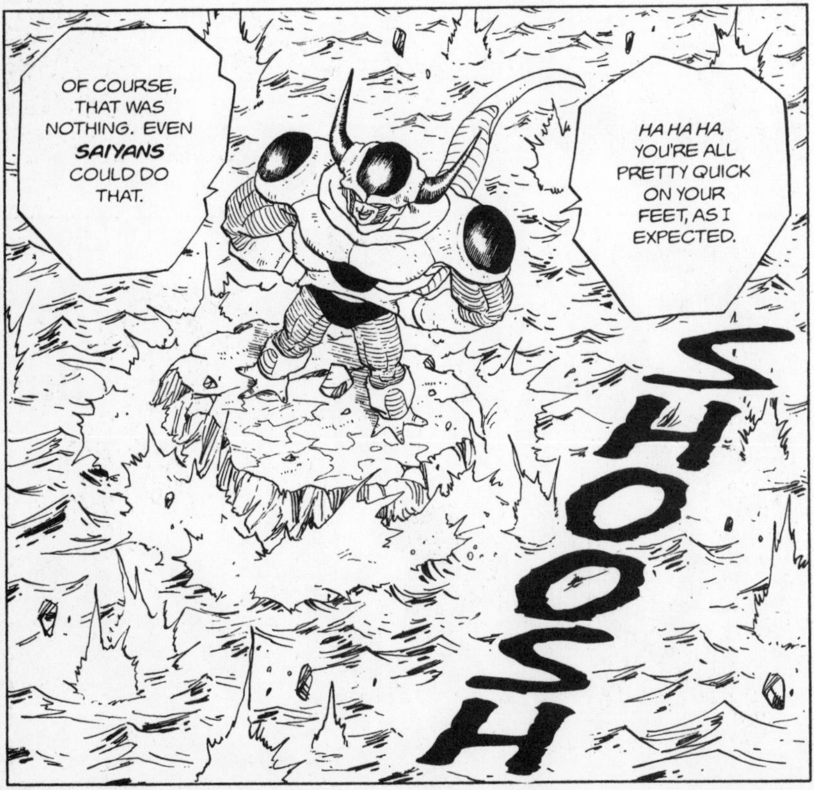
HA HA HA. YOU'RE ALL PRETTY QUICK ON YOUR FEET, AS I EXPECTED.
OF COURSE, THAT WAS NOTHING. EVEN ***SAIYANS*** COULD DO THAT.
SHOOSH

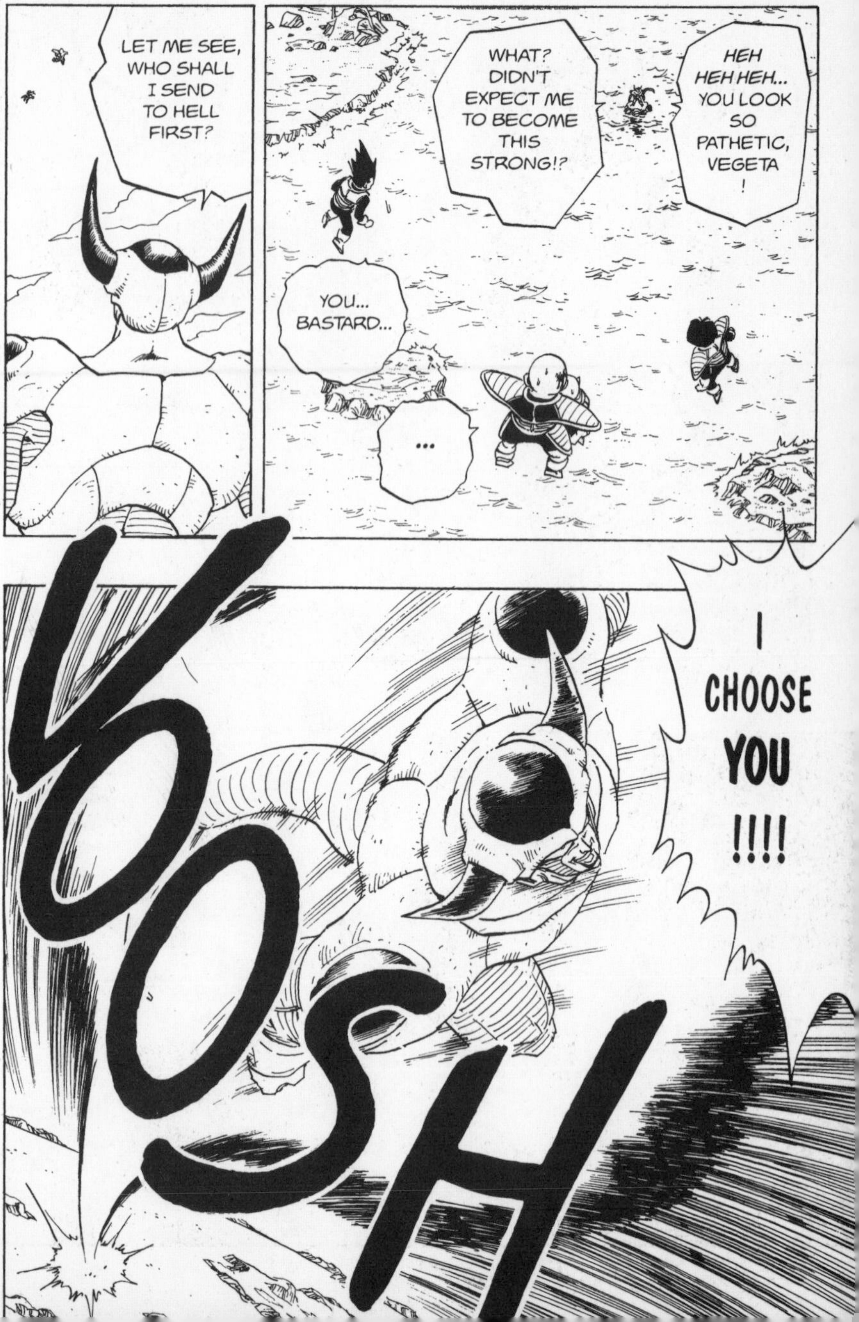
HEH HEH HEH... YOU LOOK SO PATHETIC, VEGETA !
WHAT? DIDN'T EXPECT ME TO BECOME THIS STRONG!?
YOU... BASTARD...
...
LET ME SEE, WHO SHALL I SEND TO HELL FIRST?
I CHOOSE YOU !!!!
VOOSH

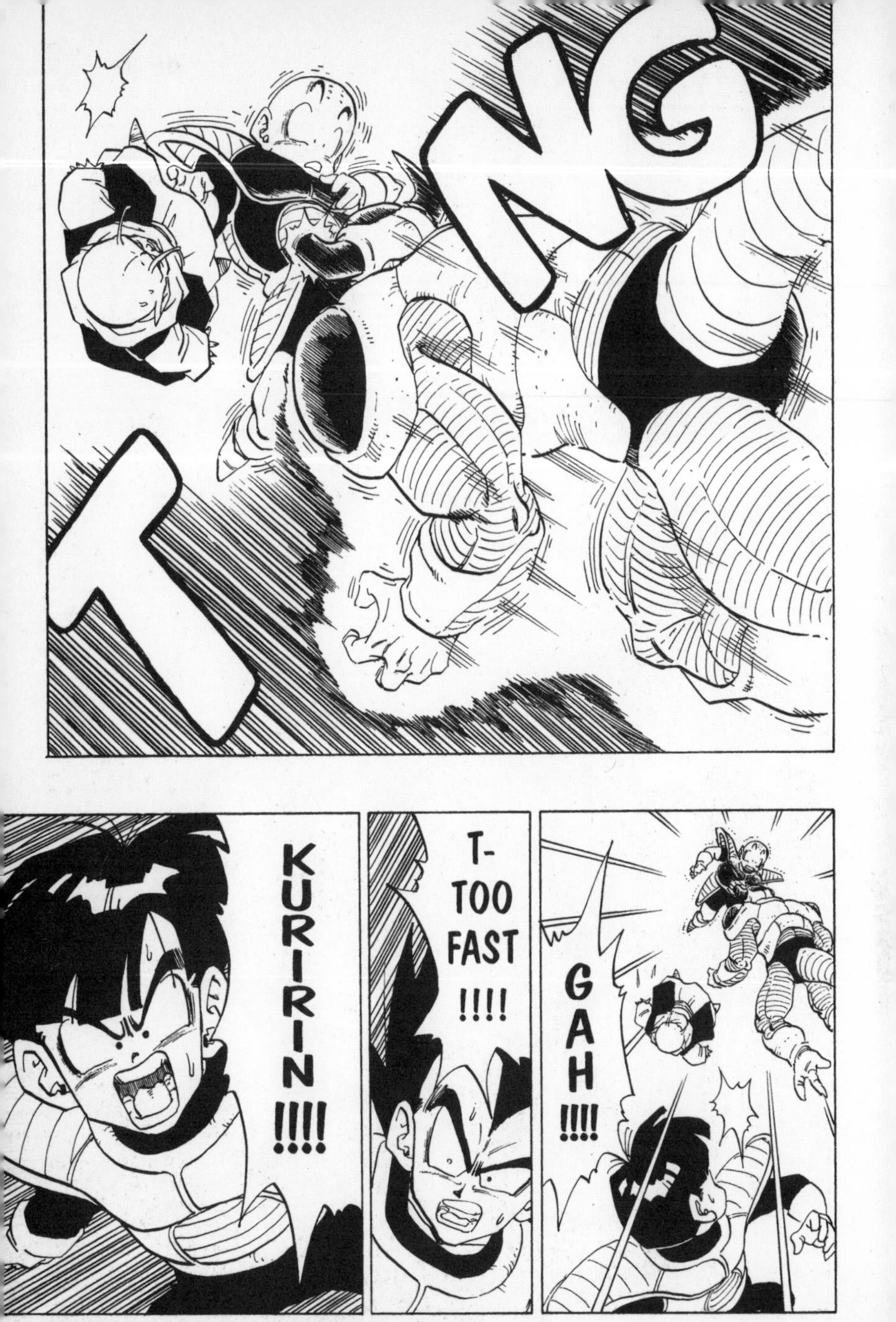
GAH!!!!
T-TOO FAST!!!!
KURIRIN!!!!

NEXT: Gohan Enraged!

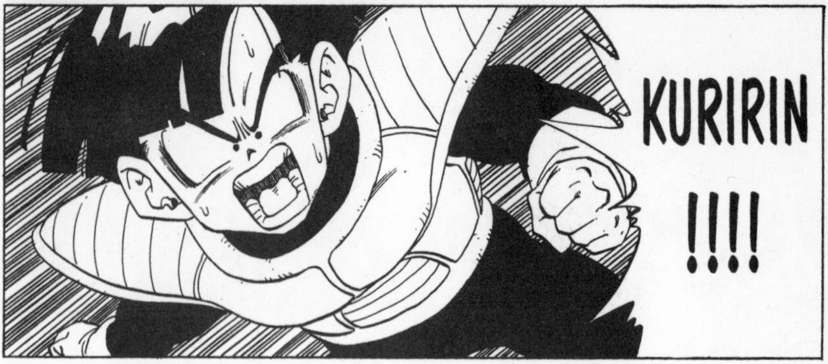
KURIRIN
!!!!

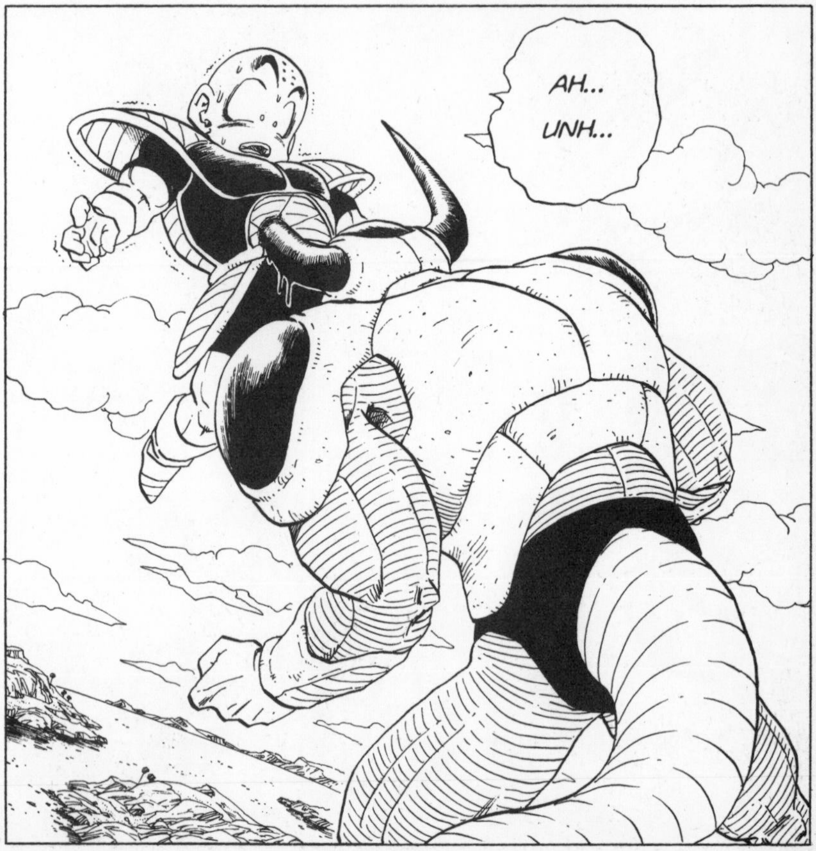
AH... UNH...

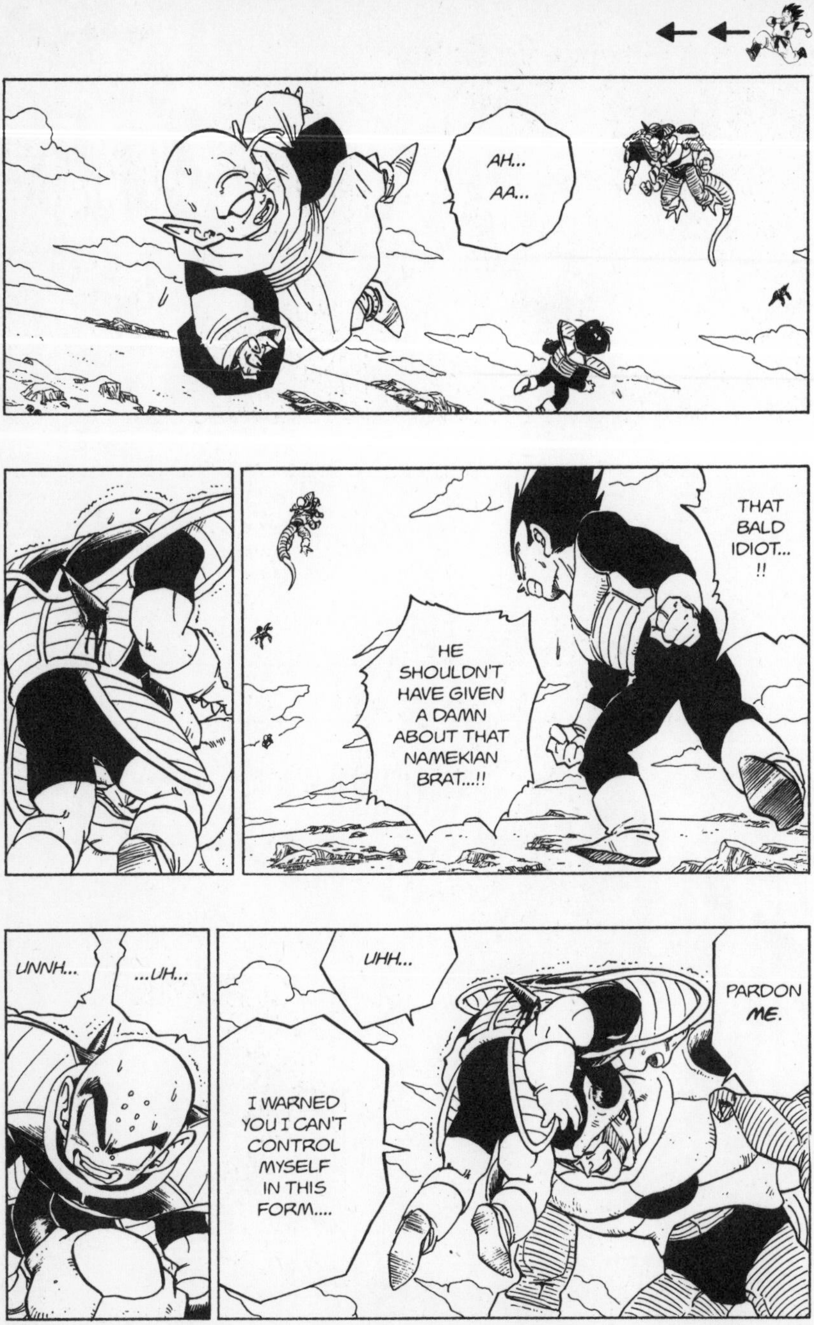
AH... AA...
THAT BALD IDIOT... !!
HE SHOULDN'T HAVE GIVEN A DAMN ABOUT THAT NAMEKIAN BRAT...!!
PARDON *ME*.
UHH...
I WARNED YOU I CAN'T CONTROL MYSELF IN THIS FORM....
UNNH...
...UH...

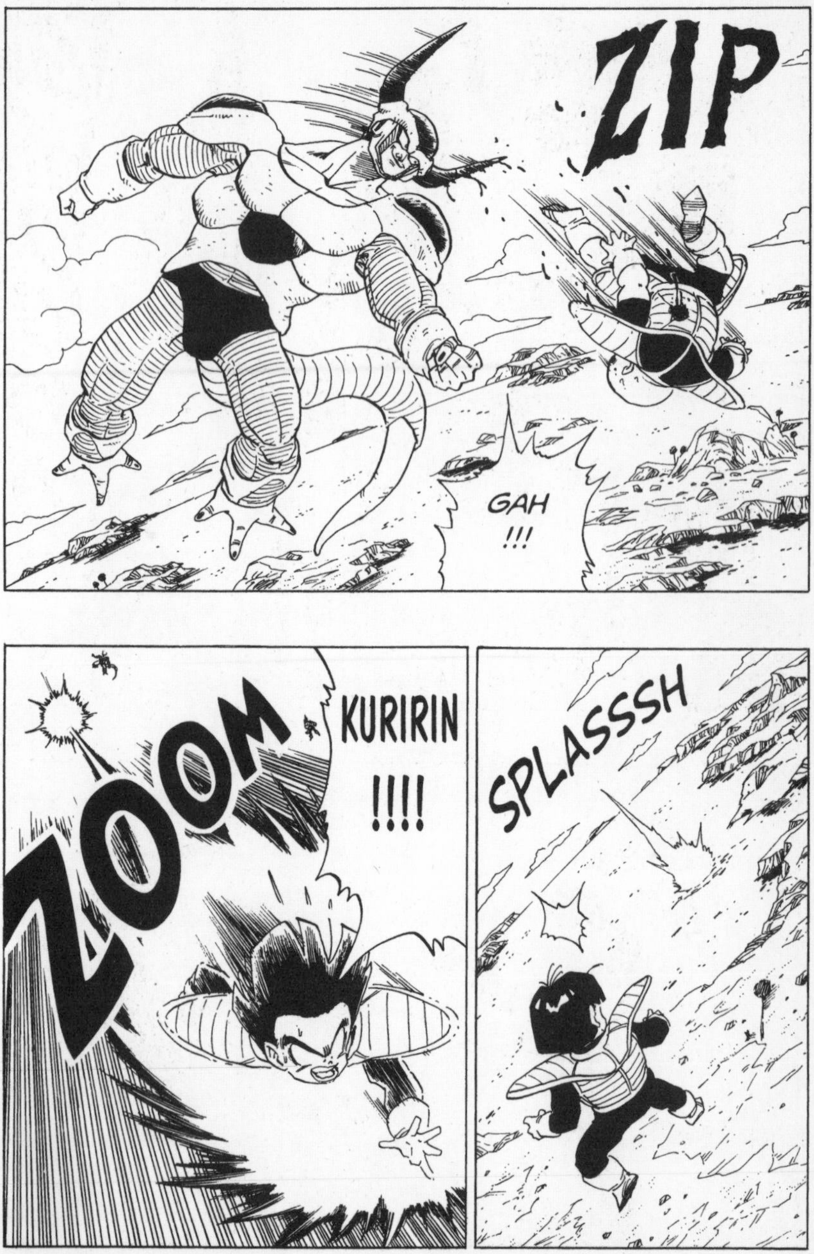
ZIP
GAH !!!
SPLASSSH
KURIRIN !!!!
ZOOM

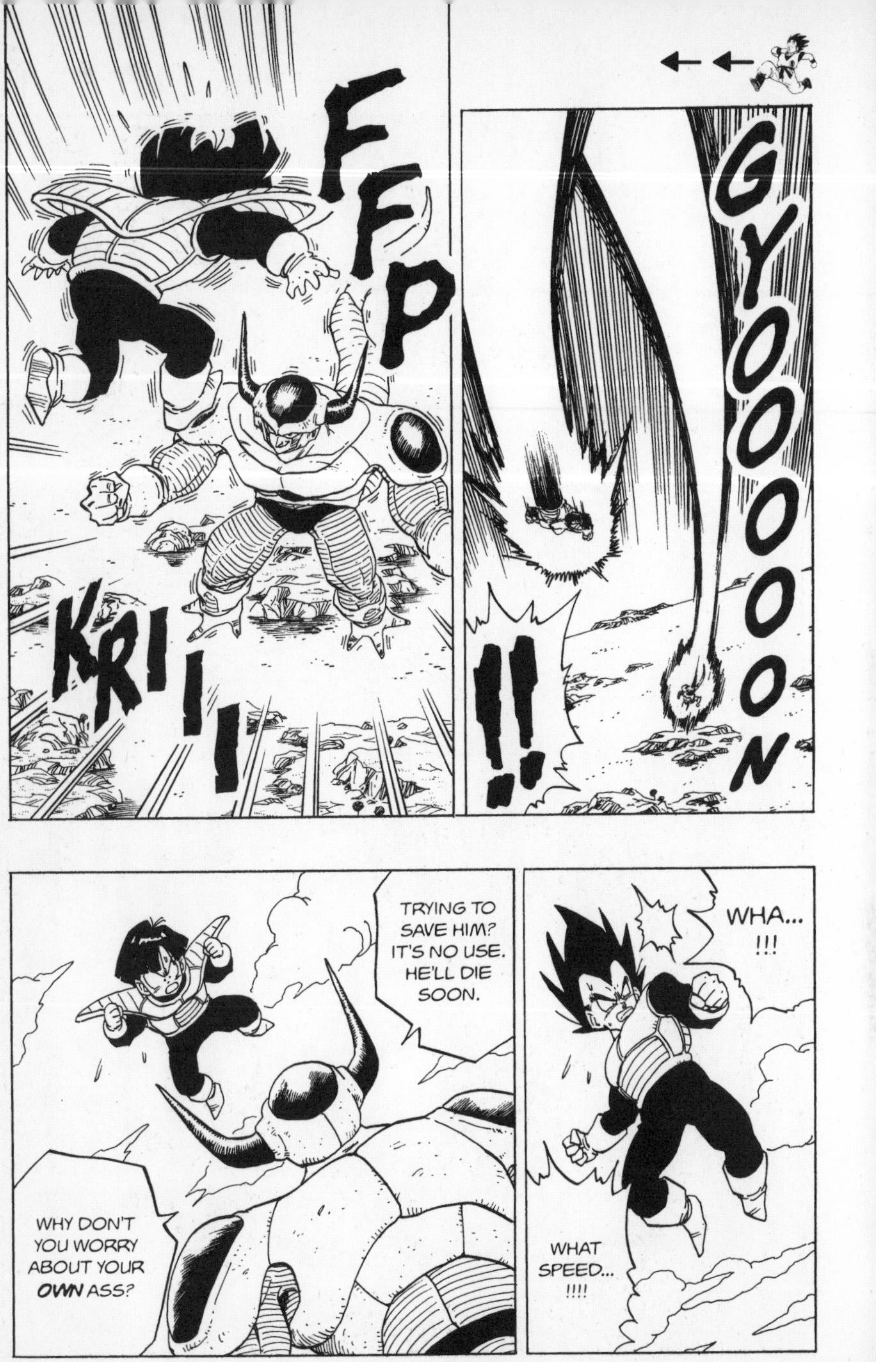
GYOOOOON
!!
FFP
KRIII
WHA... !!!
WHAT SPEED... !!!!
TRYING TO SAVE HIM? IT'S NO USE. HE'LL DIE SOON.
WHY DON'T YOU WORRY ABOUT YOUR OWN ASS?

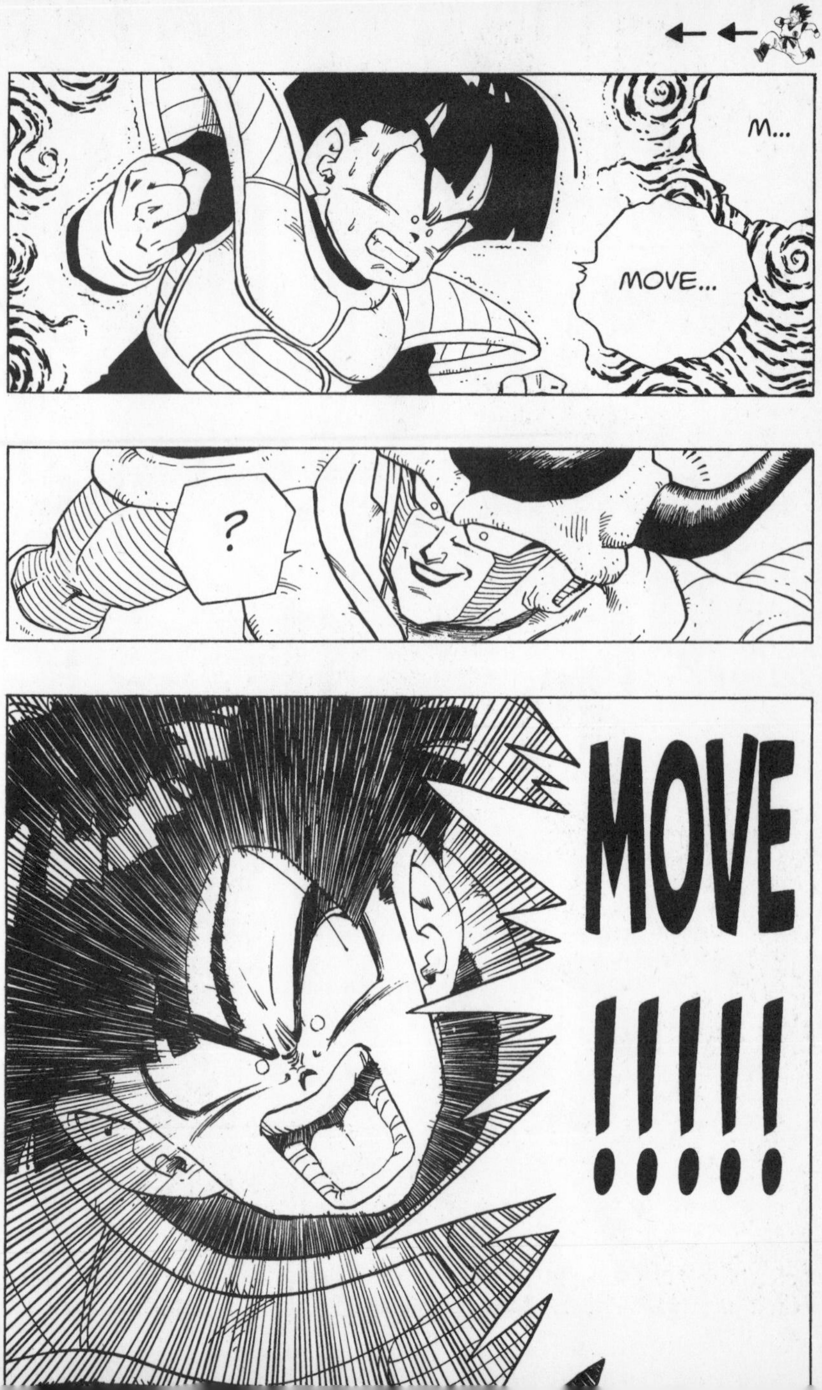
M...
MOVE...
?
MOVE !!!!!

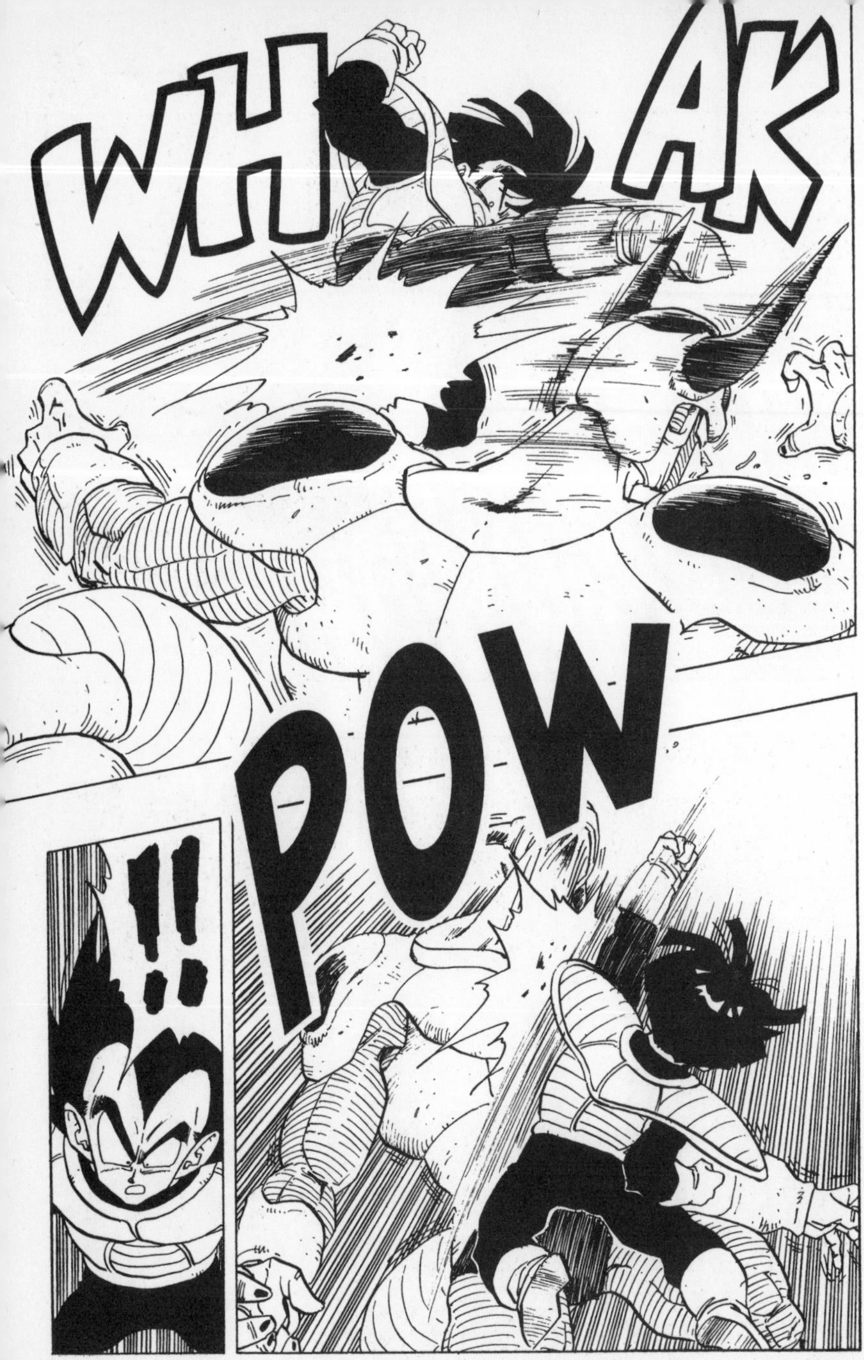
WHAK
POW
!!

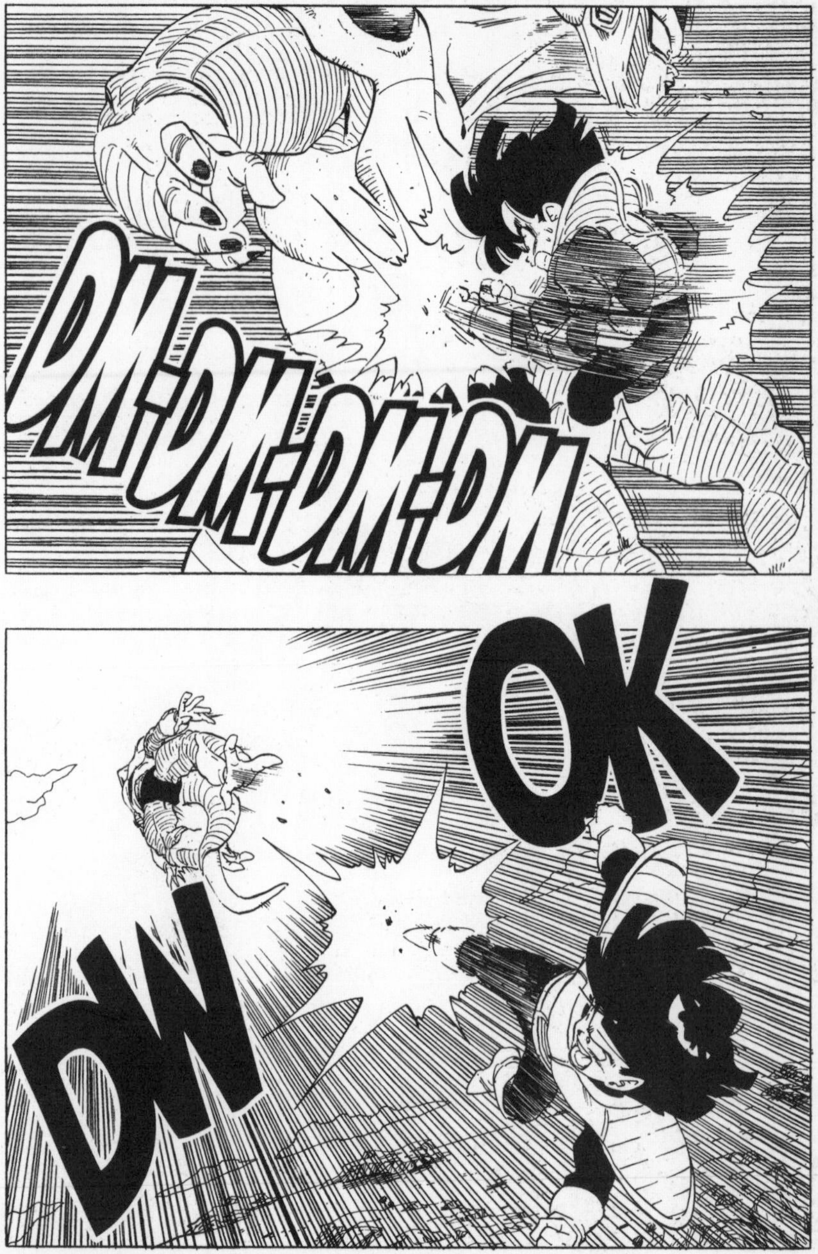
DM-DM-DM-DM-DM
DWOK

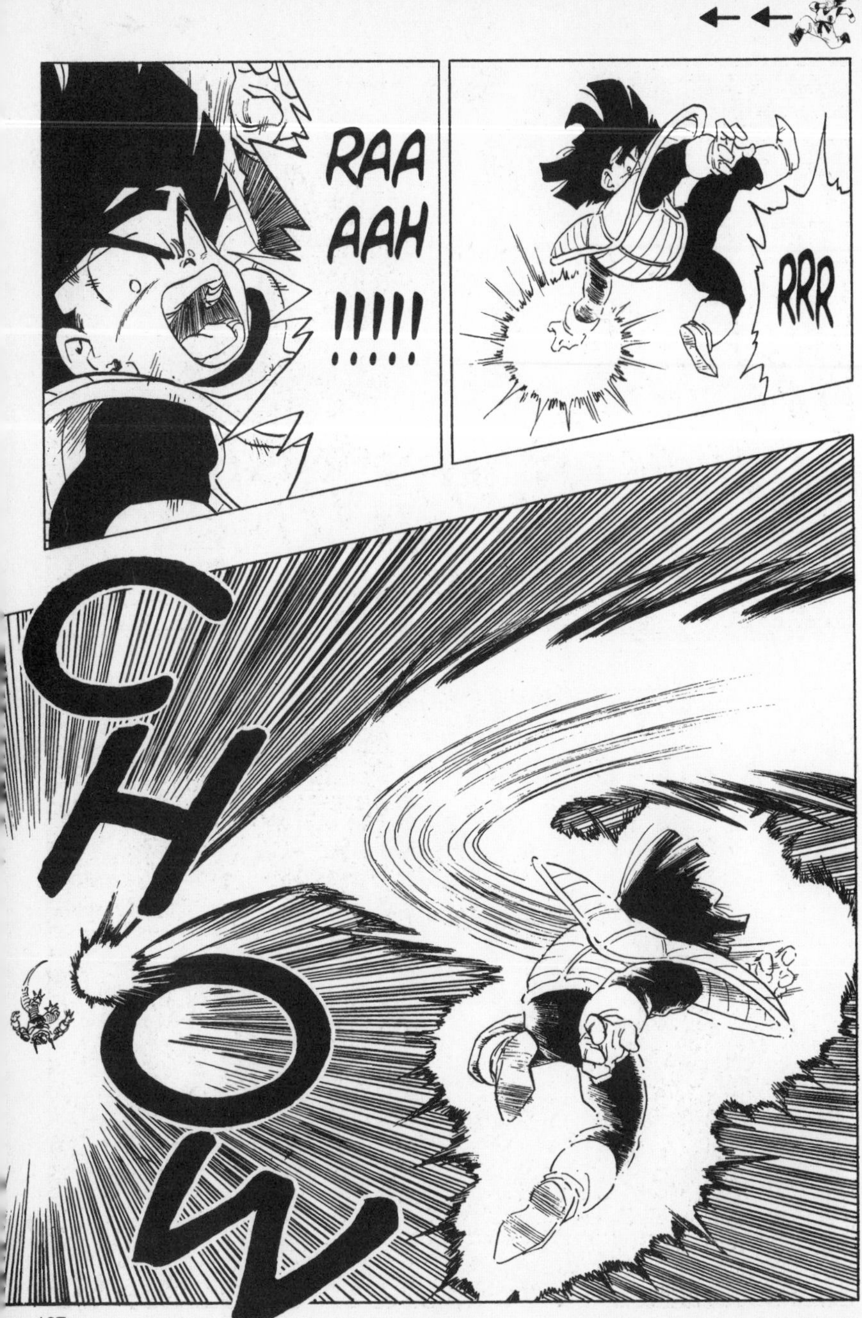
RRR
RAA
AAH
!!!!!
SHOO

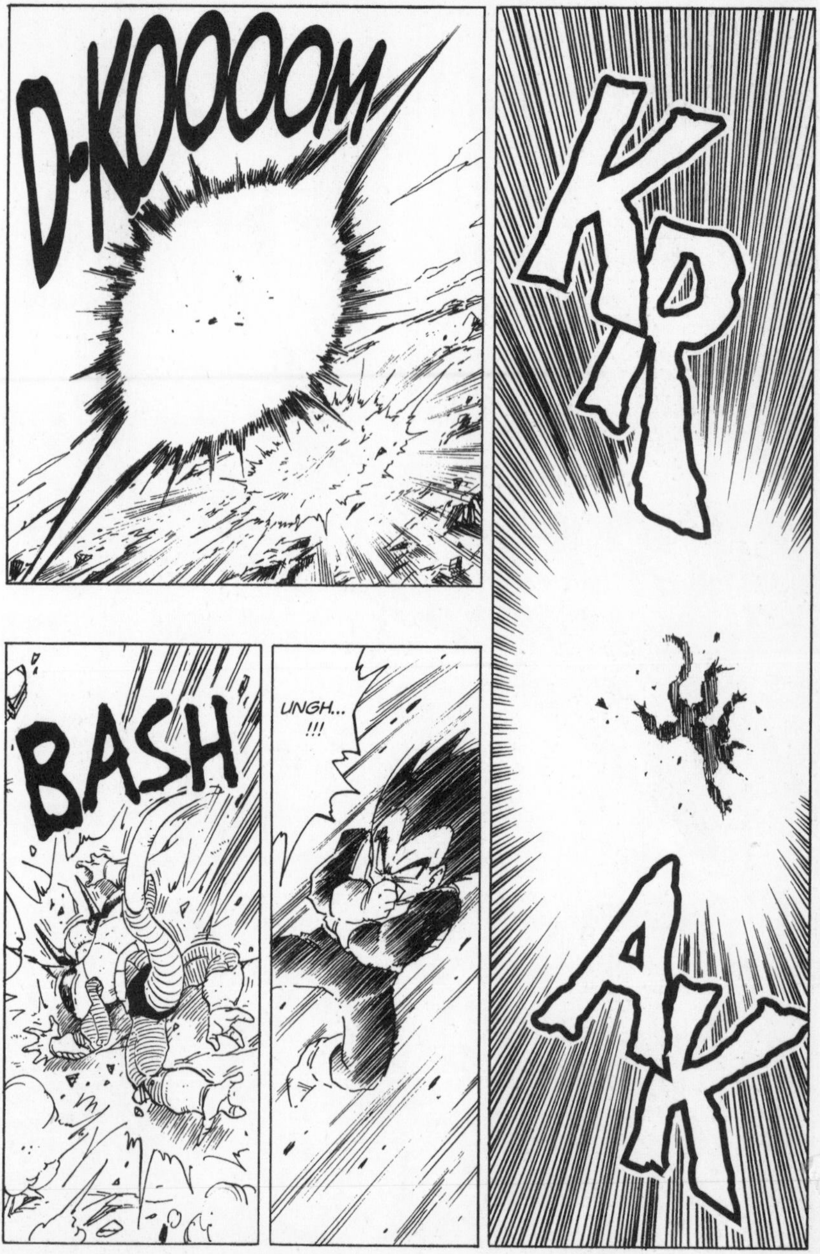
KPAK
D-KOOOOM
UNGH... !!!
BASH

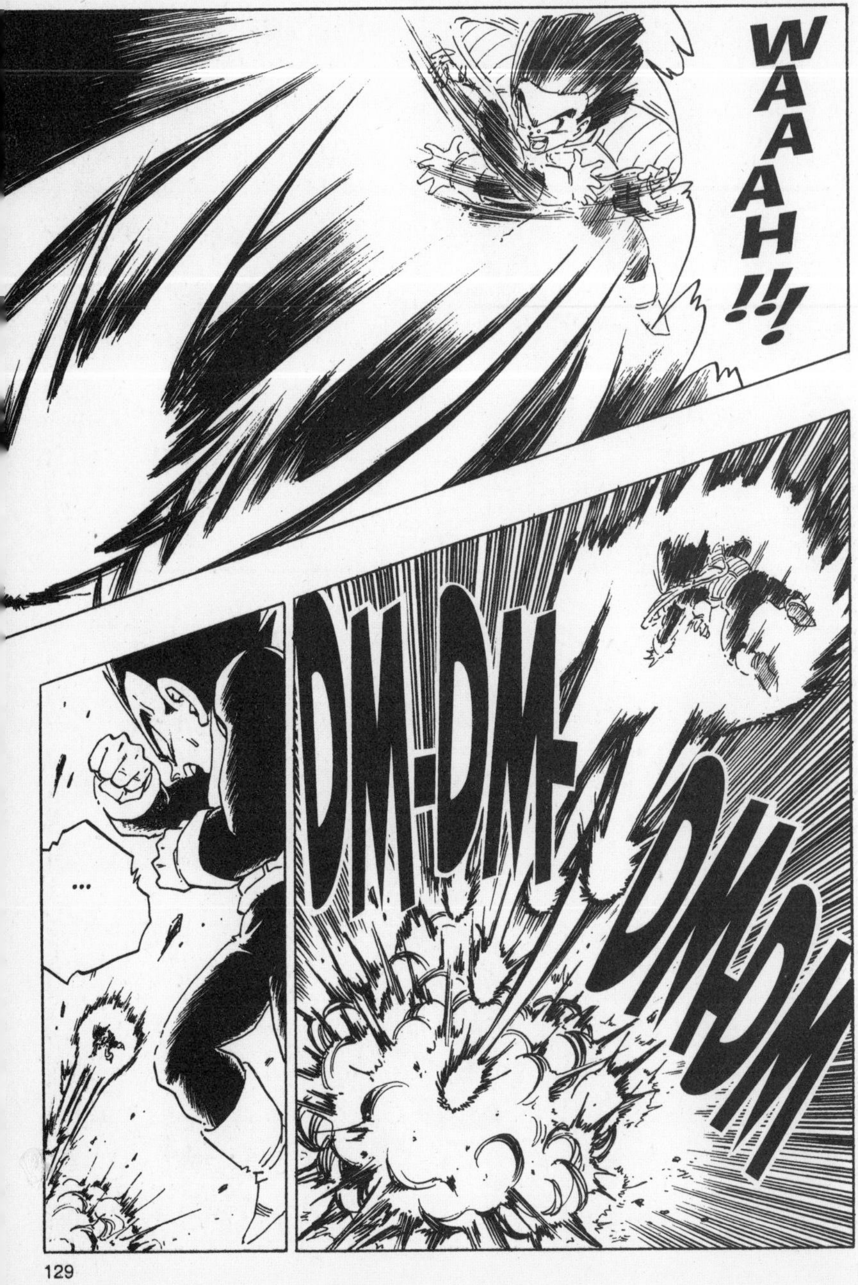
WAAAAH!!!
DM-DM
DHOM
...

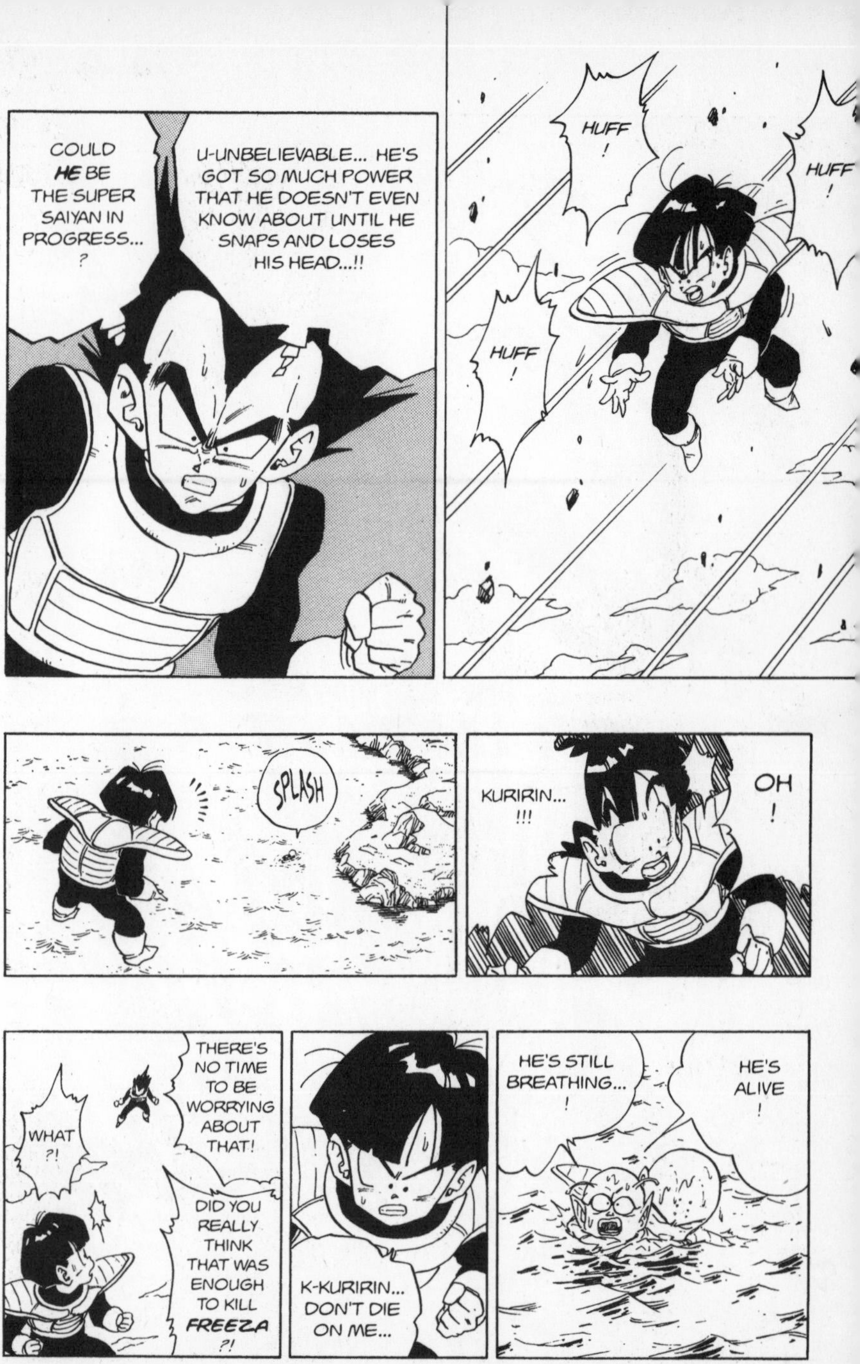
HUFF!
HUFF!
HUFF!
U-UNBELIEVABLE... HE'S GOT SO MUCH POWER THAT HE DOESN'T EVEN KNOW ABOUT UNTIL HE SNAPS AND LOSES HIS HEAD...!!
COULD **HE** BE THE SUPER SAIYAN IN PROGRESS...?
OH!
KURIRIN...!!!
SPLASH
HE'S ALIVE!
HE'S STILL BREATHING...!
K-KURIRIN... DON'T DIE ON ME...
THERE'S NO TIME TO BE WORRYING ABOUT THAT!
WHAT?!
DID YOU REALLY THINK THAT WAS ENOUGH TO KILL **FREEZA**?!

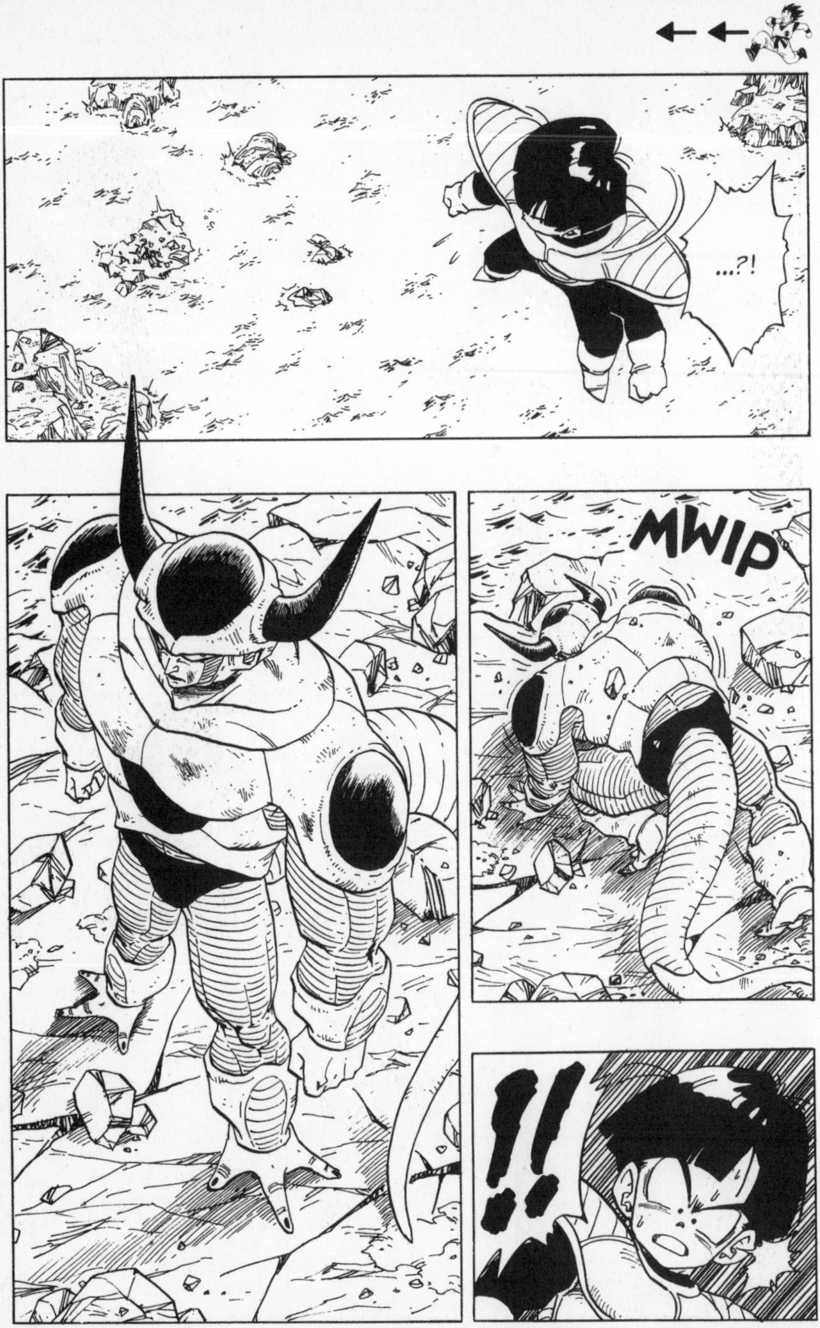
...?!
MWIP
!!

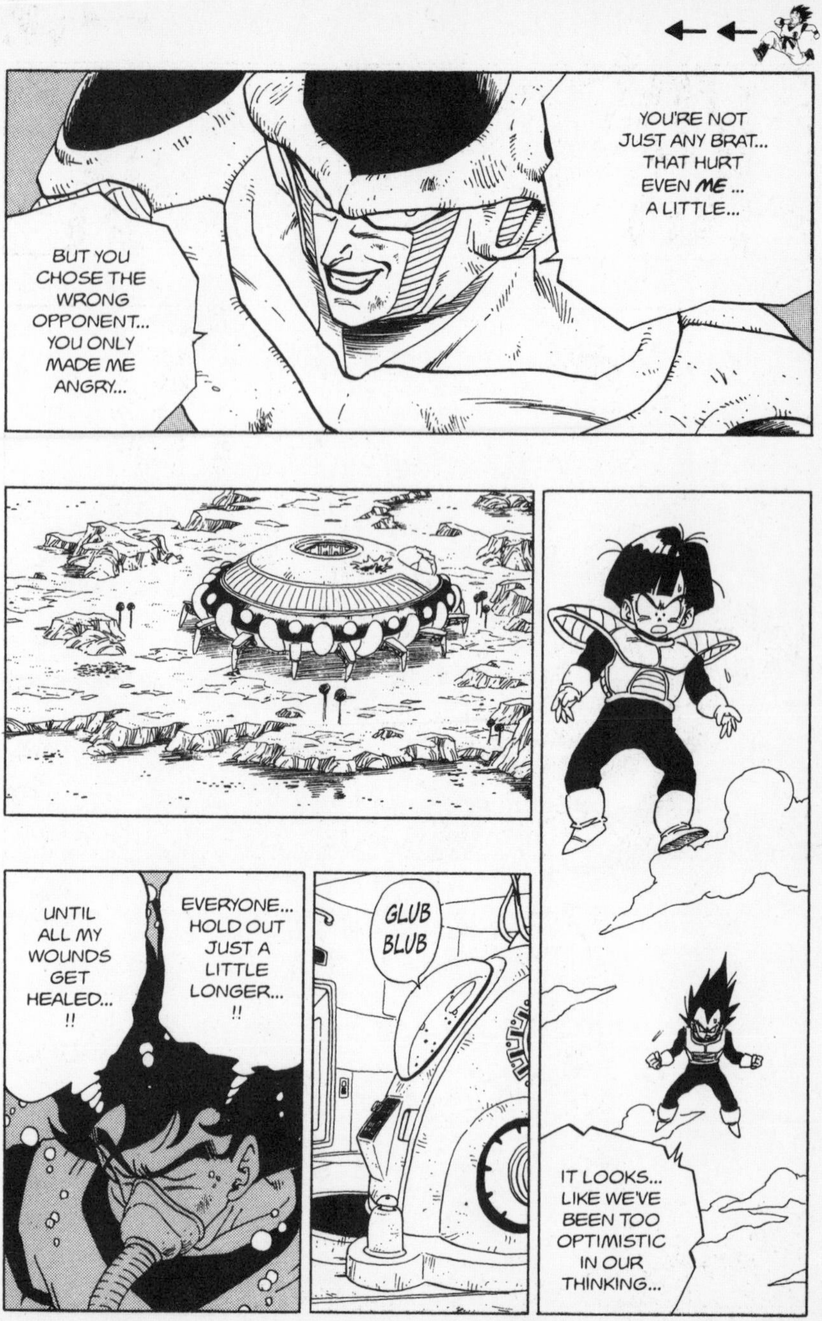
YOU'RE NOT JUST ANY BRAT... THAT HURT EVEN *ME*... A LITTLE...
BUT YOU CHOSE THE WRONG OPPONENT... YOU ONLY MADE ME ANGRY...
IT LOOKS... LIKE WE'VE BEEN TOO OPTIMISTIC IN OUR THINKING...
GLUB BLUB
EVERYONE... HOLD OUT JUST A LITTLE LONGER... !!
UNTIL ALL MY WOUNDS GET HEALED... !!

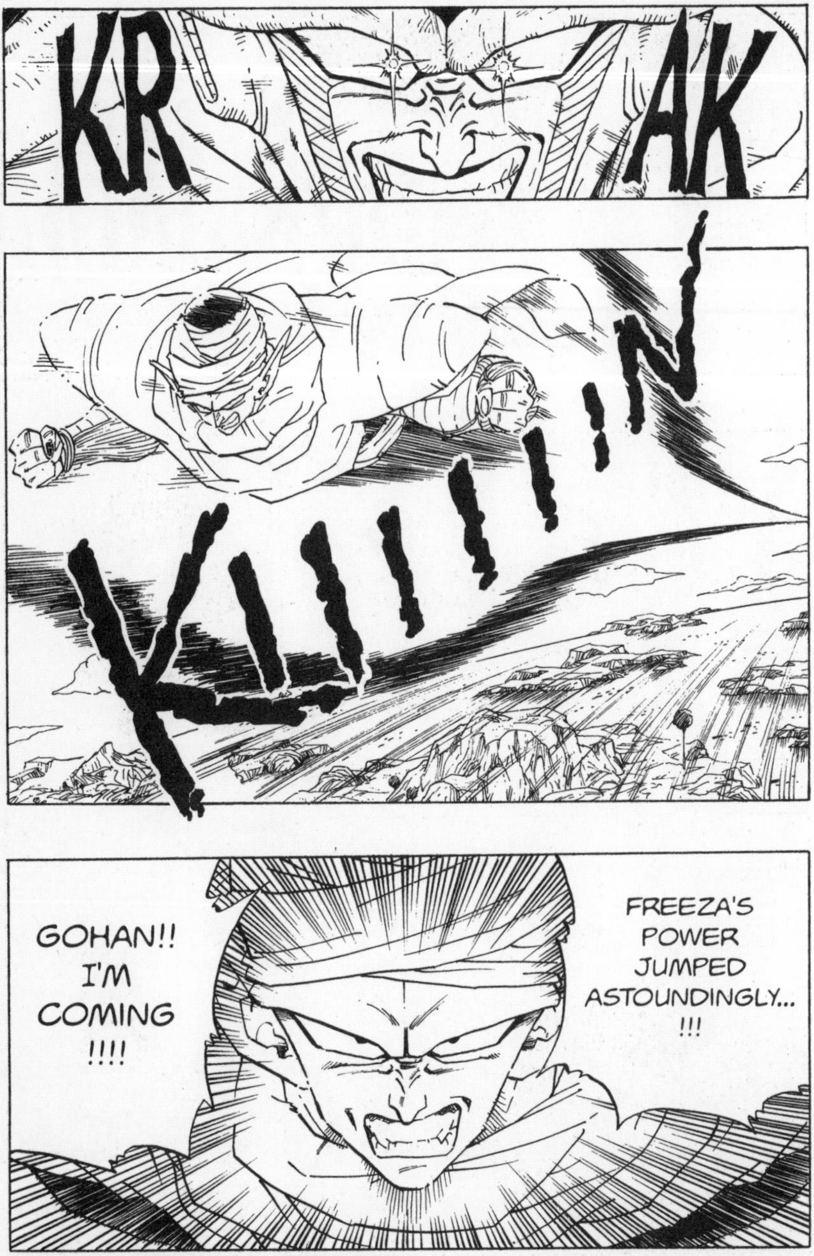
KRAK
KYIIIIN
FREEZA'S POWER JUMPED ASTOUNDINGLY... !!!
GOHAN!! I'M COMING !!!!

NEXT: *Gohan in Tatters*

DBZ:104
Freeza vs. Gohan, Part 2

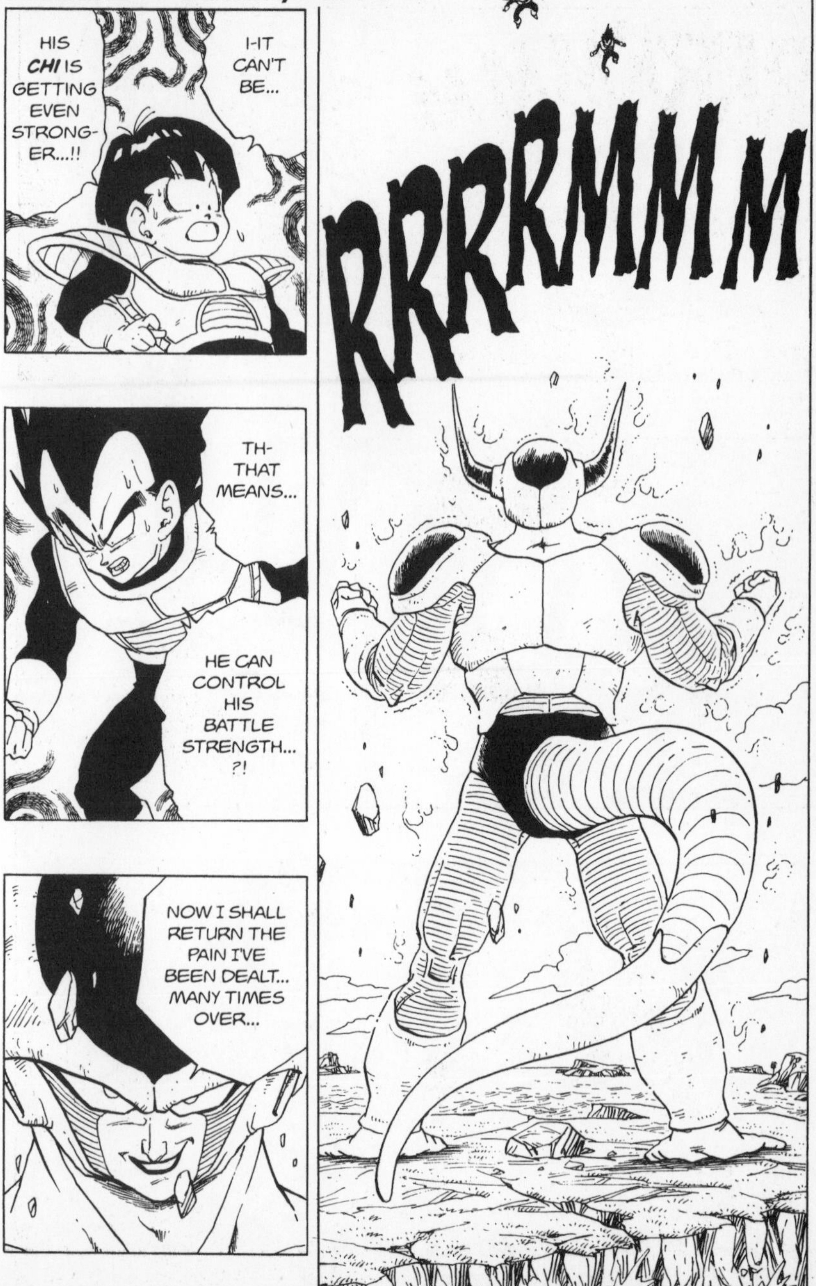
RRRRMMM M
I-IT CAN'T BE...
HIS CHI IS GETTING EVEN STRONG-ER...!!
TH-THAT MEANS...
HE CAN CONTROL HIS BATTLE STRENGTH...?!
NOW I SHALL RETURN THE PAIN I'VE BEEN DEALT... MANY TIMES OVER...

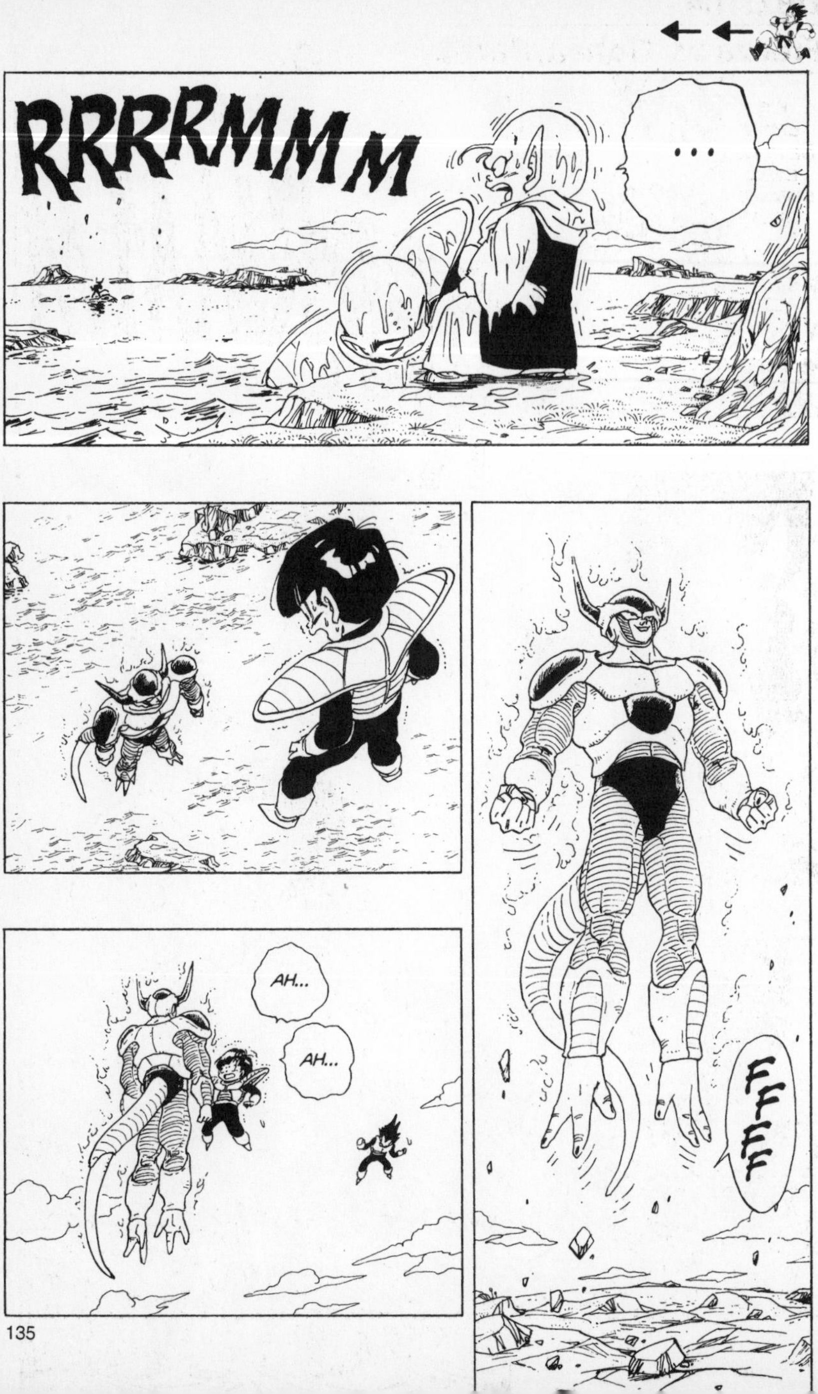

RRRRMMM M
...
FFFF
AH...
AH...

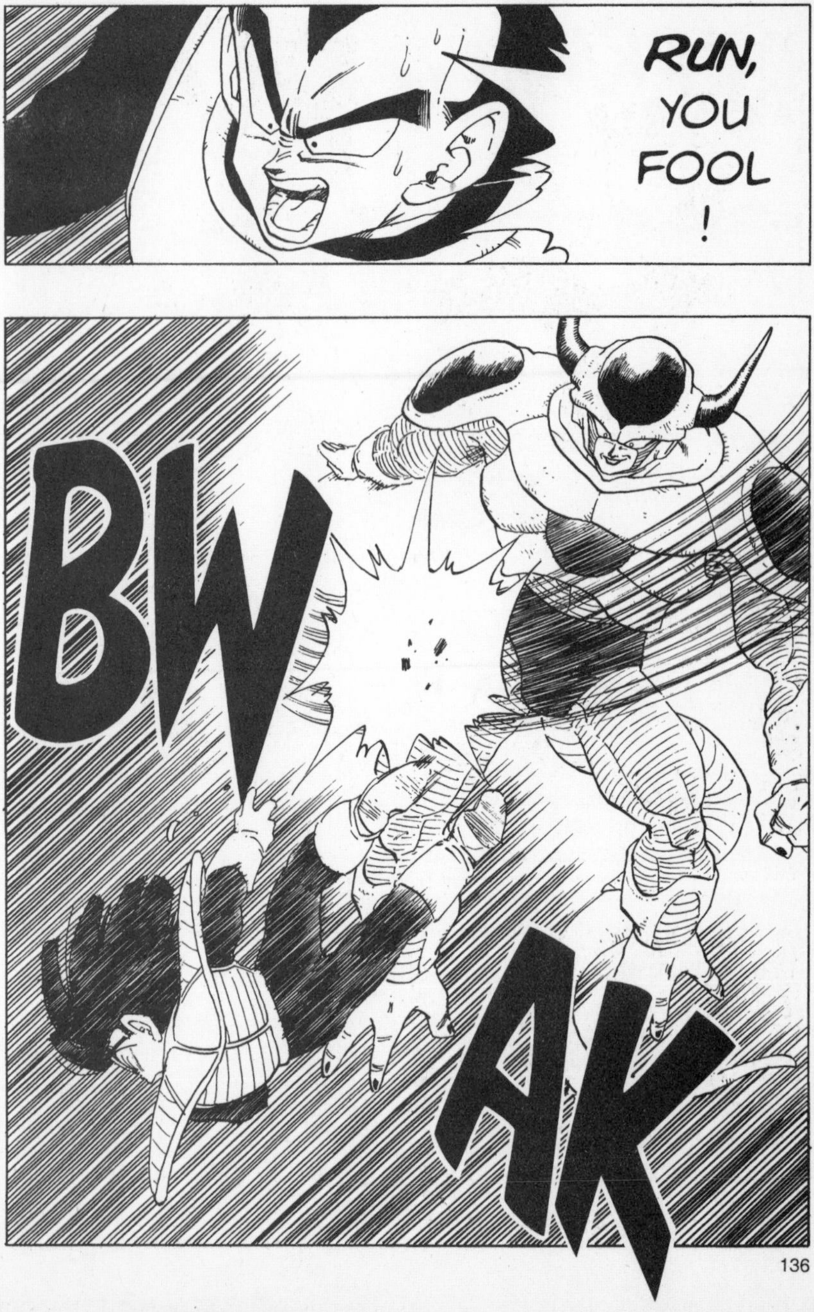
RUN, YOU FOOL!
BWAK

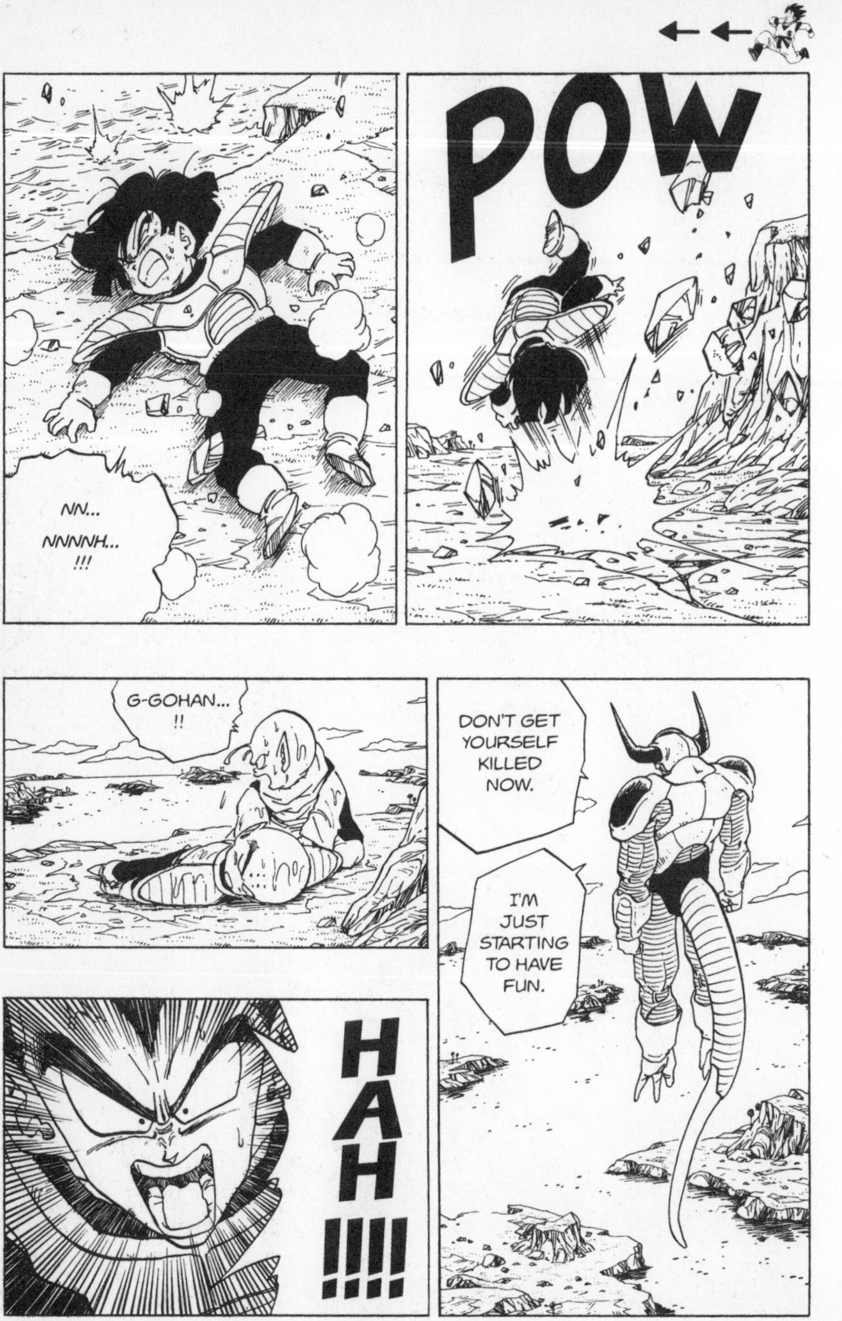
POW
NN... NNNNH... !!!
DON'T GET YOURSELF KILLED NOW.
I'M JUST STARTING TO HAVE FUN.
G-GOHAN... !!
HAH !!!!!

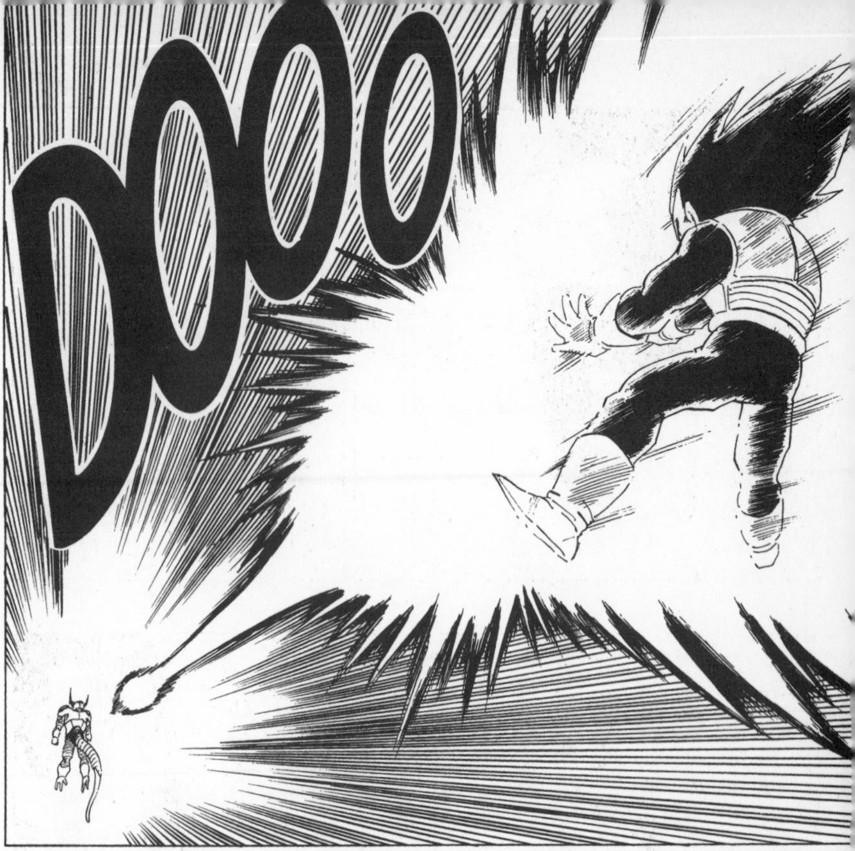
DOOO

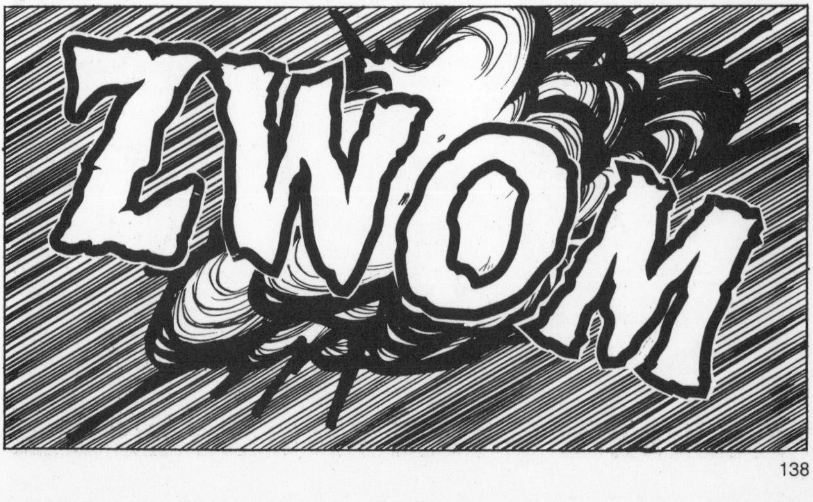
ZWOM

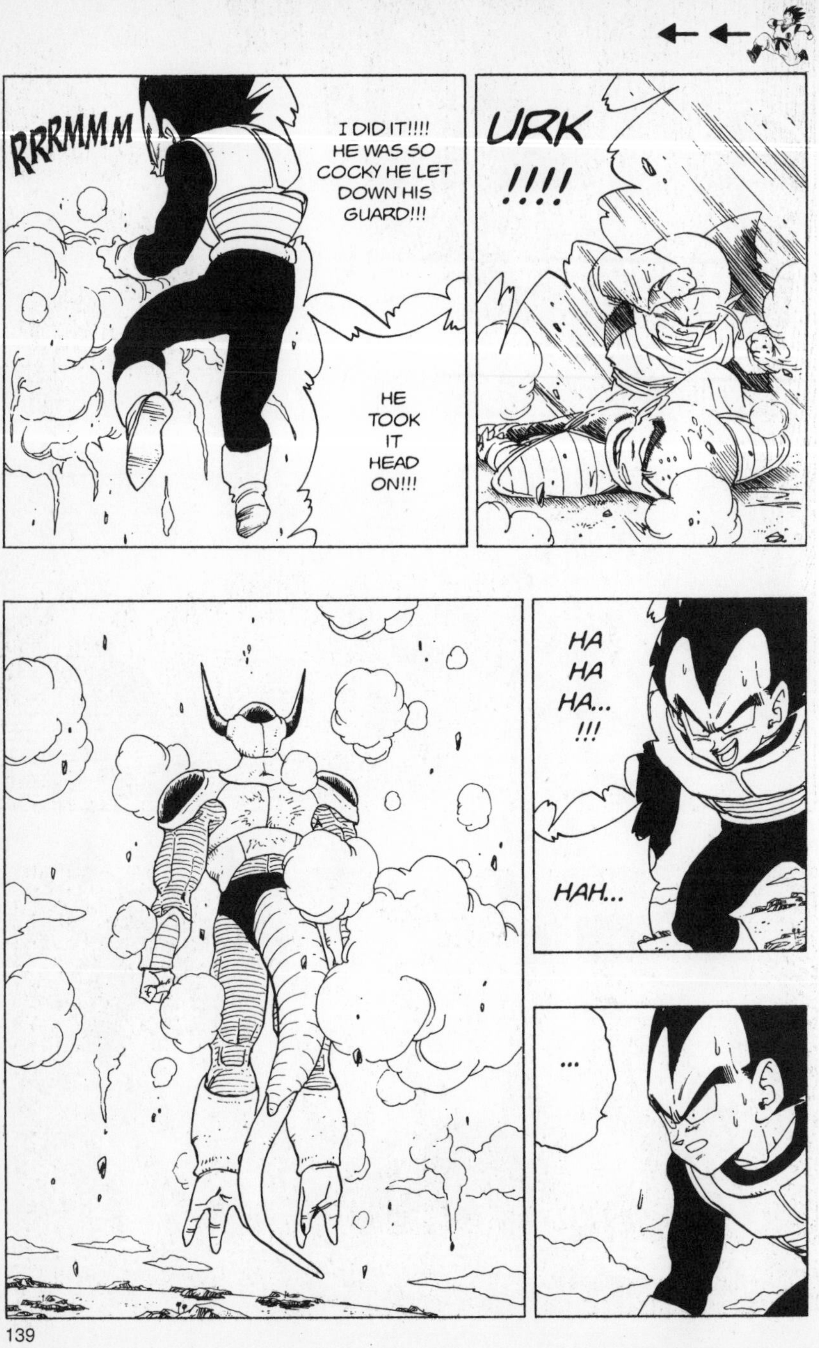
URK
!!!!
I DID IT!!!! HE WAS SO COCKY HE LET DOWN HIS GUARD!!!
RRRMMM
HE TOOK IT HEAD ON!!!
HA HA HA... !!!
HAH...
...

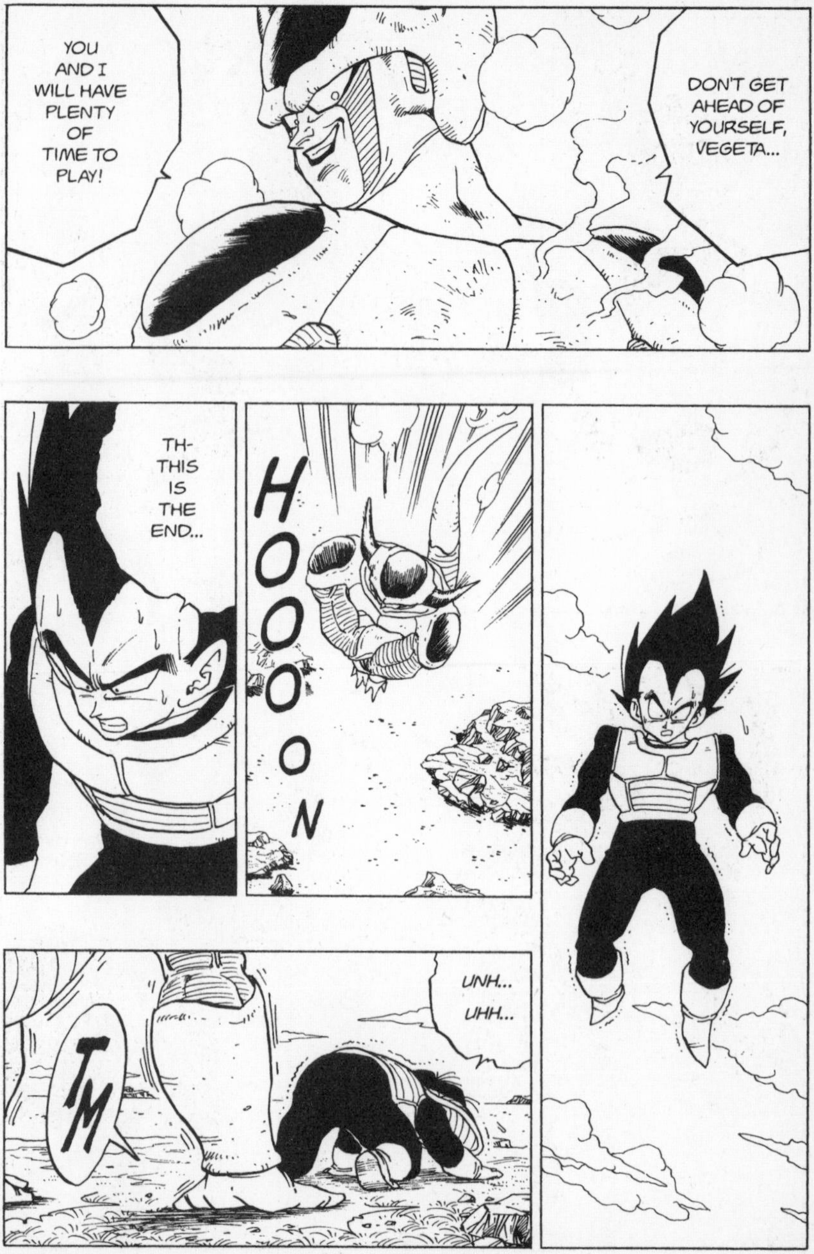
DON'T GET AHEAD OF YOURSELF, VEGETA...
YOU AND I WILL HAVE PLENTY OF TIME TO PLAY!
HOOOOON
TH-THIS IS THE END...
UNH... UHH...
TM

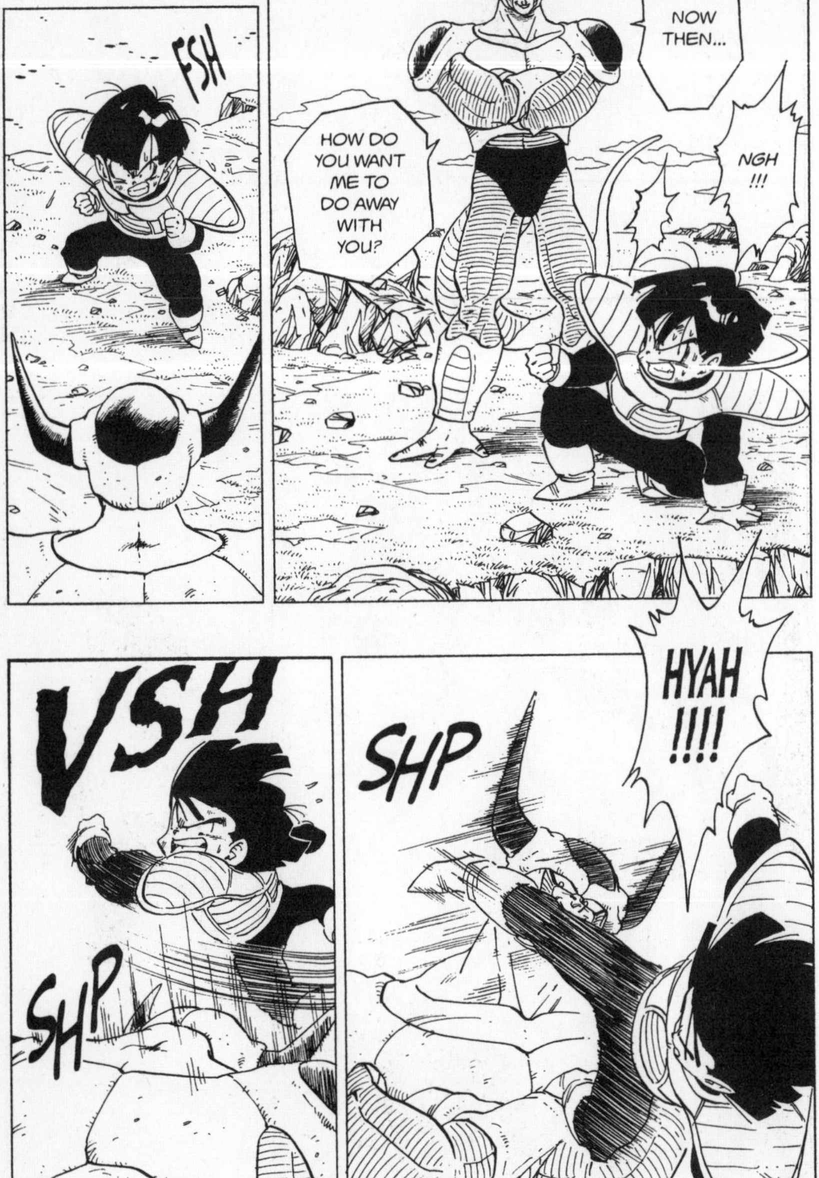
NOW THEN...
HOW DO YOU WANT ME TO DO AWAY WITH YOU?
NGH !!!
FSH
HYAH !!!!
SHP
VSH
SHP

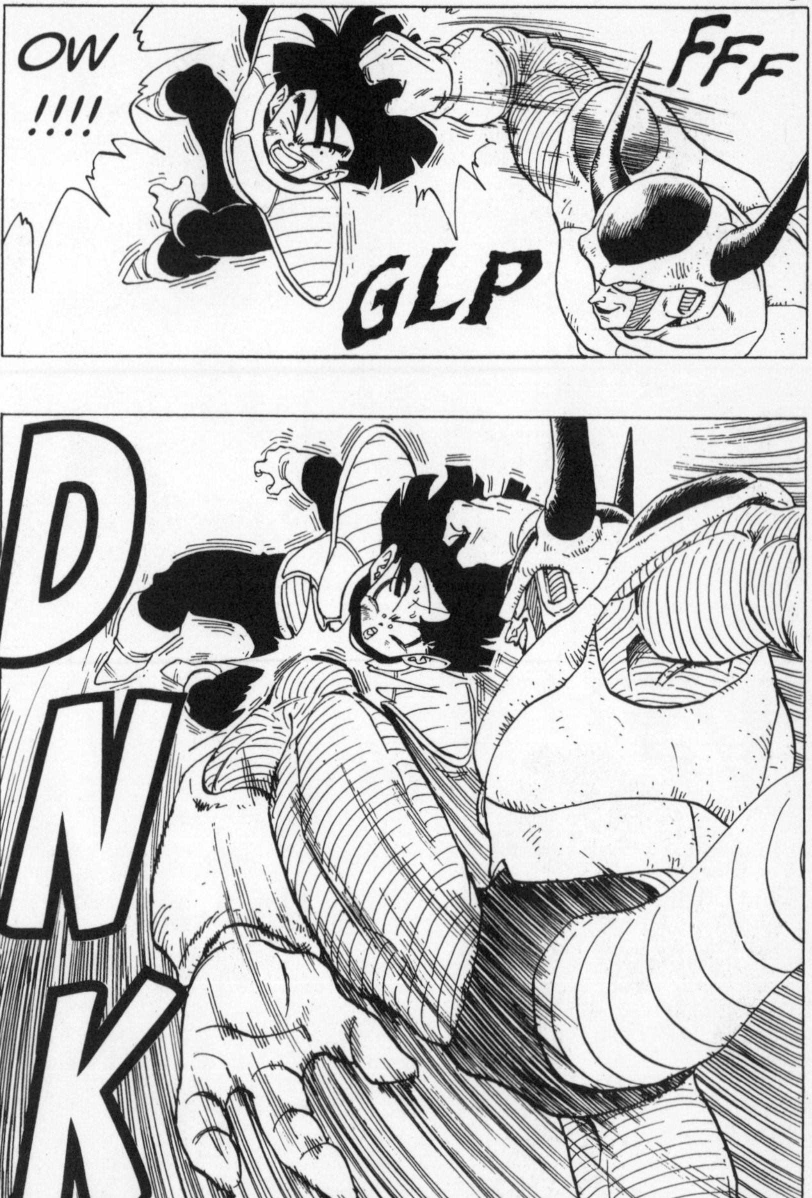
FFF
OW !!!!
GLP
DNK

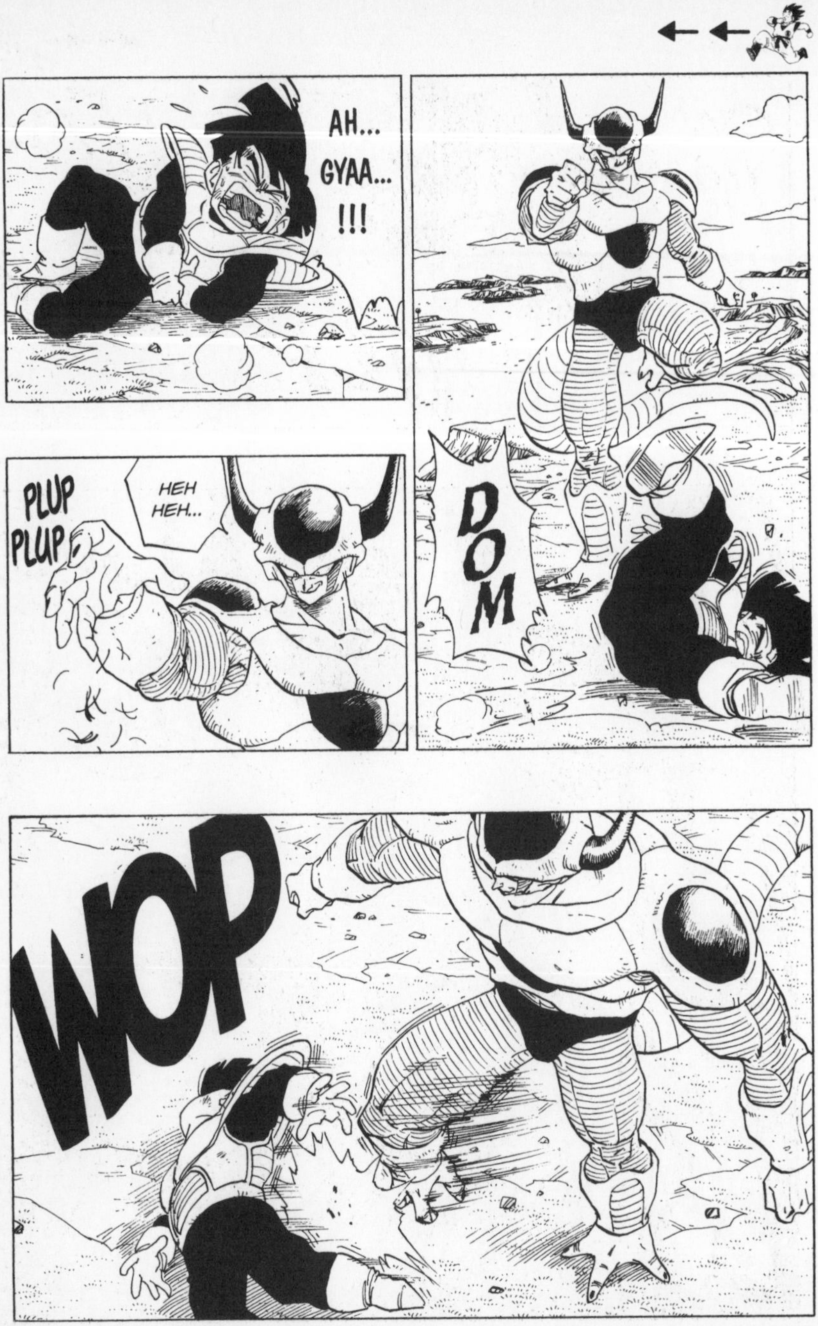
DOM
AH... GYAA... !!!
HEH HEH...
PLUP PLUP
WOP

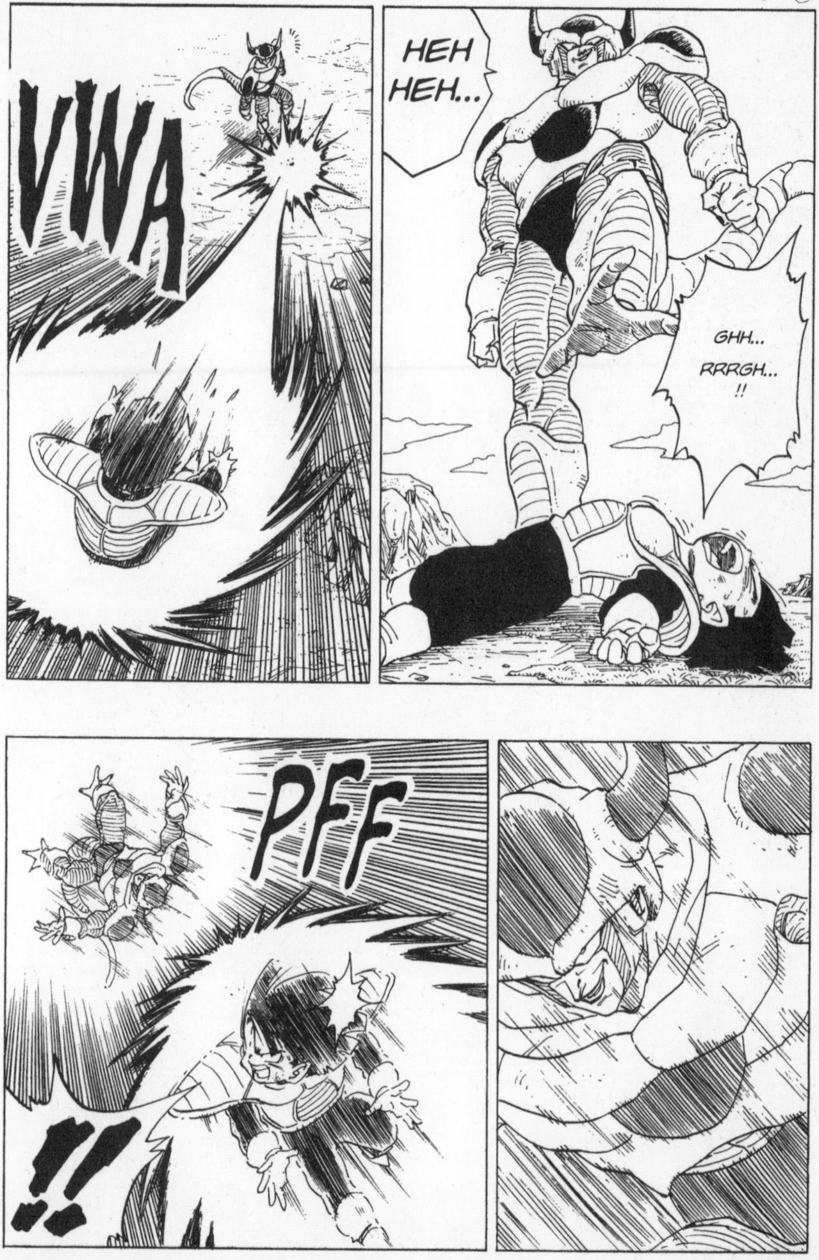
HEH HEH...
GHH... RRRGH... !!
VWA
PFF
!!

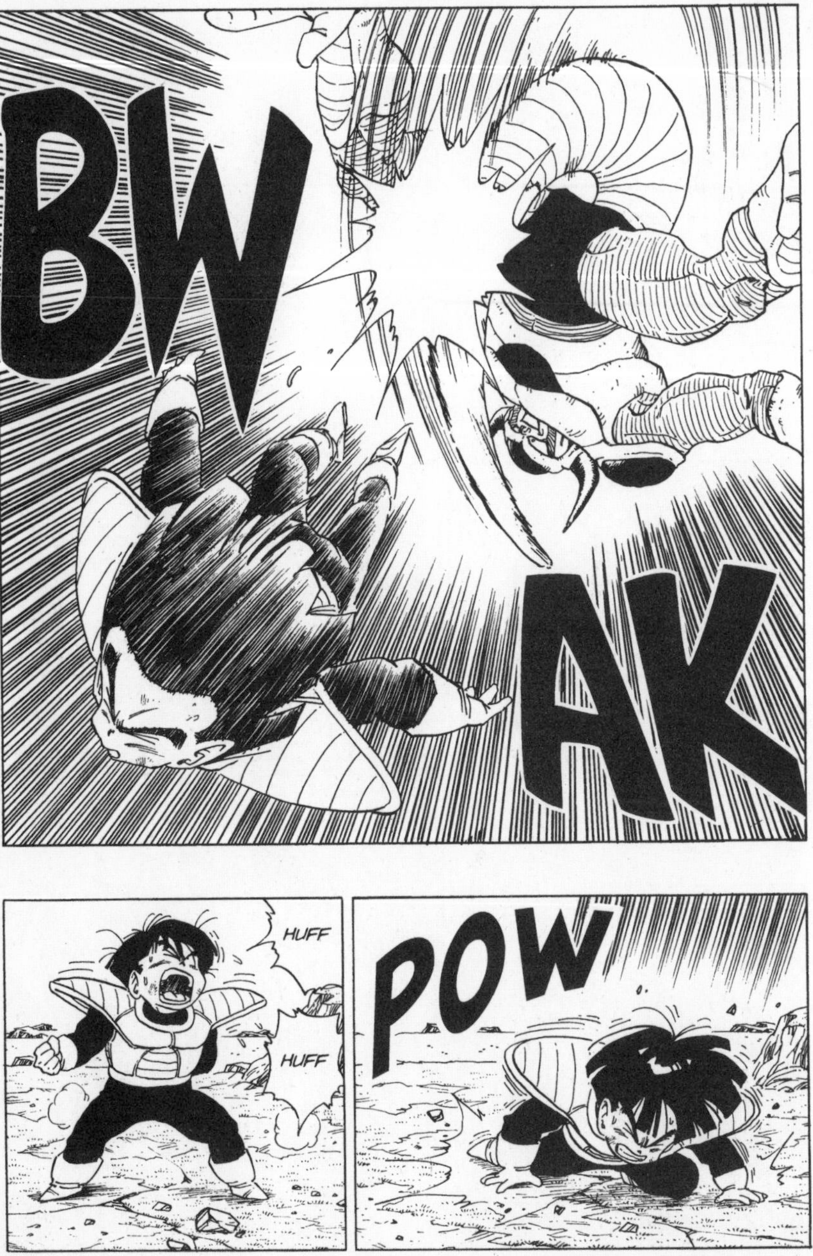
BW
AK
POW
HUFF
HUFF

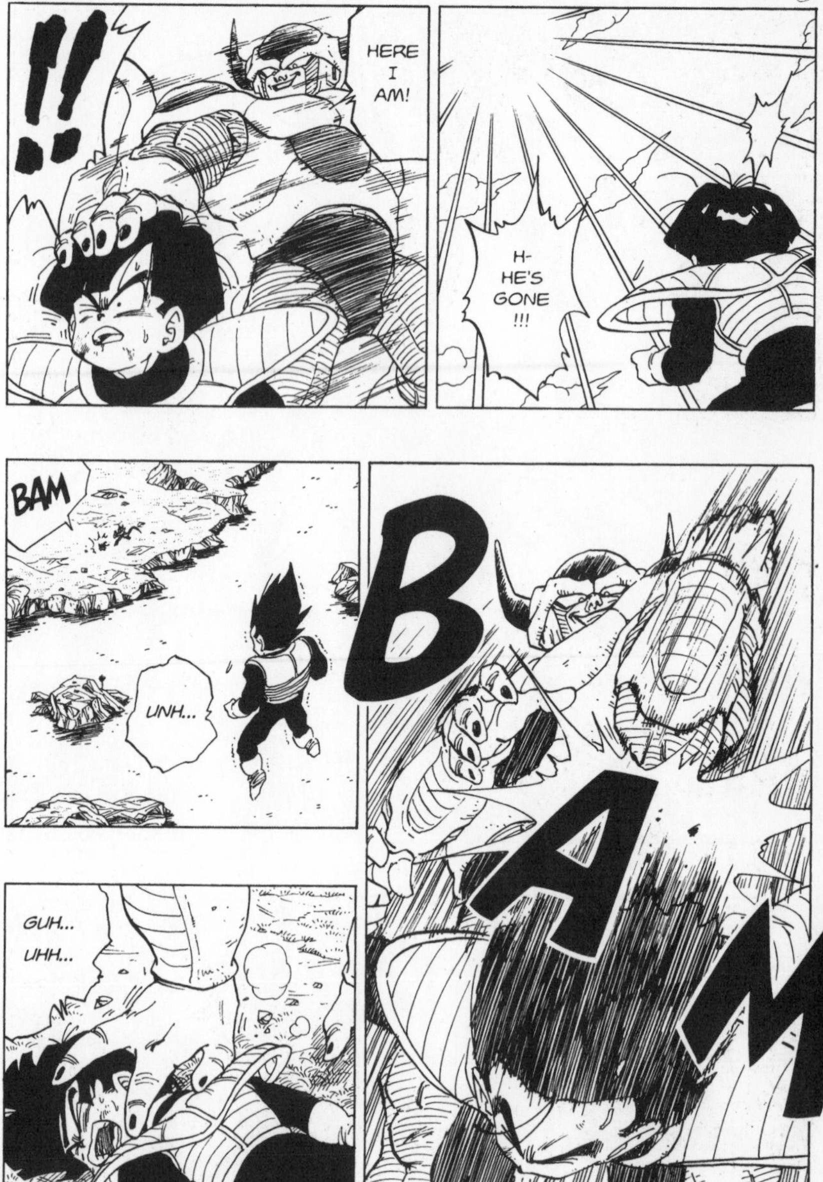
H-
HE'S
GONE
!!!
!!
HERE
I
AM!
BAM
BAM
UNH...
GUH...
UHH...

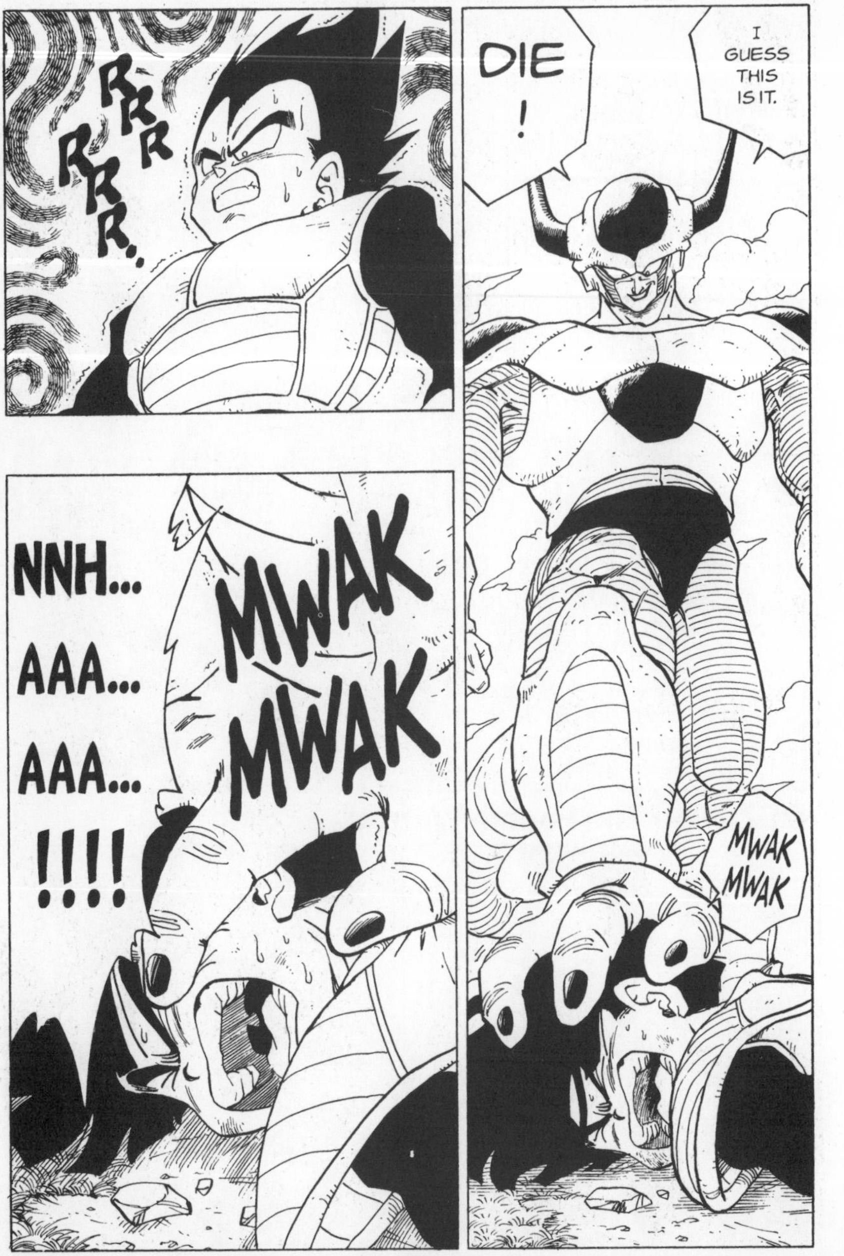
I GUESS THIS IS IT.
DIE!
MWAK MWAK
RRRRRR..
MWAK MWAK
NNH... AAA... AAA... !!!!

NEXT: Dende to the Rescue?

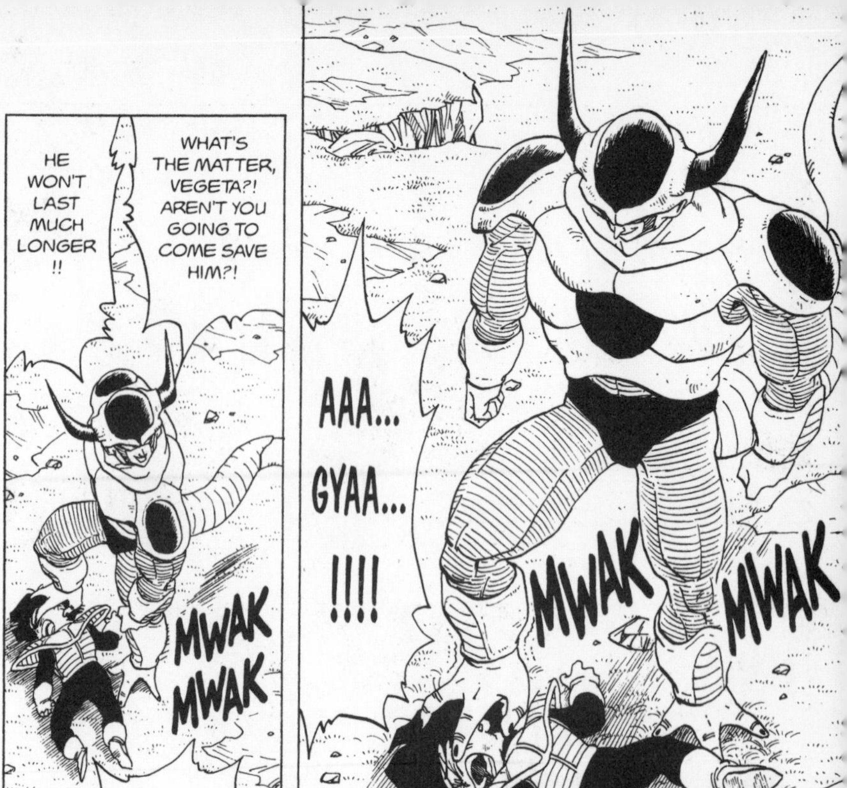
AAA... GYAA... !!!!
MWAK
MWAK
WHAT'S THE MATTER, VEGETA?! AREN'T YOU GOING TO COME SAVE HIM?!
HE WON'T LAST MUCH LONGER !!
MWAK MWAK
UHH...!! GUH...

DBZ:105 • The Fourth Warrior

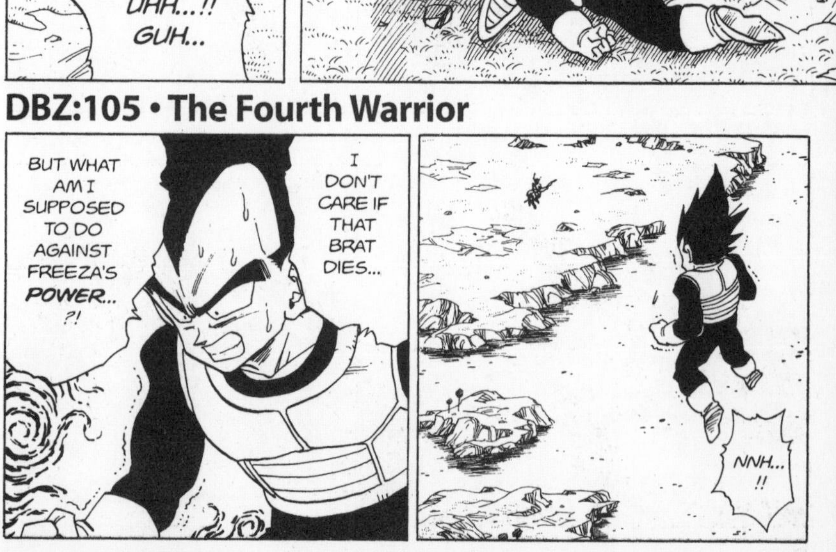
NNH... !!
I DON'T CARE IF THAT BRAT DIES...
BUT WHAT AM I SUPPOSED TO DO AGAINST FREEZA'S POWER... ?!

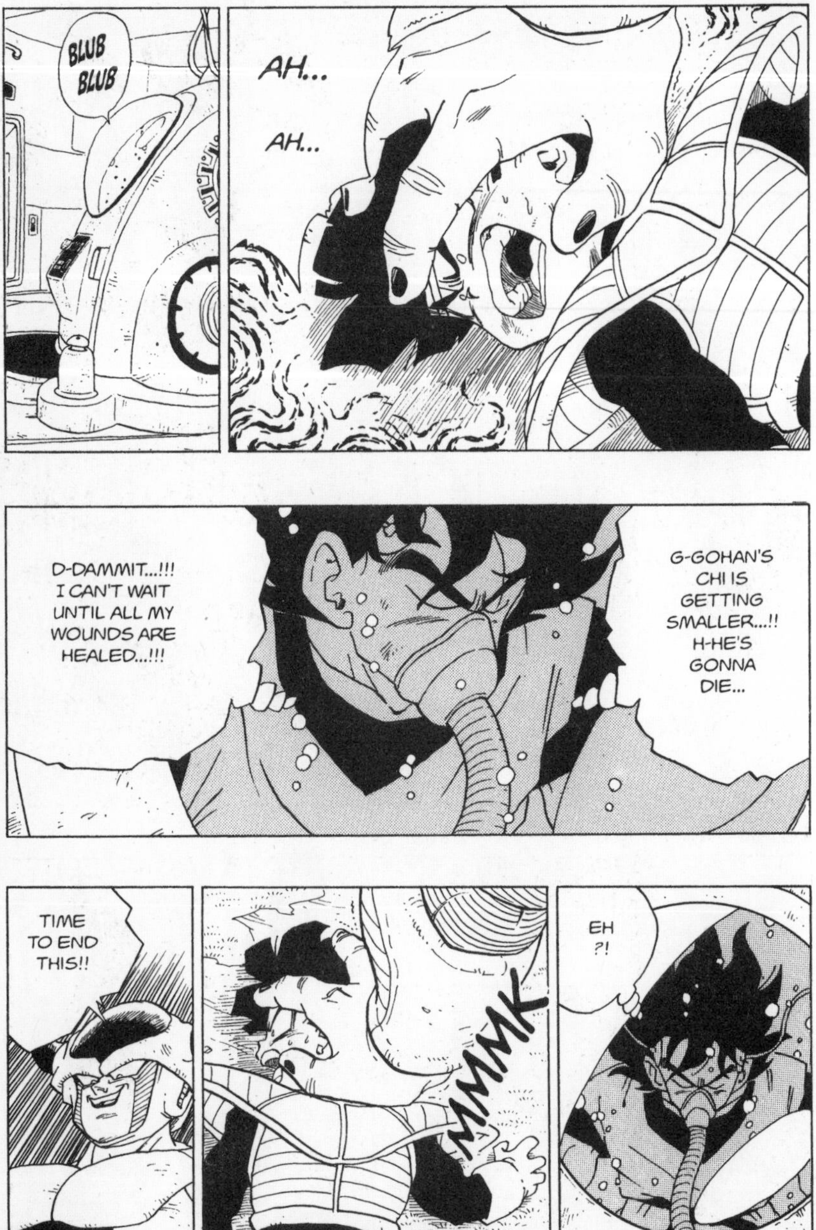
AH...
AH...
BLUB BLUB
G-GOHAN'S CHI IS GETTING SMALLER...!! H-HE'S GONNA DIE...
D-DAMMIT...!!! I CAN'T WAIT UNTIL ALL MY WOUNDS ARE HEALED...!!!
EH ?!
MMMK
TIME TO END THIS!!

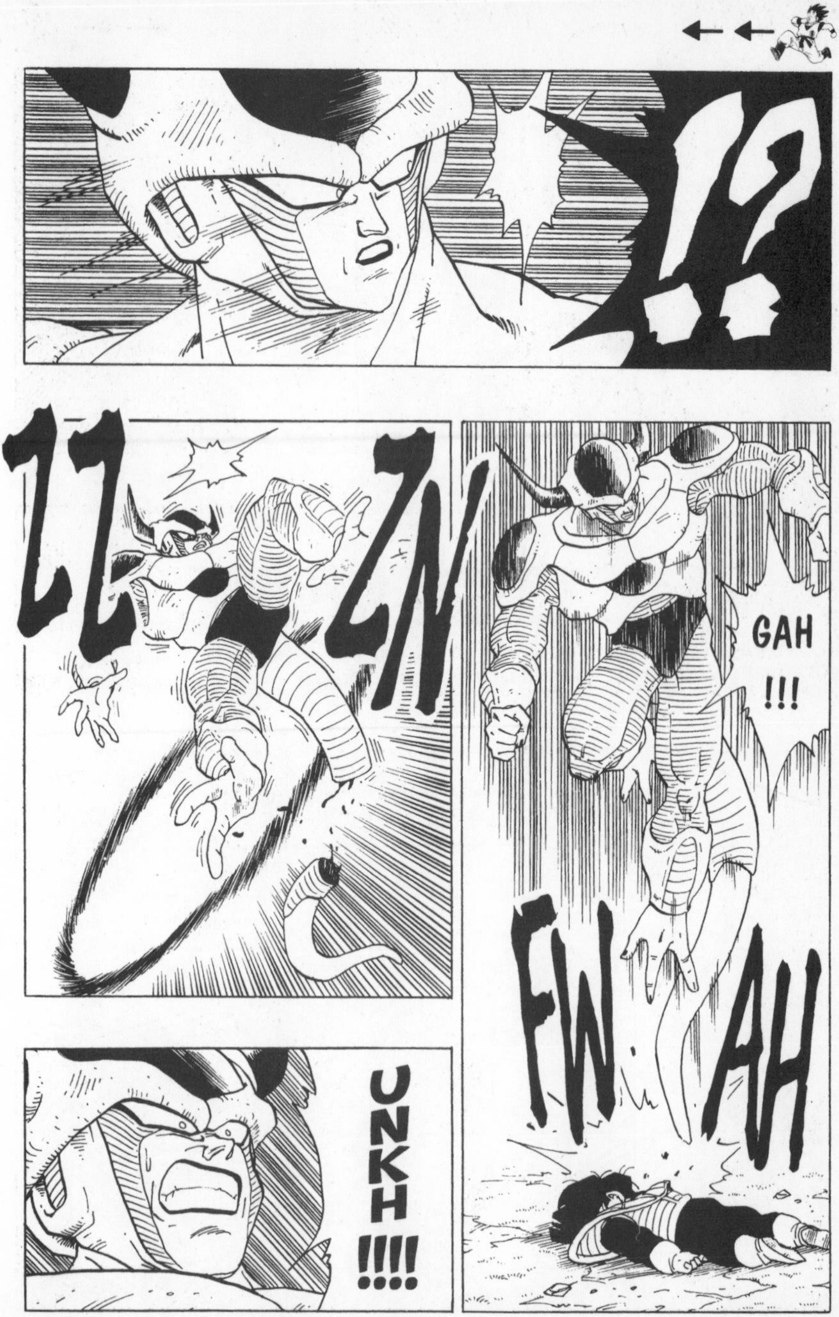
!?
GAH !!!
FW AH
ZZ ZN
UNKH !!!!

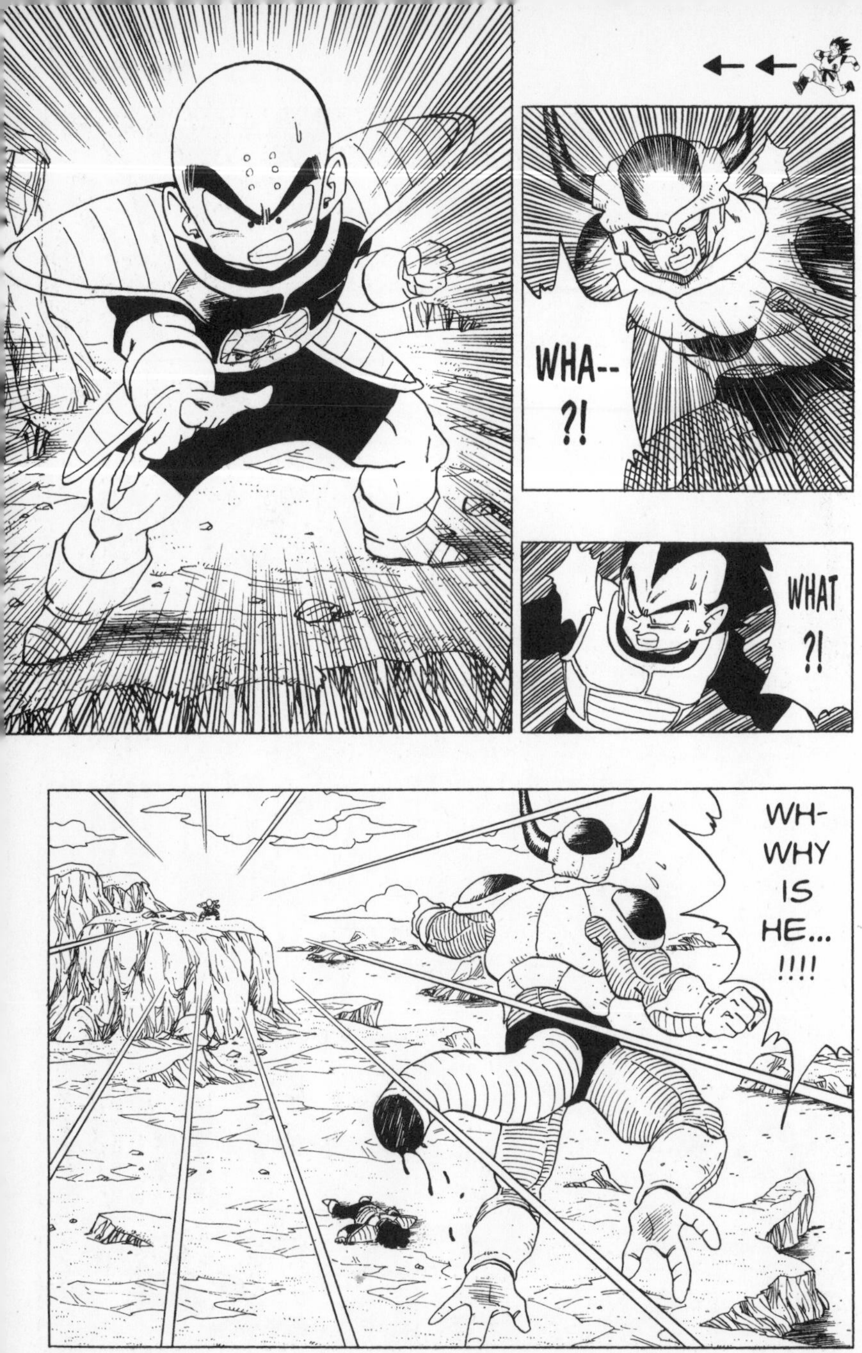
WHA-- ?!
WHAT ?!
WH- WHY IS HE... !!!!

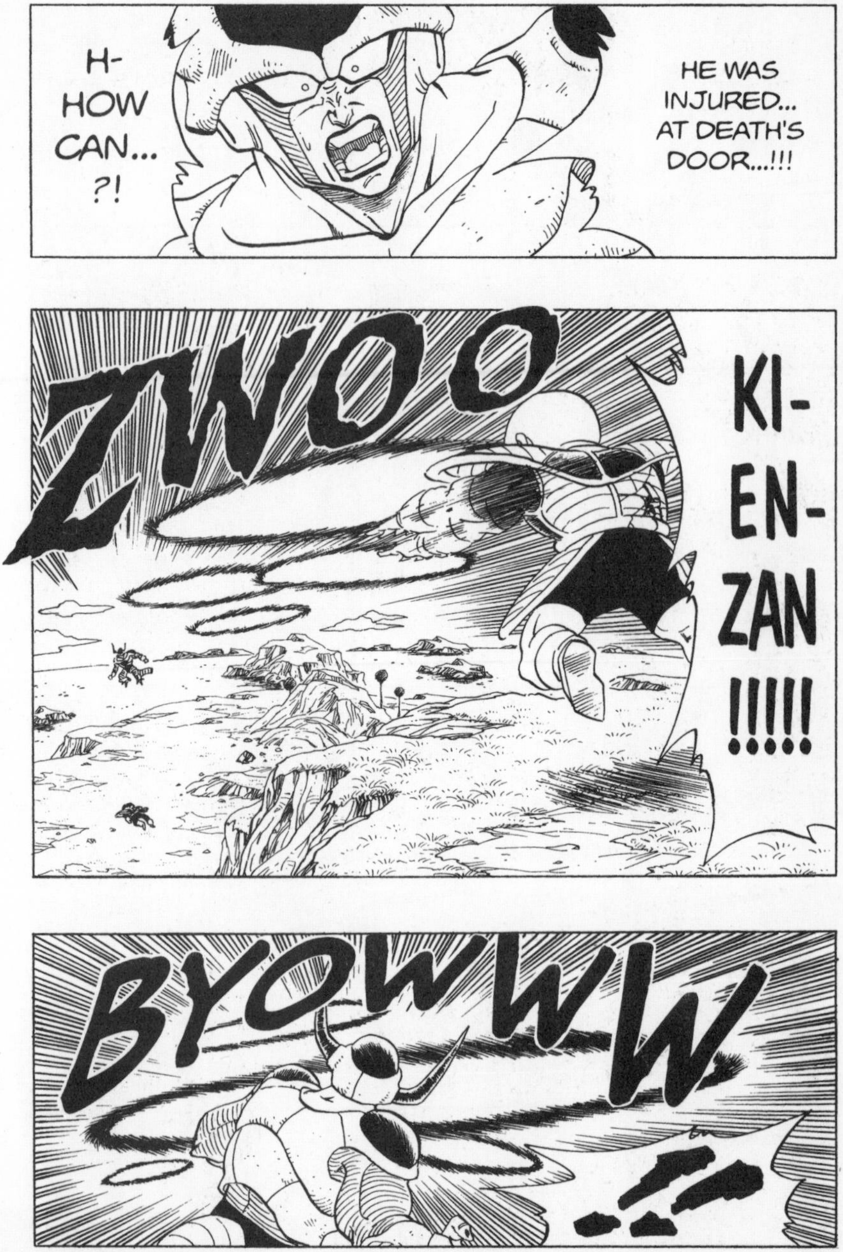
HE WAS INJURED... AT DEATH'S DOOR...!!!
H- HOW CAN... ?!
KI- EN- ZAN !!!!!
ZWOOO
BYOWWW

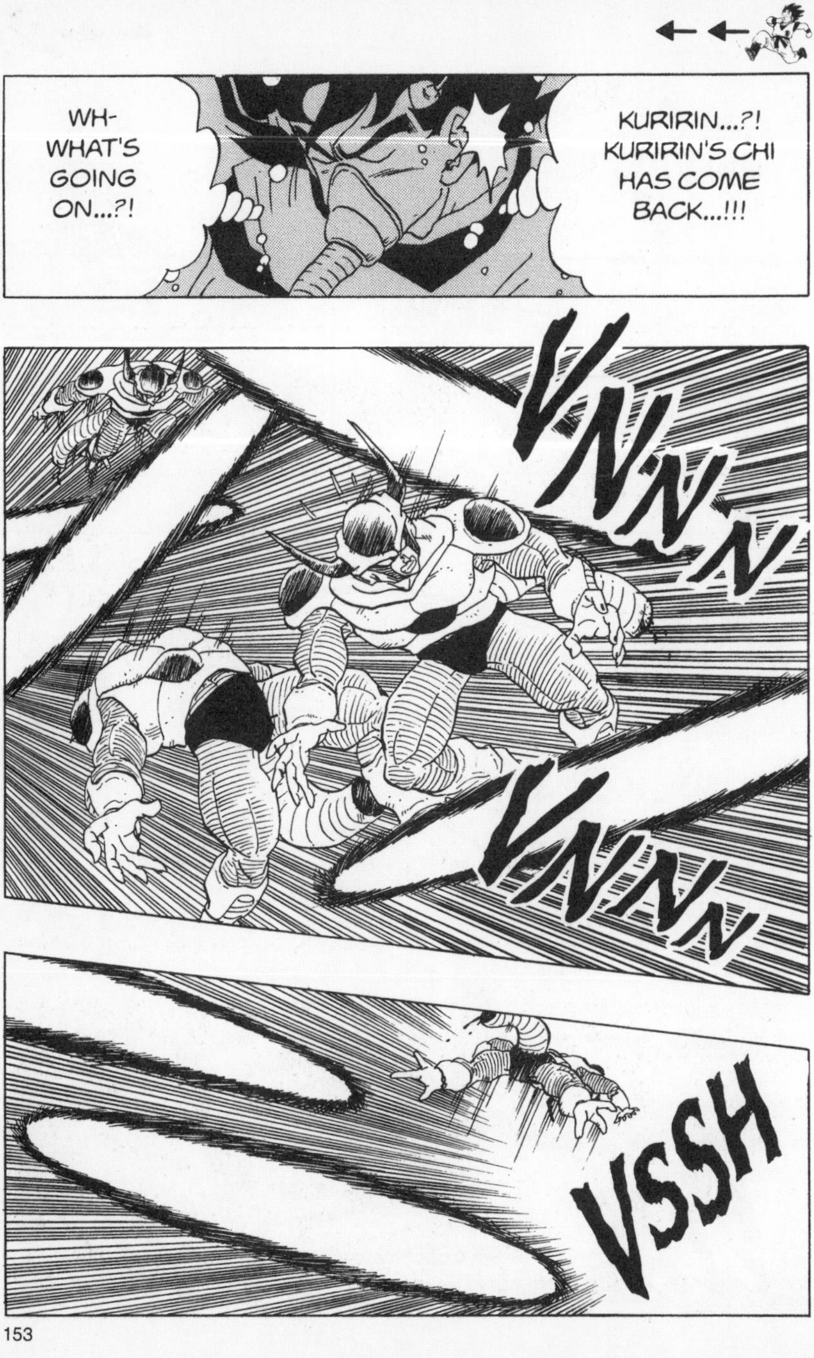
KURIRIN...?! KURIRIN'S CHI HAS COME BACK...!!!
WH- WHAT'S GOING ON...?!
VNNNN
VNNNNN
VSSH

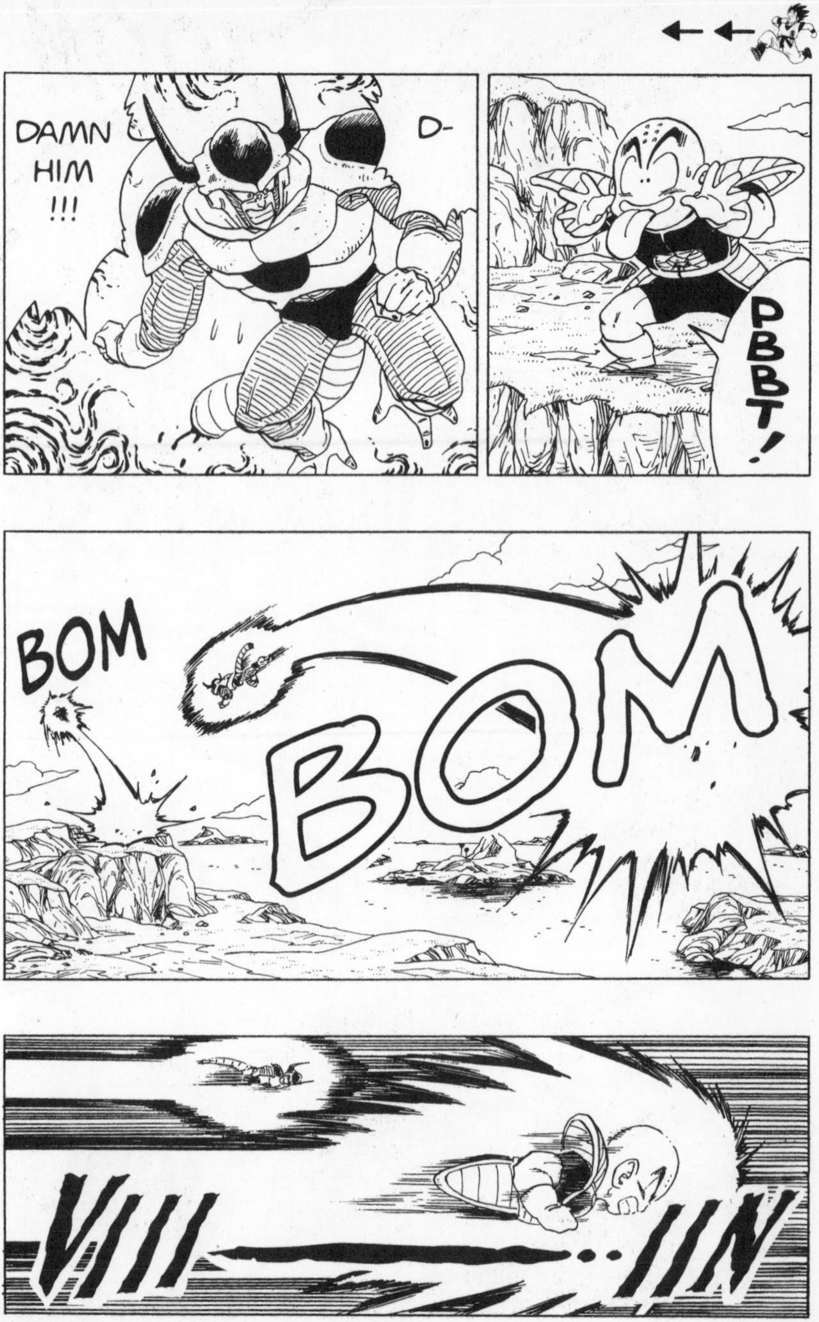
PBBT!
D-
DAMN HIM!!!
BOM
BOM
VII……IIN

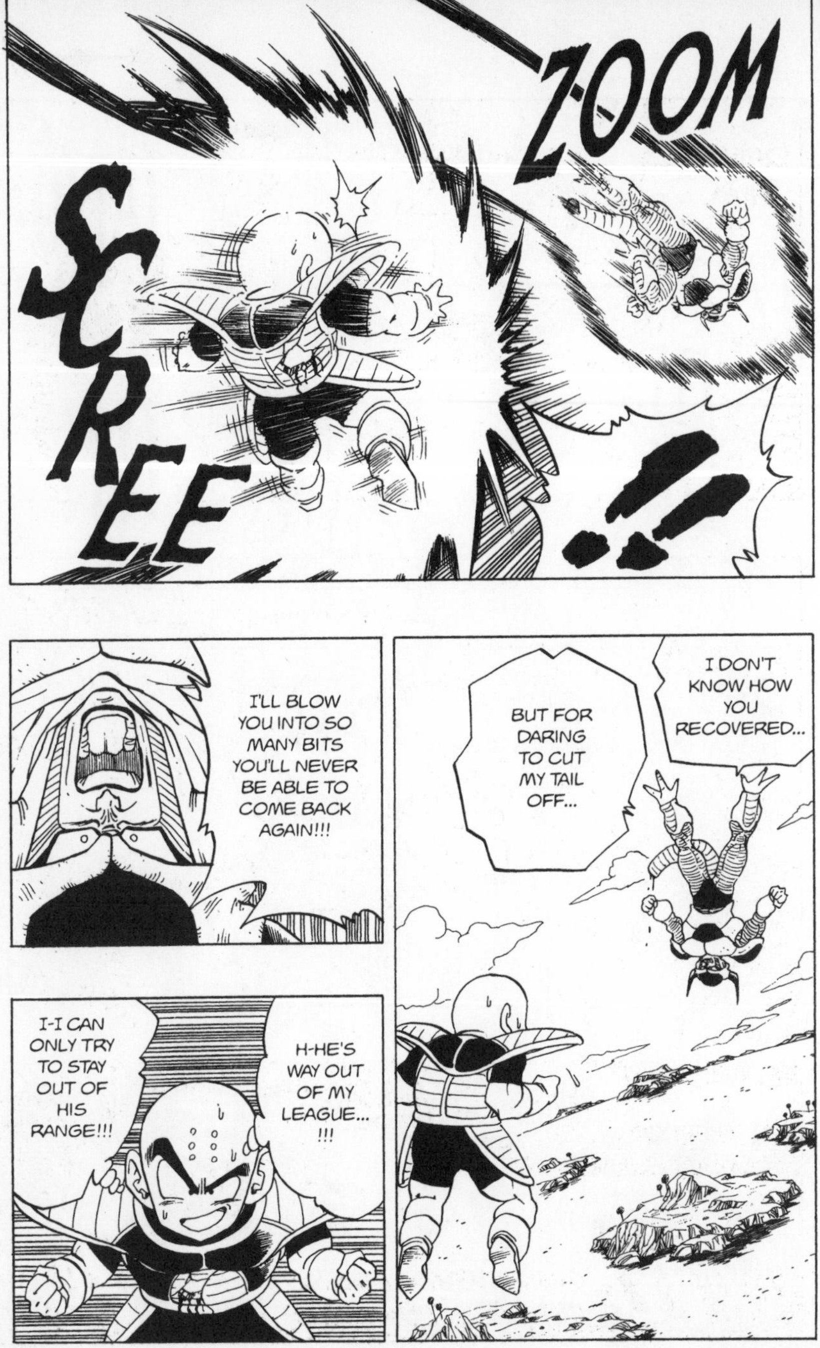
ZOOM
SCREE
!!
I DON'T KNOW HOW YOU RECOVERED...
BUT FOR DARING TO CUT MY TAIL OFF...
I'LL BLOW YOU INTO SO MANY BITS YOU'LL NEVER BE ABLE TO COME BACK AGAIN!!!
H-HE'S WAY OUT OF MY LEAGUE... !!!
I-I CAN ONLY TRY TO STAY OUT OF HIS RANGE!!!

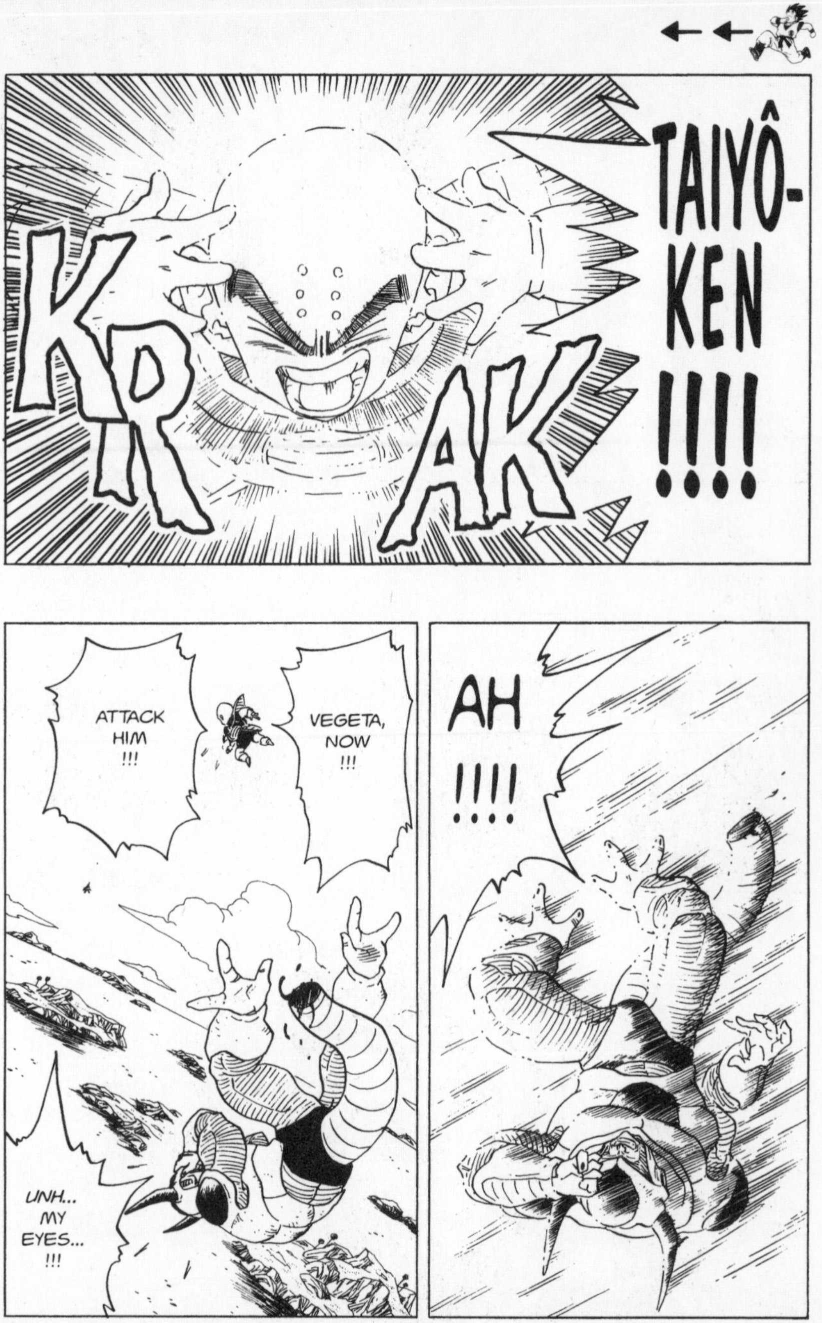
TAIYÔ-KEN !!!!
KRAK
AH !!!!
VEGETA, NOW !!!
ATTACK HIM !!!
UNH... MY EYES... !!!

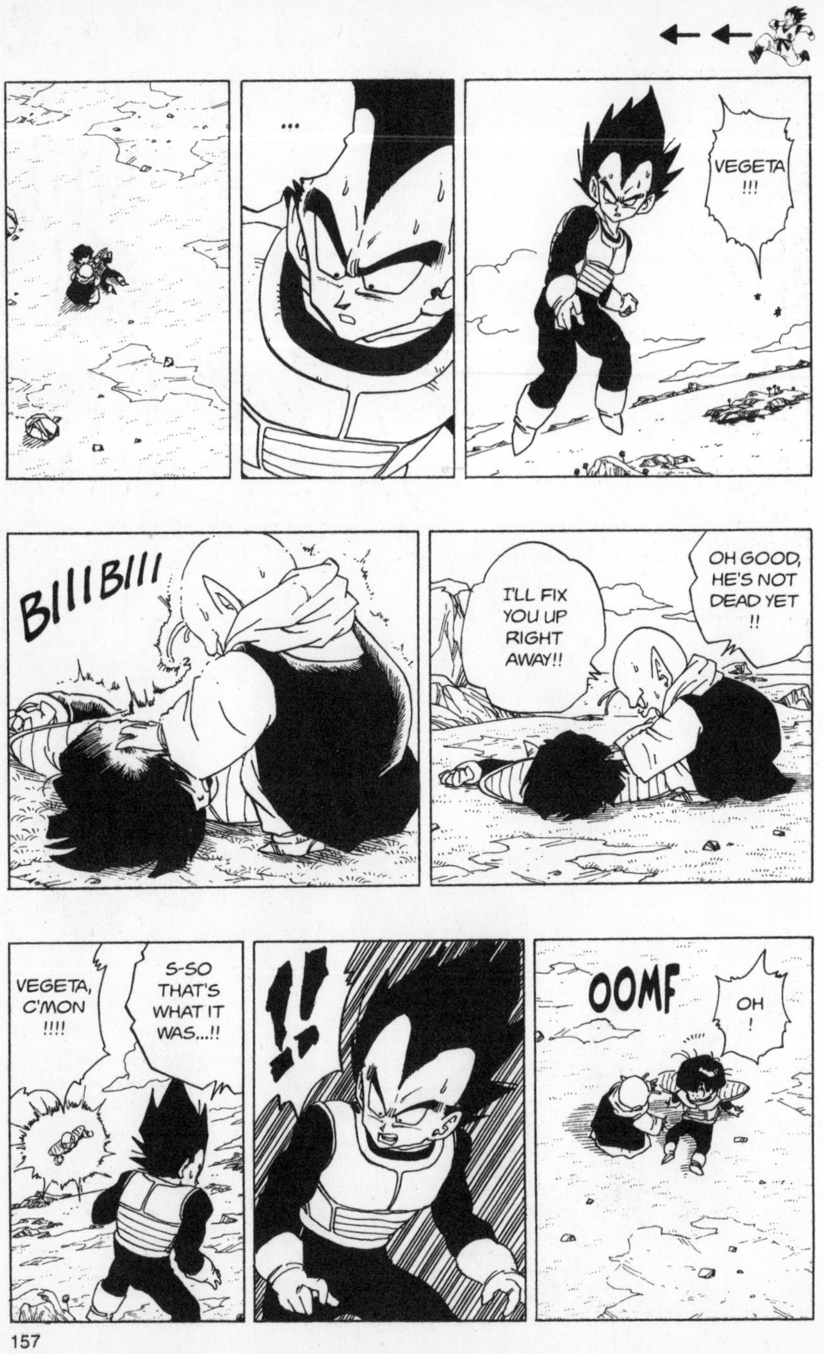
VEGETA !!!
...
OH GOOD, HE'S NOT DEAD YET !!
I'LL FIX YOU UP RIGHT AWAY!!
BIIIBIII
OOMF
OH !
!!
S-SO THAT'S WHAT IT WAS...!!
VEGETA, C'MON !!!!

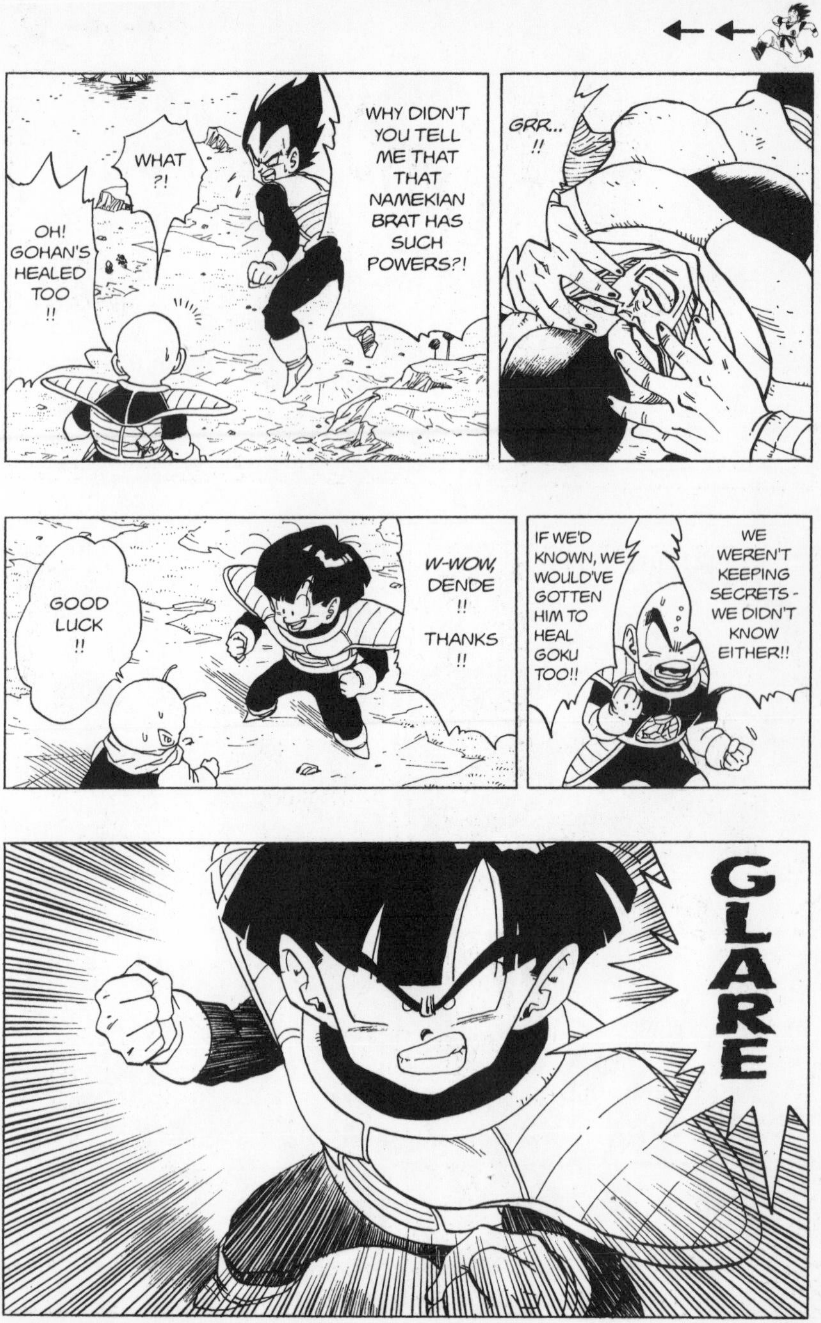
GRR... !!
WHY DIDN'T YOU TELL ME THAT THAT NAMEKIAN BRAT HAS SUCH POWERS?!
WHAT ?!
OH! GOHAN'S HEALED TOO !!
WE WEREN'T KEEPING SECRETS - WE DIDN'T KNOW EITHER!!
IF WE'D KNOWN, WE WOULD'VE GOTTEN HIM TO HEAL GOKU TOO!!
W-WOW, DENDE !!
THANKS !!
GOOD LUCK !!
GLARE

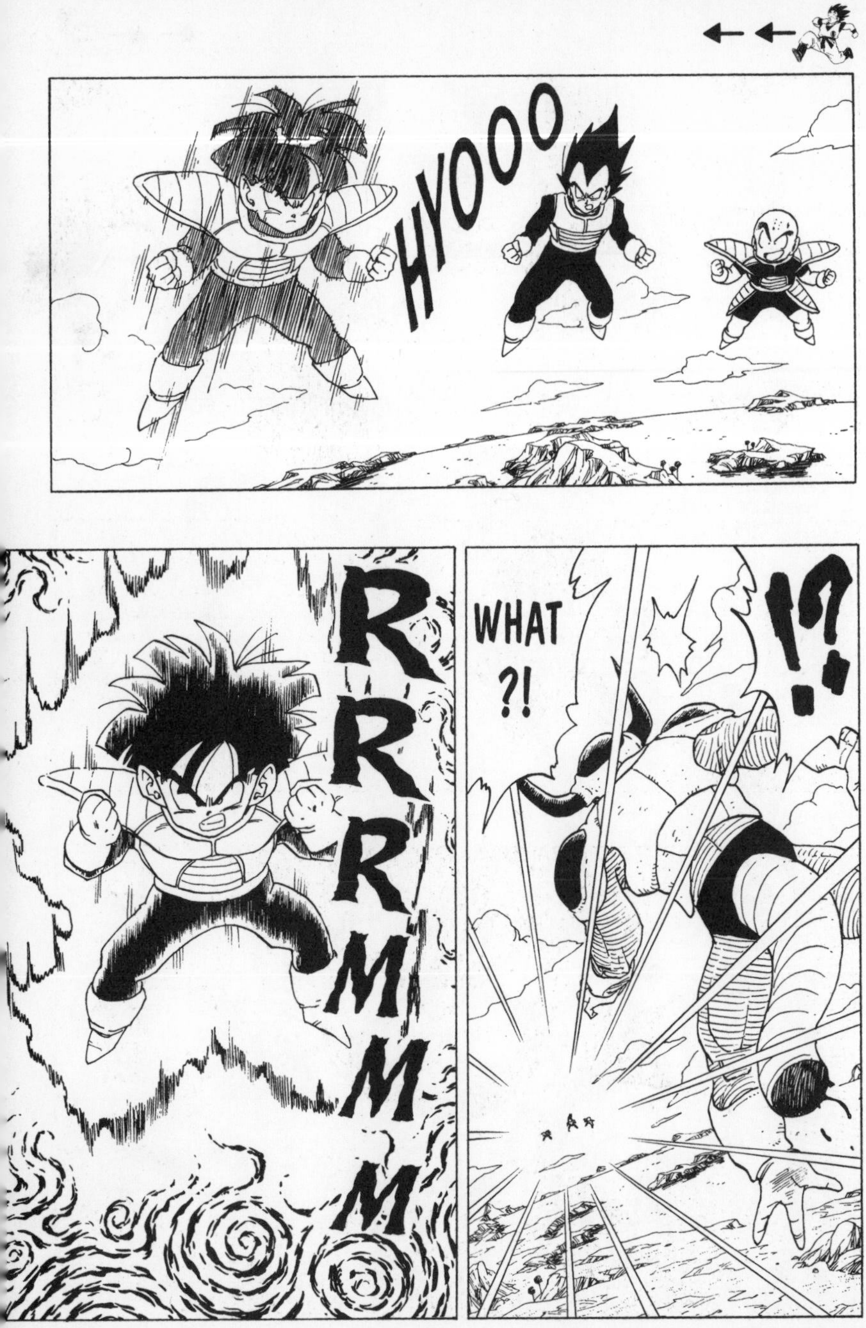

HYOOO
WHAT ?!
!?
RRRMMMM

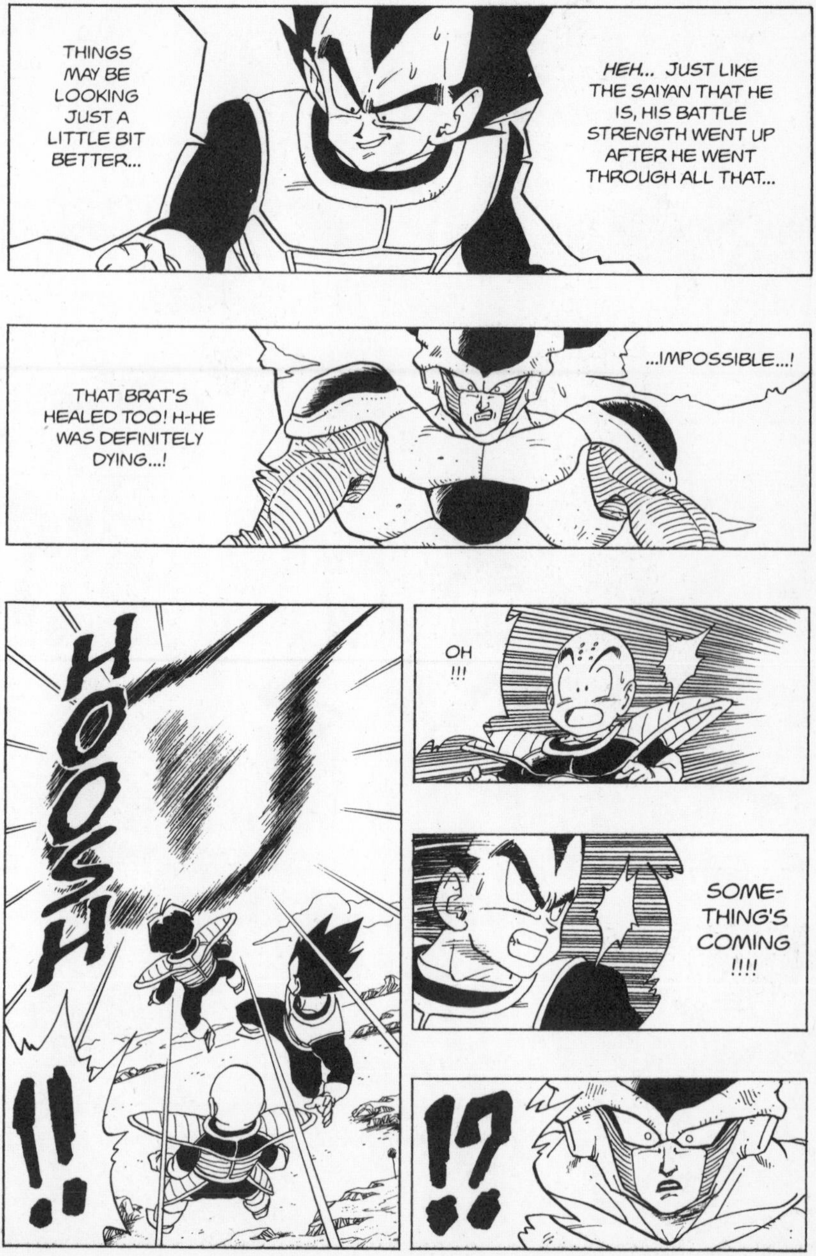
HEH... JUST LIKE THE SAIYAN THAT HE IS, HIS BATTLE STRENGTH WENT UP AFTER HE WENT THROUGH ALL THAT...
THINGS MAY BE LOOKING JUST A LITTLE BIT BETTER...
...IMPOSSIBLE...!
THAT BRAT'S HEALED TOO! H-HE WAS DEFINITELY DYING...!
OH !!!
SOME-THING'S COMING !!!!
!?
HOOSH
!!

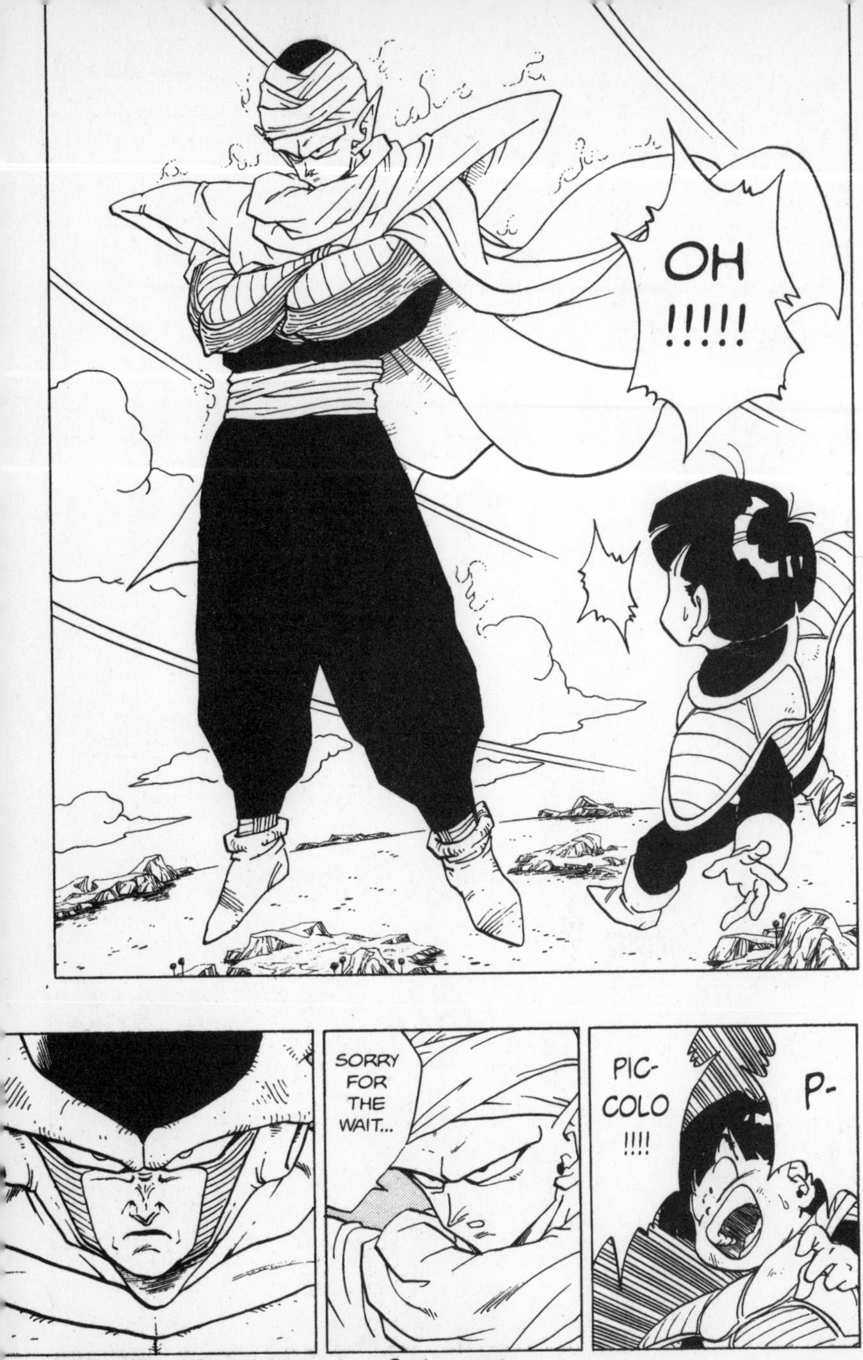
OH !!!!!
P-
PIC-COLO !!!!
SORRY FOR THE WAIT...

NEXT: The Wrath of Namek

DBZ:106 • Freeza vs. Piccolo

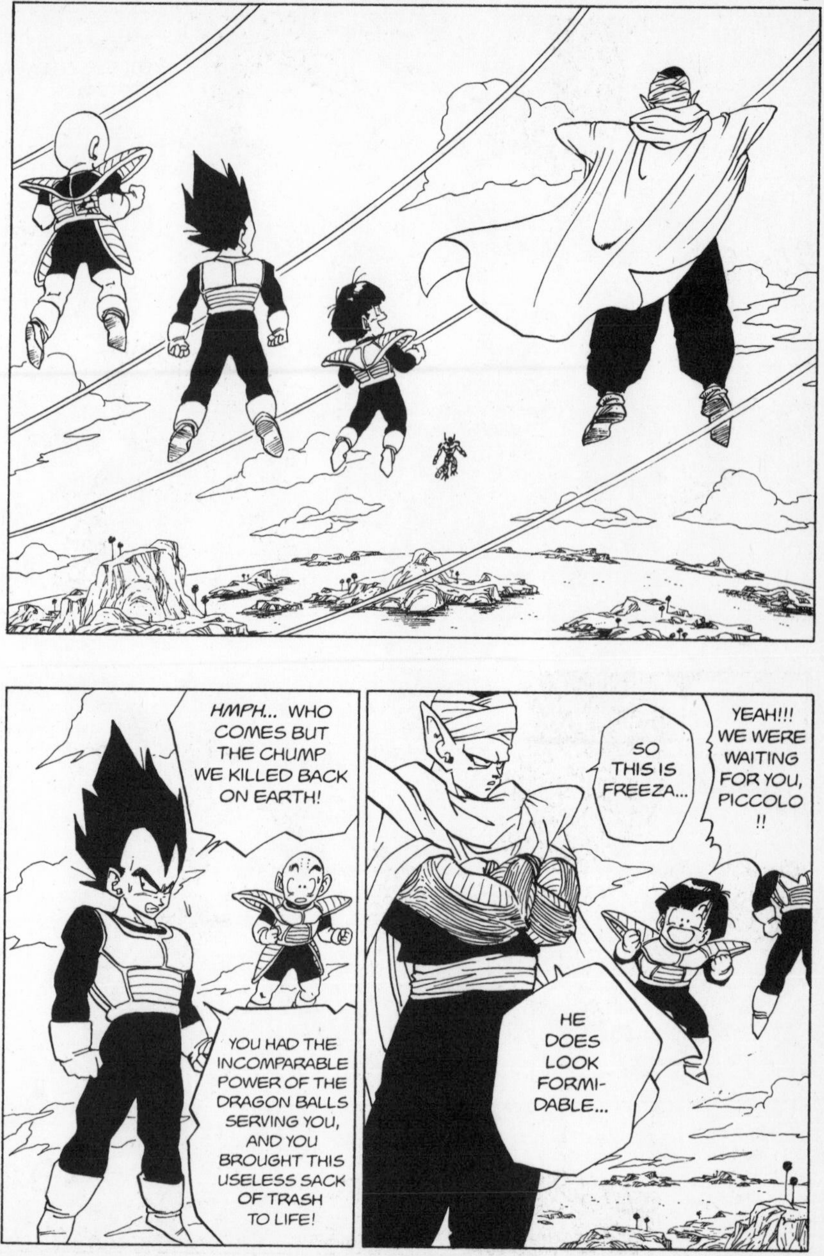

YEAH!!! WE WERE WAITING FOR YOU, PICCOLO !!
SO THIS IS FREEZA...
HE DOES LOOK FORMIDABLE...
HMPH... WHO COMES BUT THE CHUMP WE KILLED BACK ON EARTH!
YOU HAD THE INCOMPARABLE POWER OF THE DRAGON BALLS SERVING YOU, AND YOU BROUGHT THIS USELESS SACK OF TRASH TO LIFE!

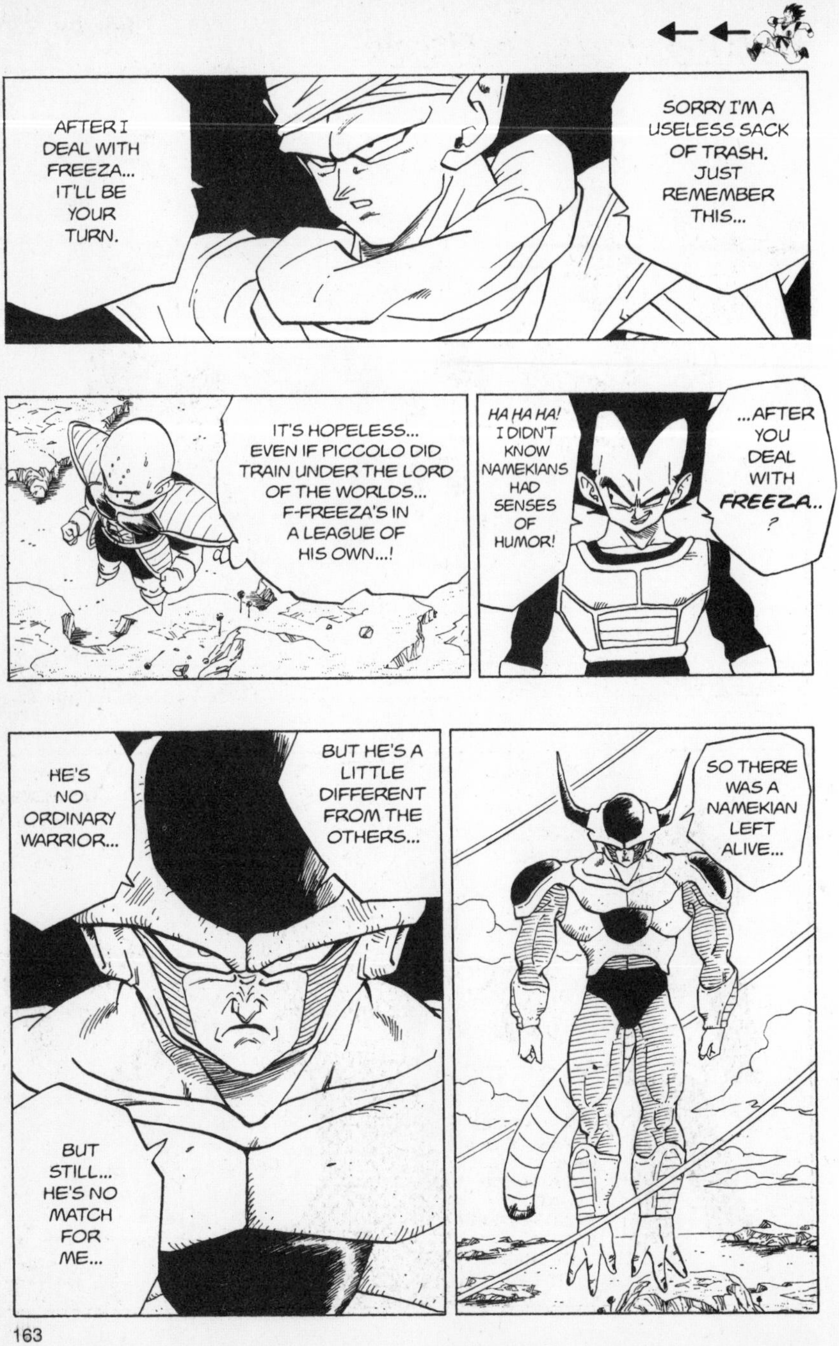
SORRY I'M A USELESS SACK OF TRASH. JUST REMEMBER THIS...
AFTER I DEAL WITH FREEZA... IT'LL BE YOUR TURN.
...AFTER YOU DEAL WITH FREEZA.. ?
HA HA HA! I DIDN'T KNOW NAMEKIANS HAD SENSES OF HUMOR!
IT'S HOPELESS... EVEN IF PICCOLO DID TRAIN UNDER THE LORD OF THE WORLDS... F-FREEZA'S IN A LEAGUE OF HIS OWN...!
SO THERE WAS A NAMEKIAN LEFT ALIVE...
BUT HE'S A LITTLE DIFFERENT FROM THE OTHERS...
HE'S NO ORDINARY WARRIOR...
BUT STILL... HE'S NO MATCH FOR ME...

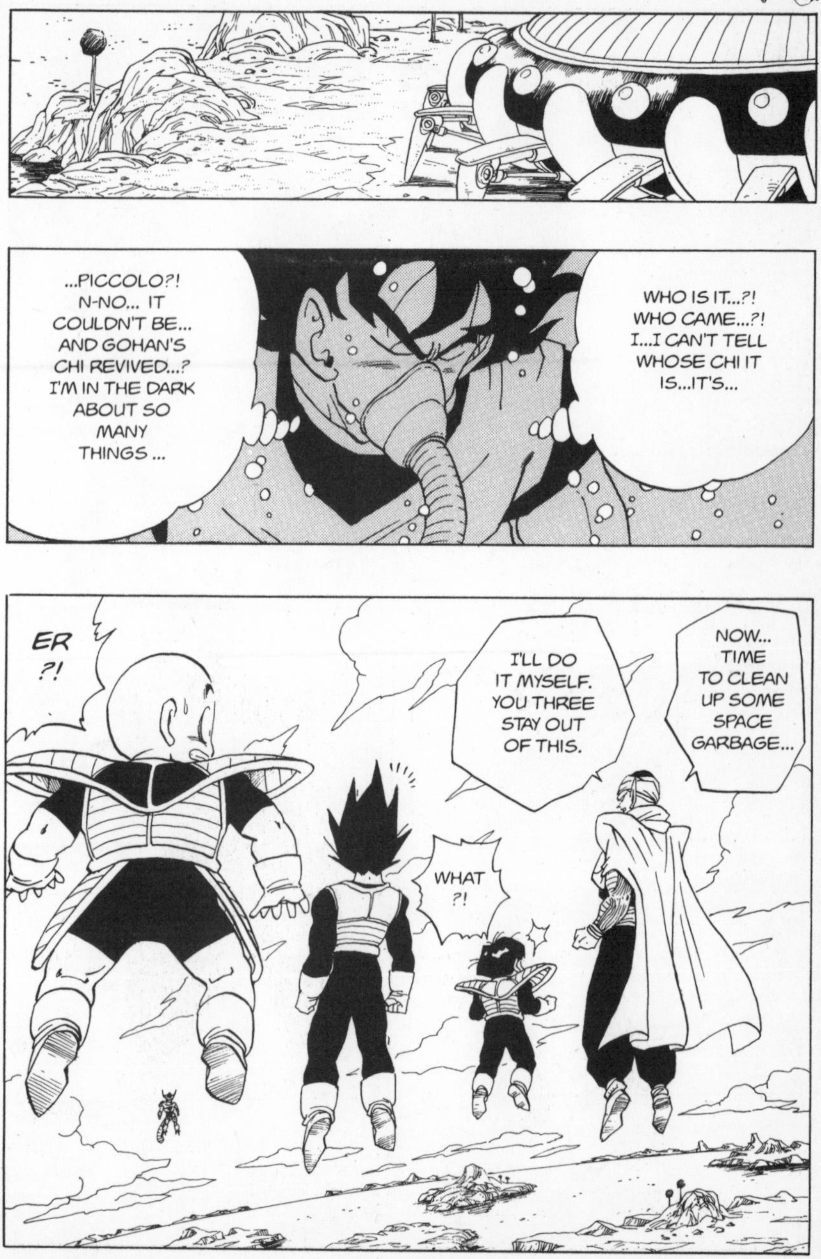
WHO IS IT...?! WHO CAME...?! I...I CAN'T TELL WHOSE CHI IT IS...IT'S...
...PICCOLO?! N-NO... IT COULDN'T BE... AND GOHAN'S CHI REVIVED...? I'M IN THE DARK ABOUT SO MANY THINGS ...
NOW... TIME TO CLEAN UP SOME SPACE GARBAGE...
I'LL DO IT MYSELF. YOU THREE STAY OUT OF THIS.
WHAT ?!
ER ?!

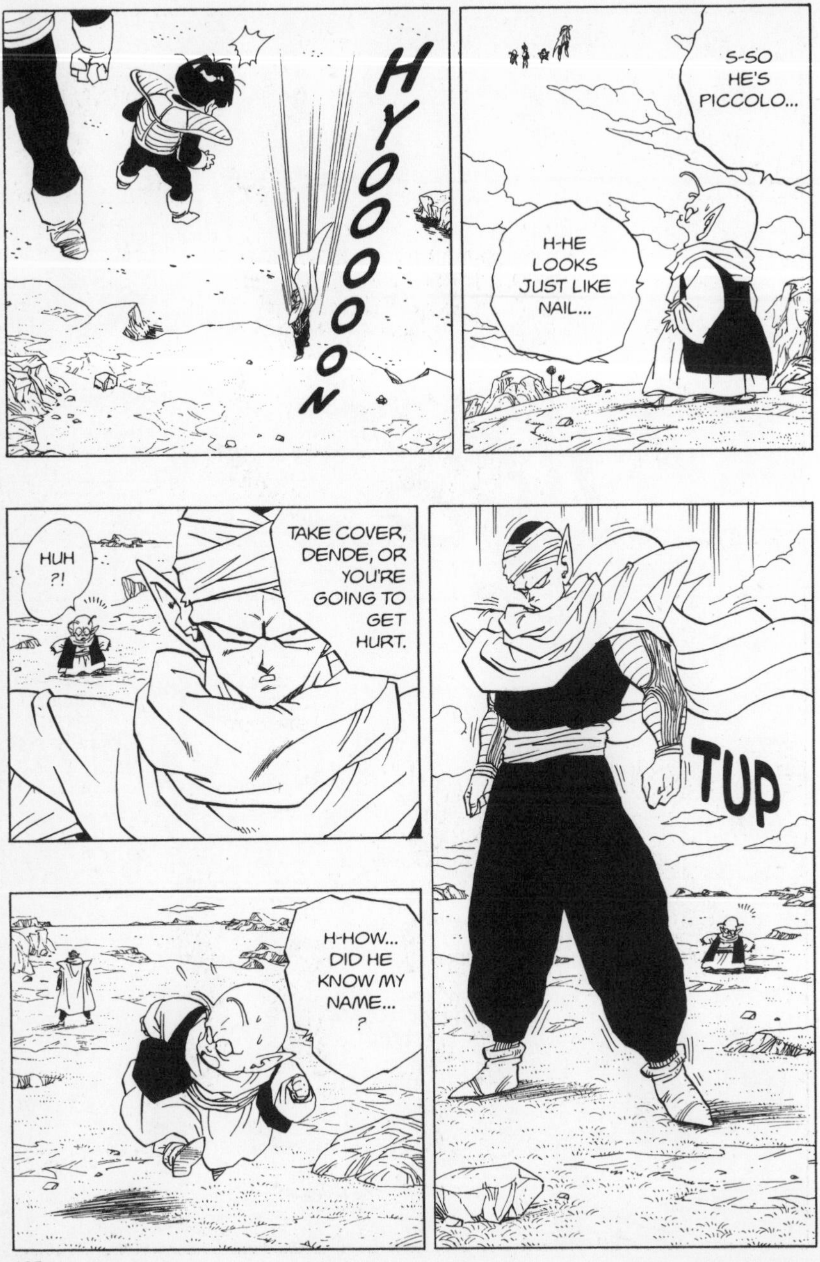
S-SO HE'S PICCOLO...
H-HE LOOKS JUST LIKE NAIL...
HYOOOOOOON
TUP
TAKE COVER, DENDE, OR YOU'RE GOING TO GET HURT.
HUH ?!
H-HOW... DID HE KNOW MY NAME... ?

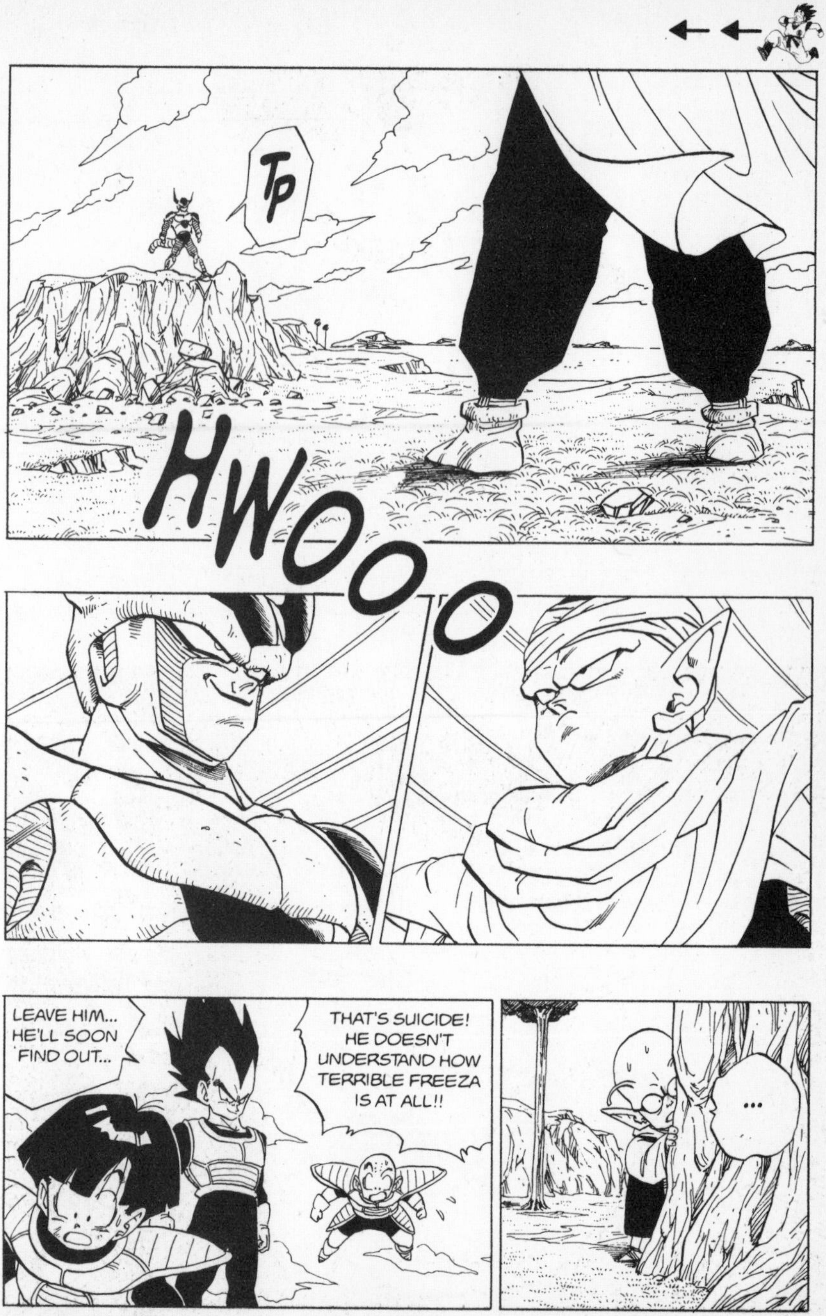
TP
HWOOOO
...
THAT'S SUICIDE! HE DOESN'T UNDERSTAND HOW TERRIBLE FREEZA IS AT ALL!!
LEAVE HIM... HE'LL SOON FIND OUT...

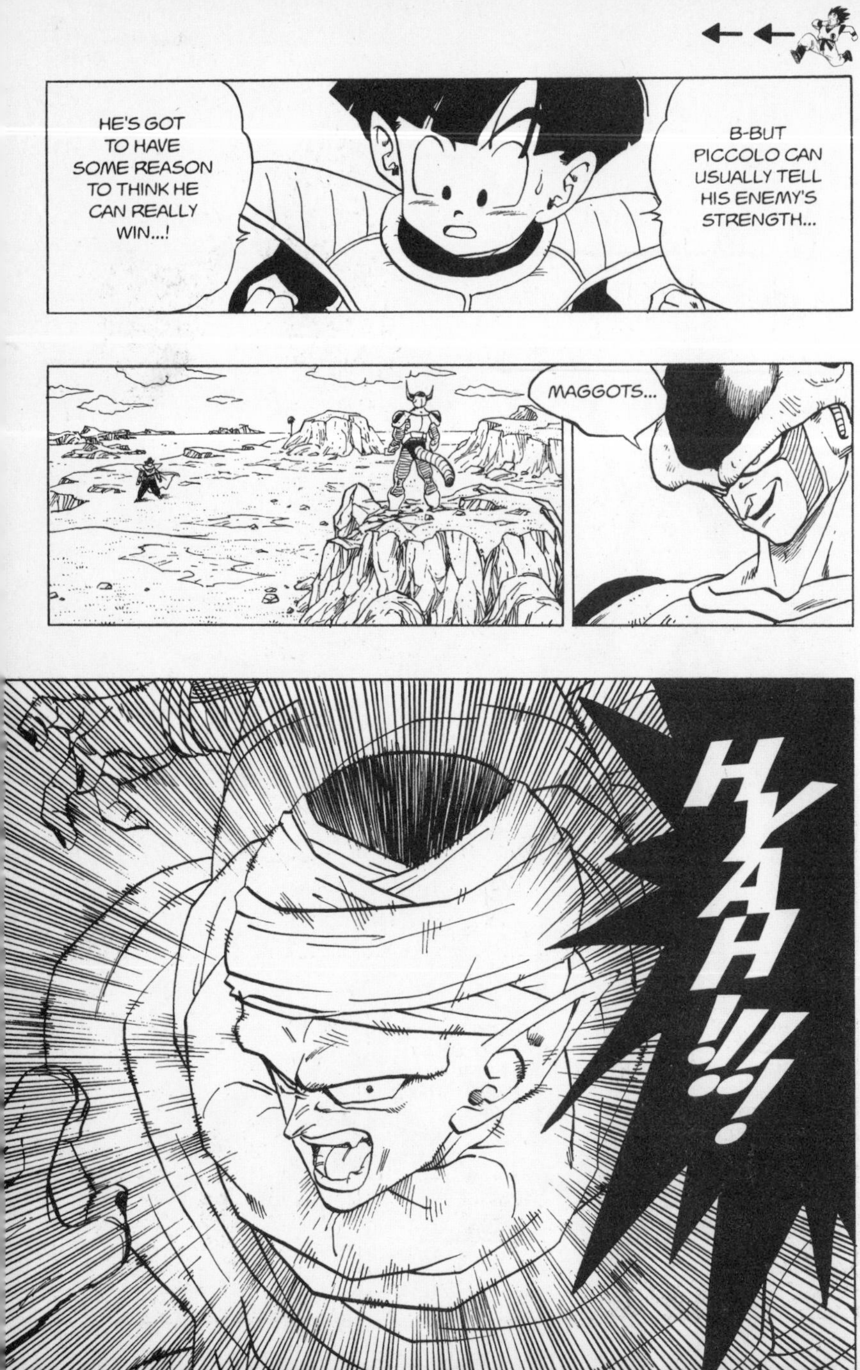
B-BUT PICCOLO CAN USUALLY TELL HIS ENEMY'S STRENGTH...
HE'S GOT TO HAVE SOME REASON TO THINK HE CAN REALLY WIN...!
MAGGOTS...
HYAAH!!!

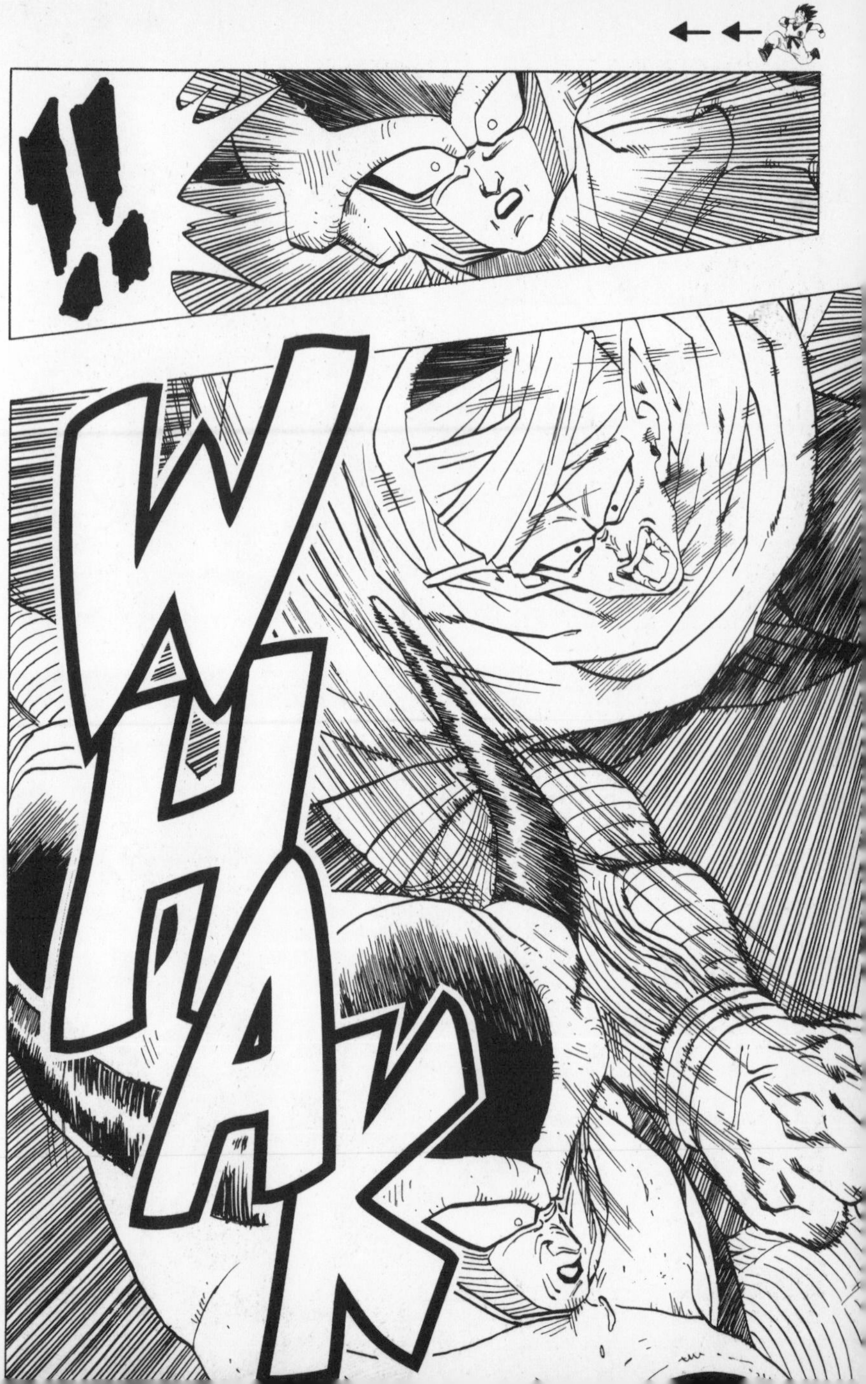
!!
WHAK

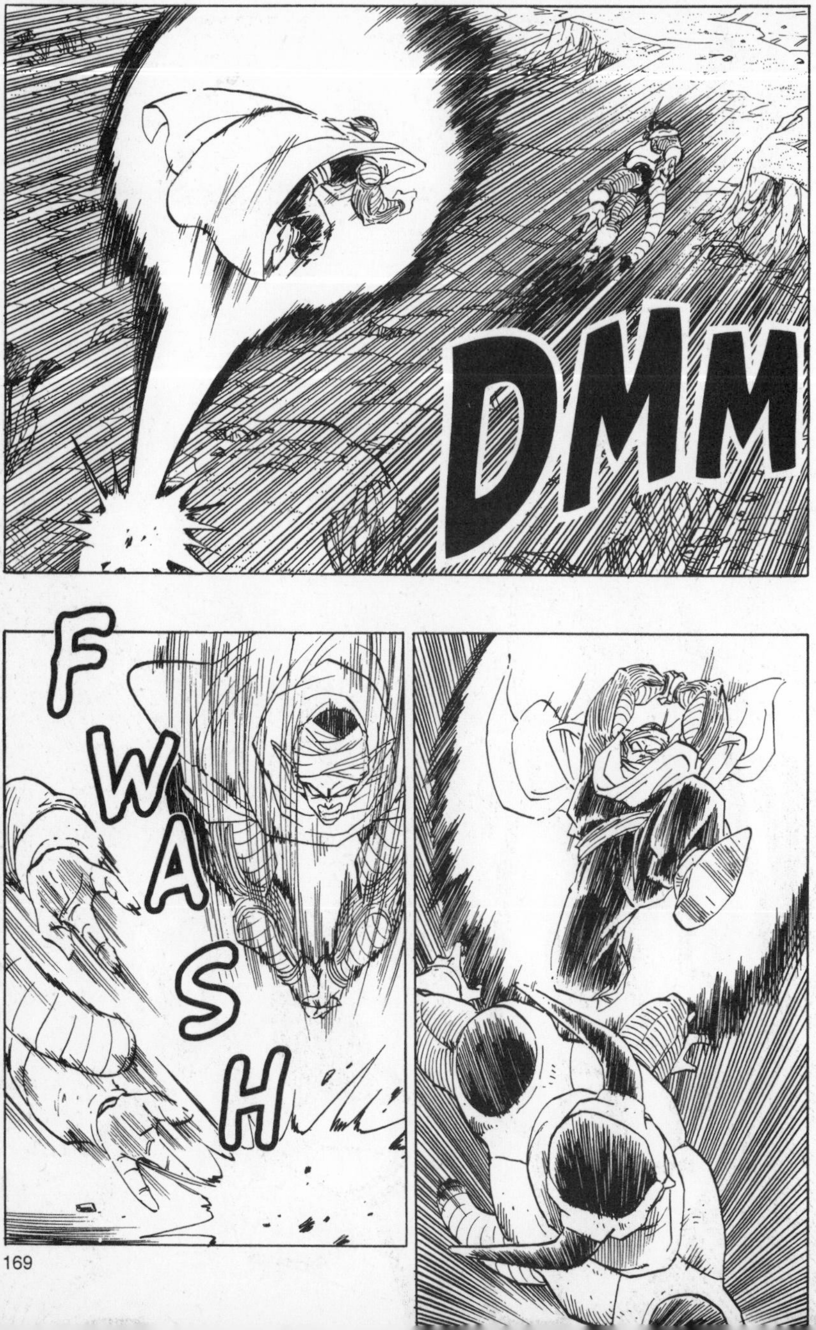
DMM
FWASH

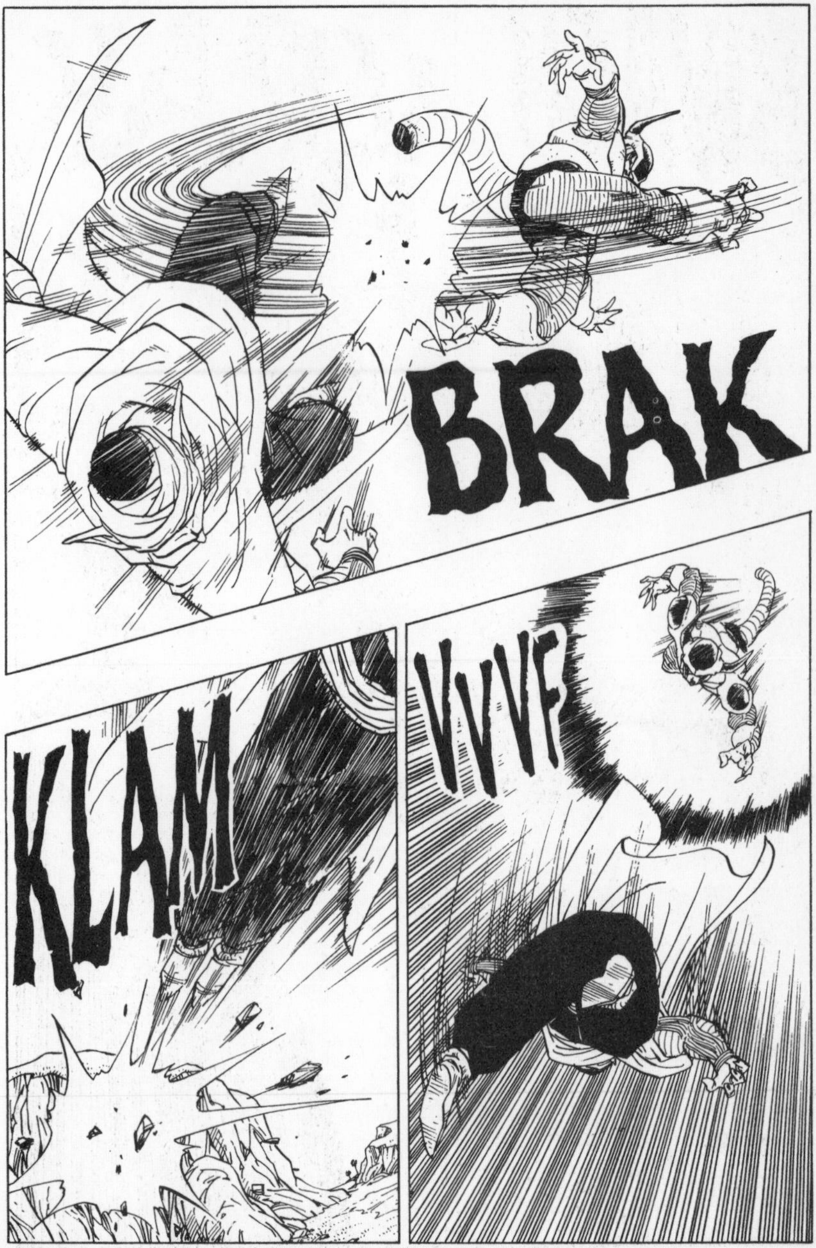
BRAK
VVVF
KLAM

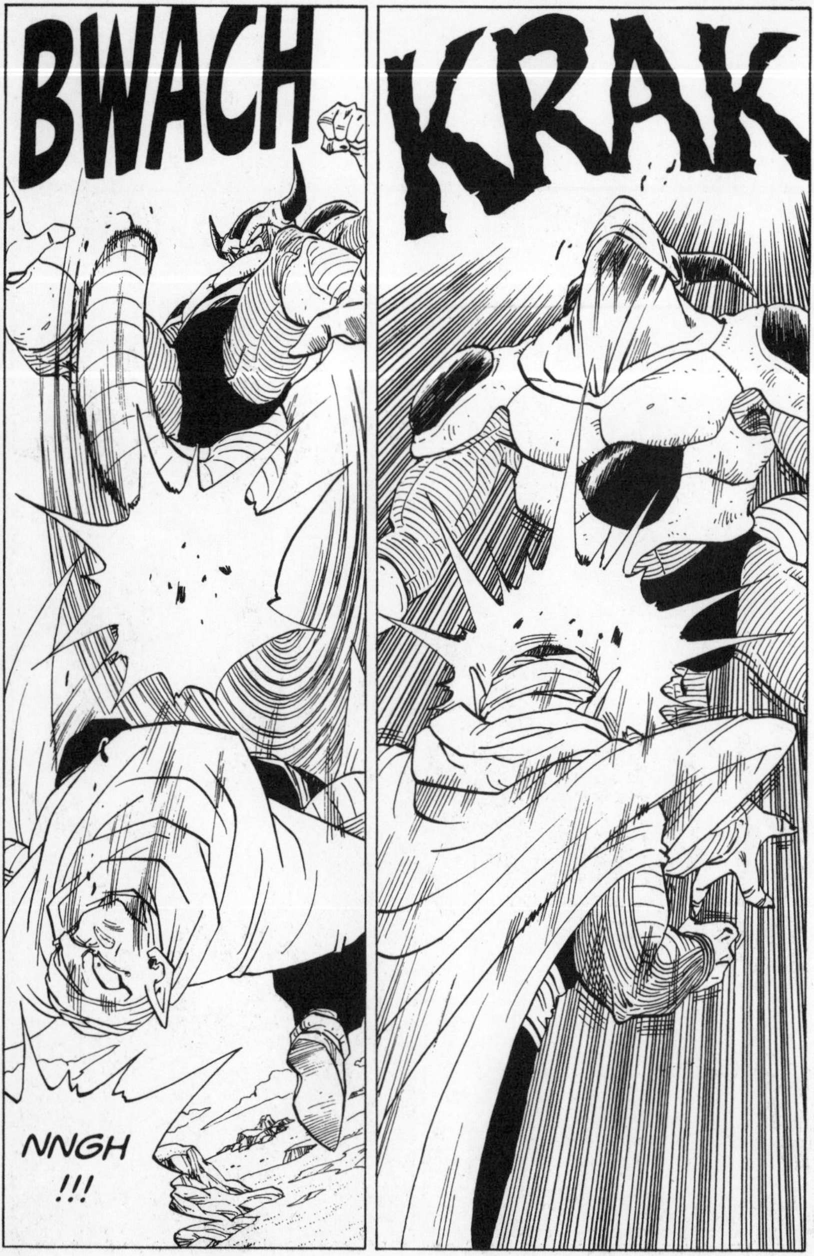
KRAK
BWACH
NNGH !!!

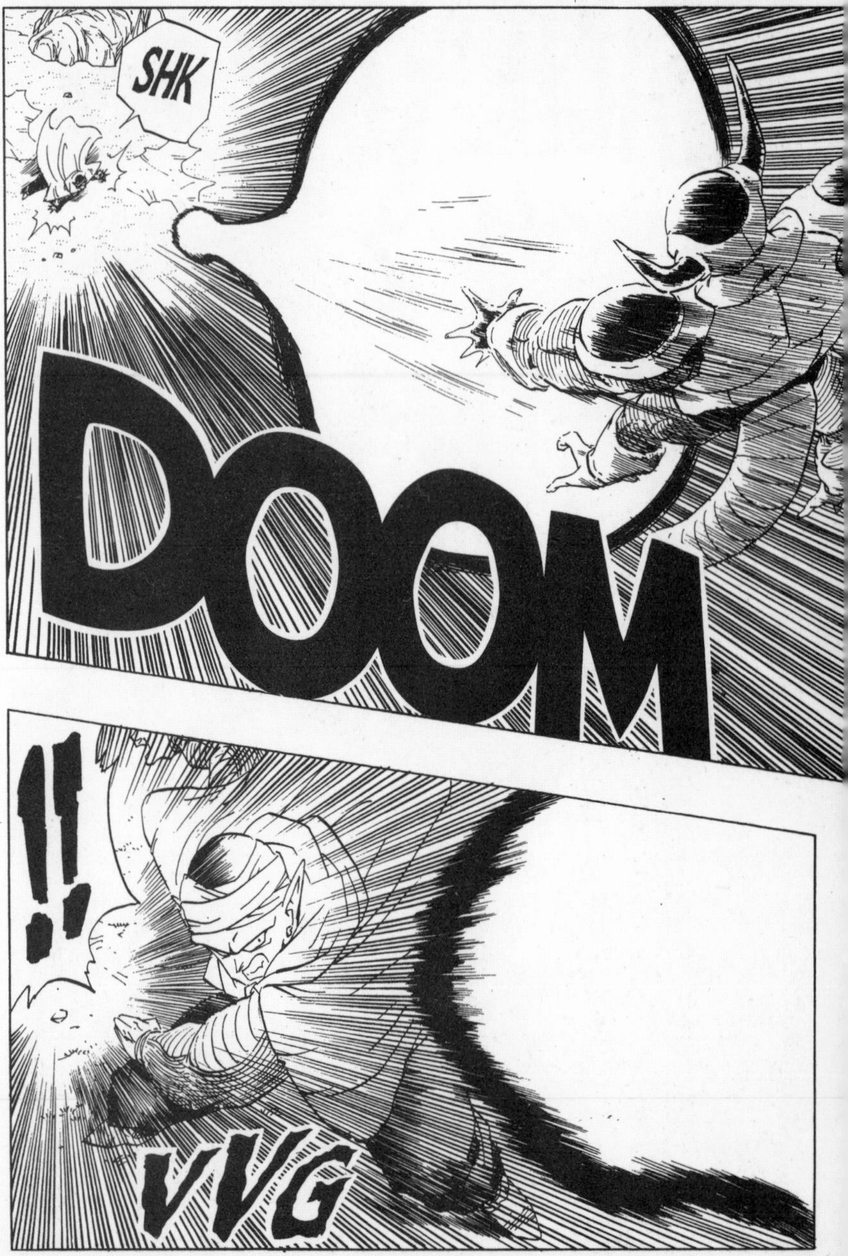
SHK
DOOM
!!
VVG

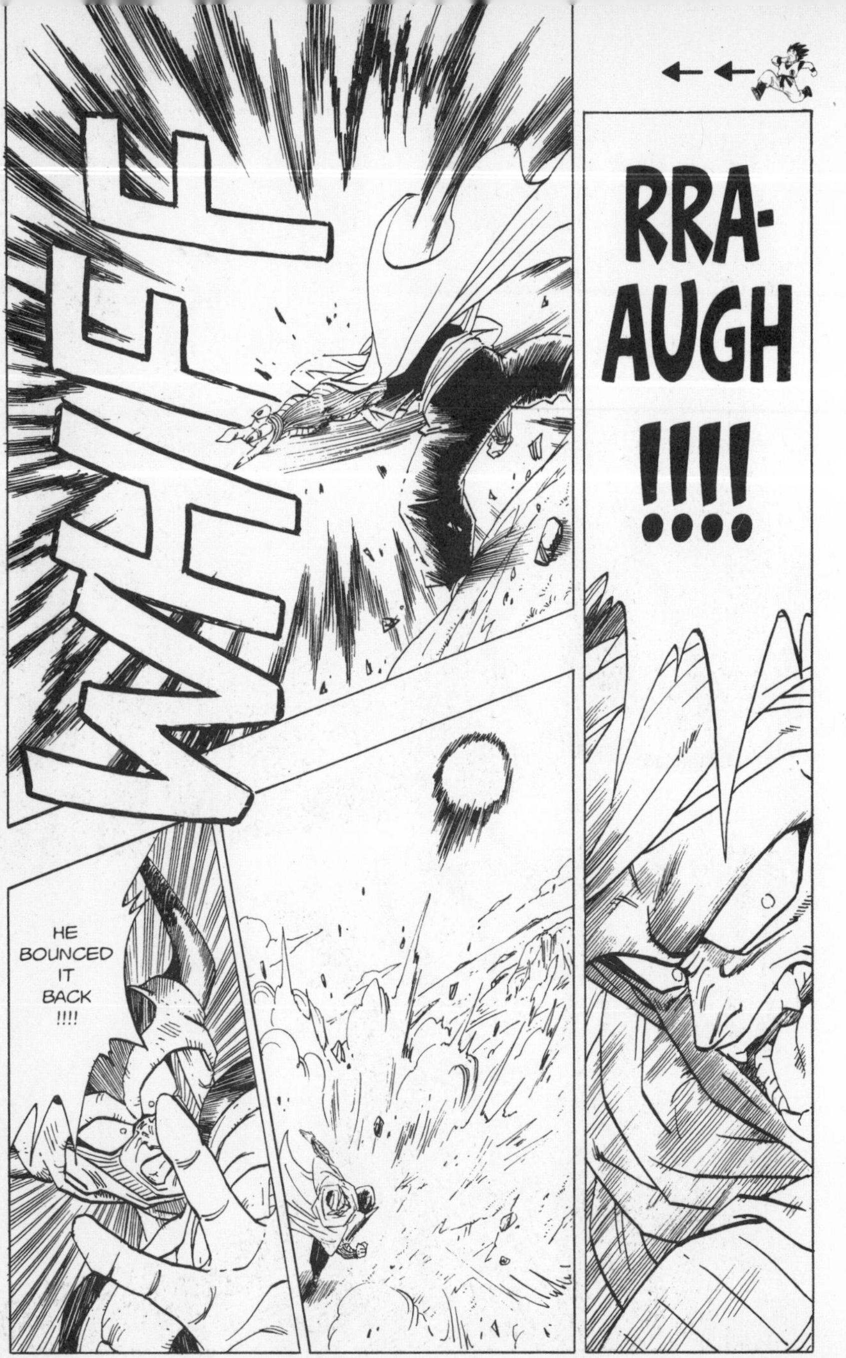
RRA-AUGH!!!!
HE BOUNCED IT BACK!!!!

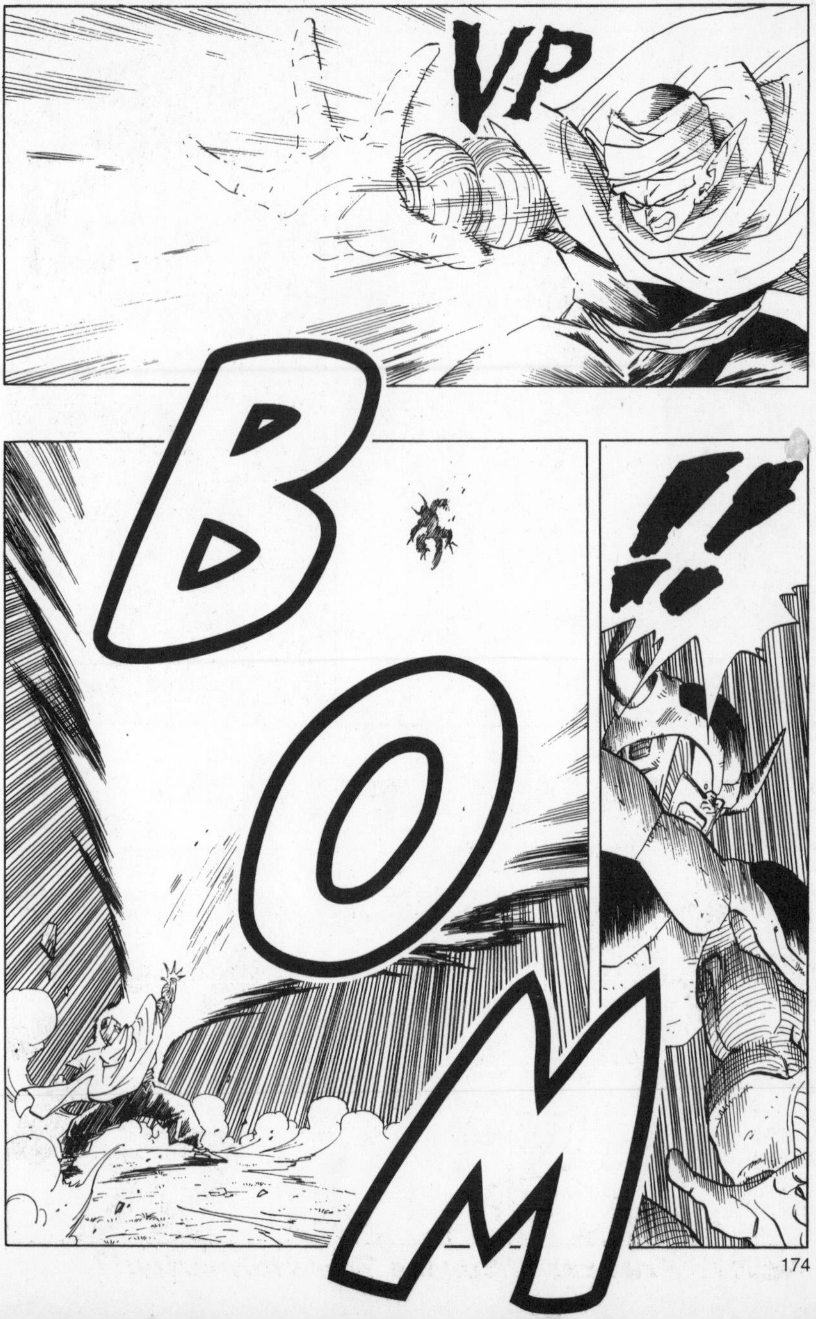
VP
!!
BOOM

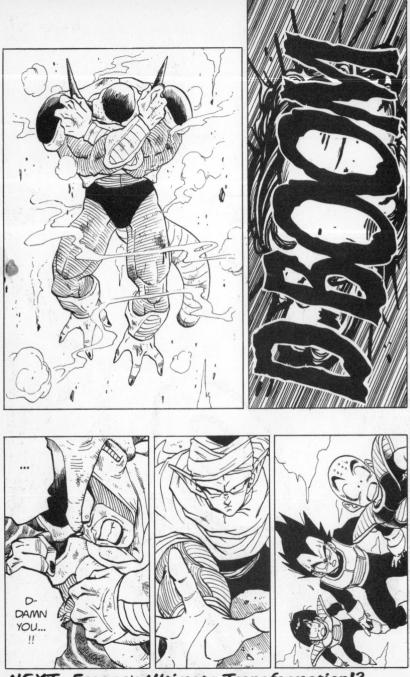

NEXT: *Freeza's Ultimate Transformation!?*

TITLE PAGE GALLERY

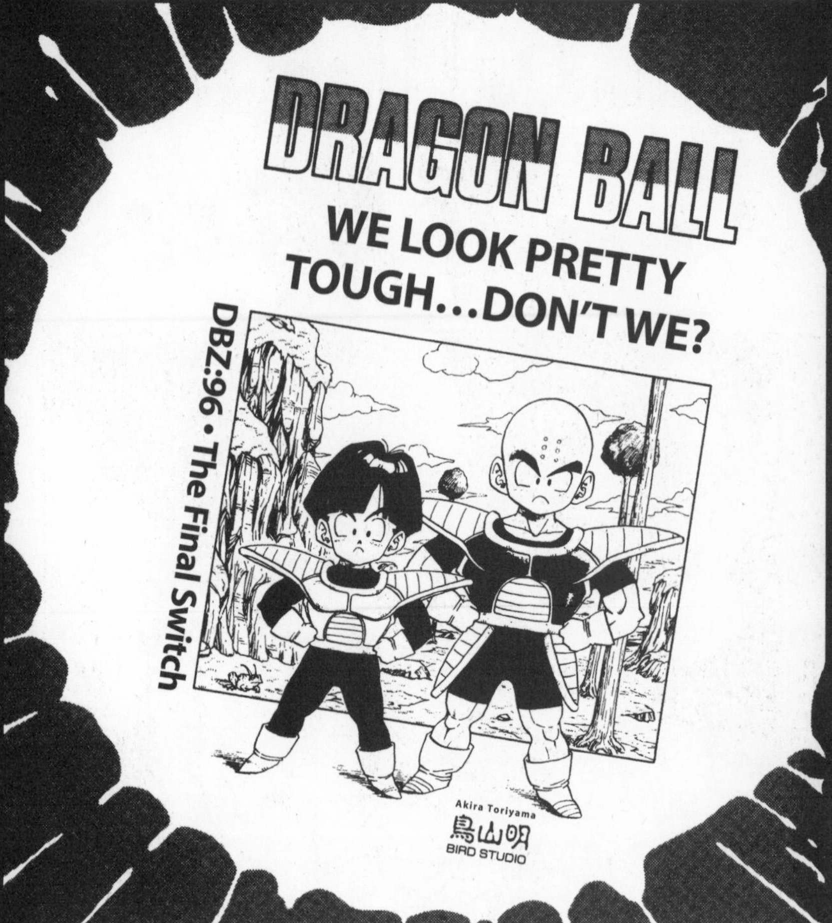
DRAGON BALL
WE LOOK PRETTY TOUGH...DON'T WE?
DBZ:96 • The Final Switch
Akira Toriyama
鳥山明
BIRD STUDIO

These title pages were used when these chapters of **Dragon Ball** were originally published in Japan from 1990 to 1991 in **Weekly Shonen Jump** magazine.

DRAGON BALL

•••!!!! !!!!•••

DBZ:97 • Nail's Sacrifice

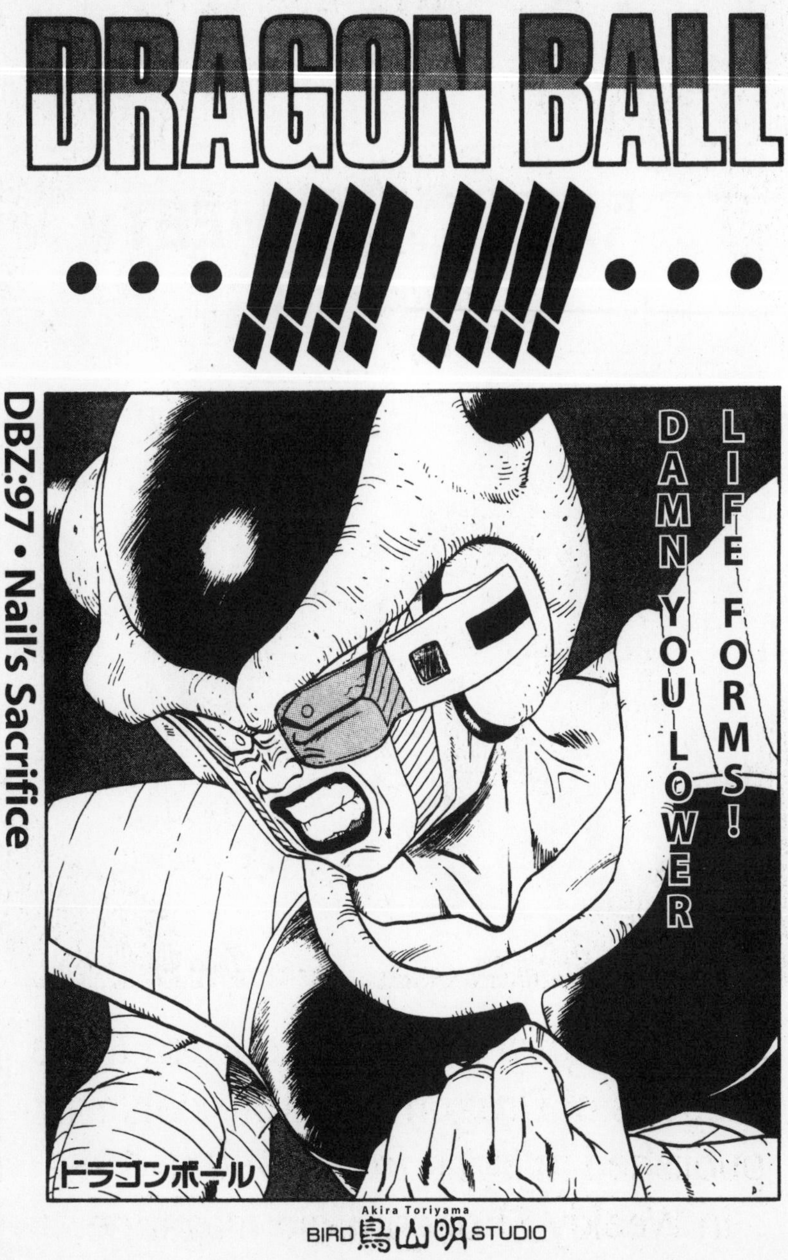
DAMN YOU LOWER LIFE FORMS!
ドラゴンボール

Akira Toriyama
BIRD 鳥山明 STUDIO

DRAGON BALL

AT LAST WE MEET SHENLONG!

Akira Toriyama
BIRD 鳥山明 STUDIO

DBZ:99

The Three Wishes

Akira Toriyama

鳥山明

BIRD STUDIO

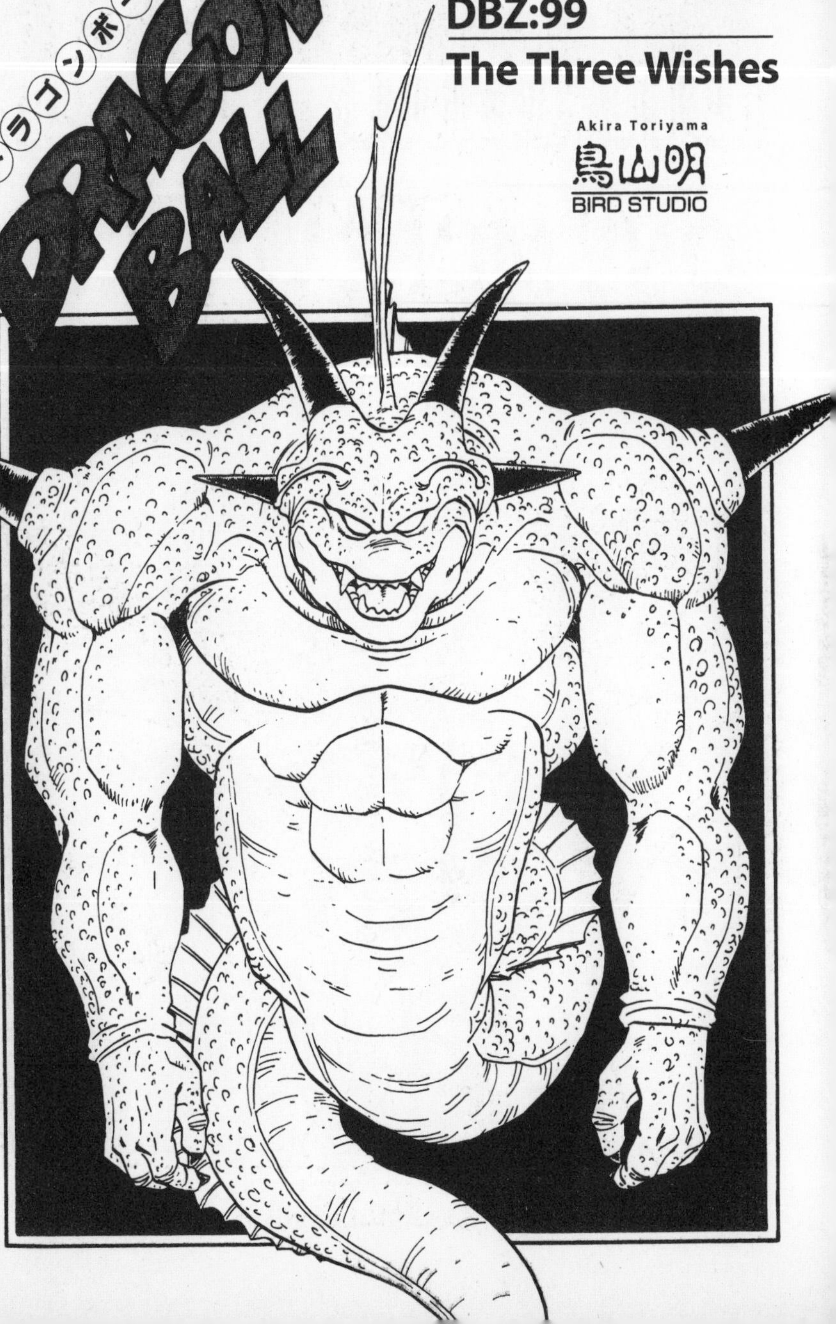

WISH FAST, BEFORE VEGETA WAKES UP!

DRAGON BALL

ONE MORE WISH... BUT FOR WHAT?

DBZ:100 • The Last Wish

Akira Toriyama
鳥山明
BIRD STUDIO

DRAGON BALL

DBZ:101 • The Assimilation

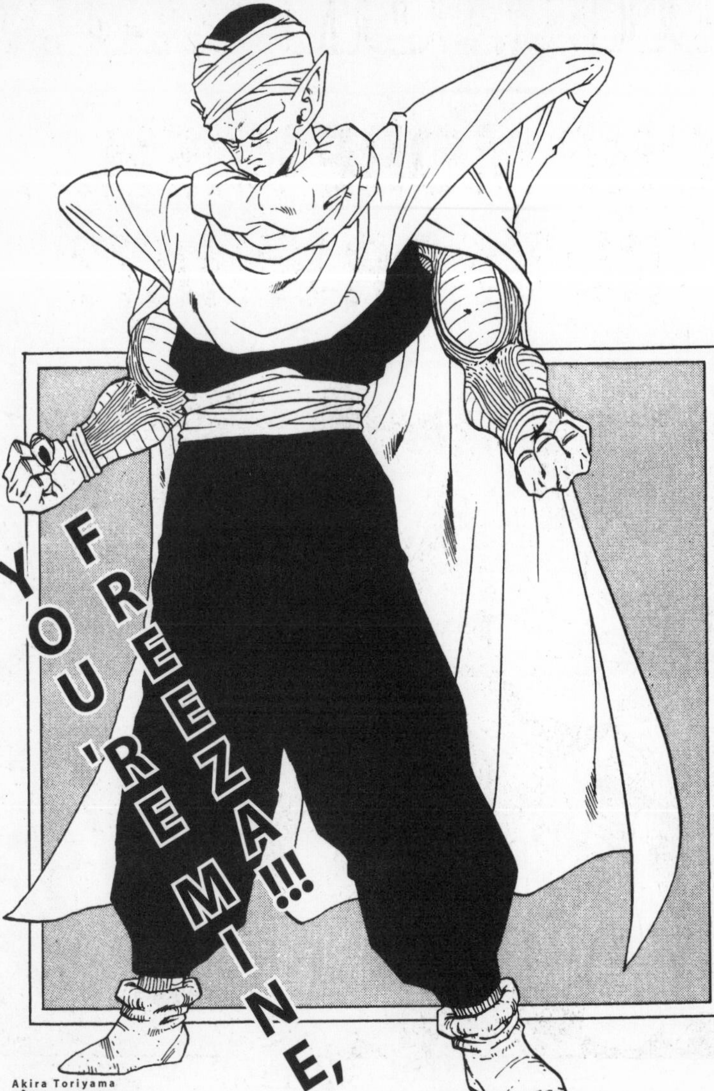
YOU'RE MINE, FREEZA!!

Akira Toriyama
鳥山明
BIRD STUDIO

WATCH CLOSELY NOW...

DBZ:102

The Transformation

Akira Toriyama

鳥山明

BIRD STUDIO

DRAGON BALL

DBZ:103

Freeza vs. Gohan

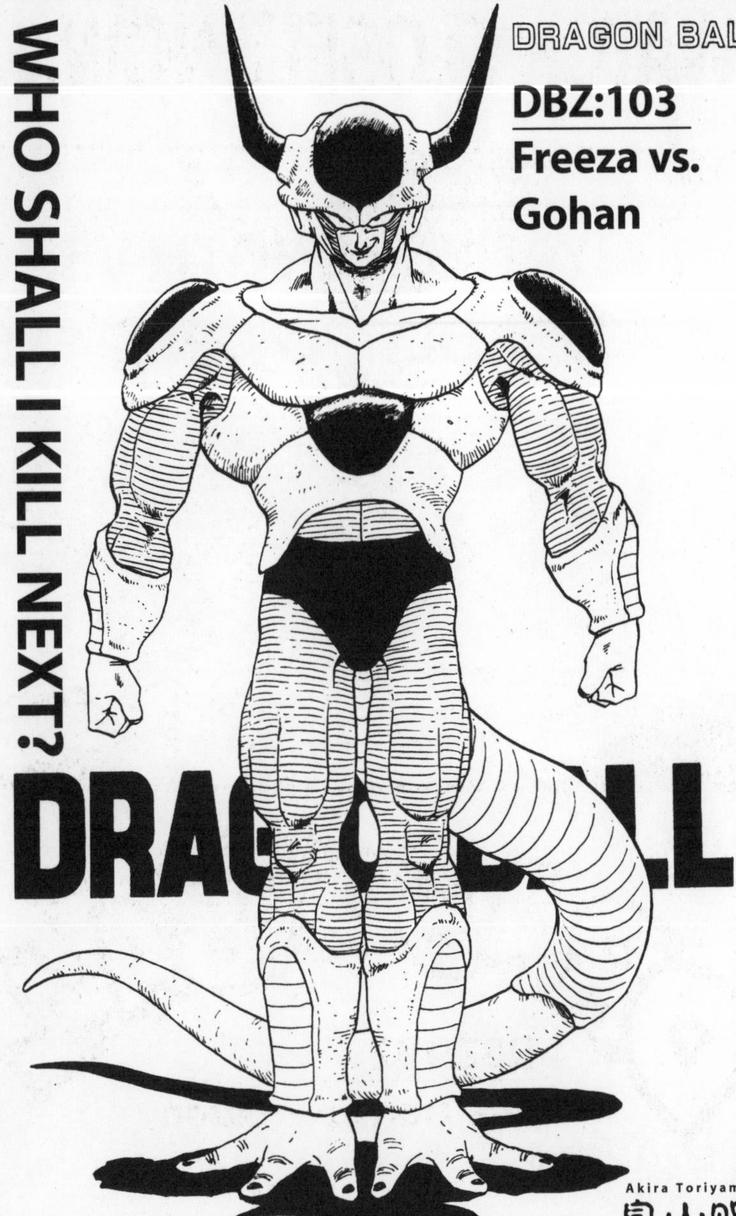
WHO SHALL I KILL NEXT?

Akira Toriyama
鳥山明
BIRD STUDIO

DRAGON BALL

SAIYAN STRENGTH VS. DEADLY POWER!

DBZ:104 • Freeza vs. Gohan, Part 2

ドラゴンボール

Akira Toriyama
BIRD 鳥山明 STUDIO

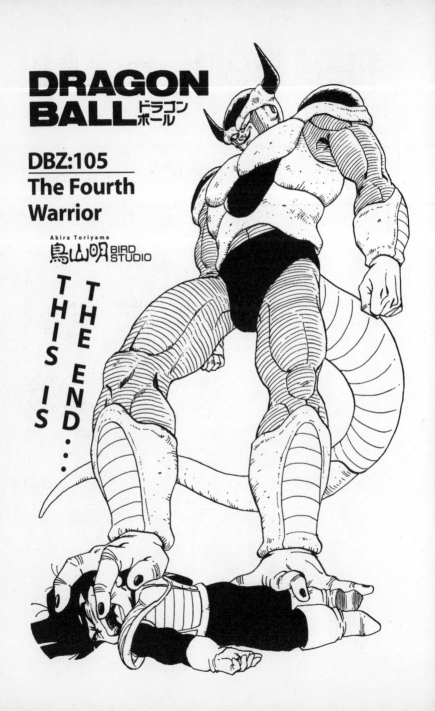

DRAGON BALL ドラゴンボール

DBZ:105
The Fourth
Warrior

Akira Toriyama
鳥山明 BIRD STUDIO

THIS IS THE END...

DRAGON BALL

DBZ:106

Freeza vs. Piccolo

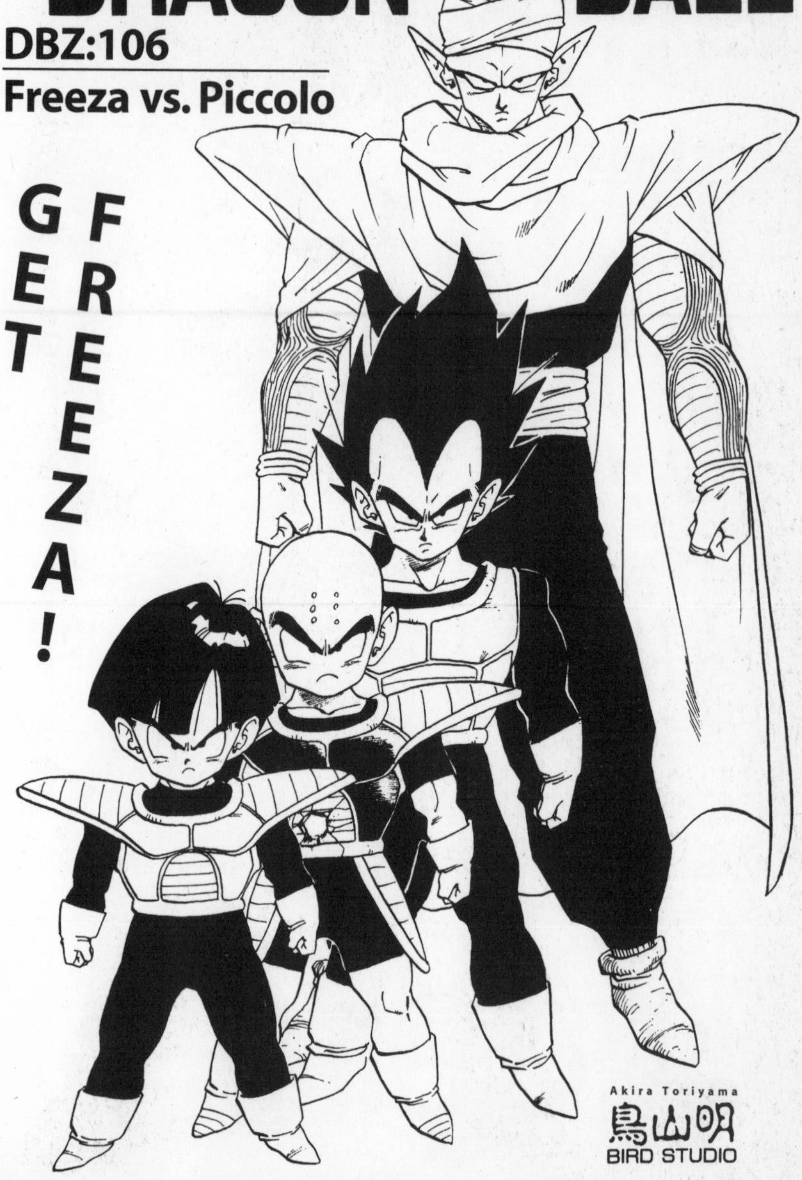
GET FREEZA!
Akira Toriyama
鳥山明
BIRD STUDIO

DBZ:110 • The Final Transformation

DRAGON BALL

Akira Toriyama
鳥山明
BIRD STUDIO

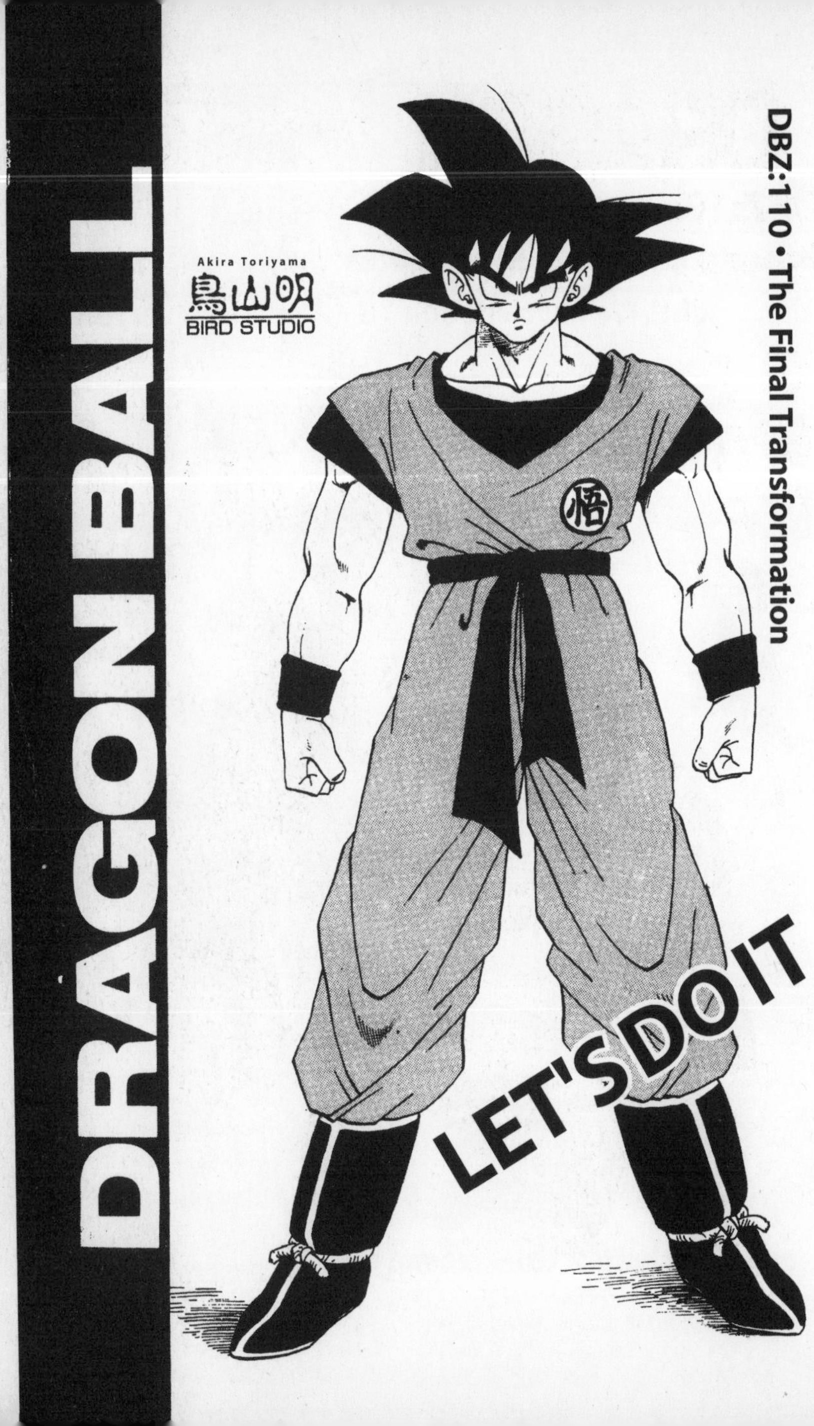
LET'S DO IT

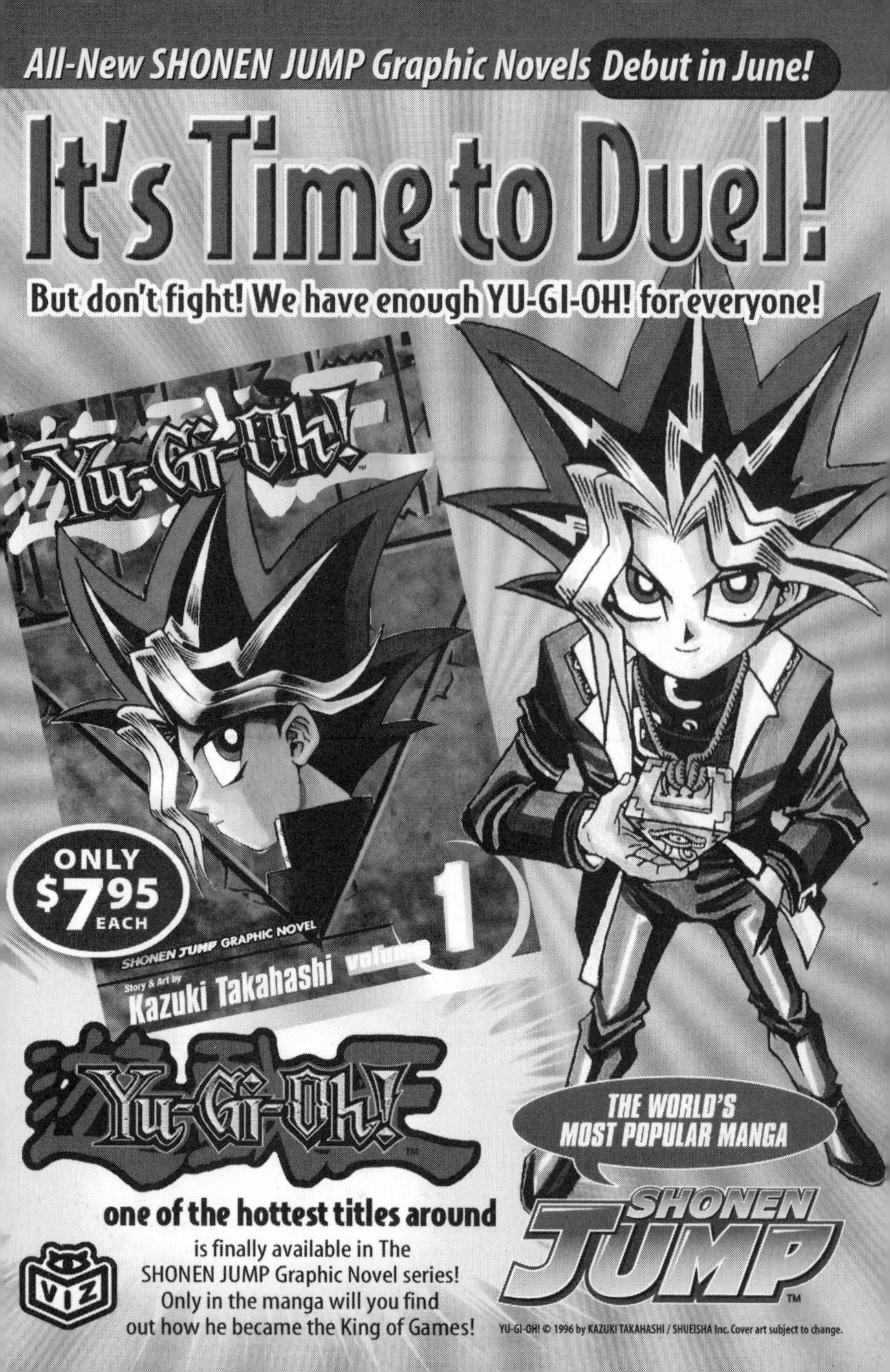
All-New SHONEN JUMP Graphic Novels Debut in June!
It's Time to Duel!
But don't fight! We have enough YU-GI-OH! for everyone!
YU-GI-OH!™
ONLY $7.95 EACH
SHONEN JUMP GRAPHIC NOVEL
volume 1
Story & Art by
Kazuki Takahashi
YU-GI-OH!™
THE WORLD'S MOST POPULAR MANGA
SHONEN JUMP™
one of the hottest titles around
is finally available in The
SHONEN JUMP Graphic Novel series!
Only in the manga will you find
out how he became the King of Games!
VIZ
YU-GI-OH! © 1996 by KAZUKI TAKAHASHI / SHUEISHA Inc. Cover art subject to change.

FREE*

DRAG🟊N BALL Z™

Collectible Display Box
FOR VOLUMES 9 THROUGH 16

Here's how you can receive a cool collectible Dragon Ball Z Display Box:

Purchase Dragon Ball Z Graphic Novels volumes 9 through 11 (purchase of volumes 12 to 16 not necessary).

1 Fill out the **Entry Form** on the reverse side.

2 Enclose the following in a postage-paid envelope:

★ This *original* completed **Entry Form** (vol.9).

★ The *original* **Validation Coupons** from Dragon Ball Z Graphic Novels volumes 10 and 11.

★ Payment in the amount of *$4.50 for shipping and handling. Payment must be made by enclosing a check or money order made payable to *Dragon Ball Display Box Offer.* (Ask your parents or legal guardian if you don't know how.)

3 Address and stuff the envelope:

ENTRY FORM (from volume 9)

+ VALIDATION COUPONS (from volumes 10 and 11)

Check or Money Order

Your return address
_____
_____

STAMP HERE

**DRAGON BALL DISPLAY BOX OFFER
P.O. Box 111238
Tacoma, WA 98411-1238**

No responsibility will be assumed for lost, late, illegible or misdirected orders or taxes arising from this offer. Limited to one product per entry form. Not valid if copied or reproduced. Consumer responsible for any applicable sales tax. Artwork subject to change. For questions, please call 415-546-7073 (x134) or email displaybox@shonenjump.com

DETACH HERE ▶

ENTRY FORM 9

DRAGON BALL Z™

DISPLAY BOX

PLEASE PRINT CLEARLY

NAME ____

ADDRESS ____

CITY __________________ **STATE** ______ **ZIP** ________

DAYTIME PHONE ____________________________________

To receive your Dragon Ball Z display box, complete this **Entry Form** from volume 9, collect the **Validation Coupons** from volumes 10 and 11, and mail them along with your payment of **$4.50** payable to:

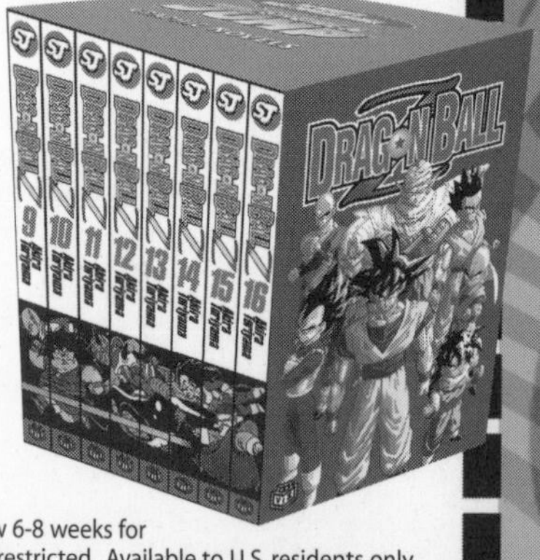

DRAGON BALL Z

DRAGON BALL DISPLAY BOX OFFER
P.O. Box 111238
Tacoma, WA 98411-1238

Replies must be postmarked no later than 06/30/2004. Please allow 6-8 weeks for delivery. Good while supplies last. Void where prohibited, taxed or restricted. Available to U.S. residents only.

◀ **DETACH HERE**